New Perspectives on

MICROSOFT® ACCESS 2002

Brief

JOSEPH J. ADAMSKI
Grand Valley State University

KATHLEEN T. FINNEGAN

Australia • Canada • Mexico • Singapore • Spain • United Kingdom • United States

New Perspectives on Microsoft® Access 2002—Brief
is published by Course Technology.

Managing Editor:
Greg Donald

Senior Editor:
Donna Gridley

Series Technology Editor:
Rachel Crapser

Senior Product Manager:
Kathy Finnegan

Product Manager:
Melissa Hathaway

Web Associate Project Manager:
Amanda Young

Editorial Assistant:
Jessica Engstrom

Marketing Manager:
Sean Teare

Developmental Editor:
Jessica Evans

Production Editor:
Daphne Barbas

Composition:
GEX Publishing Services

Text Designer:
Meral Dabcovich

Cover Designer:
Efrat Reis

COPYRIGHT © 2002 Course Technology, a division of Thomson Learning, Inc. Thomson Learning™ is a trademark used herein under license.

Printed in the United States of America

2 3 4 5 6 7 8 9 BM 05 04 03 02

For more information, contact Course Technology, 25 Thomson Place, Boston, Massachusetts, 02210.

Or find us on the World Wide Web at: www.course.com

ALL RIGHTS RESERVED. No part of this work covered by the copyright hereon may be reproduced or used in any form or by any means—graphic, electronic, or mechanical, including photocopying, recording, taping, Web distribution, or information storage and retrieval systems—without the written permission of the publisher.

For permission to use material from this text or product, contact us by
Tel (800) 730-2214
Fax (800) 730-2215
www.thomsonrights.com

Disclaimer
Course Technology reserves the right to revise this publication and make changes from time to time in its content without notice.

Some of the product names and company names used in this book have been used for identification purposes only and may be trademarks or registered trademarks of their respective manufacturers and sellers.

Microsoft and the Office logo are either registered trademarks or trademarks of Microsoft Corporation in the United States and/or other countries. Course Technology is an independent entity from the Microsoft Corporation, and not affiliated with Microsoft in any manner.

ISBN 0-619-02087-3

New Perspectives Preface

Course Technology is the world leader in information technology education. The New Perspectives Series is an integral part of Course Technology's success. Visit our Web site to see a whole new perspective on teaching and learning solutions.

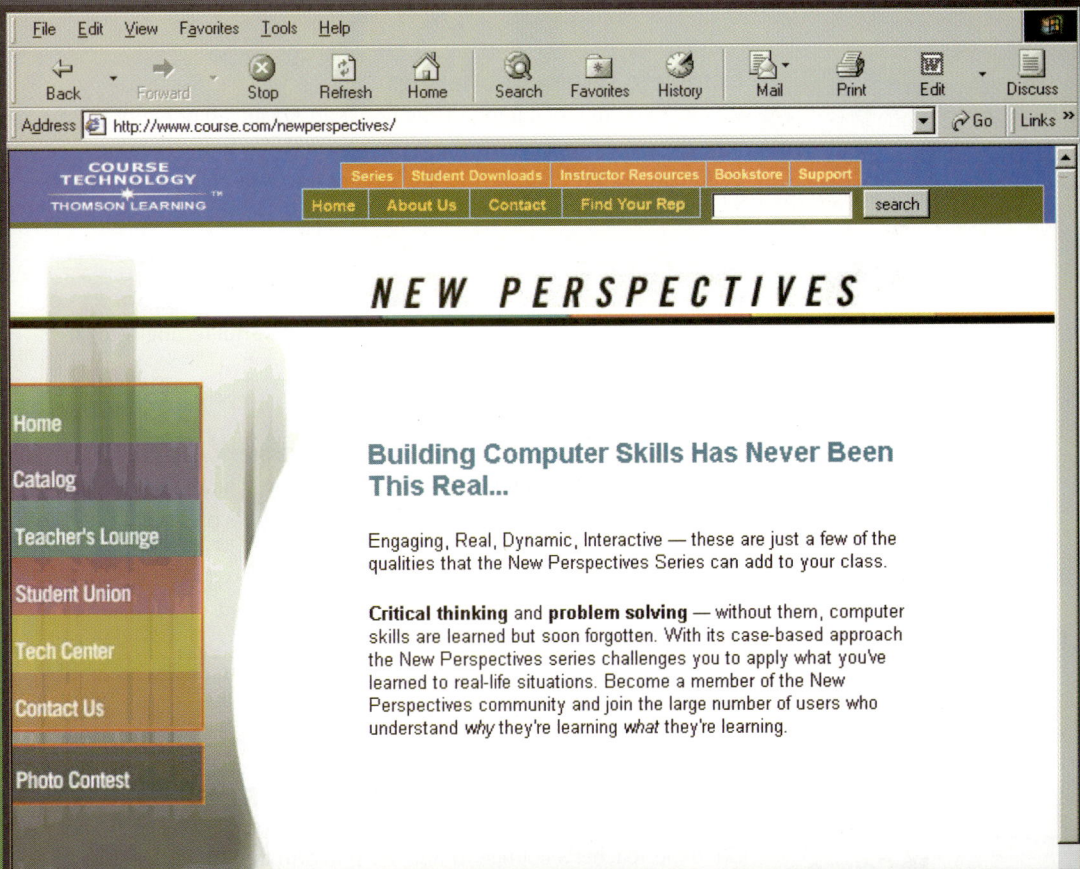

New Perspectives—Building Computer Skills Has Never Been This Real

Why New Perspectives will work for you.

Critical thinking and **problem solving**—without them, computer skills are learned but soon forgotten. With its **case-based** approach, the New Perspectives Series challenges students to apply what they've learned to real-life situations. Become a member of the New Perspectives community and watch your students not only **master** computer skills, but also **retain** and carry this **knowledge** into the world.

New Perspectives catalog
Our online catalog is never out of date! Go to the Catalog button on our Web site to check out our available titles, request a desk copy, download a book preview, or locate online files.

Complete system of offerings
Whether you're looking for a Brief book, an Advanced book, or something in between, we've got you covered. Go to the Catalog button on our Web site to find the level of coverage that's right for you.

Instructor materials
We have all the tools you need—data files, solution files, figure files, a sample syllabus, and ExamView, our powerful testing software package.

How well do your students know Microsoft Office?
Find out with performance-based testing software that measures your students' proficiency in the application. Click the Tech Center button to learn more.

Get certified
If you want to get certified, we have the titles for you. Find out more by clicking the Teacher's Lounge button.

Interested in distance learning?
Enhance your course with any one of our distance learning platforms. Go to the Teacher's Lounge to find the platform that's right for you.

Your link to the future is at www.course.com/NewPerspectives

What you need to know about this book.

"I really like the story line you've chosen for the book. I think the students will relate to it."
Rebekah L. Tidwell, Carson Newman College and Lee University

"The greatest strength of Tutorial 2 is its consistent clarity and adherence to training the students in all skills listed in the objectives. The clarity of this chapter is unusual for an early chapter and is a tremendous strength for students to build on as they continue through the rest of the book."
Michael Feiler, Merritt College

"Tutorial 4 does an excellent job of explaining the relationship between forms and reports. In addition it simplifies the relationship between forms and subforms, which had been confusing for students in the past."
Lorraine N. Bergkvist, College of Notre Dame

- Student Online Companion takes students to the Web for additional work.
- ExamView testing software gives you the option of generating a printed test, LAN-based test, or test over the Internet.
- New Perspectives Labs provide students with self-paced practice on computer-related topics.
- All cases are NEW to this edition!
- Our clear and concise coverage of database concepts provides students with the solid foundation they need as they progress to creating and working with database objects.
- Students will appreciate the in-depth explanation of creating and modifying queries, which proceeds logically from simple to more complex queries involving calculated and aggregate functions.
- The scenarios in our end-of-tutorial exercises will hold students' interest, and the number of exploratory exercises will challenge students and give them a sense of accomplishment.

CASE	TROUBLE?	SESSION 1.1	QUICK CHECK	RW
Tutorial Case Each tutorial begins with a problem presented in a case that is meaningful to students. The case sets the scene to help students understand what they will do in the tutorial.	**TROUBLE? Paragraphs** These paragraphs anticipate the mistakes or problems that students may have and help them continue with the tutorial.	**Sessions** Each tutorial is divided into sessions designed to be completed in about 45 minutes each. Students should take as much time as they need and take a break between sessions.	**Quick Check Questions** Each session concludes with conceptual Quick Check questions that test students' understanding of what they learned in the session.	**Reference Windows** Reference Windows are succinct summaries of the most important tasks covered in a tutorial. They preview actions students will perform in the steps to follow.

www.course.com/NewPerspectives

TABLE OF CONTENTS

Preface	iii
Microsoft Office XP	**OFF 1**
Read This Before You Begin	OFF 2

Tutorial 1 — OFF 3

Introducing Microsoft Office XP

Preparing Promotional Materials for Delmar Office Supplies

Exploring Microsoft Office XP	OFF 4
Integrating Programs	OFF 7
Starting Office Programs	OFF 9
Switching Between Open Programs and Files	OFF 12
Using Personalized Menus and Toolbars	OFF 13
Using Speech Recognition	OFF 15
Saving and Closing a File	OFF 16
Opening a File	OFF 18
Printing a File	OFF 20
Getting Help	OFF 21
Exiting Programs	OFF 23
Quick Check	OFF 23
Review Assignments	OFF 23
Quick Check Answers	OFF 24

Microsoft Access 2002

Level I Tutorials	**AC 1.01**
Read This Before You Begin	AC 1.02

Tutorial 1 — AC 1.03

Introduction to Microsoft Access 2002

Viewing and Working with a Table Containing Employer Data

SESSION 1.1	**AC 1.04**
Introduction to Database Concepts	AC 1.04
Organizing Data	AC 1.04
Databases and Relationships	AC 1.04
Relational Database Management Systems	AC 1.06
Opening an Existing Database	AC 1.07
The Access and Database Windows	AC 1.10
Opening an Access Table	AC 1.10
Navigating an Access Datasheet	AC 1.11
Saving a Database	AC 1.12
Session 1.1 Quick Check	AC 1.13
SESSION 1.2	**AC 1.13**
Working with Queries	AC 1.13
Opening an Existing Query	AC 1.13
Creating, Sorting, and Navigating a Query	AC 1.15
Creating and Navigating a Form	AC 1.18
Creating, Previewing, and Navigating a Report	AC 1.20
Managing a Database	AC 1.23
Backing Up and Restoring a Database	AC 1.23
Compacting and Repairing a Database	AC 1.24
Compacting a Database Automatically	AC 1.24
Converting an Access 2000 Database	AC 1.25
Session 1.2 Quick Check	AC 1.26
Review Assignments	AC 1.27
Case Problems	AC 1.28
Lab Assignments	AC 1.31
Internet Assignments	AC 1.32
Quick Check Answers	AC 1.32

Tutorial 2 — AC 2.01

Creating and Maintaining a Database

Creating the Northeast Database, and Creating, Modifying, and Updating the Position Table

SESSION 2.1	**AC 2.02**
Guidelines for Designing Databases	AC 2.02
Guidelines for Setting Field Properties	AC 2.04
Naming Fields and Objects	AC 2.04
Assigning Field Data Types	AC 2.05
Setting Field Sizes	AC 2.06
Creating a New Database	AC 2.07
Creating a Table	AC 2.08
Defining Fields	AC 2.09
Specifying the Primary Key	AC 2.16
Saving the Table Structure	AC 2.17
Session 2.1 Quick Check	AC 2.18
SESSION 2.2	**AC 2.19**
Adding Records to a Table	AC 2.19
Modifying the Structure of an Access Table	AC 2.22
Deleting a Field	AC 2.23
Moving a Field	AC 2.24
Adding a Field	AC 2.24
Changing Field Properties	AC 2.26
Obtaining Data from Another Access Database	AC 2.29
Copying Records from Another Access Database	AC 2.29
Importing a Table from Another Access Database	AC 2.32
Updating a Database	AC 2.33

Deleting Records	AC 2.33
Changing Records	AC 2.34
Session 2.2 Quick Check	AC 2.35
Review Asssignments	AC 2.36
Case Problems	AC 2.37
Internet Assignments	AC 2.42
Quick Check Answers	AC 2.42

Tutorial 3   AC 3.01

Querying a Database

Retrieving Information About Employers and Their Positions

SESSION 3.1	**AC 3.01**
Introduction to Queries	AC 3.02
Query Window	AC 3.02
Creating and Running a Query	AC 3.05
Updating Data Using a Query	AC 3.07
Defining Table Relationships	AC 3.08
One-to-Many Relationships	AC 3.08
Referential Integrity	AC 3.09
Defining a Relationship Between Two Tables	AC 3.09
Creating a Multi-table Query	AC 3.13
Sorting Data in a Query	AC 3.14
Using a Toolbar Button to Sort Data	AC 3.15
Sorting Multiple Fields in Design View	AC 3.16
Filtering Data	AC 3.19
Session 3.1 Quick Check	AC 3.21
SESSION 3.2	**AC 3.22**
Defining Record Selection Criteria for Queries	AC 3.22
Specifying an Exact Match	AC 3.22
Changing a Datasheet's Appearance	AC 3.25
Using a Comparison Operator to Match a Range of Values	AC 3.26
Defining Multiple Selection Criteria for Queries	AC 3.28
The And Logical Operator	AC 3.29
Using Multiple Undo and Redo	AC 3.30
The Or Logical Operator	AC 3.31
Performing Calculations	AC 3.33
Creating a Calculated Field	AC 3.34
Using Aggregate Functions	AC 3.38
Using Record Group Calculations	AC 3.40
Session 3.2 Quick Check	AC 3.41

Review Assignments	AC 3.42
Case Problems	AC 3.43
Internet Assignments	AC 3.46
Quick Check Answers	AC 3.46

Tutorial 4   AC 4.01

Creating Forms and Reports

Creating a Position Data Form, an Employer Positions Form, and an Employers and Positions Report

SESSION 4.1	**AC 4.02**
Creating a Form Using the Form Wizard	AC 4.02
Changing a Form's AutoFormat	AC 4.05
Finding Data Using a Form	AC 4.08
Previewing and Printing Selected Form Records	AC 4.11
Maintaining Table Data Using a Form	AC 4.12
Checking the Spelling of Table Data Using a Form	AC 4.14
Session 4.1 Quick Check	AC 4.16
SESSION 4.2	**AC 4.16**
Creating a Form with a Main Form and a Subform	AC 4.16
Modifying a Form in Design View	AC 4.19
Creating a Report Using the Report Wizard	AC 4.22
Inserting a Picture in a Report	AC 4.30
Session 4.2 Quick Check	AC 4.34
Review Assignments	AC 4.34
Case Problems	AC 4.36
Internet Assignments	AC 4.40
Quick Check Answers	AC 4.40

Creating Web Pages with Access   WEB 1

Creating Web Pages to Display Employer and Position Data

Working with the Web	WEB 2
Creating and Viewing a Static Web Page	WEB 2
Creating and Viewing a Data Access Page	WEB 5
Review Assignments	WEB 8

Index   1

Task Reference   6

File Finder   8

Acknowledgments

I would like to thank the following reviewers for their helpful and thorough feedback: Lorraine Bergkvist, College of Notre Dame; Michael Feiler, Merritt College; Eric Johnston, Vatterott College; Donna Occhifinto, County College of Morris; and Rebekah Tidwell, Carson Newman College and Lee University. Many thanks to all the Course Technology staff, especially Greg Donald and Donna Gridley for their leadership and encouragement; Melissa Hathaway and Jessica Engstrom for their tireless support and good humor; Daphne Barbas for her excellent management of the production process; and John Bosco, John Freitas, and Marianne Broughey for ensuring the quality and accuracy of this text. Special thanks to Jessica Evans for her exceptional editorial and technical skills in developing this text and her willingness to go the extra mile; and to Joe Adamski for his continued guidance and expertise. This book is dedicated with love to my two terrific sons, Connor and Devon, who always keep me both hopping and grounded at the same time.

Kathleen T. Finnegan

Thank you to all the people who contributed to developing and completing this book, with special thanks to Susan Solomon, who started it all and asked me to join the team nearly ten years ago; Greg Donald for making a smooth transition to the team; the marketing staff for supporting the series over the years; Kathy Finnegan for her many contributions; Jessica Evans for her thoughtfulness, attention to quality, perseverance, friendship, and exceptional skills; and Judy for making it all worthwhile.

Joseph J. Adamski

www.course.com/NewPerspectives

New Perspectives on

MICROSOFT® OFFICE XP

TUTORIAL 1 OFF 3

Introducing Microsoft Office XP

Delmar Office Supplies
Exploring Microsoft Office XP — 4
Starting Office Programs — 9
Using Personalized Menus and Toolbars — 13
Saving and Closing a File — 16
Opening a File — 18
Printing a File — 20
Getting Help — 21
Exiting Programs — 23

Read This Before You Begin

To the Student

Data Disks
To complete this tutorial and the Review Assignments, you need one Data Disk. Your instructor will either provide you with the Data Disk or ask you to make your own.

If you are making your own Data Disk, you will need **one** blank, formatted high-density disk. You will need to copy a set of files and/or folders from a file server, standalone computer, or the Web onto your disk. Your instructor will tell you which computer, drive letter, and folder contain the files you need. You could also download the files by going to www.course.com and following the instructions on the screen.

The information below shows you which folder goes on your disk, so that you will have enough disk space to complete the tutorial and Review Assignments:

Data Disk 1
Write this on the disk label:
Data Disk 1: Introducing Office XP
Put this folder on the disk:
Tutorial.01

When you begin the tutorial, be sure you are using the correct Data Disk. Refer to the "File Finder" chart at the back of this text for more detailed information on which files are used in the tutorial. See the inside front or inside back cover of this book for more information on Data Disk files, or ask your instructor or technical support person for assistance.

Using Your Own Computer
If you are going to work through this tutorial using your own computer, you need:

- **Computer System** Microsoft Windows 98, NT, 2000 Professional, or higher must be installed on your computer. This book assumes a typical installation of Microsoft Office XP.

- **Data Disk** You will not be able to complete this tutorial or Review Assignments using your own computer until you have your Data Disk.

Visit Our World Wide Web Site
Additional materials designed especially for you are available on the World Wide Web.
Go to www.course.com/NewPerspectives.

To the Instructor

The Data Disk Files are available on the Instructor's Resource Kit for this title. Follow the instructions in the Help file on the CD-ROM to install the programs to your network or standalone computer. For information on creating the Data Disk, see the "To the Student" section above.

You are granted a license to copy the Data Disk Files to any computer or computer network used by students who have purchased this book.

OBJECTIVES

In this tutorial you will:

- Explore the programs that comprise Microsoft Office
- Explore the benefits of integrating data between programs
- Start programs and switch between them
- Use personalized menus and toolbars
- Save and close a file
- Open an existing file
- Print a file
- Get Help
- Close files and exit programs

INTRODUCING MICROSOFT OFFICE XP

Preparing Promotional Materials for Delmar Office Supplies

CASE

Delmar Office Supplies

Delmar Office Supplies, a company in Wisconsin founded by Nicole Delmar in 1996, sells recycled office supplies to businesses and home-based offices around the world. The demand for quality recycled papers, reconditioned toner cartridges, and renovated office furniture has been growing each year. Nicole and all her employees use Microsoft Office XP, which provides everyone in the company the power and flexibility to store a variety of information, create consistent documents, and share data. In this tutorial, you'll review some of the latest documents the company's employees have created using Microsoft Office XP.

Exploring Microsoft Office XP

Microsoft Office XP, or simply **Office**, is a collection of the most popular Microsoft programs: Word, Excel, PowerPoint, Access, and Outlook. Each Office program contains valuable tools to help you accomplish many tasks, such as composing reports, analyzing data, preparing presentations, and compiling information.

Microsoft Word 2002, or simply **Word**, is a **word processing program** you use to create text documents. The files you create in Word are called **documents**. Word offers many special features that help you compose and update all types of documents, ranging from letters and newsletters to reports, fliers, faxes, and even books—all in attractive and readable formats. You also can use Word to create, insert, and position figures, tables, and other graphics to enhance the look of your documents. Figure 1 shows a business letter that a sales representative composed with Word.

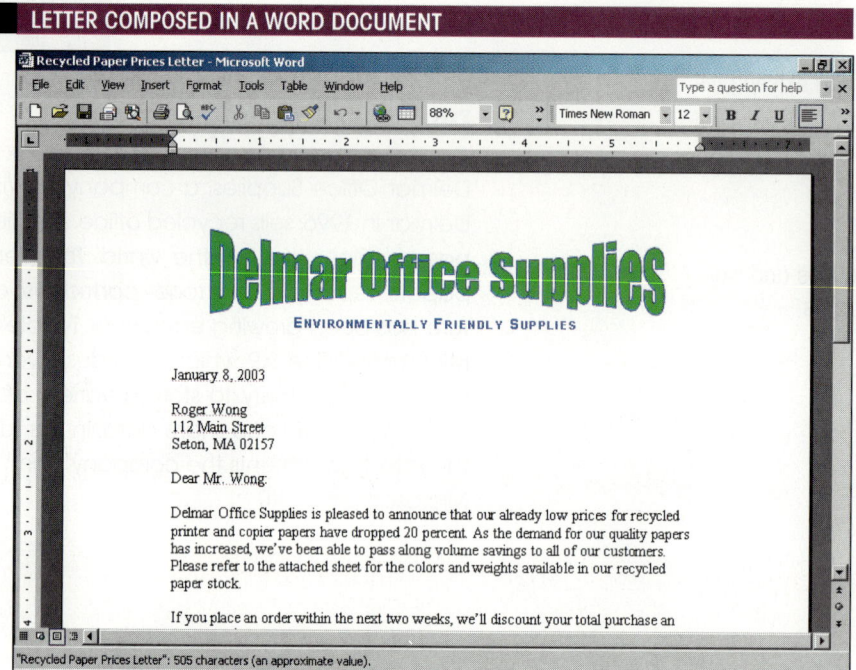

Figure 1 LETTER COMPOSED IN A WORD DOCUMENT

Microsoft Excel 2002, or simply **Excel**, is a **spreadsheet program** you use to display, organize, and analyze numerical information. You can do some of this in Word with tables, but Excel provides many more tools for performing calculations than Word does. Its graphics capabilities also enable you to display data visually. You might, for example, generate a pie chart or bar chart to help readers quickly see the significance of and the connections between information. The files you create in Excel are called **workbooks**. Figure 2 shows an Excel workbook with a line chart that the Operations Department uses to track the company's financial performance.

Figure 2   FINANCIAL DATA IN AN EXCEL WORKBOOK

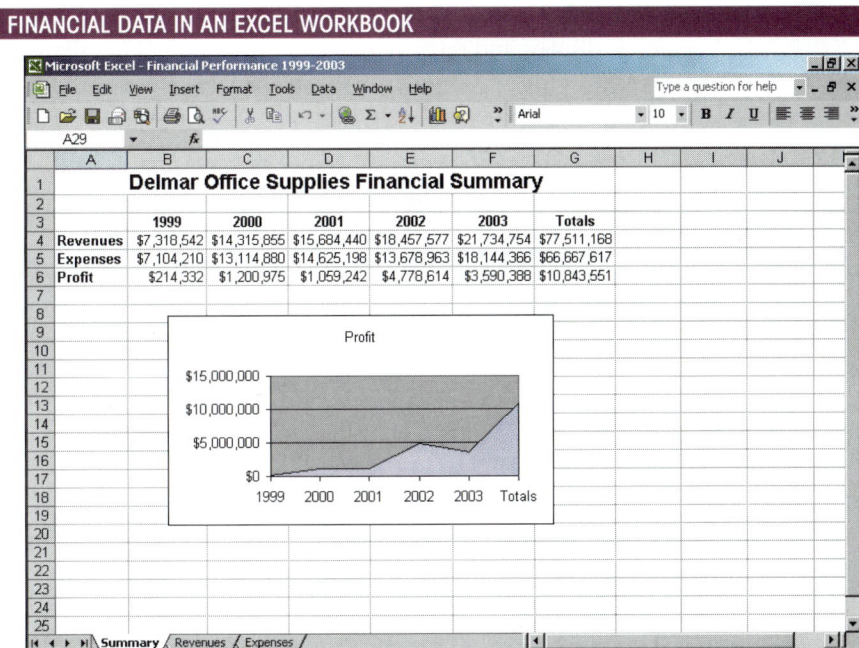

Microsoft PowerPoint 2002, or simply **PowerPoint**, is a **presentation graphics program** you use to create a collection of "slides" that can contain text, charts, pictures, and so on. The files you create in PowerPoint are called **presentations**. You can show these presentations on your computer monitor, project them onto a screen as a slide show, print them, share them over the Internet, or display them on the World Wide Web. You also can use PowerPoint to generate presentation-related documents such as audience handouts, outlines, and speakers' notes. Figure 3 shows an effective slide presentation the Sales Department created with PowerPoint to promote the latest product line.

Figure 3   SLIDE PRESENTATION CREATED IN POWERPOINT

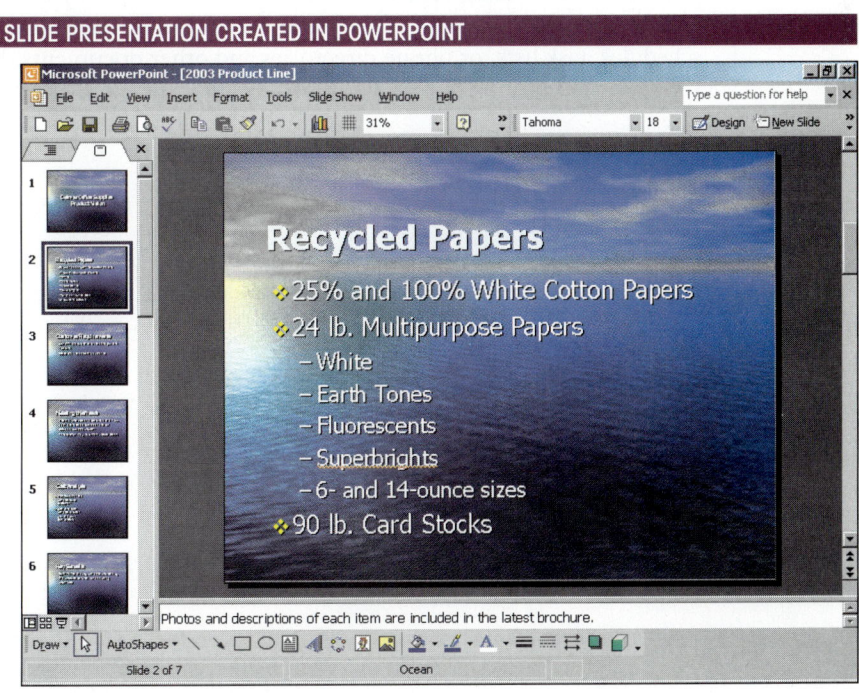

Microsoft Access 2002, or simply **Access**, is a **database program** you use to enter, organize, display, and retrieve related information. The files you create in Access are called **databases**. With Access you can create data entry forms to make data entry easier, and you can create professional reports to improve the readability of your data. Figure 4 shows a table in an Access database with customer names and addresses compiled by the Sales Department.

Figure 4: CUSTOMER ADDRESSES COMPILED IN AN ACCESS DATABASE

Customer Num	Name	Street	City	State/Prov	Postal Code
501	Wonder Supplies	5499 Alpine Lane	Gardner	MA	01440
285	The Best Supplies	2837 Commonwealth Avenue	Cambridge	MA	02142
129	Office World	95 North Bay Boulevard	Warwick	RI	02287
135	Supplies Plus	2840 Cascade Road	Laconia	NH	03246
104	American Office	Pond Hill Road	Millinocket	ME	04462
515	Pens and Paper	8200 Baldwin Boulevard	Burlington	VT	05406
165	Pen and Ink	1935 Snow Street	Nagatuck	CT	06770
423	Wonderful World of Work	H 1055	Budapest	Hungary	1/A
83	Sophia's Supplies	87 Weeping Willow Road	Brooklyn	NY	11201
17	Supplies and More	132-A Old Country Road	Bellport	NY	11763
322	Supply Closet	114 Lexington	Plattsburgh	NY	12901
302	Blackburg's Stationers	4489 Perlman Avenue	Blacksburg	VA	24060
136	Home Office Needs	4090 Division Stret NW	Fort Lauderdale	FL	33302
131	Supplies 4 U	14832 Old Bedford Trail	Mishawaka	IN	46544
122	VIP Stationery	8401 E. Fletcher Road	Clare	MI	48617
164	Supply Depot	1355 39th Street	Roscommon	MI	48653
325	Max Office Supplies	56 Four Mile Road	Grand Rapids	MI	49505
133	Supply Your Office	2874 Western Avenue	Sioux Falls	SD	57057
107	A+ Supplies	82 Mix Avenue	Bonners Ferry	ID	83805
203	Discount Supplies	28320 Fruitland Street	Studio City	CA	94106
536	One Stop Shop	31 Union Street	San Francisco	CA	94123
82	Supply Stop	2159 Causewayside	Edinburgh	Scotland	EH9 1PH
202	Office Products	3130 Edgwood Parkway	Thunder Bay	Ontario	L5B 1X2
407	Paper and More	44 Tower Lane	Leeds	England	LS12 3SD
394	The Office Store	397 Pine Road	Toronto	Ontario	M4J1B5

Microsoft Outlook 2002, or simply **Outlook**, is an **information management program** you use to send, receive, and organize e-mail; plan your schedule; arrange meetings; organize contacts; create a to-do list; and jot down notes. You also can use Outlook to print schedules, task lists, or phone directories and other documents. Figure 5 shows how Nicole Delmar uses Outlook to plan her schedule and create a to-do list.

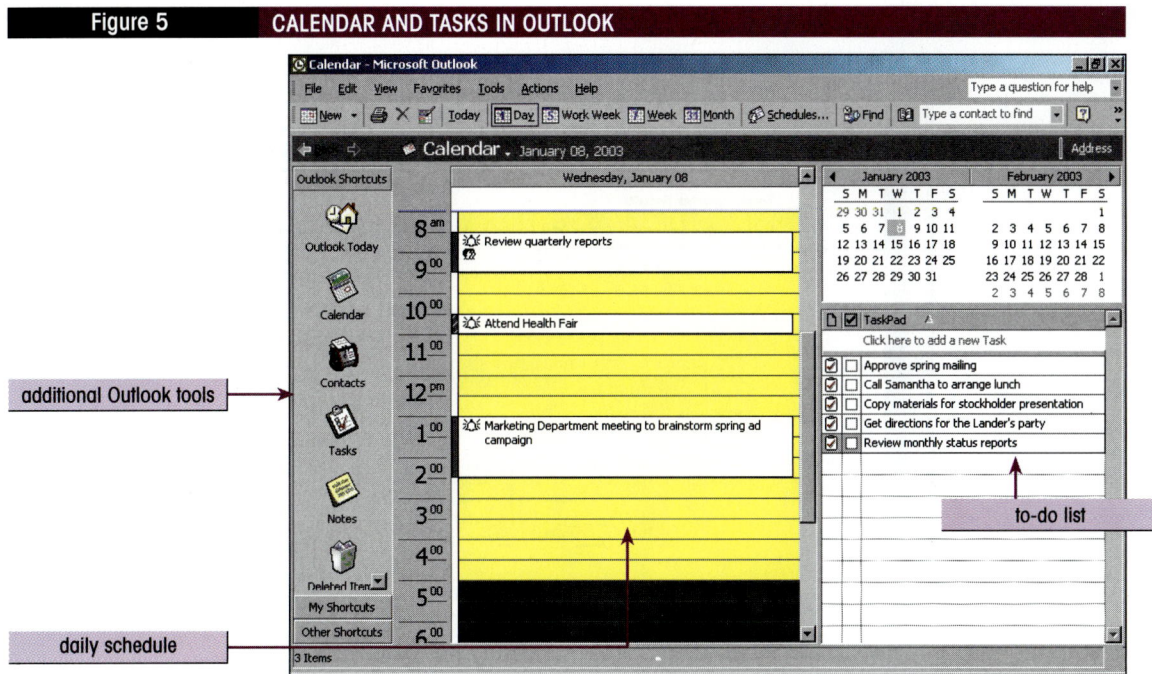

Figure 5 — CALENDAR AND TASKS IN OUTLOOK

Although each Office program individually is a strong tool, their potential is even greater when used together.

Integrating Programs

One of the main advantages of Office is **integration**, the ability to share information between programs. Integration ensures consistency and accuracy, and it saves time because you don't have to re-enter the same information in several Office programs. The staff at Delmar Office Supplies uses the integration features of Office daily, including the following examples:

- The Accounting Department created an Excel bar chart on the last two years' fourth-quarter results, which they inserted into the quarterly financial report, created in Word. They added a hyperlink to the Word report that employees can click to open the Excel workbook and view the original data. See Figure 6.

Figure 6 — WORD DOCUMENT WITH AN EXCEL CHART

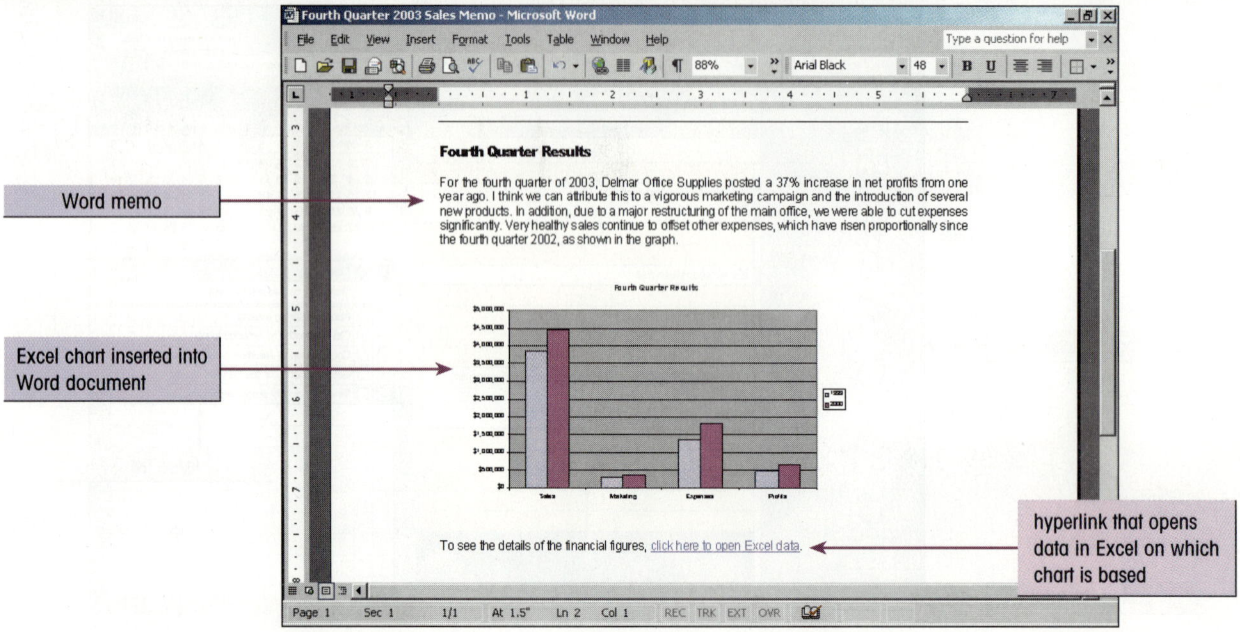

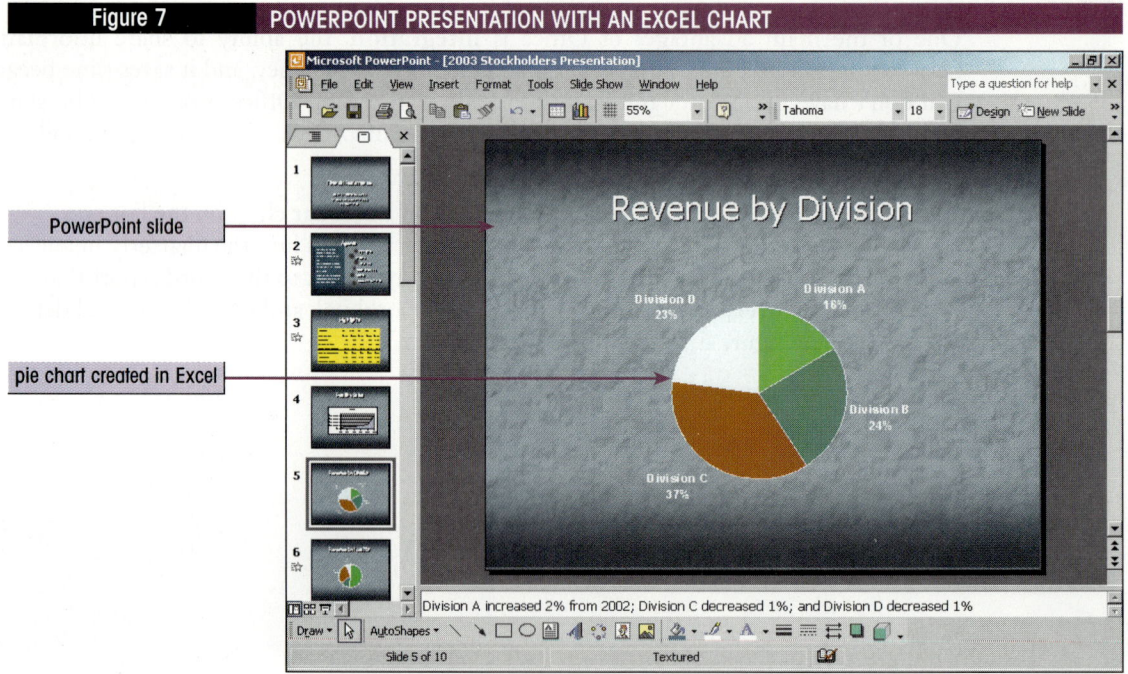

- An Excel pie chart of sales percentages by divisions of Delmar Office Supplies can be duplicated on a PowerPoint slide. The slide is part of the Operations Department's presentation to stockholders. See Figure 7.

Figure 7 — POWERPOINT PRESENTATION WITH AN EXCEL CHART

- An Access database or an Outlook contact list that stores the names and addresses of customers can be combined with a form letter that the Marketing Department created in Word, to produce a mailing promoting the company's newest products. See Figure 8.

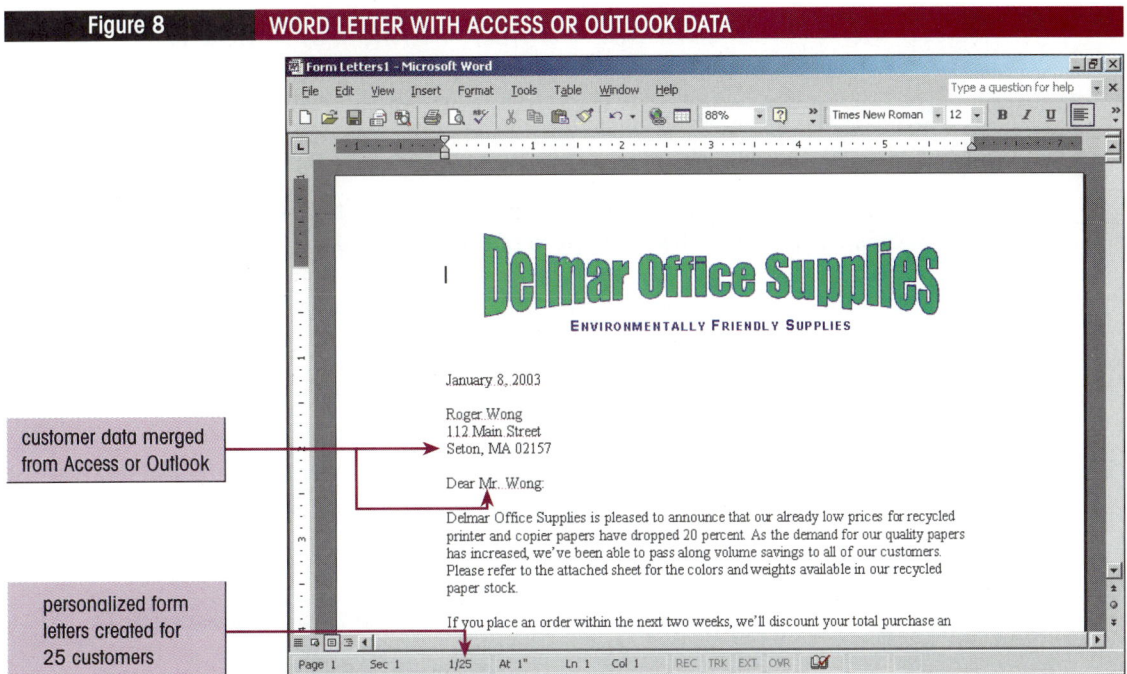

Figure 8 — WORD LETTER WITH ACCESS OR OUTLOOK DATA

customer data merged from Access or Outlook

personalized form letters created for 25 customers

These are just a few examples of how you can take information from one Office program and integrate it into another.

Starting Office Programs

All Office programs start the same way—from the Programs menu on the Start button. You select the program you want, and then the program starts so you can immediately begin to create new files or work with existing ones.

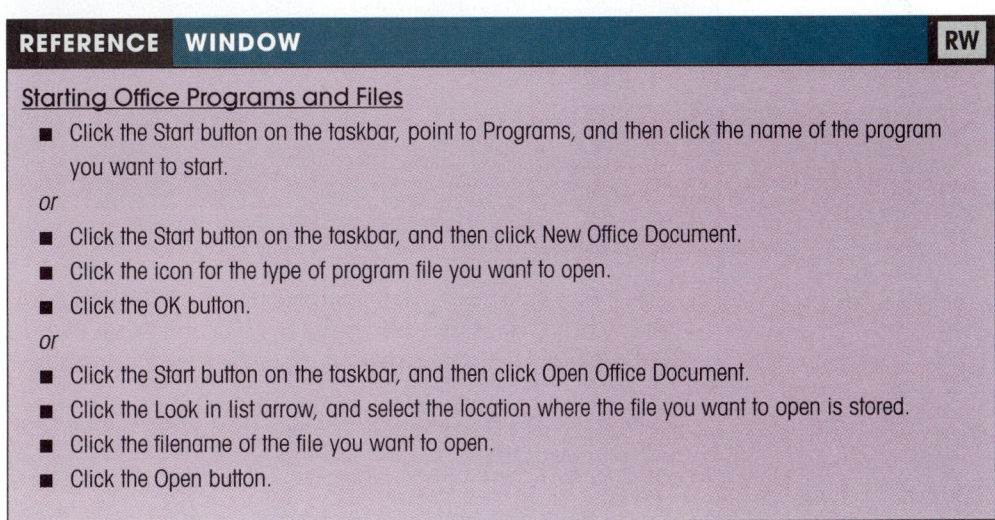

REFERENCE WINDOW

Starting Office Programs and Files
- Click the Start button on the taskbar, point to Programs, and then click the name of the program you want to start.

or
- Click the Start button on the taskbar, and then click New Office Document.
- Click the icon for the type of program file you want to open.
- Click the OK button.

or
- Click the Start button on the taskbar, and then click Open Office Document.
- Click the Look in list arrow, and select the location where the file you want to open is stored.
- Click the filename of the file you want to open.
- Click the Open button.

You'll start Excel using the Start button.

To start Excel and open a new, blank workbook from the Start menu:

1. Make sure your computer is on and the Windows desktop appears on your screen.

   TROUBLE? Don't worry if your screen differs slightly from those shown in the figures. The figures in this book were created while running Windows 2000 in its default settings, but Office runs equally well using Windows 98 or later or Windows NT 4 with Service Pack 5. These operating systems share the same basic user interface.

2. Click the **Start** button on the taskbar, and then point to **Programs** to display the Programs menu.

3. Point to **Microsoft Excel** on the Programs menu. See Figure 9. Depending on how your computer is set up, your desktop and menu might contain different icons and commands.

Figure 9 — START MENU WITH PROGRAMS MENU DISPLAYED

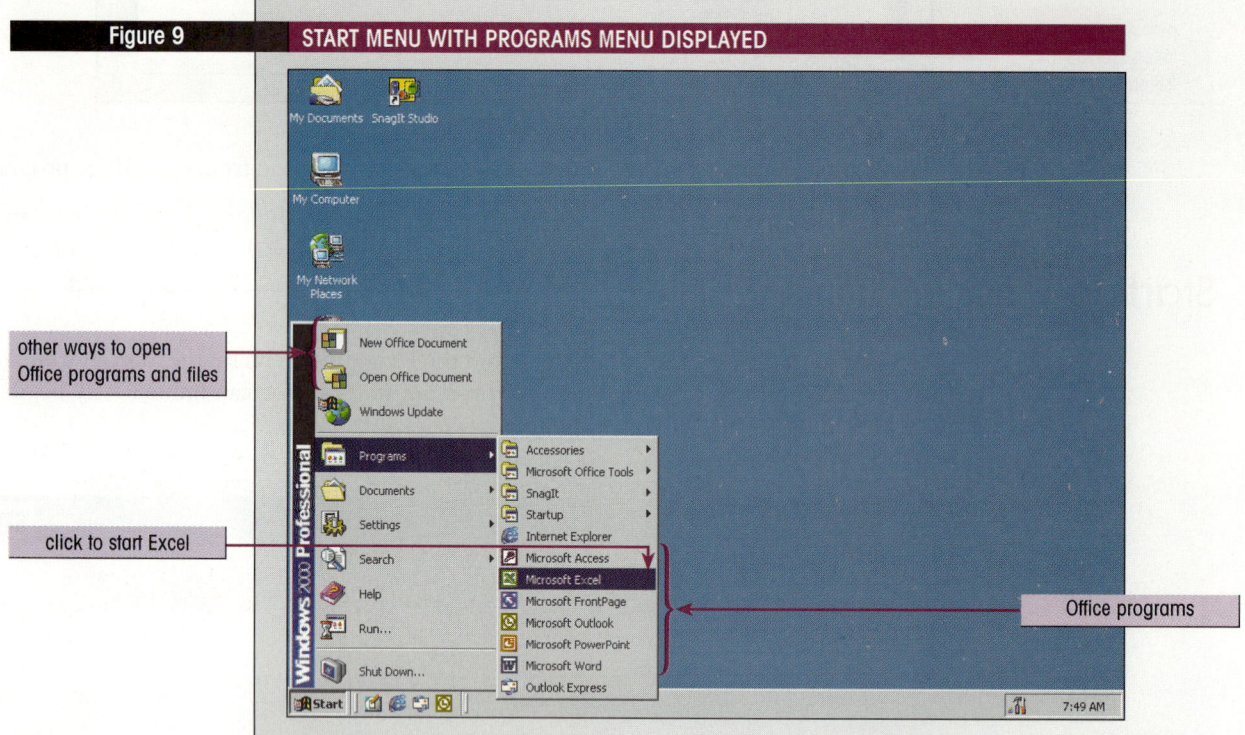

other ways to open Office programs and files

click to start Excel

Office programs

   TROUBLE? If you don't see Microsoft Excel on the Programs menu, point to Microsoft Office, and then point to Microsoft Excel. If you still don't see Microsoft Excel, ask your instructor or technical support person for help.

4. Click **Microsoft Excel** to start Excel and open a new, blank workbook. See Figure 10.

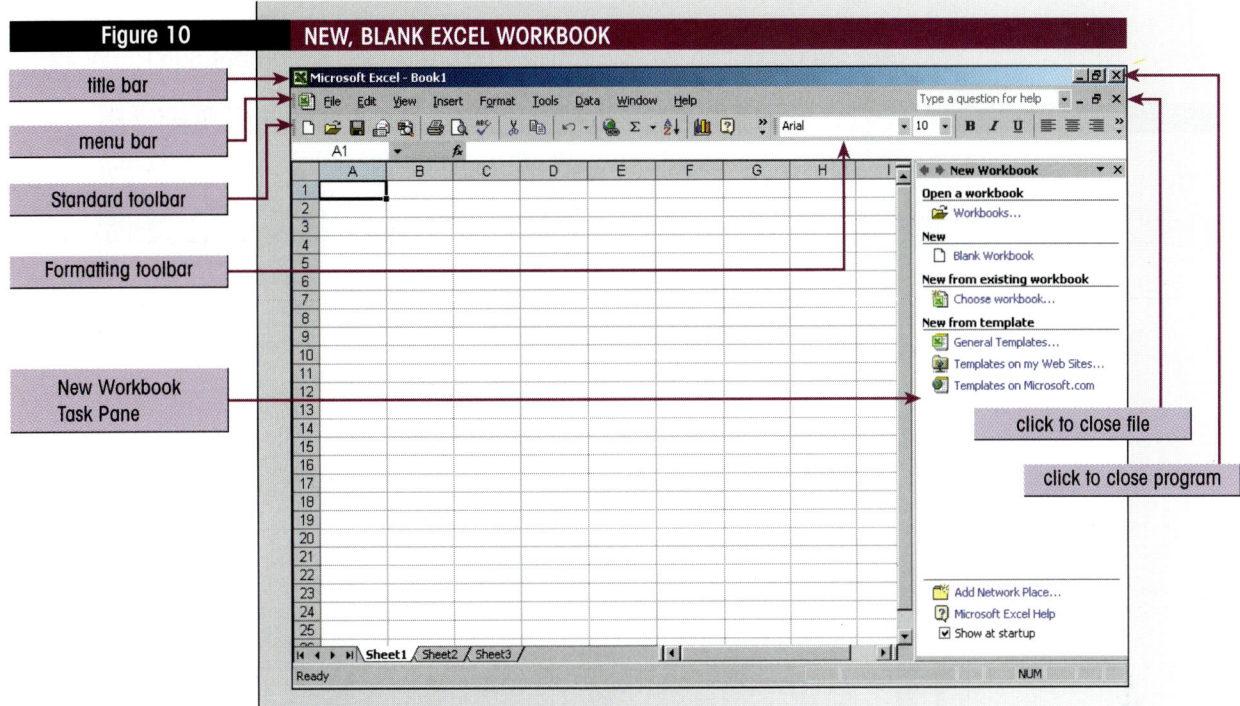

Figure 10 NEW, BLANK EXCEL WORKBOOK

An alternate method for starting programs with a blank file is to click the New Office Document command on the Start menu; the kind of file you choose determines which program opens. You'll use this method to start Word and open a new, blank document.

To start Word and open a new, blank document with the New Office Document command:

1. Leaving Excel open, click the **Start** button on the taskbar, and then click **New Office Document**. The New Office Document dialog box opens, providing another way to start Office programs. See Figure 11.

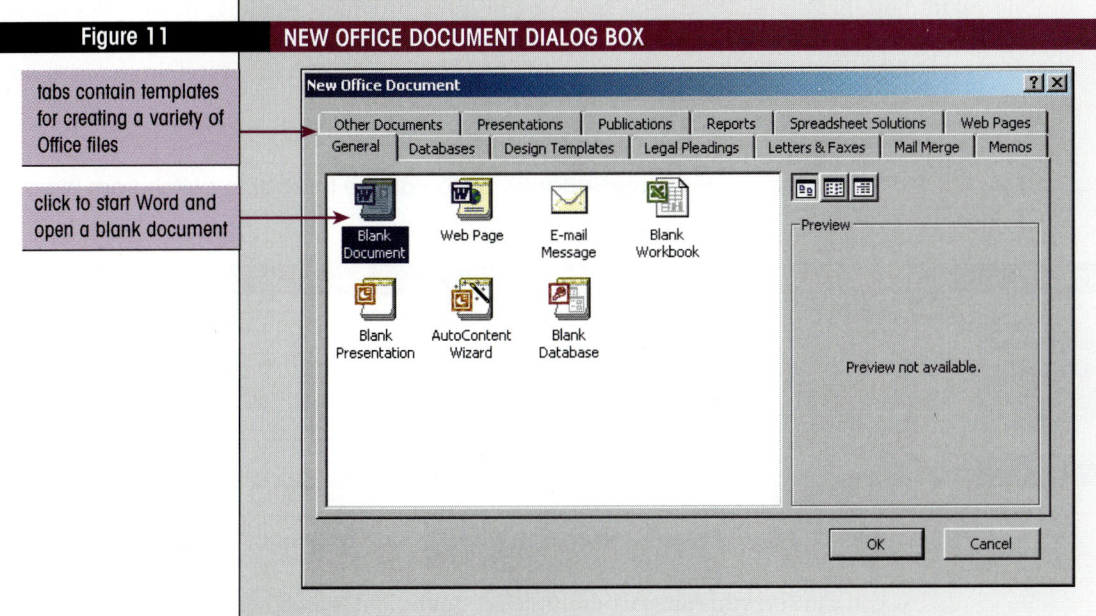

Figure 11 NEW OFFICE DOCUMENT DIALOG BOX

2. If necessary, click the **General** tab, click the **Blank Document** icon, and then click the **OK** button. Word opens with a new, blank document. See Figure 12.

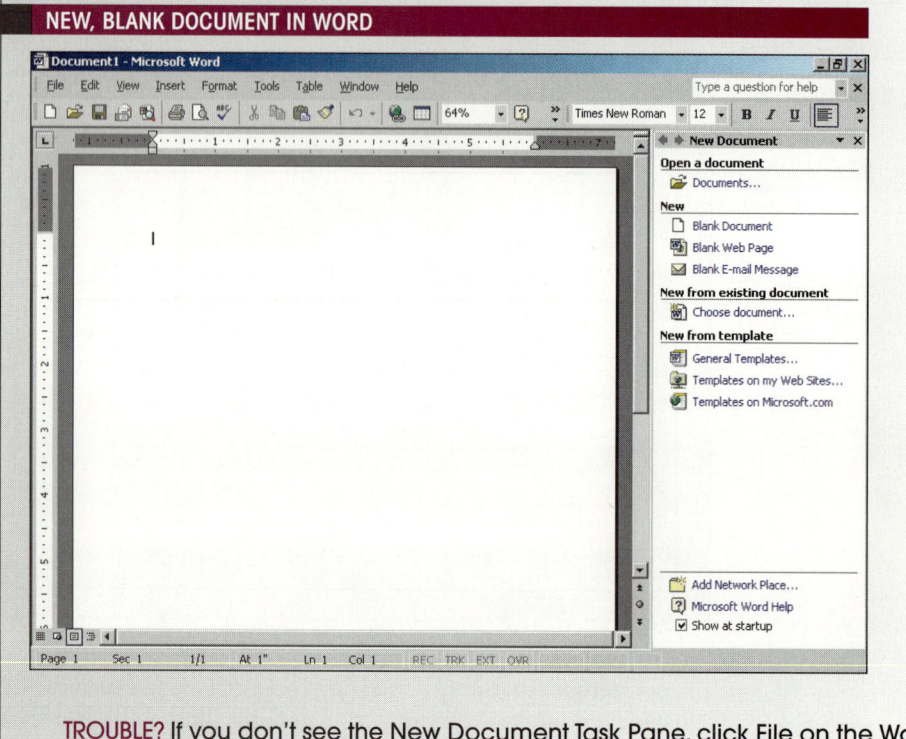

Figure 12 NEW, BLANK DOCUMENT IN WORD

TROUBLE? If you don't see the New Document Task Pane, click File on the Word menu bar, and then click New.

You've tried two ways to start a program. There are several methods for performing most tasks in Office. This flexibility enables you to use Office in the way that fits how you like to work.

Switching Between Open Programs and Files

Two programs are running at the same time—Excel and Word. The taskbar contains buttons for both programs. When you have two or more programs running, or two files within the same program open, you can use the taskbar buttons to switch from one program or file to another. The employees at Delmar Office Supplies often work in several programs at once.

To switch between Word and Excel:

1. Click the **Microsoft Excel - Book1** button on the taskbar to switch from Word to Excel. See Figure 13.

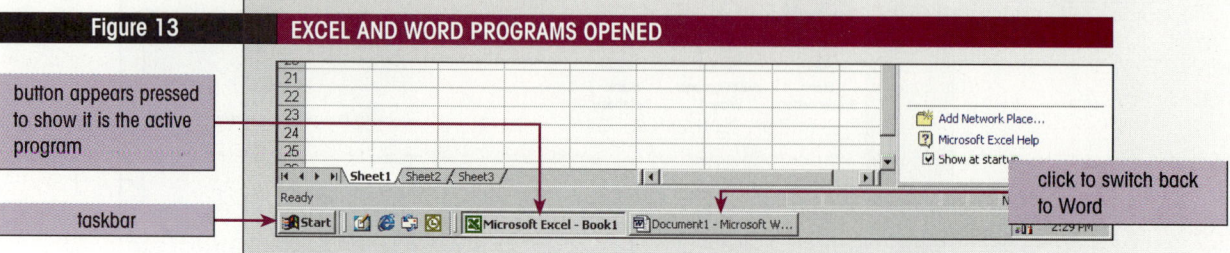

Figure 13 EXCEL AND WORD PROGRAMS OPENED

- button appears pressed to show it is the active program
- taskbar
- click to switch back to Word

2. Click the **Document1 - Microsoft Word** button on the taskbar to return to Word.

As you can see, you can start multiple programs and switch between them in seconds.

The Office programs also share many features, so once you've learned one program, it's easy to learn the others. One of the most visible similarities among all the programs is the "personalized" menus and toolbars.

Using Personalized Menus and Toolbars

In each Office program, you perform tasks using a menu command, a toolbar button, or a keyboard shortcut. A **menu command** is a word on a menu that you click to execute a task; a **menu** is a group of related commands. For example, the File menu contains commands for managing files, such as the Open command and the Save command. A **toolbar** is a collection of **buttons** that correspond to commonly used menu commands. For example, the Standard toolbar contains an Open button and a Save button. **Keyboard shortcuts** are combinations of keys you press to perform a command. For example, Ctrl+S is the keyboard shortcut for the Save command (you hold down the Ctrl key while you press the S key). Keyboard shortcuts are displayed to the right of many menu commands.

When you first use a newly installed Office program, the menus and toolbars display only the basic and most commonly used commands and buttons, streamlining the program window. The other commands and buttons are available, but you have to click an extra button to see them (the double-arrow button on a menu and the Toolbar Options button on a toolbar). As you select commands and click buttons, the ones you use often are put on the short, personalized menu and on the visible part of the toolbars. The ones you don't use remain available on the full menus and toolbars. This means that the Office menus and toolbars might display different commands and buttons on each person's computer.

To view a personalized and full menu:

1. Click **Insert** on the Word menu bar to display the short, personalized menu. See Figure 14. The Bookmark command, for example, does not appear on the short menu.

Figure 14   SHORT, PERSONALIZED MENU

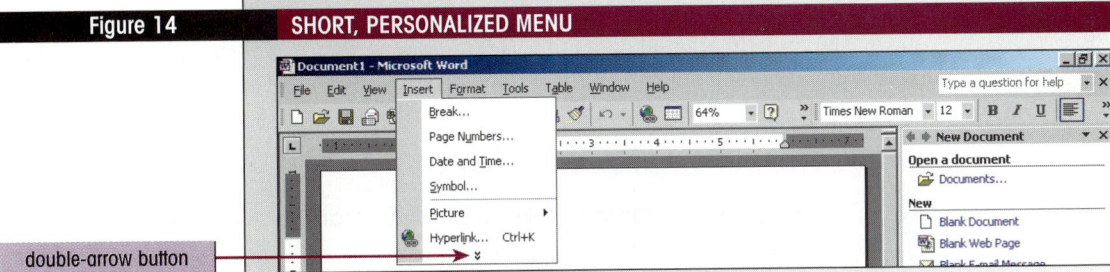

double-arrow button

TROUBLE? If the Insert menu displays different commands than shown in Figure 14, you need to reset the menus. Click Tools on the menu bar, click Customize (you might need to pause until the full menu appears to see that command), and then click the Options tab in the Customize dialog box. Click the Always show full menus check box to remove the check mark if necessary, and then click the Show full menus after a short delay check box to insert a check mark if necessary. Click the Reset my usage data button, and then click the Yes button to confirm that you want to reset the commands. Click the Close button. Repeat Step 1.

You can display the full menu in one of three ways: (1) pause until the full menu appears, which might happen as you read this; (2) click the double-arrow button at the bottom of the menu; or (3) double-click the menu name on the menu bar.

2. Pause until the full Insert menu appears, as shown in Figure 15. The Bookmark command and other commands are now visible.

Figure 15   EXPANDED, FULL MENU

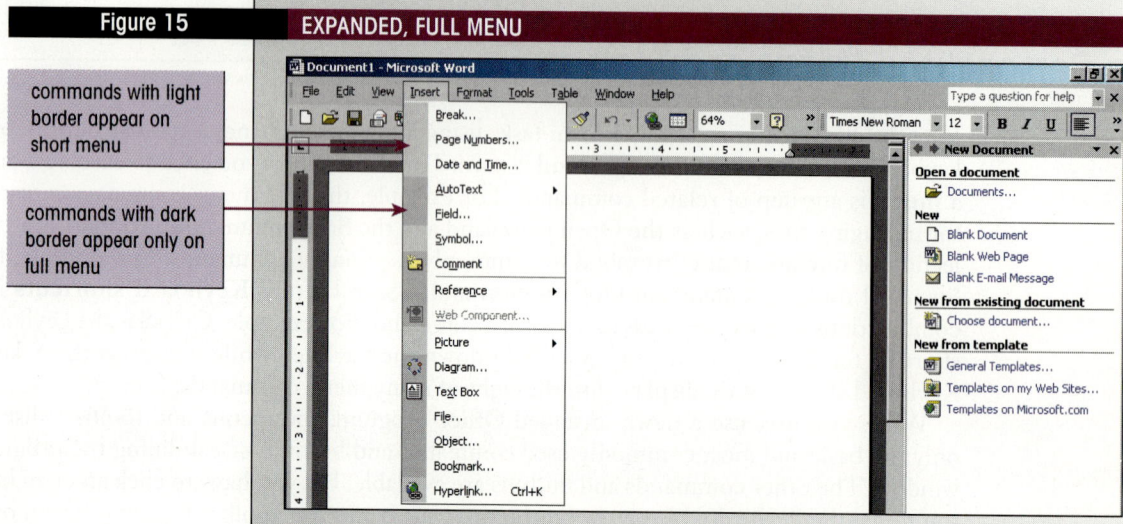

commands with light border appear on short menu

commands with dark border appear only on full menu

3. Click the **Bookmark** command. A dialog box opens when you click a command whose name is followed by an ellipsis (...). In this case, the Bookmark dialog box opens.

4. Click the **Cancel** button to close the Bookmark dialog box.

5. Click **Insert** on the menu bar again to display the short, personalized menu. The Bookmark command appears on the short, personalized menu because you used it.

6. Press the **Esc** key to close the menu.

As you can see, the menu changed based on your actions. Over time, only the commands you use frequently will appear on the personalized menu. The toolbars work similarly.

To use the personalized toolbars:

1. Observe that the Standard and Formatting toolbars appear side by side below the menu bar.

   TROUBLE? If the toolbars appear on two rows, you need to reset them. Click Tools on the menu bar, click Customize, and then click the Options tab in the Customize dialog box. Click the Show Standard and Formatting toolbars on two rows check box to remove the check mark. Click the Reset my data usage button, and then click the Yes button to confirm you want to reset the commands. Click the Close button. Repeat Step 1.

   The Formatting toolbar sits to the right of the Standard toolbar. You can see most of the Standard toolbar buttons, but only a few Formatting toolbar buttons.

2. Click the **Toolbar Options** button at the right side of the Standard toolbar. See Figure 16.

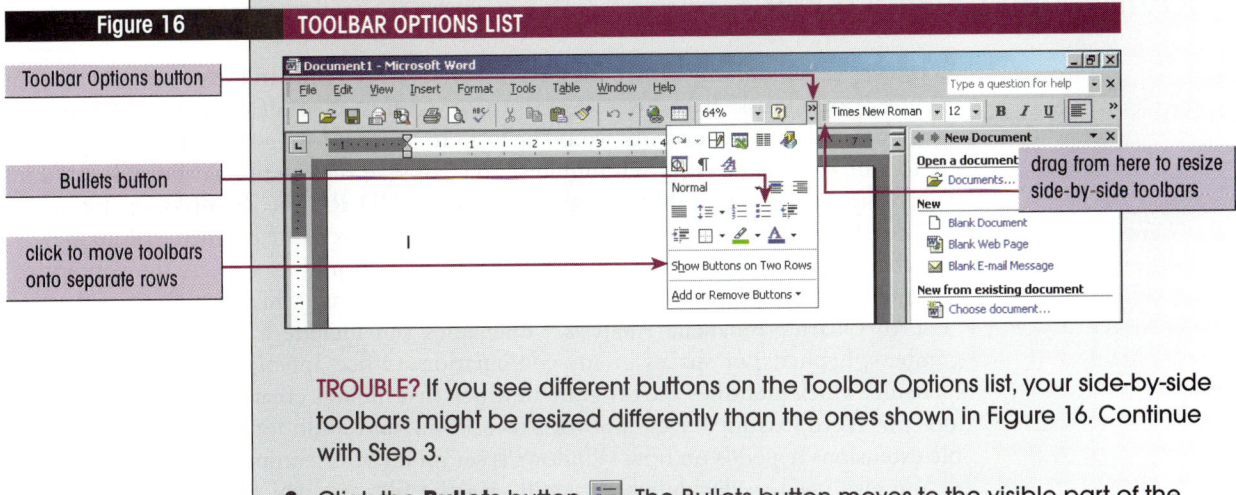

Figure 16 TOOLBAR OPTIONS LIST

- Toolbar Options button
- Bullets button
- click to move toolbars onto separate rows
- drag from here to resize side-by-side toolbars

TROUBLE? If you see different buttons on the Toolbar Options list, your side-by-side toolbars might be resized differently than the ones shown in Figure 16. Continue with Step 3.

3. Click the **Bullets** button. The Bullets button moves to the visible part of the Formatting toolbar, and another button is moved onto the Toolbar Options list to make room for the new button.

TROUBLE? If the Bullets button already appears on the Formatting toolbar, click another button on the Toolbar Options list. Then click that same button again in Step 4 to turn off that formatting.

4. Click again to turn off the Bullets formatting.

Some people like that the menus and toolbars change to meet their work habits. Others prefer to see all the menu commands or to display the toolbars on different rows so that all the buttons are always visible. You'll change the toolbar setting now.

To turn off the personalized toolbars:

1. Click the **Toolbar Options** button at the right side of the Standard toolbar.
2. Click the **Show Buttons on Two Rows command**. The toolbars move to separate rows (the Standard toolbar on top) and you can see all the buttons on each toolbar.

You can easily access any button on the toolbars with one mouse click. The drawback is that the toolbars take up more space in the program window.

Using Speech Recognition

Another way to perform tasks in Office is with your voice. Office's **speech recognition technology** enables you to say the names of the toolbar buttons, menus, menu commands, dialog box items, and so forth, rather than clicking the mouse or pressing keys to select them. The Language toolbar includes the Speech Balloon, which displays the voice command equivalents of a selected button or command. If you switch from Voice mode to Dictation mode, you can dictate the contents of your files rather than typing the text or numbers. For better accuracy, complete the Training Wizard, which helps Office learn your vocal quality, rate of talking, and speech patterns. To start using speech recognition, click Tools on the menu bar in any Office program, and then click Speech. The first time you start this feature, the Training Wizard guides you through the setup process.

Saving and Closing a File

As you create and modify Office files, your work is stored only in the computer's temporary memory, not on disk. If you were to exit the programs, turn off your computer, or experience a power failure, your work would be lost. To prevent losing work, frequently save your file to a disk—at least every ten minutes. You can save files to the hard disk located inside your computer or to portable storage disks, such as CD-ROMs, Zip disks, or floppy disks.

The first time you save a file, you need to name it. This name is called a **filename**. When you choose a filename, select a descriptive one that accurately reflects the content of the document, workbook, presentation, or database, such as "Shipping Options Letter" or "Fourth Quarter Financial Analysis." Filenames can include a maximum of 255 letters, numbers, hyphens, or spaces in any combination. Office appends a **file extension** to the filename, which identifies the program in which that file was created. The file extensions are .doc for Word, .xls for Excel, .ppt for PowerPoint, and .mdb for Access. Whether you see file extensions depends on how Windows is set up for your computer.

You also need to decide where you'll save the file—on which disk and in what folder. Choose a logical location that you'll remember whenever you want to use the file again.

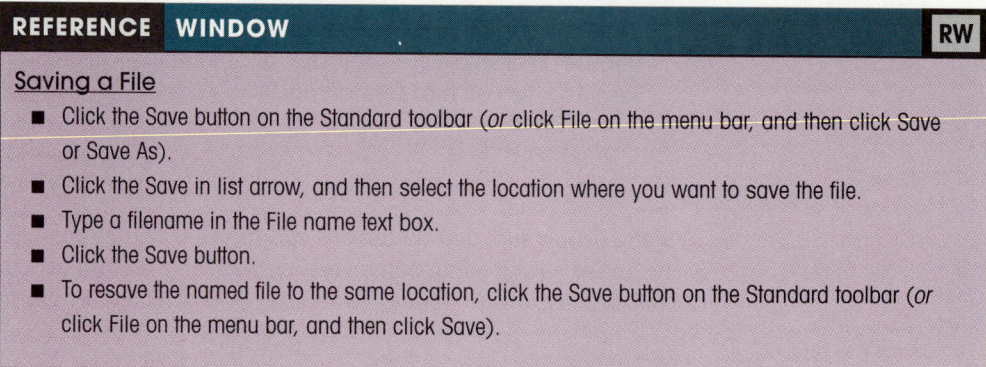

REFERENCE WINDOW | **RW**

<u>Saving a File</u>
- Click the Save button on the Standard toolbar (*or* click File on the menu bar, and then click Save or Save As).
- Click the Save in list arrow, and then select the location where you want to save the file.
- Type a filename in the File name text box.
- Click the Save button.
- To resave the named file to the same location, click the Save button on the Standard toolbar (*or* click File on the menu bar, and then click Save).

Nicole has asked you to start working on the agenda for the stockholder meeting. You enter text in a Word document by typing. After you type some text, you'll save the file.

To enter text in a document:

1. Type **Delmar Office Supplies**, and then press the **Enter** key. The text you typed appears on one line in the Word document.

    TROUBLE? If you make a typing error, press the Backspace key to delete the incorrect letters, and then retype the text.

2. Type **Stockholder Meeting Agenda**, and then press the **Enter** key. The text you typed appears on the second line.

The two lines of text you typed are not yet saved on disk. You'll do that now.

To save a file for the first time:

1. Insert your Data Disk in the appropriate drive.

   TROUBLE? If you don't have a Data Disk, you need to get one before you can proceed. Your instructor or technical support person will either give you one or ask you to make your own by following the instructions on the "Read This Before You Begin" page at the beginning of this tutorial. See your instructor or technical support person for more information.

2. Click the **Save** button on the Standard toolbar. The Save As dialog box opens. See Figure 17. The first few words of the first line appear in the File name text box, as a suggested filename. You'll replace this with a more descriptive filename.

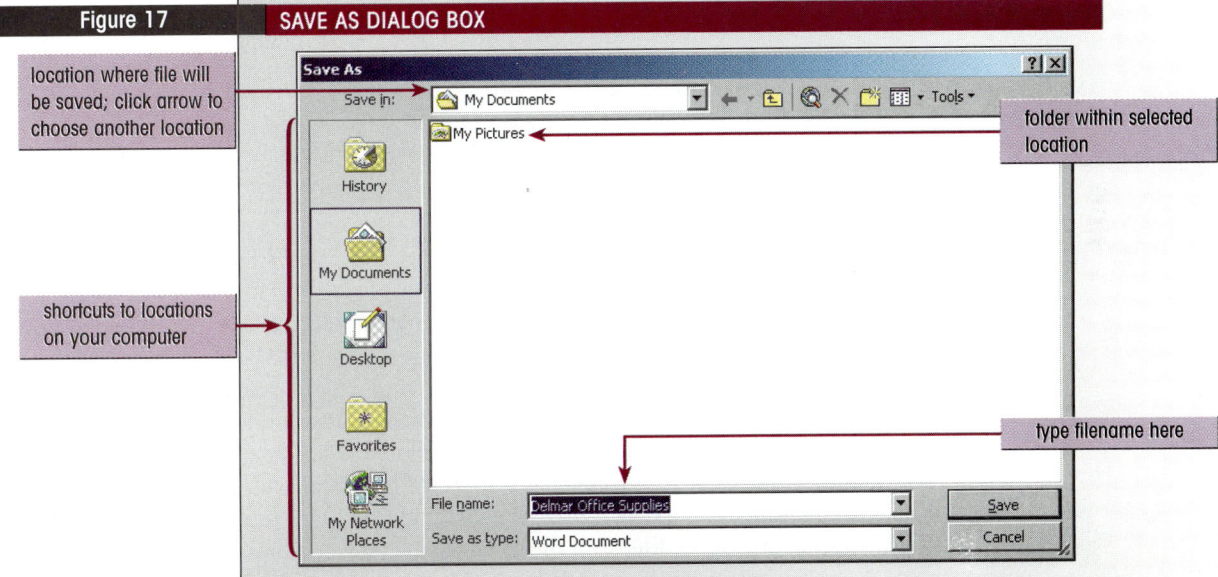

Figure 17 — SAVE AS DIALOG BOX

   TROUBLE? If the .doc file extension appears after the filename, then your computer is configured to show file extensions. Just continue with Step 3.

3. Type **Stockholder Meeting Agenda** in the File name text box.

4. Click the **Save in** list arrow, and then click the drive that contains your Data Disk.

5. Double-click the **Tutorial.01** folder in the list box, and then double-click the **Tutorial** folder. This is the location where you want to save the document.

6. Click the **Save** button. The Save As dialog box closes, and the name of your file appears in the program window title bar.

The saved file includes everything in the document at the time you saved. Any edits or additions you then make to the document exist only in the computer's memory and are not saved in the file on the disk. As you work, remember to save frequently so that the file is updated to reflect the latest content of the document.

Because you already named the document and selected a storage location, the second and subsequent times you save, the Save As dialog box doesn't open. If you wanted to save a copy of the file with a different filename or to a different location, you would reopen the Save As dialog box by clicking File on the menu bar, and then clicking Save As. The previous version of the file remains on your disk as well.

You need to add your name to the agenda. Then you'll save your changes and close the file. You can close a file by clicking the Close command on the File menu or by clicking the Close Window button in the upper-right corner of the menu bar.

> ### To modify, save, and close a file:
> 1. Type your name, and then press the **Enter** key. The text you typed appears on the next line.
> 2. Click the **Save** button 🖫 on the Standard toolbar.
>
>   The updated document is saved to the file. When you're done with a file, you can close it. Although you can keep multiple files open at one time, you should close any file you are no longer working on to conserve system resources.
> 3. Click the **Close Window** button ☒ on the Word menu bar to close the document. Word is still running, but no documents are open.
>
>   **TROUBLE?** If a dialog box opens and asks whether you want to save the changes you made to the document, you modified the document since you last saved. Click the Yes button to save the current version and close it.

Opening a File

Once you have a program open, you can create additional new files for the open programs or you can open previously created and saved files. You can do both of these from the New Task Pane. The New Task Pane enables you to create new files and open existing ones. The name of the Task Pane varies, depending on the program you are using: Word has the New Document Task Pane, Excel has the New Workbook Task Pane, PowerPoint has the New Presentation Task Pane, and Access has the New File Task Pane.

When you want to work on a previously created file, you must open it first. Opening a file transfers a copy of the file from the storage disk (either a hard disk or a portable disk) to the computer's memory and displays it on your screen. The file is then in your computer's memory and on the disk.

> ### REFERENCE WINDOW   RW
>
> Opening an Existing or New File
> - Click File on the menu bar, click New, and then (depending on the program) click the More documents, More workbooks, More presentations, or More files link in the New Task Pane (*or* click the Open button on the Standard toolbar *or* click File on the menu bar, and then click Open).
> - Click the Look in list arrow, and then select the storage location of the file you want to open.
> - Click the filename of the file you want to open.
> - Click the Open button.
>
> *or*
> - Click File on the menu bar, click New, and then (depending on the program) click the Blank Document, Blank Workbook, Blank Presentation, or Blank Database link in the New Task Pane (*or* click the New button on the Standard toolbar).

Nicole asks you to print the agenda. To do that, you'll reopen the file. Because Word is still open, you'll use the New Document Task Pane.

To open an existing file:

1. If necessary, click **File** on the menu bar, and then click **New** to display the New Document Task Pane. See Figure 18.

Figure 18   **NEW DOCUMENT TASK PANE**

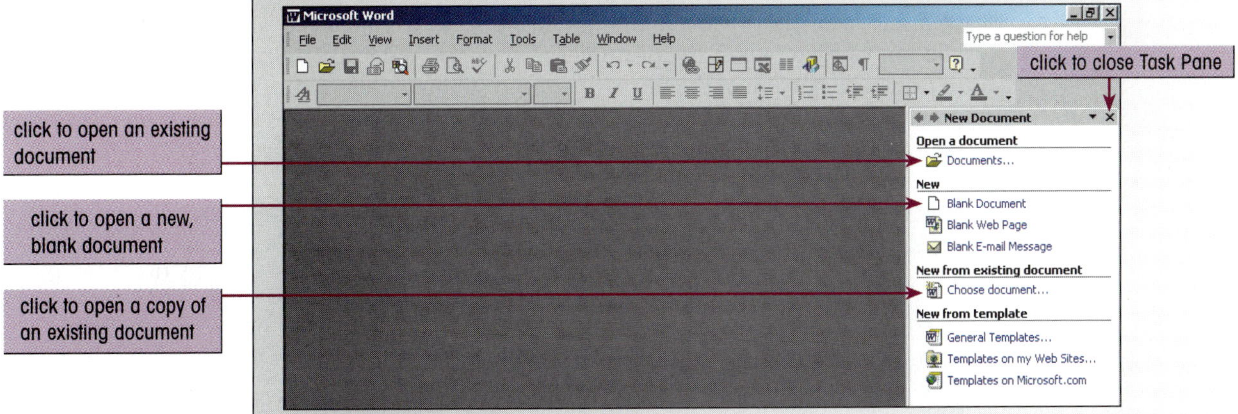

2. Click the **Documents** link in the Open a document area of the New Document Task Pane. The Open dialog box, which works similarly to the Save As dialog box, opens.

   TROUBLE? If you don't see the Documents link, look for a More Documents link below a list of recently opened files. The link name changes from Documents to More Documents after you have opened a file.

3. Click the **Look in** list arrow, and then select the **Tutorial** folder within the **Tutorial.01** folder on your Data Disk. This is the location where you saved the agenda document.

4. Click **Stockholder Meeting Agenda** in the file list. See Figure 19.

Figure 19   **OPEN DIALOG BOX**

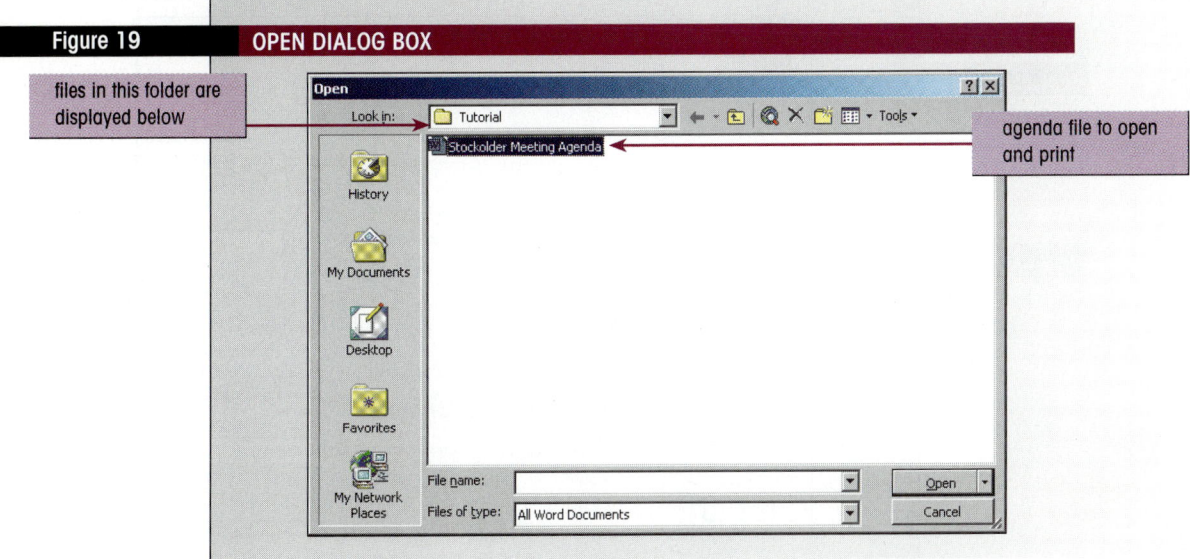

5. Click the **Open** button. The file you saved earlier reopens in the Word program window, and the New Document Task Pane closes.

After the file is open, you can view, edit, print, or resave it.

Printing a File

At times, you'll want a paper copy of your Office file. The first time you print during each computer session, you should use the Print menu command to open the Print dialog box so you can verify or adjust the printing settings. You can select a printer, the number of copies to print, the portion of the file to print, and so forth; the printing settings vary slightly from program to program. For subsequent print jobs you can use the Print button to print without opening the dialog box, if you want to use the same default settings.

REFERENCE WINDOW

Printing a File
- Click File on the menu bar, and then click Print.
- Verify the print settings in the Print dialog box.
- Click the OK button.

or
- Click the Print button on the Standard toolbar.

You'll print the agenda document.

To print a file:

1. Make sure your printer is turned on and contains paper.
2. Click **File** on the menu bar, and then click **Print**. The Print dialog box opens. See Figure 20.

Figure 20   PRINT DIALOG BOX

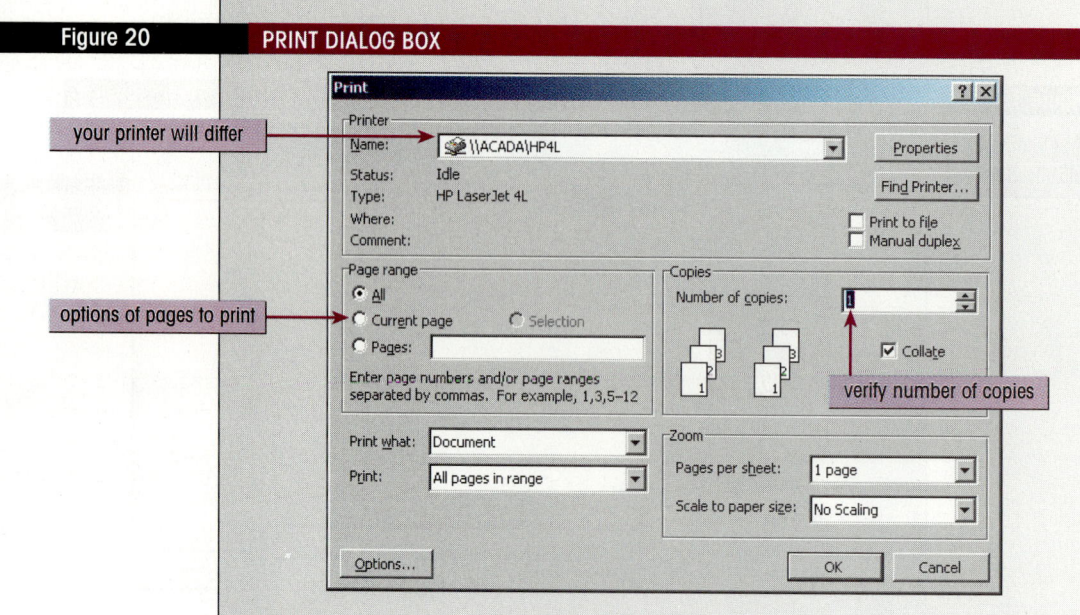

3. Verify that the correct printer appears in the Name list box. If the wrong printer appears, click the **Name** list arrow, and then click the correct printer from the list of available printers.

4. Verify that **1** appears in the Number of copies text box.

5. Click the **OK** button to print the document. See Figure 21.

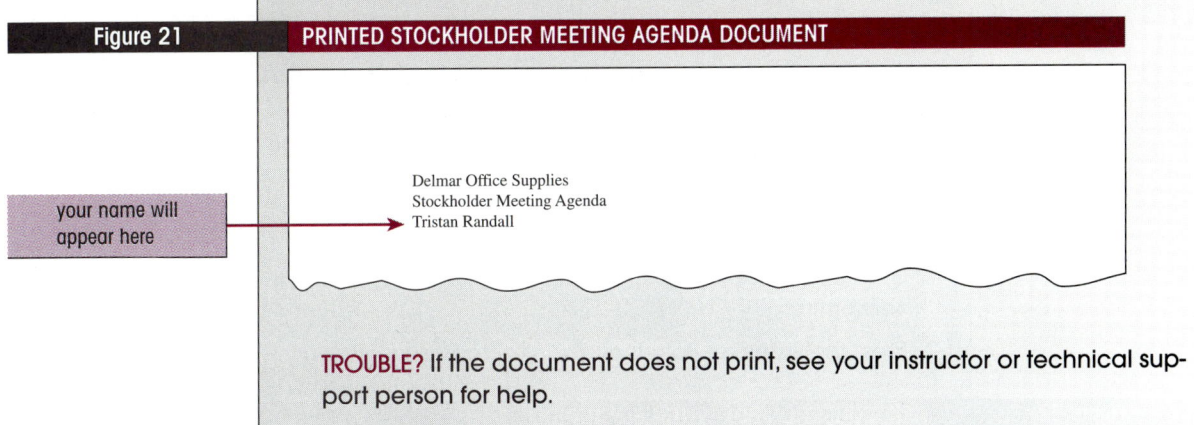

Figure 21 — PRINTED STOCKHOLDER MEETING AGENDA DOCUMENT

your name will appear here

Delmar Office Supplies
Stockholder Meeting Agenda
Tristan Randall

TROUBLE? If the document does not print, see your instructor or technical support person for help.

Another important aspect of Office is the ability to get help right from your computer.

Getting Help

If you don't know how to perform a task or want more information about a feature, you can turn to Office itself for information on how to use it. This information, referred to simply as **Help**, is like a huge encyclopedia stored on your computer. You can access it in a variety of ways.

There are two fast and simple methods you can use to get Help about objects you see on the screen. First, you can position the mouse pointer over a toolbar button to view its **ScreenTip**, a yellow box with the button's name. Second, you can click the **What's This?** command on the Help menu to change the pointer to ?, which you can click on any toolbar button, menu command, dialog box option, worksheet cell, or anything else you can see on your screen to view a brief description of that item.

For more in-depth help, you can use the **Ask a Question** box, located on the menu bar of every Office program, to find information in the Help system. You simply type a question using everyday language about a task you want to perform or a topic you need help with, and then press the Enter key to search the Help system. The Ask a Question box expands to show Help topics related to your query. You click a topic to open a Help window with step-by-step instructions that guide you through a specific procedure and explanations of difficult concepts in clear, easy-to-understand language. For example, you might ask how to format a cell in an Excel worksheet; a list of Help topics related to the words you typed will appear. The Help window also has Contents, Answer Wizard, and Index tabs, which you can use to look up information directly from the Help window.

If you prefer, you can ask questions of the **Office Assistant**, an interactive guide to finding information from the Help system. In addition, the Office Assistant can provide Help topics and tips on tasks as you work. For example, it might offer a tip when you select a menu command instead of clicking the corresponding toolbar button. You can turn on or off the tips, depending on your personal preference.

> **REFERENCE WINDOW** RW
>
> **Getting Help from the Ask a Question Box**
> - Click in the Ask a Question box on the menu bar.
> - Type your question, and then press the Enter key.
> - Click a Help topic.
> - Read the information in the Help window. For more information, click other topics or links.
> - Click the Close button in the Help window title bar.

You'll use the Ask a Question box to obtain more information about Help.

To use the Ask a Question box:

1. Click in the **Ask a Question** box on the menu bar, and then type **How do I search help?**.
2. Press the **Enter** key to retrieve a list of topics, as shown in Figure 22.

Figure 22 — ASK A QUESTION BOX WITH HELP TOPICS

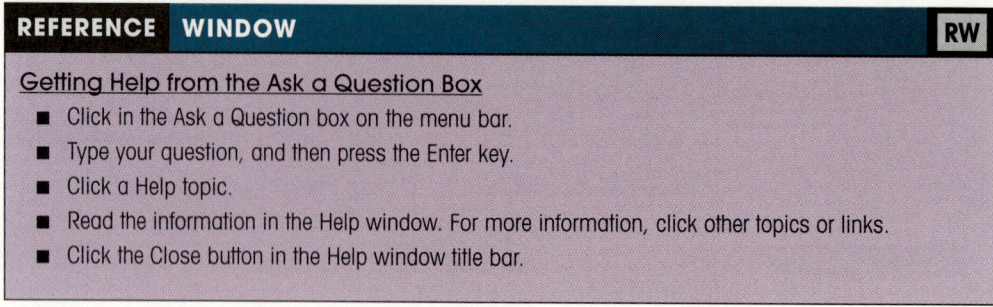

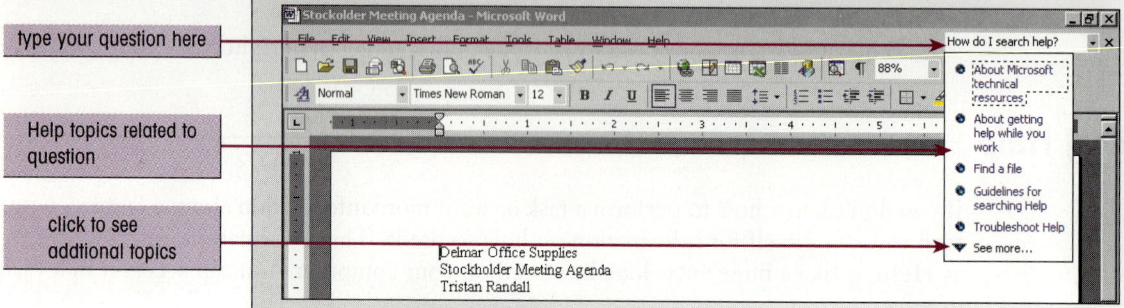

- type your question here
- Help topics related to question
- click to see addtional topics

3. Click the **See more** link, review the additional Help topics, and then click the **See previous** link.
4. Click **About getting help while you work** to open the Help window and learn more about the various ways to obtain assistance in Office. See Figure 23.

Figure 23 — HELP WINDOW

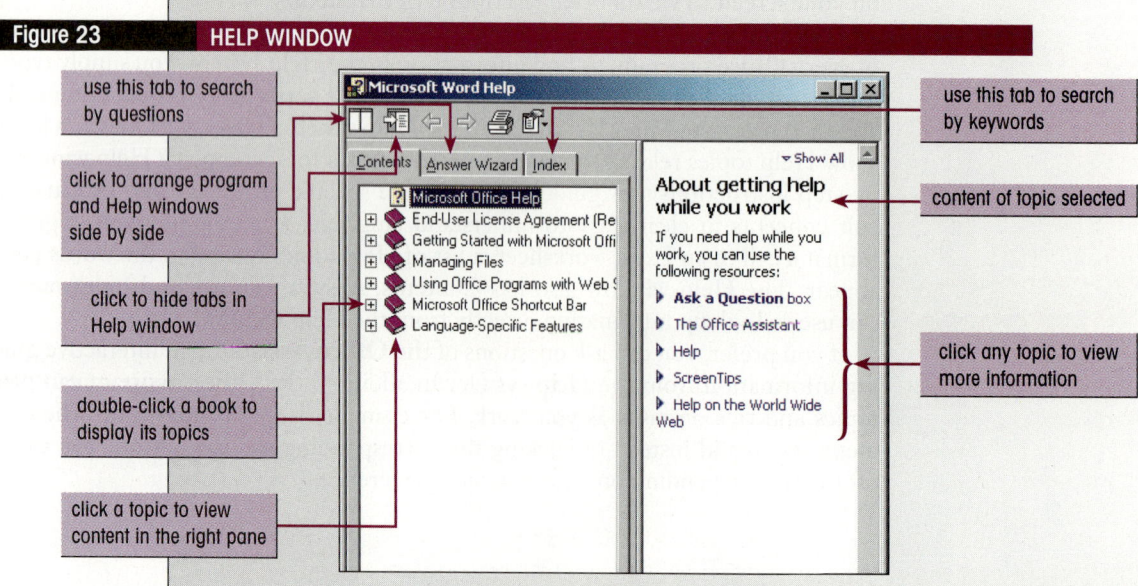

- use this tab to search by questions
- click to arrange program and Help windows side by side
- click to hide tabs in Help window
- double-click a book to display its topics
- click a topic to view content in the right pane
- use this tab to search by keywords
- content of topic selected
- click any topic to view more information

5. Click **Help** in the right pane to display information about that topic.
6. Click the other links about Help features and read the information.
7. When you're done, click the **Close** button ⨯ in the Help window title bar to return to the Word window.

The Help features enable the staff at Delmar Office Supplies to get answers to questions they have about any task or procedure when they need it. The more you practice getting information from the Help system, the more effective you will be at using Office to its full potential.

Exiting Programs

Whenever you finish working with a program, you should exit it. As with many other aspects of Office, you can exit programs with a button or from a menu. You'll use both methods to close Word and Excel.

To exit a program:

1. Click the **Close** button ⨯ in the upper-right corner of the screen to exit Word. Word exits, and the Excel window is visible again on your screen.

   TROUBLE? If a dialog box opens, asking whether you want to save the document, you may have inadvertently made a change to the document. Click the No button.

2. Click **File** on the menu bar, and then click **Exit**. The Excel program exits.

Exiting programs after you are done using them keeps your Windows desktop uncluttered for the next person using the computer, frees up your system's resources, and prevents data from being lost accidentally.

QUICK CHECK

1. Which Office program would you use to write a letter?
2. Which Office programs could you use to store customer names and addresses?
3. What is integration?
4. Explain the difference between Save As and Save.
5. What is the purpose of the New Task Pane?
6. When would you use the Ask a Question box?

REVIEW ASSIGNMENTS

Before the stockholders meeting at Delmar Office Supplies, you'll open and print documents for the upcoming presentation.

1. Start PowerPoint using the Start button and the Programs menu.
2. Use the Ask a Question box to learn how to change the toolbar buttons from small to large, and then do it. Use the same procedure to change the buttons back to regular size. Close the Help window when you're done.

3. Open a blank Excel workbook using the New Office Document command on the Start menu.

Explore 4. Switch to the PowerPoint window using the taskbar, and then close the presentation but leave open the PowerPoint program. (*Hint:* Click the Close Window button in the menu bar.)

Explore 5. Open a new, blank PowerPoint presentation from the New Presentation Task Pane. (*Hint:* Click Blank Presentation in the New area of the New Presentation Task Pane.)

6. Close the PowerPoint presentation and program using the Close button in the PowerPoint title bar; do not save changes if asked.

Explore 7. Open a copy of the Excel **Finances** workbook located in the **Review** folder within the **Tutorial.01** folder on your Data Disk using the New Workbook Task Pane. (*Hint:* Click File on the Excel menu bar and then click New to open the Task Pane. Click Choose Workbook in the New from existing workbook area of the New Workbook Task Pane; the dialog box functions similarly to the Open dialog box.)

8. Type your name, and then press the Enter key to insert your name at the top of the worksheet.

9. Save the worksheet as **Delmar Finances** in the **Review** folder within the **Tutorial.01** folder on your Data Disk.

10. Print one copy of the worksheet using the Print command on the File menu.

11. Exit Excel using the File menu.

Explore 12. Open the **Letter** document located in the **Review** folder within the **Tutorial.01** folder on your Data Disk using the Open Office Document command on the Start menu.

13. Use the Save As command to save the document with the filename **Delmar Letter** in the **Review** folder within the **Tutorial.01** folder on your Data Disk.

Explore 14. Press and hold the Ctrl key, press the End key, and then release both keys to move the insertion point to the end of the letter, and then type your name.

15. Use the Save button on the Standard toolbar to save the change to the Delmar Letter document.

16. Print one copy of the document, and then close the document.

17. Exit the Word program using the Close button on the title bar.

QUICK CHECK ANSWERS

1. Word
2. Access or Outlook
3. the ability to share information between programs
4. Save As enables you to change the filename and save location of a file. Save updates a file to reflect its latest contents using its current filename and location.
5. enables you to create new files and open existing files
6. when you don't know how to perform a task or want more information about a feature

LEVEL I

New Perspectives on

MICROSOFT® ACCESS 2002

TUTORIAL 1   AC 1.03

Introduction to Microsoft Access 2002
Viewing and Working with a Table Containing Employer Data

TUTORIAL 2   AC 2.01

Creating and Maintaining a Database
Creating the Northeast Database, and Creating, Modifying, and Updating the Position Table

TUTORIAL 3   AC 3.01

Querying a Database
Retrieving Information About Employers and Their Positions

TUTORIAL 4   AC 4.01

Creating Forms and Reports
Creating a Position Data Form, an Employer Positions Form, and an Employers and Positions Report

CREATING WEB PAGES WITH ACCESS   WEB 1

Creating Web Pages to Display Employer and Position Data

Read This Before You Begin

To the Student

Data Disks

To complete the Level I tutorials, Review Assignments, and Case Problems, you need six Data Disks. Your instructor will either provide you with these Data Disks or ask you to make your own.

If you are making your own Data Disks, you will need **six** blank, formatted high-density disks. You will need to copy a set of files and/or folders from a file server, standalone computer, or the Web onto your disks. Your instructor will tell you which computer, drive letter, and folders contain the files you need. You could also download the files by going to www.course.com and following the instructions on the screen.

The information below shows you which folders go on each of your disks, so that you will have enough disk space to complete all the tutorials, Review Assignments, and Case Problems:

Data Disk 1
Write this on the disk label:
Data Disk 1: Access Tutorial Files
Put this folder on the disk:
Tutorial

Data Disk 2
Write this on the disk label:
Data Disk 2: Access Review Assignments
Put this folder on the disk:
Review

Data Disk 3
Write this on the disk label:
Data Disk 3: Access Case Problem 1
Put this folder on the disk:
Cases

Data Disk 4
Write this on the disk label:
Data Disk 4: Access Case Problem 2
Put this folder on the disk:
Cases

Data Disk 5
Write this on the disk label:
Data Disk 5: Access Case Problem 3
Put this folder on the disk:
Cases

Data Disk 6
Write this on the disk label:
Data Disk 6: Access Case Problem 4
Put this folder on the disk:
Cases

When you begin each tutorial, be sure you are using the correct Data Disk. Refer to the "File Finder" chart at the back of this text for more detailed information on which files are used in which tutorials, and make sure you carefully read the note above the chart. See the inside front or inside back cover of this book for more information on Data Disk files, or ask your instructor or technical support person for assistance.

Course Labs

The Access Level I tutorials feature an interactive Course Lab to help you understand database concepts. There are Lab Assignments at the end of Tutorial 1 that relate to this Lab.

To start a Lab, click the **Start** button on the Windows taskbar, point to **Programs**, point to **Course Labs**, point to **New Perspectives Course Labs**, and then click the name of the Lab you want to use.

Using Your Own Computer

If you are going to work through this book using your own computer, you need:

- **Computer System** Microsoft Windows 98, NT, 2000 Professional, or higher must be installed on your computer. This book assumes a typical installation of Microsoft Access.

- **Data Disks** You will not be able to complete the tutorials or exercises in this book using your own computer until you have your Data Disks.

- **Course Labs** See your instructor or technical support person to obtain the Course Lab software for use on your own computer.

Visit Our World Wide Web Site

Additional materials designed especially for you are available on the World Wide Web.
Go to www.course.com/NewPerspectives.

To the Instructor

The Data Disk Files and Course Labs are available on the Instructor's Resource Kit for this title. Follow the instructions in the Help file on the CD-ROM to install the programs to your network or standalone computer. For information on creating Data Disks or the Course Labs, see the "To the Student" section above.

You are granted a license to copy the Data Files and Course Labs to any computer or computer network used by students who have purchased this book.

TUTORIAL 1

OBJECTIVES

In this tutorial you will:

- Define the terms field, record, table, relational database, primary key, and foreign key

- Open an existing database

- Identify the components of the Access and Database windows

- Open and navigate a table

- Learn how Access saves a database

- Open an existing query, and create, sort, and navigate a new query

- Create and navigate a form

- Create, preview, and navigate a report

- Learn how to manage a database by backing up, restoring, compacting, and converting a database

LAB

Databases

INTRODUCTION TO MICROSOFT ACCESS 2002

Viewing and Working with a Table Containing Employer Data

CASE

Northeast Seasonal Jobs International (NSJI)

During her high school and college years, Elsa Jensen spent her summers working as a lifeguard for some of the most popular beaches on Cape Cod, Massachusetts. Throughout those years, Elsa met many foreign students who had come to the United States to work for the summer, both at the beaches and at other seasonal businesses, such as restaurants and hotels. Elsa formed friendships with several students and kept in contact with them beyond college. Through discussions with her friends, Elsa realized that foreign students often have a difficult time finding appropriate seasonal work, relying mainly on "word-of-mouth" references to locate jobs. Elsa became convinced that there must be an easier way.

Several years ago, Elsa founded Northeast Seasonal Jobs, a small firm located in Boston that served as a job broker between foreign students seeking part-time, seasonal work and resort businesses located in New England. Recently Elsa expanded her business to include resorts in the eastern provinces of Canada, and consequently she changed her company's name to Northeast Seasonal Jobs International (NSJI). At first the company focused mainly on summer employment, but as the business continued to grow, Elsa increased the scope of operations to include all types of seasonal opportunities, including foliage tour companies in the fall and ski resorts in the winter.

Elsa depends on computers to help her manage all areas of NSJI's operations, including financial management, sales, and information management. Several months ago the company upgraded to Microsoft Windows and **Microsoft Access 2002** (or simply **Access**), a computer program used to enter, maintain, and retrieve related data in a format known as a database. Elsa and her staff use Access to maintain data such as information about employers, positions they have available for seasonal work, and foreign students seeking employment. Elsa recently created a database named Seasonal to track the company's employer customers and data about their available positions. She asks for your help in completing and maintaining this database.

AC 1.03

SESSION 1.1

In this session, you will learn key database terms and concepts, open an existing database, identify components of the Access and Database windows, open and navigate a table, and learn how Access saves a database.

Introduction to Database Concepts

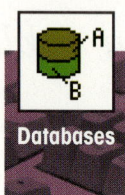

Before you begin working on Elsa's database and using Access, you need to understand a few key terms and concepts associated with databases.

Organizing Data

Data is a valuable resource to any business. At NSJI, for example, important data includes employers' names and addresses, and available positions and wages. Organizing, storing, maintaining, retrieving, and sorting this type of data are critical activities that enable a business to find and use information effectively. Before storing data on a computer, however, you first must organize the data.

Your first step in organizing data is to identify the individual fields. A **field** is a single characteristic or attribute of a person, place, object, event, or idea. For example, some of the many fields that NSJI tracks are employer ID, employer name, employer address, employer phone number, position, wage, and start date.

Next, you group related fields together into tables. A **table** is a collection of fields that describe a person, place, object, event, or idea. Figure 1-1 shows an example of an Employer table consisting of four fields: EmployerID, EmployerName, EmployerAddress, and PhoneNumber.

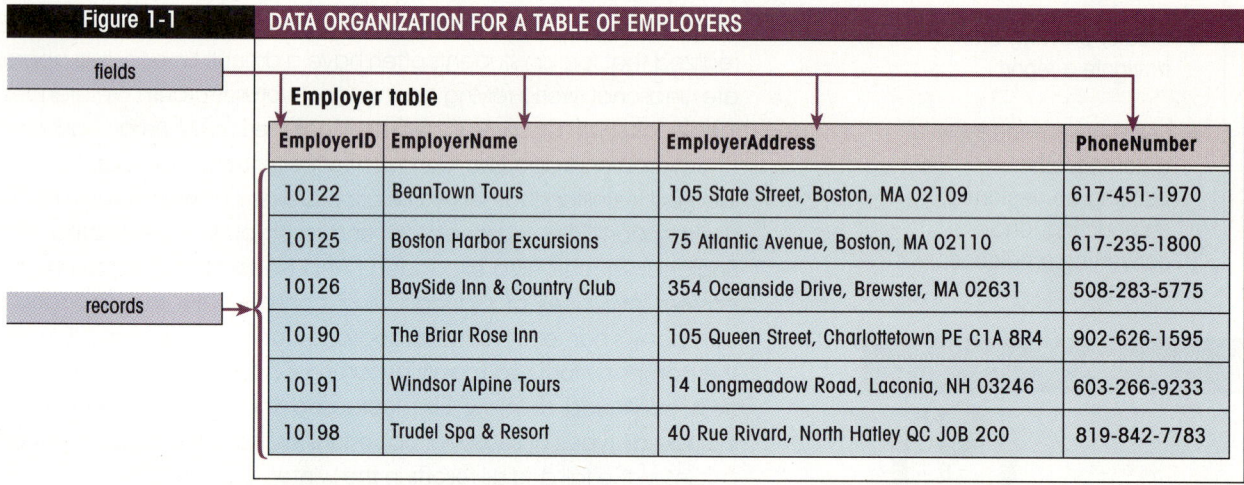

Figure 1-1 DATA ORGANIZATION FOR A TABLE OF EMPLOYERS

The specific value, or content, of a field is called the **field value**. In Figure 1-1, the first set of field values for EmployerID, EmployerName, EmployerAddress, and PhoneNumber are, respectively: 10122; BeanTown Tours; 105 State Street, Boston, MA 02109; and 617-451-1970. This set of field values is called a **record**. In the Employer table, the data for each employer is stored as a separate record. Figure 1-1 shows six records; each row of field values is a record.

Databases and Relationships

A collection of related tables is called a **database**, or a **relational database**. NSJI's Seasonal database contains two related tables: the Employer and NAICS tables, which Elsa created. (The NAICS table contains North American Industry Classification System codes, which are used to classify businesses by the type of activity in which they are engaged.) In Tutorial 2, you will create a Position table to store information about the available positions at NSJI's employer clients.

Sometimes you might want information about employers and their available positions. To obtain this information, you must have a way to connect records in the Employer table to records in the Position table. You connect the records in the separate tables through a **common field** that appears in both tables.

In the sample database shown in Figure 1-2, each record in the Employer table has a field named EmployerID, which is also a field in the Position table. For example, BaySide Inn & Country Club is the third employer in the Employer table and has an EmployerID of 10126. This same EmployerID field value, 10126, appears in three records in the Position table. Therefore, BaySide Inn & Country Club is the employer with these three positions available.

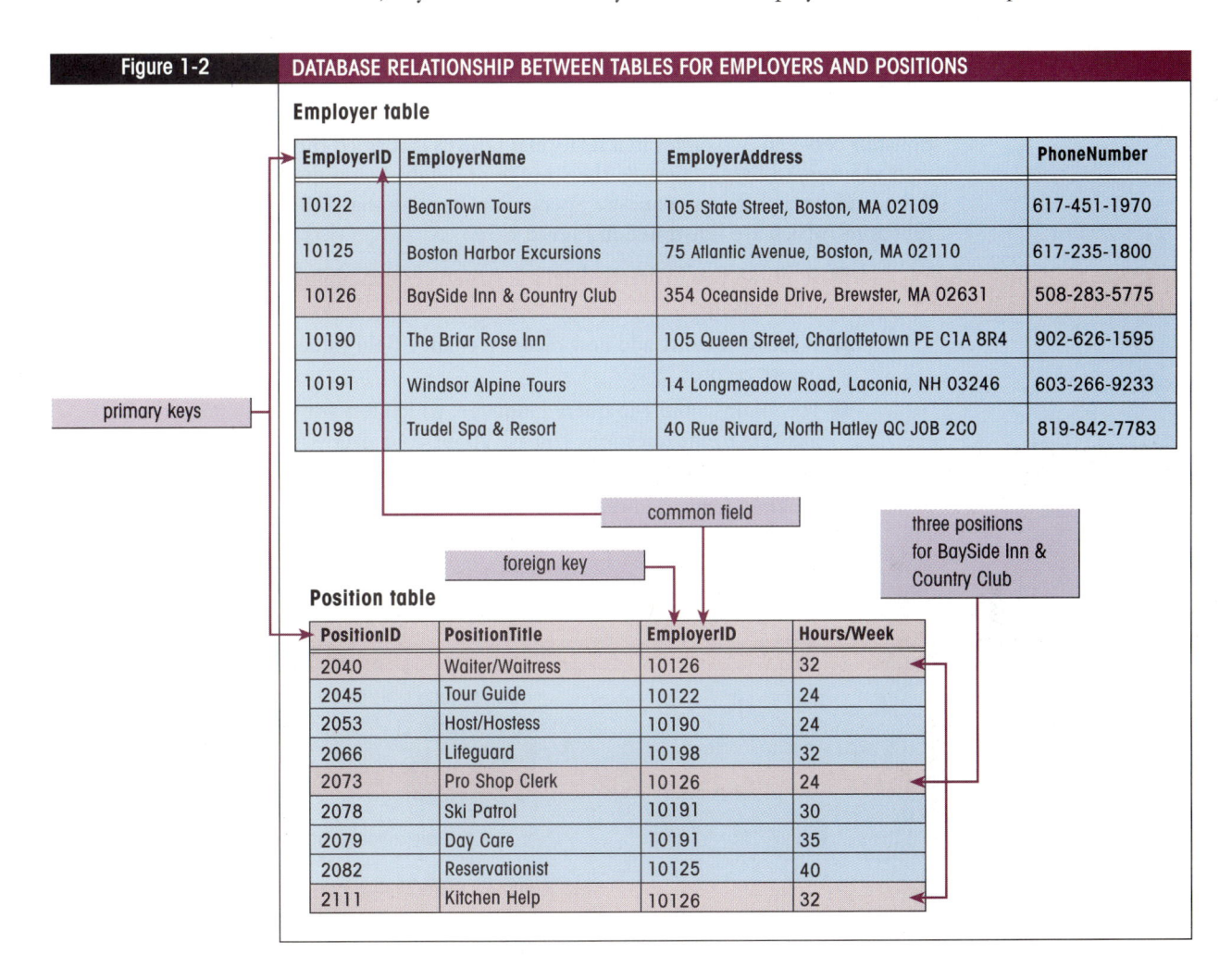

Figure 1-2   DATABASE RELATIONSHIP BETWEEN TABLES FOR EMPLOYERS AND POSITIONS

Employer table

EmployerID	EmployerName	EmployerAddress	PhoneNumber
10122	BeanTown Tours	105 State Street, Boston, MA 02109	617-451-1970
10125	Boston Harbor Excursions	75 Atlantic Avenue, Boston, MA 02110	617-235-1800
10126	BaySide Inn & Country Club	354 Oceanside Drive, Brewster, MA 02631	508-283-5775
10190	The Briar Rose Inn	105 Queen Street, Charlottetown PE C1A 8R4	902-626-1595
10191	Windsor Alpine Tours	14 Longmeadow Road, Laconia, NH 03246	603-266-9233
10198	Trudel Spa & Resort	40 Rue Rivard, North Hatley QC J0B 2C0	819-842-7783

primary keys

common field · foreign key · three positions for BaySide Inn & Country Club

Position table

PositionID	PositionTitle	EmployerID	Hours/Week
2040	Waiter/Waitress	10126	32
2045	Tour Guide	10122	24
2053	Host/Hostess	10190	24
2066	Lifeguard	10198	32
2073	Pro Shop Clerk	10126	24
2078	Ski Patrol	10191	30
2079	Day Care	10191	35
2082	Reservationist	10125	40
2111	Kitchen Help	10126	32

Each EmployerID in the Employer table must be unique, so that you can distinguish one employer from another and identify the employer's specific positions available in the Position table. The EmployerID field is referred to as the primary key of the Employer table. A **primary key** is a field, or a collection of fields, whose values uniquely identify each record in a table. In the Position table, PositionID is the primary key.

When you include the primary key from one table as a field in a second table to form a relationship between the two tables, it is called a **foreign key** in the second table, as shown in Figure 1-2. For example, EmployerID is the primary key in the Employer table and a foreign key in the Position table. Although the primary key EmployerID has unique values in the Employer table, the same field as a foreign key in the Position table does not have unique values. The EmployerID value 10126, for example, appears three times in the Position table because the BaySide Inn & Country Club has three available positions. Each foreign key value, however, must match one of the field values for the primary key in the other table. In the example shown in Figure 1-2, each EmployerID value in the Position table must match an EmployerID value in the Employer table. The two tables are related, enabling users to connect the facts about employers with the facts about their employment positions.

Relational Database Management Systems

To manage its databases, a company purchases a database management system. A **database management system (DBMS)** is a software program that lets you create databases and then manipulate data in them. Most of today's database management systems, including Access, are called relational database management systems. In a **relational database management system**, data is organized as a collection of tables. As stated earlier, a relationship between two tables in a relational DBMS is formed through a common field.

A relational DBMS controls the storage of databases on disk by carrying out data creation and manipulation requests. Specifically, a relational DBMS provides the following functions, which are illustrated in Figure 1-3:

- It allows you to create database structures containing fields, tables, and table relationships.
- It lets you easily add new records, change field values in existing records, and delete records.
- It contains a built-in query language, which lets you obtain immediate answers to the questions you ask about your data.
- It contains a built-in report generator, which lets you produce professional-looking, formatted reports from your data.
- It provides protection of databases through security, control, and recovery facilities.

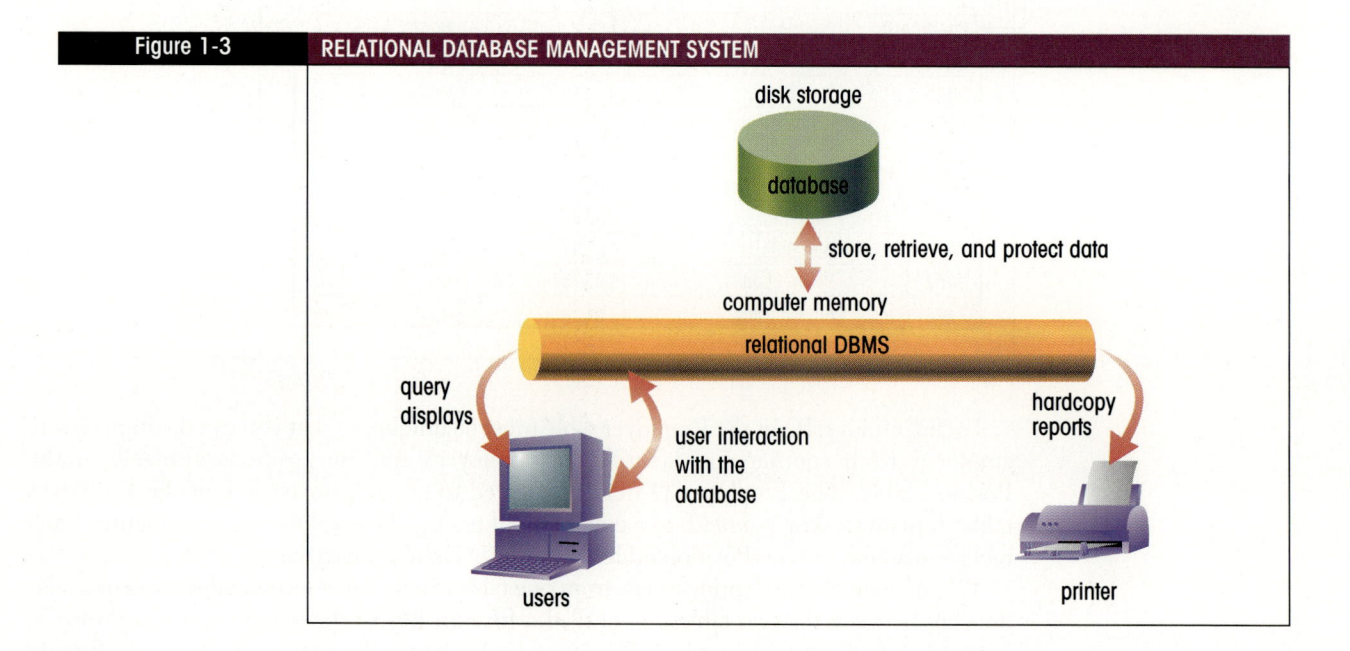

Figure 1-3   RELATIONAL DATABASE MANAGEMENT SYSTEM

A company such as NSJI benefits from a relational DBMS because it allows users working in different departments to share the same data. More than one user can enter data into a database, and more than one user can retrieve and analyze data that was entered by others. For example, NSJI will store only one copy of the Employer table, and all employees will be able to use it to meet their specific requests for employer information.

Finally, unlike other software programs, such as spreadsheets, a DBMS can handle massive amounts of data and can easily form relationships among multiple tables. Each Access database, for example, can be up to two gigabytes in size and can contain up to 32,768 objects (tables, queries, and so on).

Opening an Existing Database

Now that you've learned some database terms and concepts, you're ready to start Access and open the Seasonal database.

To start Access and open the Seasonal database:

1. Click the **Start** button on the taskbar, point to **Programs**, and then point to **Microsoft Access**. See Figure 1-4.

Figure 1-4   STARTING MICROSOFT ACCESS

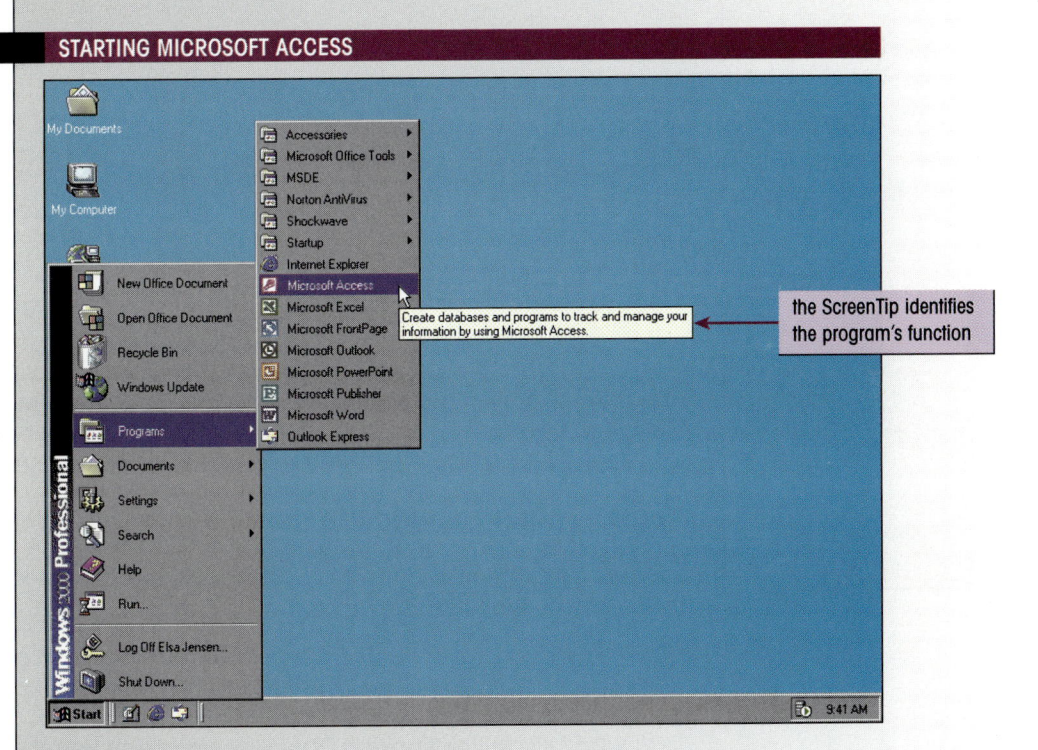

the ScreenTip identifies the program's function

TROUBLE? If your screen differs slightly from the figure, don't worry. Although the figures in this tutorial were created on a computer running Windows 2000 in its default settings, the different Windows operating systems share the same basic user interface, and Microsoft Access runs equally well using Windows 98, Windows NT, Windows 2000, or Windows XP.

TROUBLE? If you don't see the Microsoft Access option on the Programs menu, you might need to click the double arrow on the Programs menu to display more options. If you still cannot find the Microsoft Access option, ask your instructor or technical support person for help.

2. Click **Microsoft Access** to start Access. After a short pause, the Access copyright information appears in a message box and remains on the screen until the Access window opens. See Figure 1-5.

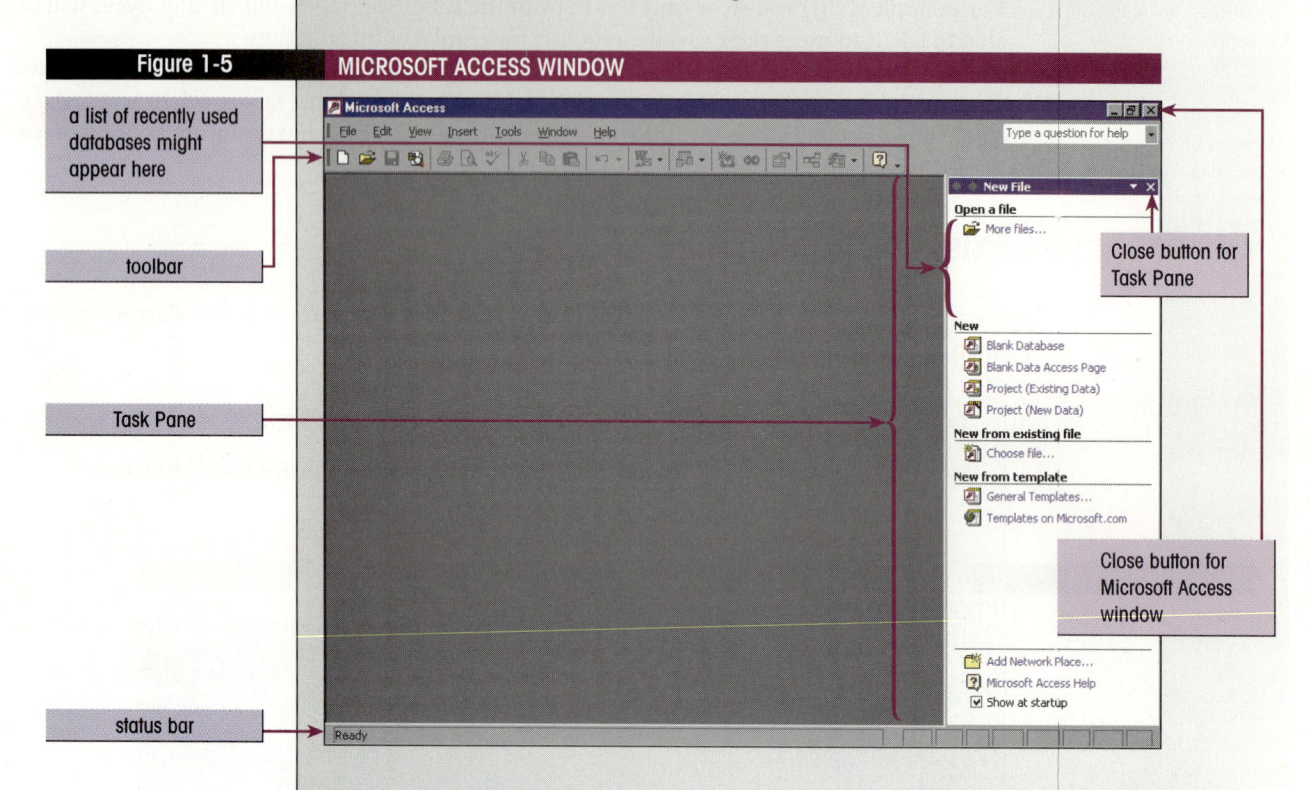

Figure 1-5   MICROSOFT ACCESS WINDOW

- a list of recently used databases might appear here
- toolbar
- Task Pane
- status bar
- Close button for Task Pane
- Close button for Microsoft Access window

When you start Access, the Access window contains a Task Pane that allows you to create a new database or to open an existing database. You can click the "Blank Database" option in the "New" section of the Task Pane to create a new database on your own, or you can click the "General Templates" option in the "New from template" section of the Task Pane to let Access guide you through the steps for creating one of the standard databases provided by Microsoft. In this case, you need to open an existing database.

To open an existing database, you can select the name of a database in the list of recently opened databases (if the list appears), or you can click the "More files" option to open a database not listed. You need to open an existing database—the Seasonal database on your Data Disk.

3. Make sure you have created your copy of the Access Data Disk, and then place your Data Disk in the appropriate disk drive.

   TROUBLE? If you don't have a Data Disk, you need to get one before you can proceed. Your instructor will either give you one or ask you to make your own. (See your instructor for more information.) In either case, be sure that you have made a backup copy of your Data Disk before you begin working, so that the original Data Files will be available on the copied disk in case you need to start over because of an error or problem.

4. In the "Open a file" section of the Task Pane, click the **More files** option. The Open dialog box is displayed. See Figure 1-6.

TUTORIAL 1 INTRODUCTION TO MICROSOFT ACCESS 2002   AC 1.09

Figure 1-6   OPEN DIALOG BOX

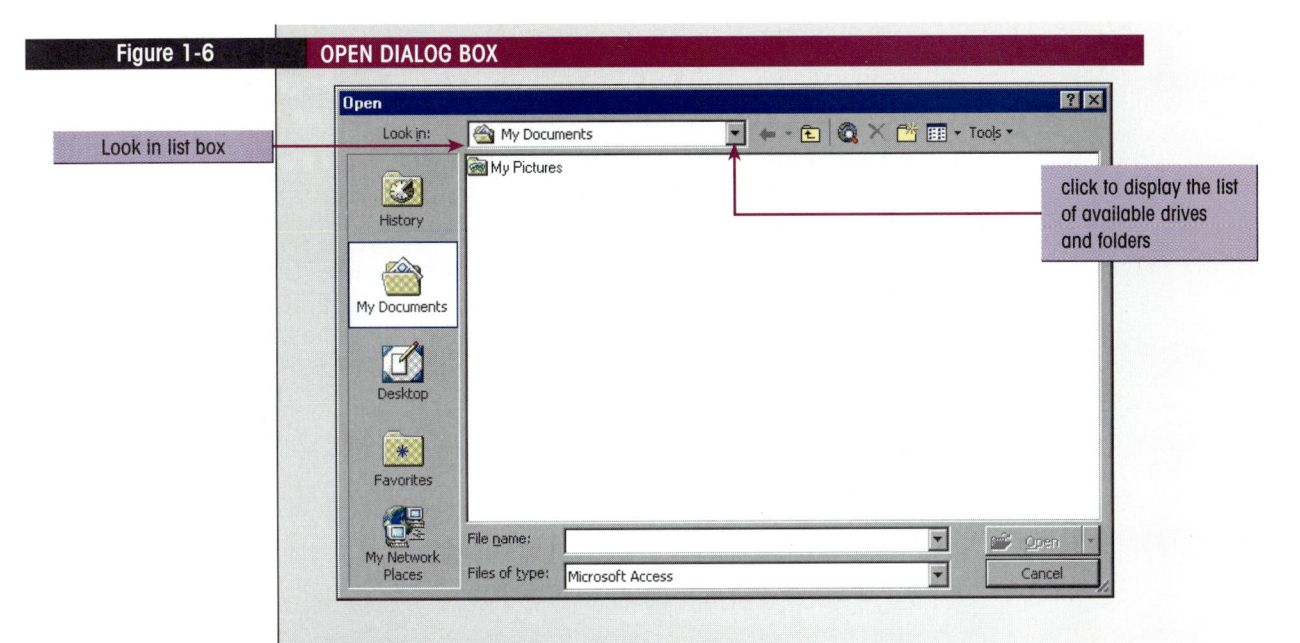

- Look in list box
- click to display the list of available drives and folders

TROUBLE? The list of folders and files on your screen might be different from the list in Figure 1-6.

5. Click the **Look in** list arrow, and then click the drive that contains your Data Disk.

6. Click **Tutorial** in the list box (if necessary), and then click the **Open** button to display a list of the files in the Tutorial folder.

7. Click **Seasonal** in the list box, and then click the **Open** button. The Seasonal database opens in the Access window. See Figure 1-7.

Figure 1-7   ACCESS AND DATABASE WINDOWS

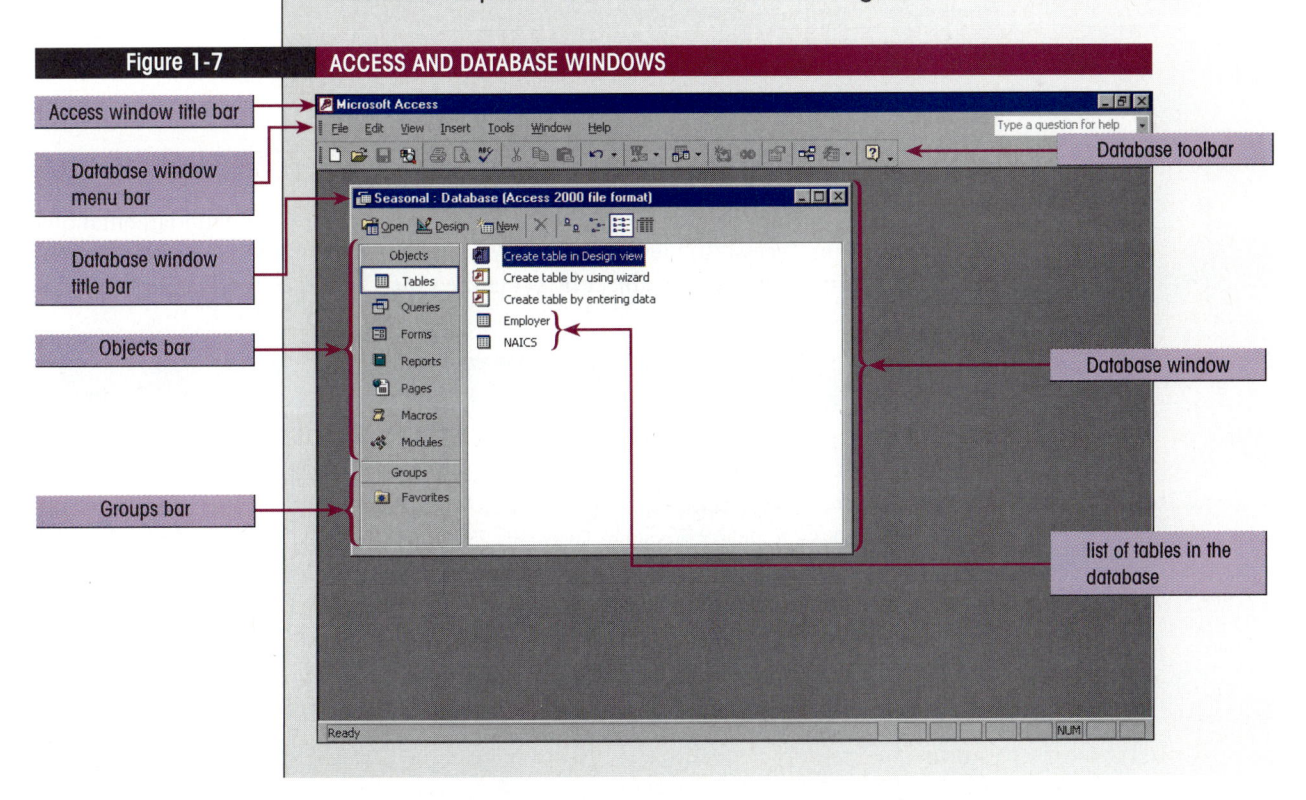

- Access window title bar
- Database window menu bar
- Database window title bar
- Objects bar
- Groups bar
- Database toolbar
- Database window
- list of tables in the database

> **TROUBLE?** The filename on your screen might be Seasonal.mdb instead of Seasonal, depending on your computer's default settings. The extension ".mdb" identifies the file as a Microsoft Access database.
>
> **TROUBLE?** If Tables is not selected in the Objects bar of the Database window, click it to display the list of tables in the database.

Before you can begin working with the database, you need to become familiar with the components of the Access and Database windows.

The Access and Database Windows

The **Access window** is the program window that appears when you start the program. The **Database window** appears when you open a database; this window is the main control center for working with an open Access database. Except for the Access window title bar, all screen components now on your screen are associated with the Database window (see Figure 1-7). Most of these screen components—including the title bars, window sizing buttons, menu bar, toolbar, and status bar—are the same as the components in other Windows programs.

Notice that the Database window title bar includes the notation "(Access 2000 file format)." By default, databases that you create in Access 2002 use the Access 2000 database file format. This feature ensures that you can use and share databases originally created in Access 2002 without converting them to Access 2000, and vice versa. (You'll learn more about database file formats and converting databases later in this tutorial.)

The Database window provides a variety of options for viewing and manipulating database objects. Each item in the **Objects bar** controls one of the major object groups—such as tables, queries, forms, and reports—in an Access database. The **Groups bar** allows you to organize different types of database objects into groups, with shortcuts to those objects, so that you can work with them more easily. The Database window also provides buttons for quickly creating, opening, and managing objects, as well as shortcut options for some of these tasks.

Elsa has already created the Employer and NAICS tables in the Seasonal database. She asks you to open the Employer table and view its contents.

Opening an Access Table

As noted earlier, tables contain all the data in a database. Tables are the fundamental objects for your work in Access. To view, add, change, or delete data in a table, you first open the table. You can open any Access object by using the Open button in the Database window.

REFERENCE WINDOW RW

Opening an Access Object
- In the Objects bar of the Database window, click the type of object you want to open.
- If necessary, scroll the object list box until the object name appears, and then click the object name.
- Click the Open button in the Database window.

You need to open the Employer table, which is one of two tables in the Seasonal database.

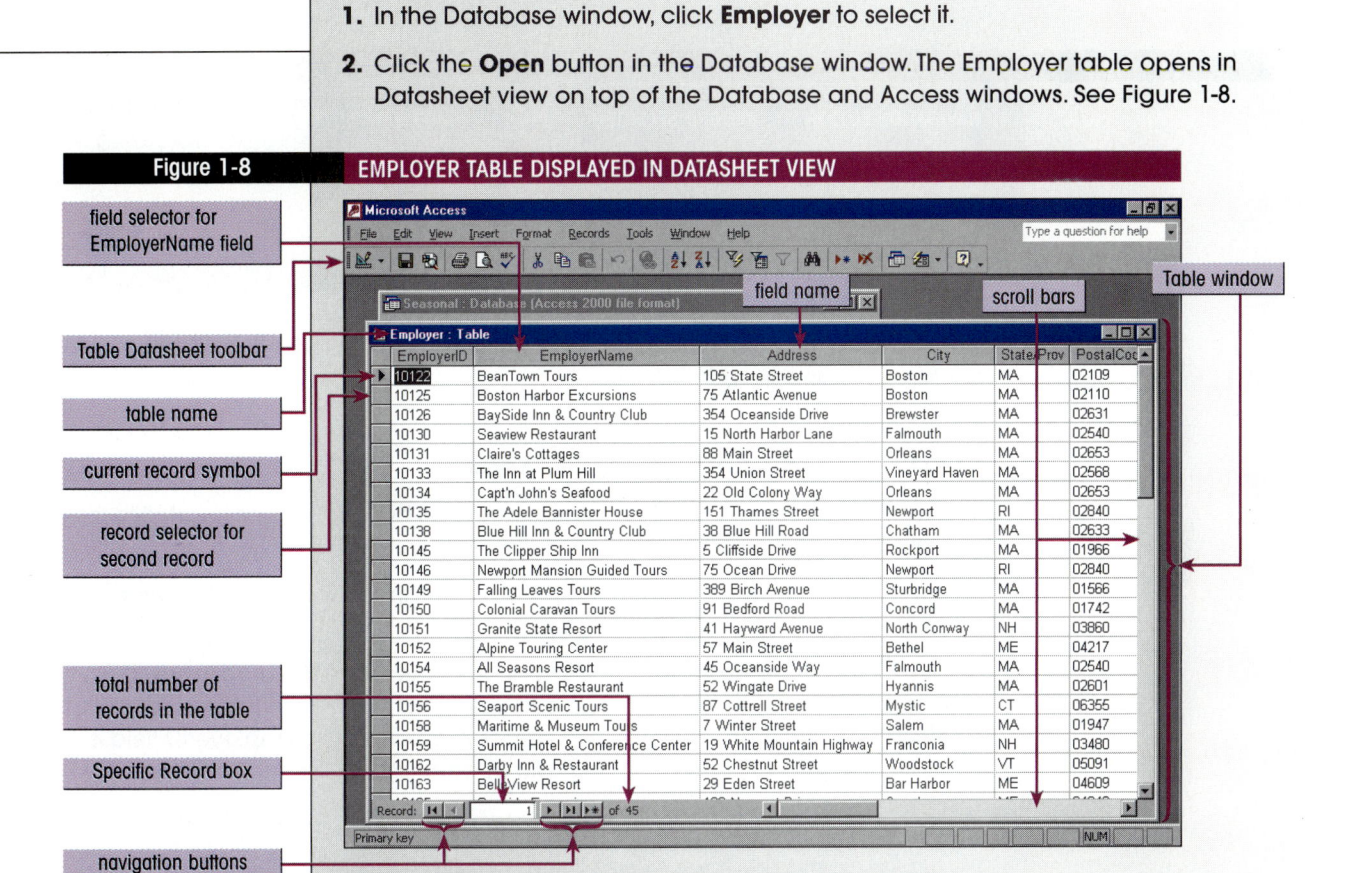

To open the Employer table:

1. In the Database window, click **Employer** to select it.

2. Click the **Open** button in the Database window. The Employer table opens in Datasheet view on top of the Database and Access windows. See Figure 1-8.

Figure 1-8   EMPLOYER TABLE DISPLAYED IN DATASHEET VIEW

Callouts: field selector for EmployerName field; Table Datasheet toolbar; table name; current record symbol; record selector for second record; total number of records in the table; Specific Record box; navigation buttons; field name; scroll bars; Table window.

Datasheet view shows a table's contents as a **datasheet** in rows and columns, similar to a table or spreadsheet. Each row is a separate record in the table, and each column contains the field values for one field in the table. Each column is headed by a field name inside a field selector, and each row has a record selector to its left. Clicking a **field selector** or a **record selector** selects that entire column or row (respectively), which you then can manipulate. A field selector is also called a **column selector**, and a record selector is also called a **row selector**.

Navigating an Access Datasheet

When you first open a datasheet, Access selects the first field value in the first record. Notice that this field value is highlighted and that a darkened triangle symbol, called the current record symbol, appears in the record selector to the left of the first record. The **current record symbol** identifies the currently selected record. Clicking a record selector or field value in another row moves the current record symbol to that row. You can also move the pointer over the data on the screen and click one of the field values to position the insertion point.

The Employer table currently has 13 fields and 45 records. To view fields or records not currently visible in the datasheet, you can use the horizontal and vertical scroll bars shown in Figure 1-8 to navigate through the data. The **navigation buttons**, also shown in Figure 1-8, provide another way to move vertically through the records. Figure 1-9 shows which record becomes the current record when you click each navigation button. The **Specific Record box**, which appears between the two sets of navigation buttons, displays the current record number. The total number of records in the table appears to the right of the navigation buttons.

Figure 1-9   **NAVIGATION BUTTONS**

NAVIGATION BUTTON	RECORD SELECTED	NAVIGATION BUTTON	RECORD SELECTED
▏◀	First Record	▶▕	Last Record
◀	Previous Record	▶✱	New Record
▶	Next Record		

Elsa suggests that you use the various navigation techniques to move through the Employer table and become familiar with its contents.

To navigate the Employer datasheet:

1. Click the right scroll arrow in the horizontal scroll bar a few times to scroll to the right and view the remaining fields in the Employer table.

2. Drag the scroll box in the horizontal scroll bar all the way to the left to return to the previous display of the datasheet.

3. Click the **Next Record** navigation button ▶ . The second record is now the current record, as indicated by the current record symbol in the second record selector. Also, notice that the second record's value for the EmployerID field is highlighted, and "2" (for record number 2) appears in the Specific Record box.

4. Click the **Last Record** navigation button ▶▕ . The last record in the table, record 45, is now the current record.

5. Click the **Previous Record** navigation button ◀ . Record 44 is now the current record.

6. Click the **First Record** navigation button ▏◀ . The first record is now the current record.

Saving a Database

Notice the Save button 🖫 on the Table Datasheet toolbar. Unlike the Save buttons in other Windows programs, this Save button does not save the active document (database) to your disk. Instead, you use the Save button to save the design of an Access object, such as a table, or to save datasheet format changes. Access does not have a button or option you can use to save the active database.

Access saves changes to the active database to your disk automatically, when a record is changed or added and when you close the database. If your database is stored on a disk in drive A, you should never remove the disk while the database file is open. If you remove the disk, Access will encounter problems when it tries to save the database, which might damage the database.

Now that you've viewed the Employer table, you can exit Access.

> **To exit Access:**
>
> 1. Click the **Close** button ⊠ on the Access window title bar. The Employer table and the Seasonal database close, Access closes, and you return to the Windows desktop.

Now that you've become familiar with Access and the Seasonal database, in the next session, you'll be ready to work with the data stored in the database.

Session 1.1 Quick Check

1. A(n) _____ is a single characteristic of a person, place, object, event, or idea.
2. You connect the records in two separate tables through a(n) _____ that appears in both tables.
3. The _____, whose values uniquely identify each record in a table, is called a(n) _____ when it is placed in a second table to form a relationship between the two tables.
4. In a table, the rows are also called _____, and the columns are also called _____.
5. The _____ identifies the selected record in an Access table.
6. Describe two methods for navigating through a table.

SESSION 1.2

In this session, you will open an existing query and create and navigate a new query; create and navigate a form; and create, preview, and navigate a report. You will also learn how to manage databases by backing up and restoring, compacting and repairing, and converting databases.

Working with Queries

A **query** is a question you ask about the data stored in a database. In response to a query, Access displays the specific records and fields that answer your question. When you create a query, you tell Access which fields you need and what criteria Access should use to select the records. Then Access displays only the information you want, so you don't have to navigate through the entire database for the information.

Before creating a new query, you will open a query that Elsa created recently so that she could view information in the Employer table in a different way.

Opening an Existing Query

Queries that you create and save appear in the Queries list of the Database window. To see the results of a query, you simply open, or run, the query. Elsa created and saved a query named "Contacts" in the Seasonal database. This query shows all the fields from the Employer table, but in a different order. Elsa suggests that you open this query to see its results.

To open the Contacts query:

1. Insert your Data Disk into the appropriate disk drive.

2. Start Access, and then click the **More files** option in the Task Pane to display the Open dialog box.

3. Click the **Look in** list arrow, click the drive that contains your Data Disk, click **Tutorial** in the list box, and then click the **Open** button to display the list of files in the Tutorial folder.

4. Click **Seasonal** in the list box, and then click the **Open** button.

5. Click **Queries** in the Objects bar of the Database window to display the Queries list. The Queries list box contains one object—the Contacts query. See Figure 1-10.

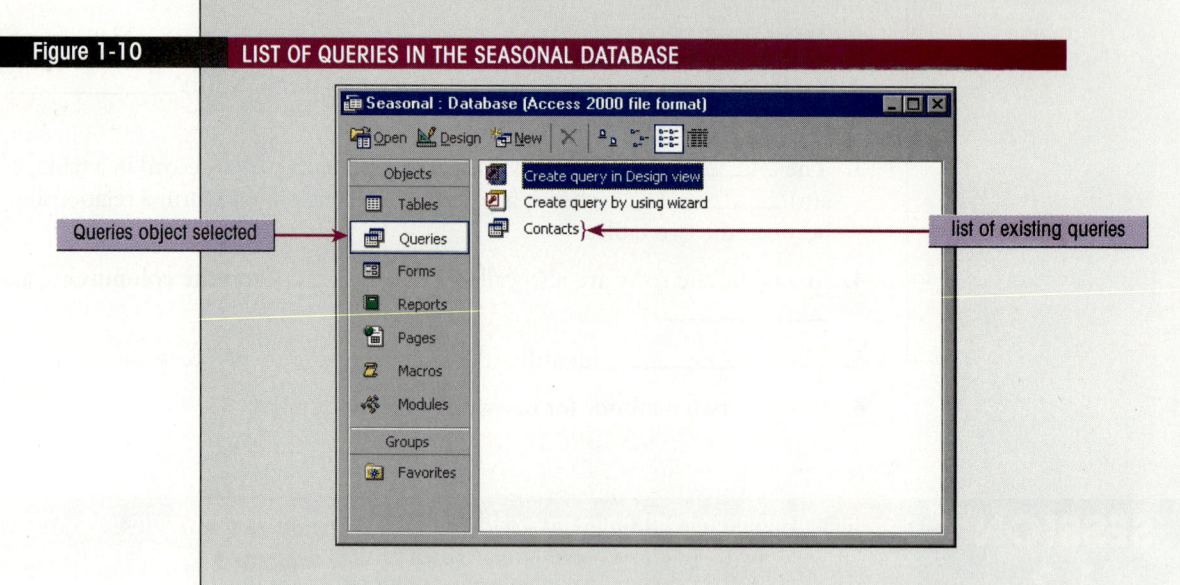

Figure 1-10 — LIST OF QUERIES IN THE SEASONAL DATABASE

Now you will run the Contacts query by opening it.

6. Click **Contacts** to select it, and then click the **Open** button in the Database window. Access displays the results of the query in Datasheet view. See Figure 1-11.

Figure 1-11 — RESULT OF RUNNING THE CONTACTS QUERY

> Notice that the query displays the fields from the Employer table, but in a different order. For example, the first and last names of each contact, as well as the contact's phone number, appear next to the employer name. This arrangement lets Elsa view pertinent contact information without having to scroll through the table. Rearranging the display of table data is one task you can perform with queries, so that table information appears in a different order to suit how you want to work with the information.
>
> 7. Click the **Close** button ☒ on the Query window title bar to close the Contacts query.

Even though a query can display table information in a different way, the information still exists in the table as it was originally entered. If you opened the Employer table, it would still show the fields in their original order.

Zack Ward, the director of marketing at NSJI, wants a list of all employers so that his staff can call them to check on their satisfaction with NSJI's services and recruits. He doesn't want the list to include all the fields in the Employer table (such as PostalCode and NAICSCode). To produce this list for Zack, you need to create a query using the Employer table.

Creating, Sorting, and Navigating a Query

You can design your own queries or use an Access **Query Wizard**, which guides you through the steps to create a query. The Simple Query Wizard allows you to select records and fields quickly, and it is an appropriate choice for producing the employer list Zack wants. You can choose this Wizard either by clicking the New button, which opens a dialog box from which you can choose among several different Wizards to create your query, or by double-clicking the "Create query by using wizard" option, which automatically starts the Simple Query Wizard.

> **To start the Simple Query Wizard:**
>
> 1. Double-click **Create query by using wizard**. The first Simple Query Wizard dialog box opens. See Figure 1-12.

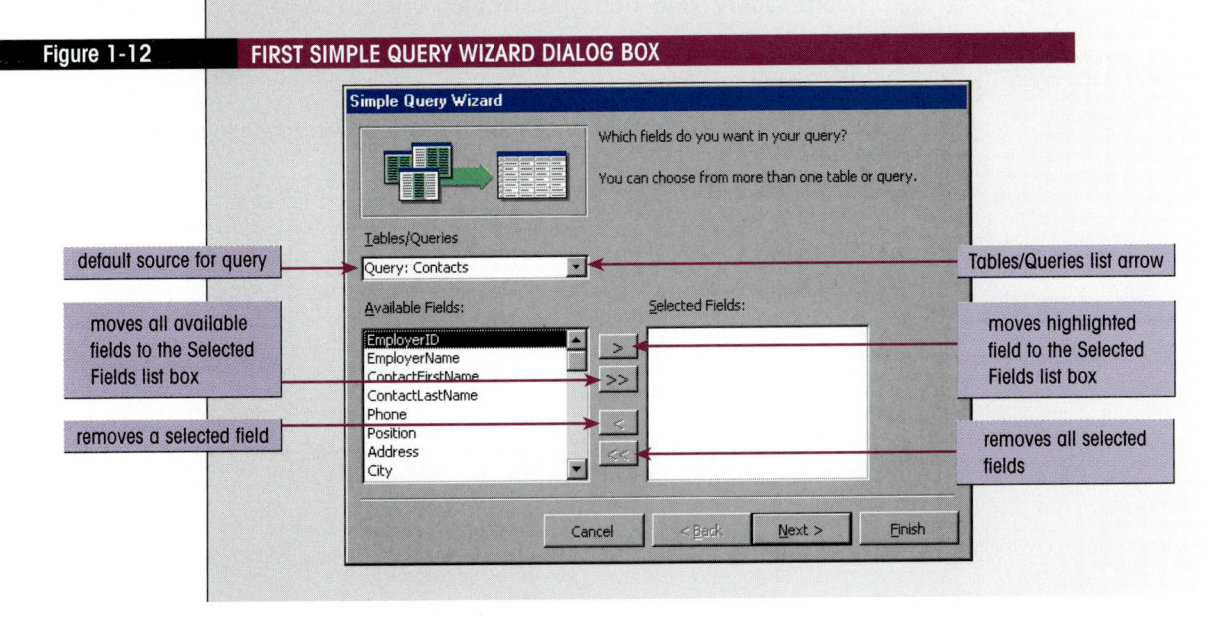

Figure 1-12   **FIRST SIMPLE QUERY WIZARD DIALOG BOX**

Because Contacts is the only query object currently in the Seasonal database, it is listed in the Tables/Queries box by default. You need to base the query you're creating on the Employer table.

2. Click the **Tables/Queries** list arrow, and then click **Table: Employer** to select the Employer table as the source for the new query. The Available Fields list box now lists the fields in the Employer table.

You need to select fields from the Available Fields list to include them in the query. To select fields one at a time, click a field and then click the > button. The selected field moves from the Available Fields list box on the left to the Selected Fields list box on the right. To select all the fields, click the >> button. If you change your mind or make a mistake, you can remove a field by clicking it in the Selected Fields list box and then clicking the < button. To remove all selected fields, click the << button.

Each Wizard dialog box contains buttons on the bottom that allow you to move to the previous dialog box (Back button), move to the next dialog box (Next button), or cancel the creation process (Cancel button) and return to the Database window. You can also finish creating the object (Finish button) and accept the Wizard's defaults for the remaining options.

Zack wants his list to include data from only the following fields: EmployerName, City, State/Prov, ContactFirstName, ContactLastName, and Phone. You need to select these fields to include them in the query.

To create the query using the Simple Query Wizard:

1. Click **EmployerName** in the Available Fields list box, and then click the > button. The EmployerName field moves to the Selected Fields list box.

2. Repeat Step 1 for the fields **City**, **State/Prov**, **ContactFirstName**, **ContactLastName**, and **Phone**, and then click the **Next** button. The second, and final, Simple Query Wizard dialog box opens and asks you to choose a name for your query. This name will appear in the Queries list in the Database window. You'll change the suggested name (Employer Query) to "Employer List."

3. Click at the end of the highlighted name, use the Backspace key to delete the word "Query," and then type **List**. Now you can view the query results.

4. Click the **Finish** button to complete the query. Access displays the query results in Datasheet view.

5. Click the **Maximize** button on the Query window title bar to maximize the window. See Figure 1-13.

Figure 1-13 QUERY RESULTS

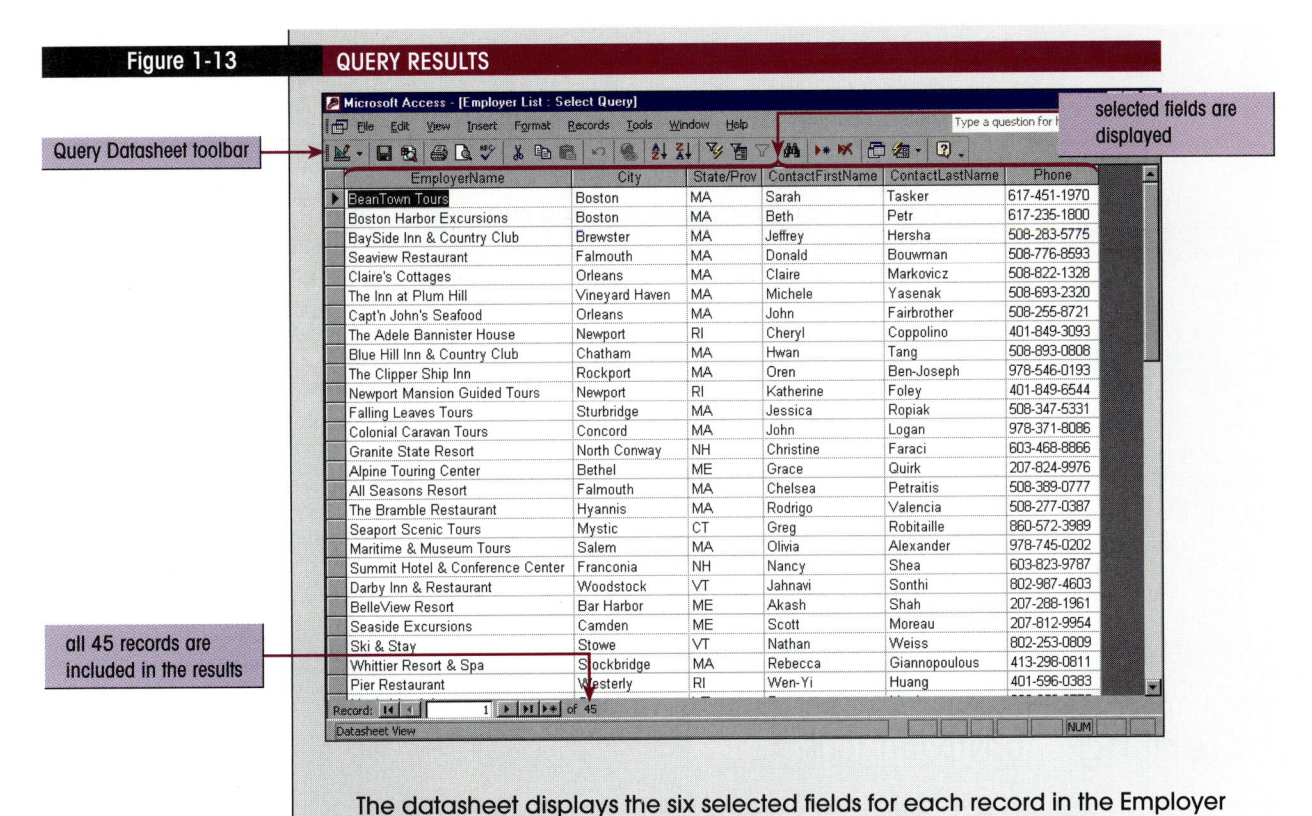

Query Datasheet toolbar

selected fields are displayed

EmployerName	City	State/Prov	ContactFirstName	ContactLastName	Phone
BeanTown Tours	Boston	MA	Sarah	Tasker	617-451-1970
Boston Harbor Excursions	Boston	MA	Beth	Petr	617-235-1800
BaySide Inn & Country Club	Brewster	MA	Jeffrey	Hersha	508-283-5775
Seaview Restaurant	Falmouth	MA	Donald	Bouwman	508-776-8593
Claire's Cottages	Orleans	MA	Claire	Markovicz	508-822-1328
The Inn at Plum Hill	Vineyard Haven	MA	Michele	Yasenak	508-693-2320
Capt'n John's Seafood	Orleans	MA	John	Fairbrother	508-255-8721
The Adele Bannister House	Newport	RI	Cheryl	Coppolino	401-849-3093
Blue Hill Inn & Country Club	Chatham	MA	Hwan	Tang	508-893-0808
The Clipper Ship Inn	Rockport	MA	Oren	Ben-Joseph	978-546-0193
Newport Mansion Guided Tours	Newport	RI	Katherine	Foley	401-849-6544
Falling Leaves Tours	Sturbridge	MA	Jessica	Ropiak	508-347-5331
Colonial Caravan Tours	Concord	MA	John	Logan	978-371-8086
Granite State Resort	North Conway	NH	Christine	Faraci	603-468-8866
Alpine Touring Center	Bethel	ME	Grace	Quirk	207-824-9976
All Seasons Resort	Falmouth	MA	Chelsea	Petraitis	508-389-0777
The Bramble Restaurant	Hyannis	MA	Rodrigo	Valencia	508-277-0387
Seaport Scenic Tours	Mystic	CT	Greg	Robitaille	860-572-3989
Maritime & Museum Tours	Salem	MA	Olivia	Alexander	978-745-0202
Summit Hotel & Conference Center	Franconia	NH	Nancy	Shea	603-823-9787
Darby Inn & Restaurant	Woodstock	VT	Jahnavi	Sonthi	802-987-4603
BelleView Resort	Bar Harbor	ME	Akash	Shah	207-288-1961
Seaside Excursions	Camden	ME	Scott	Moreau	207-812-9954
Ski & Stay	Stowe	VT	Nathan	Weiss	802-253-0809
Whittier Resort & Spa	Stockbridge	MA	Rebecca	Giannopoulous	413-298-0811
Pier Restaurant	Westerly	RI	Wen-Yi	Huang	401-596-0383

Record: 1 of 45

all 45 records are included in the results

The datasheet displays the six selected fields for each record in the Employer table. The fields are shown in the order you selected them, from left to right.

The records are currently listed in order by the primary key field (EmployerID from the Employer table). This is true even though the EmployerID field is not included in the display of the query results. Zack prefers the records listed in order by state or province, so that his staff members can focus on all records for the employers in a particular state or province. To display the records in the order Zack wants, you need to sort the query results by the State/Prov field.

To sort the query results:

1. Click to position the insertion point anywhere in the State/Prov column. This establishes the State/Prov column as the current field.

2. Click the **Sort Ascending** button on the Query Datasheet toolbar. Now the records are sorted in ascending alphabetical order by the values in the State/Prov field. All the records for Connecticut (CT) are listed first, followed by the records for Massachusetts (MA), Maine (ME), and so on.

   Notice that the navigation buttons are located at the bottom of the window. You navigate through a query datasheet in the same way that you navigate through a table datasheet.

3. Click the **Last Record** navigation button. The last record in the query datasheet, for the Darby Inn & Restaurant, is now the current record.

4. Click the **Previous Record** navigation button. Record 44 in the query datasheet is now the current record.

> 5. Click the **First Record** navigation button [◄]. The first record is now the current record.
>
> 6. Click the **Close Window** button [X] on the menu bar to close the query.
>
>   A dialog box opens and asks if you want to save changes to the design of the query. This box opens because you changed the sort order of the query results.
>
> 7. Click the **Yes** button to save the query design changes and return to the Database window. Notice that the Employer List query now appears in the Queries list box. In addition, because you maximized the Query window, now the Database window is also maximized. You need to restore the window.
>
> 8. Click the **Restore Window** button on the menu bar to restore the Database window.

The query results are not stored in the database; however, the query design is stored as part of the database with the name you specified. You can re-create the query results at any time by running the query again. You'll learn more about creating and running queries in Tutorial 3.

After Zack views the query results, Elsa then asks you to create a form for the Employer table so that her staff members can use the form to enter and work with data in the table easily.

Creating and Navigating a Form

A **form** is an object you use to maintain, view, and print records in a database. Although you can perform these same functions with tables and queries, forms can present data in many customized and useful ways.

In Access, you can design your own forms or use a Form Wizard to create your forms automatically. A **Form Wizard** is an Access tool that asks you a series of questions, and then creates a form based on your answers. The quickest way to create a form is to use an **AutoForm Wizard**, which places all the fields from a selected table (or query) on a form automatically, without asking you any questions, and then displays the form on the screen.

Elsa wants a form for the Employer table that will show all the fields for one record at a time, with fields listed one below another in a column. This type of form will make it easier for her staff to focus on all the data for a particular employer. You'll use the AutoForm: Columnar Wizard to create the form.

> ### To create the form using an AutoForm Wizard:
>
> 1. Click **Forms** in the Objects bar of the Database window to display the Forms list. The Forms list box does not contain any forms yet.
>
> 2. Click the **New** button in the Database window to open the New Form dialog box. See Figure 1-14.

TUTORIAL 1 INTRODUCTION TO MICROSOFT ACCESS 2002   AC 1.19

Figure 1-14   **NEW FORM DIALOG BOX**

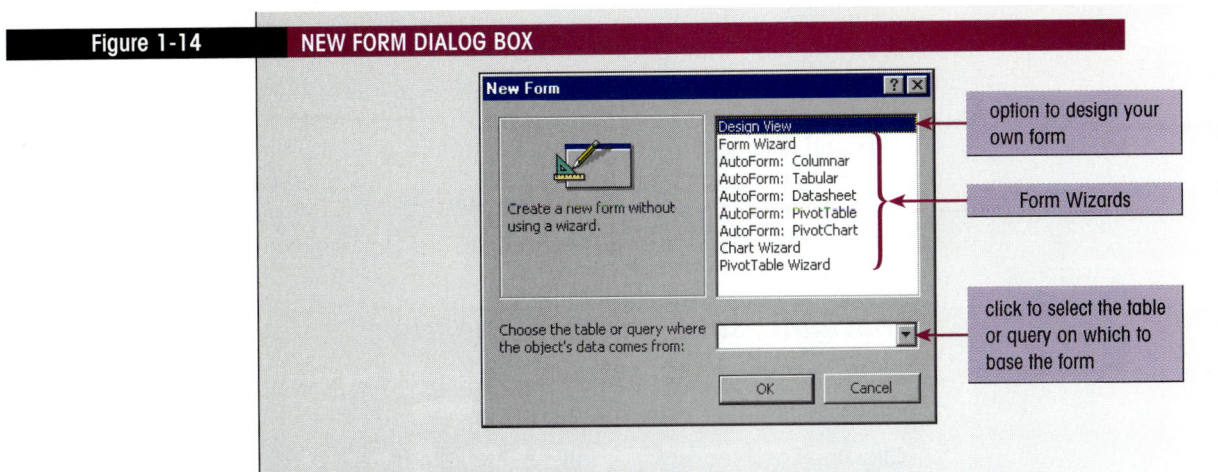

The top list box provides options for designing your own form or creating a form using one of the Form Wizards. In the bottom list box, you choose the table or query that will supply the data for the form.

3. Click **AutoForm: Columnar** to select this AutoForm Wizard.

4. Click the list arrow for choosing the table or query on which to base the form, and then click **Employer**.

5. Click the **OK** button. The AutoForm Wizard creates the form and displays it in Form view. See Figure 1-15.

Figure 1-15   **FORM CREATED BY THE AUTOFORM: COLUMNAR WIZARD**

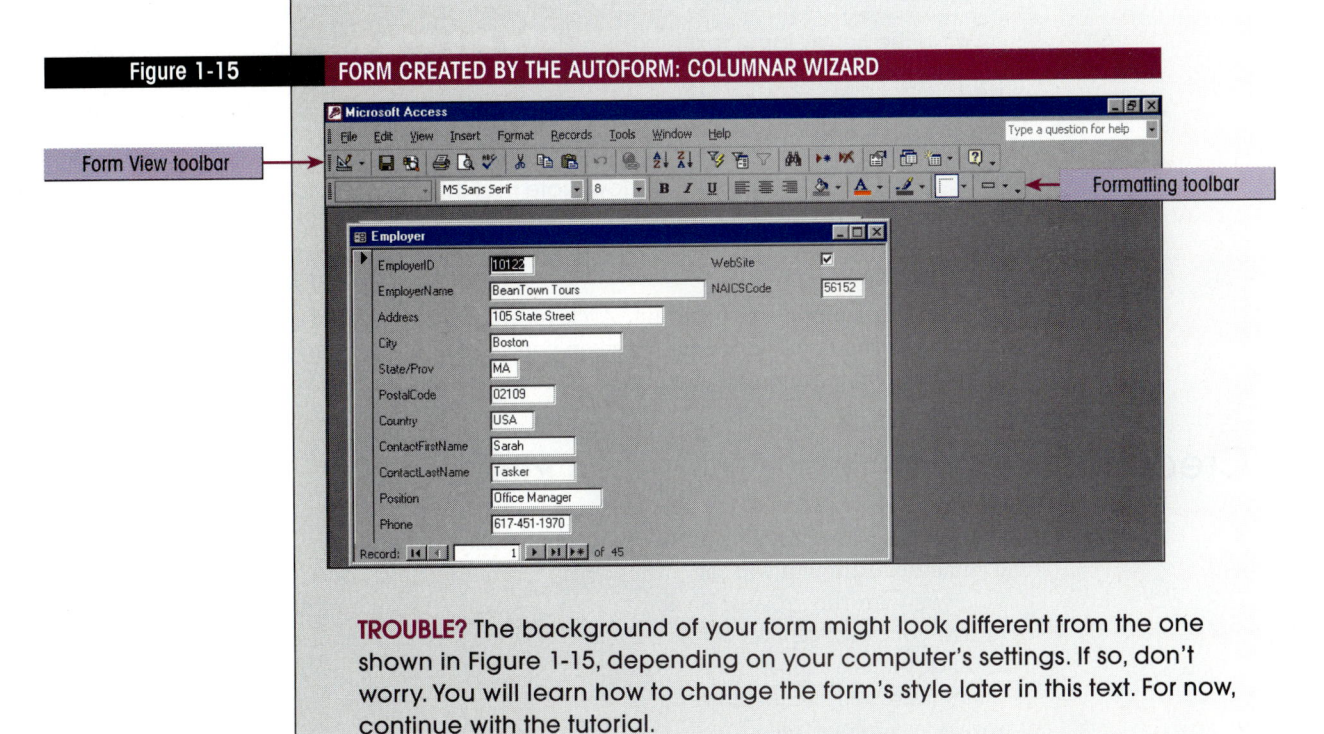

TROUBLE? The background of your form might look different from the one shown in Figure 1-15, depending on your computer's settings. If so, don't worry. You will learn how to change the form's style later in this text. For now, continue with the tutorial.

The form displays one record at a time in the Employer table. Access displays the field values for the first record in the table and selects the first field value (EmployerID). Each field name appears on a separate line (spread over two columns) and on the same line as its field value, which appears in a box. The widths of the boxes are different to accommodate the different sizes of the displayed field values; for example, compare the small box for the State/Prov field value with the larger box for the EmployerName field value. The AutoForm: Columnar Wizard automatically placed the field names and values on the form and supplied the background style.

To view and maintain data using a form, you must know how to move from field to field and from record to record. Notice that the Form window contains navigation buttons, similar to those available in Datasheet view, which you can use to display different records in the form. You'll use these now to navigate through the form; then you'll save and close the form.

To navigate, save, and close the form:

1. Click the **Next Record** navigation button ▶. The form now displays the values for the second record in the Employer table.

2. Click the **Last Record** navigation button ▶| to move to the last record in the table. The form displays the information for record 45, Lighthouse Tours.

3. Click the **Previous Record** navigation button ◀ to move to record 44.

4. Click the **First Record** navigation button |◀ to return to the first record in the Employer table.

   Next, you'll save the form with the name "Employer Data" in the Seasonal database. Then the form will be available for later use. You'll learn more about creating and customizing forms in Tutorial 4.

5. Click the **Save** button on the Form View toolbar. The Save As dialog box opens.

6. In the Form Name text box, click at the end of the highlighted word "Employer," press the **spacebar**, type **Data**, and then press the **Enter** key. Access saves the form as Employer Data in the Seasonal database and closes the dialog box.

7. Click the **Close** button ✕ on the Form window title bar to close the form and return to the Database window. Note that the Employer Data form is now listed in the Forms list box.

After attending a staff meeting, Zack returns with another request. He wants the same employer list you produced earlier when you created the Employer List query, but he'd like the information presented in a more readable format. You'll help Zack by creating a report.

Creating, Previewing, and Navigating a Report

A **report** is a formatted printout (or screen display) of the contents of one or more tables in a database. Although you can print data appearing in tables, queries, and forms, reports provide you with the greatest flexibility for formatting printed output. As with forms, you can design your own reports or use a Report Wizard to create reports automatically.

Zack wants a report showing the same information contained in the Employer List query that you created earlier. However, he wants the data for each employer to be grouped together, with one employer record below another, as shown in the report sketch in Figure 1-16.

Figure 1-16   SKETCH OF ZACK'S REPORT

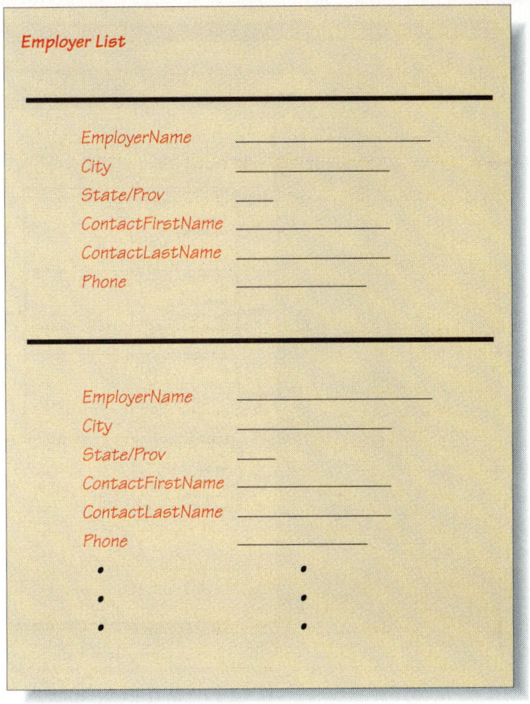

Employer List

EmployerName
City
State/Prov
ContactFirstName
ContactLastName
Phone

EmployerName
City
State/Prov
ContactFirstName
ContactLastName
Phone

To produce the report for Zack, you'll use the AutoReport: Columnar Wizard, which is similar to the AutoForm: Columnar Wizard you used earlier when creating the Employer Data form.

To create the report using the AutoReport: Columnar Wizard:

1. Click **Reports** in the Objects bar of the Database window, and then click the **New** button in the Database window to open the New Report dialog box, which is similar to the New Form dialog box you saw earlier.

2. Click **AutoReport: Columnar** to select this Wizard for creating the report.

   Because Zack wants the same data as in the Employer List query, you need to choose that query as the basis for the report.

3. Click the list arrow for choosing the table or query on which to base the report, and then click **Employer List**.

4. Click the **OK** button. The AutoReport Wizard creates the report and displays it in Print Preview, which shows exactly how the report will look when printed.

   To view the report better, you'll maximize the window and change the Zoom setting so that you can see the entire page.

5. Click the **Maximize** button on the Report window title bar, click the **Zoom** list arrow (to the right of the value 100%) on the Print Preview toolbar, and then click **Fit**. The entire first page of the report is displayed in the window. See Figure 1-17.

Figure 1-17   **FIRST PAGE OF THE REPORT IN PRINT PREVIEW**

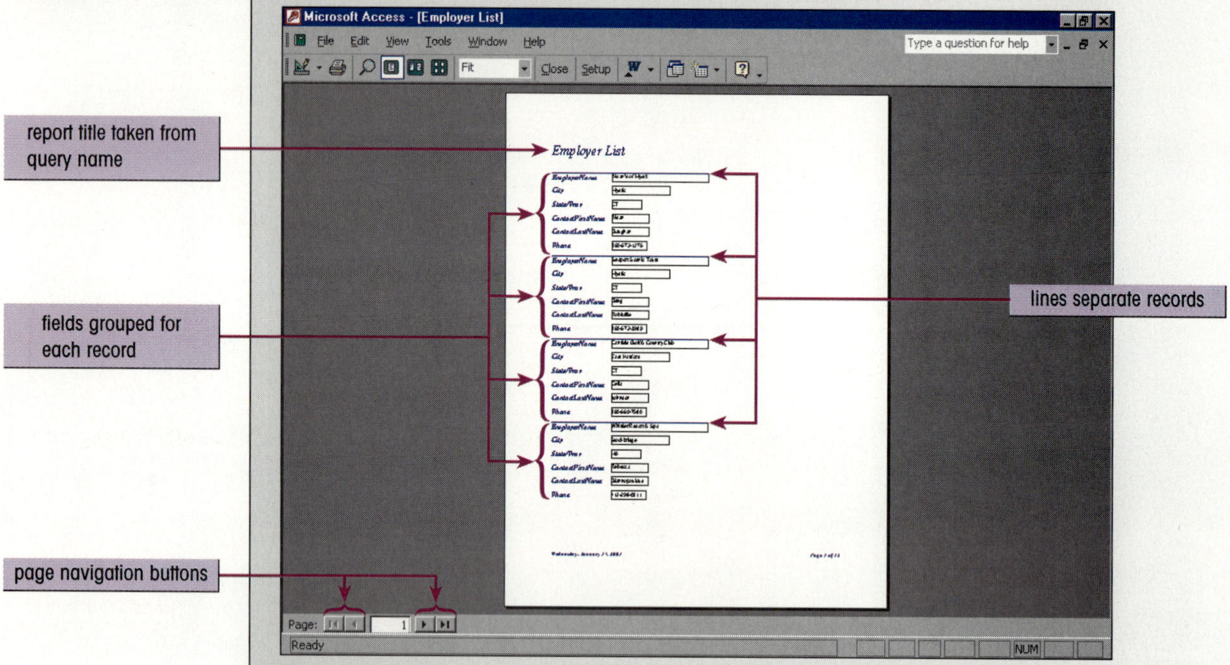

- report title taken from query name
- fields grouped for each record
- lines separate records
- page navigation buttons

TROUBLE? The fonts used in your report might look different from the ones shown in Figure 1-17, depending on your computer's settings. If so, don't worry. You will learn how to change the report's style later in this text.

Each field from the Employer List query appears on its own line, with the corresponding field value to the right and in a box. Horizontal lines separate one record from the next, visually grouping all the fields for each record. The name of the query—Employer List—appears as the report's title.

Notice that the Print Preview window provides page navigation buttons at the bottom of the window, similar to the navigation buttons you've used to move through records in a table, query, and form. You use these buttons to move through the pages of a report.

6. Click the **Next Page** navigation button ▶. The second page of the report is displayed in Print Preview.

7. Click the **Last Page** navigation button ▶| to move to the last page of the report. Note that this page contains the fields for only one record. Also note that the box in the middle of the navigation buttons displays the number "12"; there are 12 pages in this report.

TROUBLE? Depending on the printer you are using, your report might have more or fewer pages. If so, don't worry. Different printers format reports in different ways, sometimes affecting the total number of pages.

8. Click the **First Page** navigation button |◀ to return to the first page of the report.

At this point, you could close the report without saving it because you can easily re-create it at any time. In general, it's best to save an object—report, form, or query—only if you anticipate using the object frequently or if it is time-consuming to create, because these objects use considerable storage space on your disk. However, Zack wants to show the report to his staff members, so he asks you to save it.

To close and save the report:

1. Click the **Close Window** button ⊠ on the menu bar. *Do not* click the Close button on the Print Preview toolbar.

   TROUBLE? If you clicked the Close button on the Print Preview toolbar, you switched to Design view. Simply click the Close Window button ⊠ on the menu bar, and then continue with the steps.

   A dialog box opens and asks if you want to save the changes to the report design.

2. Click the **Yes** button. The Save As dialog box opens.

3. Click to the right of the highlighted text in the Report Name text box, press the **spacebar** once, type **Report**, and then click the **OK** button. Access saves the report as "Employer List Report" and returns to the Database window.

You'll learn more about creating and customizing reports in Tutorial 4.

Managing a Database

One of the main tasks involved in working with database software is managing your databases and the data they contain. By managing your databases, you can ensure that they operate in the most efficient way, that the data they contain is secure, and that you can work with the data effectively. Some of the activities involved in database management include backing up and restoring a database, compacting and repairing a database, and converting a database for use in other versions of Access.

Backing Up and Restoring a Database

You make a backup copy of a database file to protect your database against loss or damage. You can make the backup copy using one of several methods: Windows Explorer, My Computer, Microsoft Backup, or other backup software. If you back up your database file to a floppy disk, and the file size exceeds the size of the disk, you cannot use Windows Explorer or My Computer; you must use Microsoft Backup or some other backup software so that you can copy the file over more than one disk.

To restore a backup database file, choose the same method you used to make the backup copy. For example, if you used the Microsoft Backup tool (which is one of the System Tools available from the Programs menu and Accessories submenu in Windows 2000), you must choose the Restore option for this tool to copy the database file to your database folder. If the existing database file and the backup copy have the same name, restoring the backup copy might replace the existing file. If you want to save the existing file, rename it before you restore it.

Compacting and Repairing a Database

Whenever you open an Access database and work in it, the size of the database increases. Likewise, when you delete records and when you delete or replace database objects—such as queries, forms, and reports—the space that had been occupied on the disk by the deleted or replaced records or objects does not become available for other records or objects. To make the space available, you must compact the database. **Compacting** a database rearranges the data and objects in a database to decrease its file size. Unlike making a copy of a database file, which you do to protect your database against loss or damage, you compact a database to make it smaller, thereby making more space available on your disk and speeding up the process of opening and closing the database. Figure 1-18 illustrates the compacting process; the orange colored elements in the figure represent database records and objects.

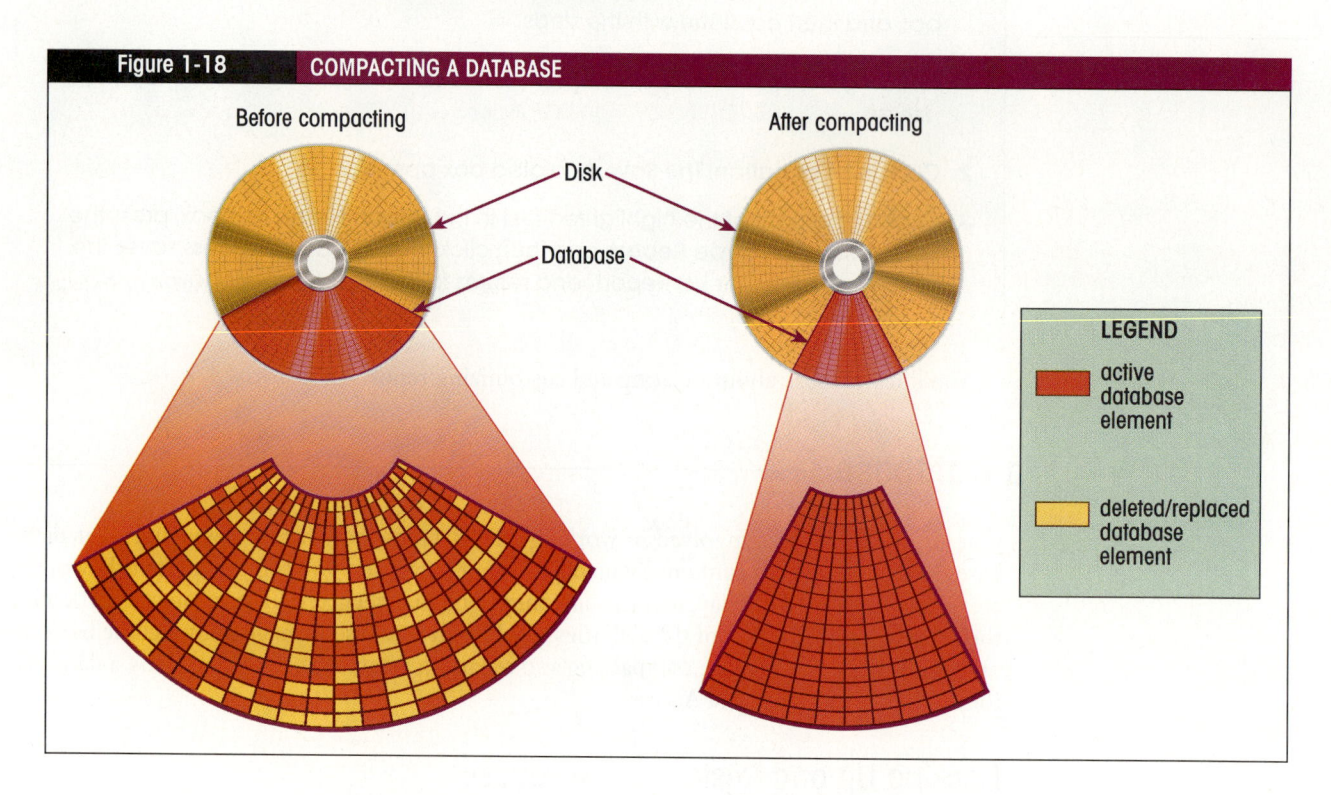

Figure 1-18   COMPACTING A DATABASE

When you compact a database, Access repairs the database at the same time. In many cases, Access detects that a database is damaged when you try to open it and gives you the option to compact and repair it at that time. If you think your database might be damaged because it is behaving unpredictably, you can use the "Compact and Repair Database" option to fix it. With your database file open, point to the Database Utilities option on the Tools menu, and then choose the Compact and Repair Database option.

Compacting a Database Automatically

Access also allows you to set an option for your database file so that every time you close the database, it will be compacted automatically.

TUTORIAL 1 INTRODUCTION TO MICROSOFT ACCESS 2002   AC 1.25   ACCESS

| REFERENCE WINDOW | RW |

Compacting a Database Automatically
- Make sure the database file you want to compact automatically is open.
- Click Tools on the menu bar, and then click Options.
- Click the General tab in the Options dialog box.
- Click the Compact on Close check box to select it.
- Click the OK button.

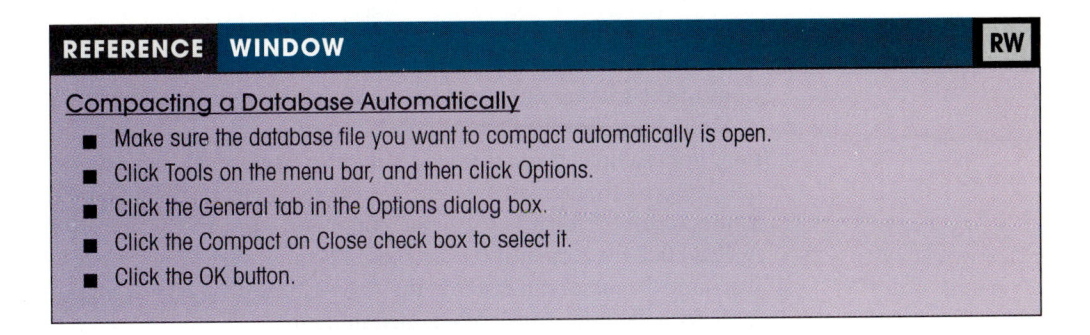

You'll set the compact option now for the Seasonal database. Then, every time you subsequently close the Seasonal database, Access will compact the database file for you. After setting this option, you'll exit Access.

To set the option for compacting the Seasonal database:

1. Make sure the Seasonal Database window is open on your screen.

2. Click **Tools** on the menu bar, and then click **Options**. The Options dialog box opens.

3. Click the **General** tab in the dialog box, and then click the **Compact on Close** check box to select it. See Figure 1-19.

Figure 1-19   GENERAL TAB OF THE OPTIONS DIALOG BOX

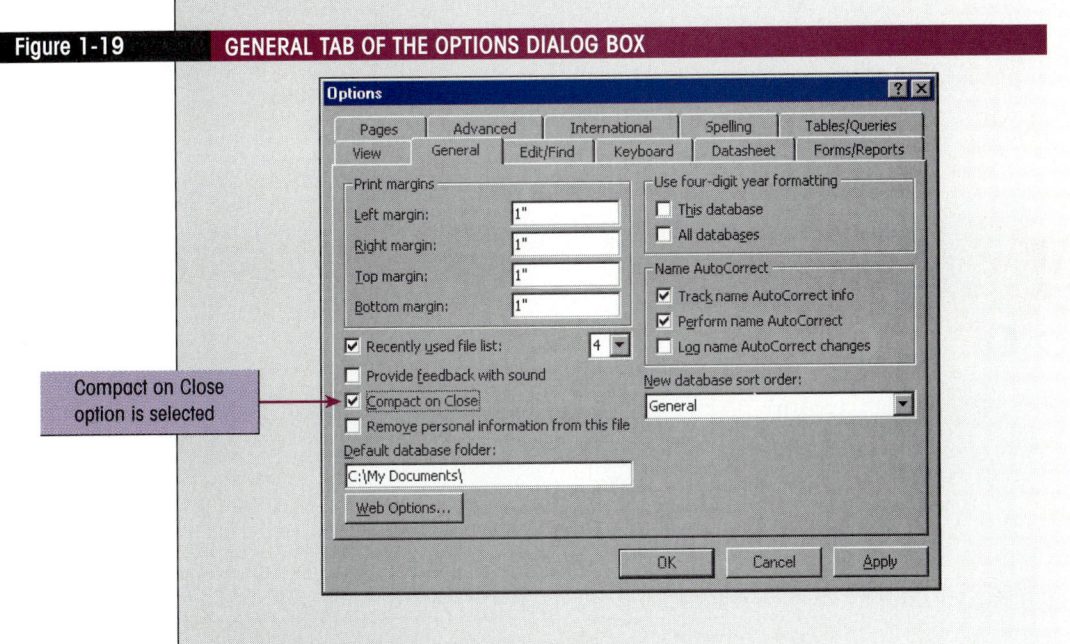

Compact on Close option is selected

4. Click the **OK** button to set the option.

5. Click the **Close** button ⊠ on the Access window title bar to exit Access. When you exit, Access closes the Seasonal database file and compacts it automatically.

Converting an Access 2000 Database

Another important database management task is converting a database so that you can work with it in a different version of Access. As noted earlier in this tutorial, the default file format for databases you create in Access 2002 is Access 2000. This enables you to work with the database in either the Access 2000 or 2002 versions of the software, without having to convert it. This compatibility makes it easy for multiple users working with different versions of the software to share the same database and work more efficiently.

Sometimes, however, you might need to convert an Access 2000 database to another version. For example, if you needed to share an Access 2000 database with a colleague who worked on a laptop computer with Access 97 installed on it, you could convert the Access 2000 database to the Access 97 format. Likewise, you might want to convert an Access 2000 database to the Access 2002 file format if the database becomes very large in size. Access 2002 is enhanced so that large databases run faster in the Access 2002 file format, making it more efficient for you to work with the information contained in them.

To convert a database, follow these steps:

1. Make sure the database you want to convert is closed and the Access window is open.

2. Click Tools on the menu bar, point to Database Utilities, point to Convert Database, and then choose the format you want to convert to—To Access 97 File Format, To Access 2000 File Format, or To Access 2002 File Format.

3. In the Database to Convert From dialog box, select the name of the database you want to convert, and then click the Convert button.

4. In the Convert Database Into dialog box, enter a new name for the converted database in the File name text box, and then click the Save button.

After converting a database, you can use it in the version of Access to which you converted the file. Note, however, that when you convert to a previous file format, such as converting from the Access 2000 file format to the Access 97 file format, you might lose some of the advanced features of the newer version and you might need to make some adjustments to the converted database.

With the Employer and NAICS tables in place, Elsa can continue to build the Seasonal database and use it to store, manipulate, and retrieve important data for NSJI. In the following tutorials, you'll help Elsa complete and maintain the database, and you'll use it to meet the specific information needs of other NSJI employees.

Session 1.2 QUICK CHECK

1. A(n) _____ is a question you ask about the data stored in a database.
2. Unless you specify otherwise, the records resulting from a query are listed in order by the _____.
3. The quickest way to create a form is to use a(n) _____.
4. Describe the form created by the AutoForm: Columnar Wizard.
5. After creating a report, the AutoReport Wizard displays the report in _____.
6. _____ a database rearranges the data and objects in a database to decrease its file size.

REVIEW ASSIGNMENTS

In the Review Assignments, you'll work with the **Seasons** database, which is similar to the database you worked with in the tutorial. Complete the following:

1. Make sure your Data Disk is in the disk drive.

2. Start Access and open the **Seasons** database, which is located in the Review folder on your Data Disk.

Explore
3. Open the Microsoft Access Help window, and then display the Contents tab. Double-click the topic "Microsoft Access Help" (if necessary), and then double-click the topic "Queries," and then click "About types of queries." Read the displayed information, and then click "Select queries." Read the displayed information. In the Contents tab, double-click the topic "Forms," and then click the topic "About forms." Read the displayed information. In the Contents tab, scroll down and double-click the topic "Reports and Report Snapshots," and then click the topic "About reports." Read the displayed information. When finished reading all the topics, close the Microsoft Access Help window. Use Notepad, Word, or some other text editor to write a brief summary of what you learned.

Explore
4. Use the "Ask a Question" box to ask the following question: "How do I rename an object?" Click the topic "Rename a database object" and read the displayed information. Close the Microsoft Access Help window. Then, in the **Seasons** database, rename the **Table1** table as **Employers**.

5. Open the **Employers** table.

Explore
6. Open the Microsoft Access Help window, and then display the Index tab. Type the keyword "print" in the Type keywords text box, and then click the Search button. Click the topic "Set page setup options for printing" and then click "For a table, query, form, or report." Read the displayed information. Close the Microsoft Access Help window. Set the option for printing in landscape orientation, and then print the first page only of the **Employers** table datasheet. Close the **Employers** table.

Explore
7. Use the Simple Query Wizard to create a query that includes the City, EmployerName, ContactFirstName, ContactLastName, and Phone fields (in that order) from the **Employers** table. Name the query **Employer Phone List**. Sort the query results in ascending order by City. Set the option for printing in landscape orientation, and then print the second page only of the query results. Close and save the query.

8. Use the AutoForm: Columnar Wizard to create a form for the **Employers** table.

Explore
9. Use context-sensitive Help to find out how to move to a particular record and display it in the form. Click the What's This? command from the Help menu, and then use the Help pointer to click the number 1 in the Specific Record box at the bottom of the form. Read the displayed information. Click to close the Help box, and then use the Specific Record box to move to record 42 (for Whitney's Resort & Spa) in the **Employers** table.

Explore
10. Print the form for the current record (42). (*Hint:* Click the Selected Record(s) option in the Print dialog box to print the current record.)

11. Save the form as **Employer Info**, and then close the form.

Explore
12. Use the AutoReport: Tabular Wizard to create a report based on the **Employers** table. Print the first page of the report, and then close and save the report as **Employers**.

13. Set the option for compacting the **Seasons** database on close.

Explore 14. Convert the **Seasons** database to Access 2002 file format, saving the converted file as **Seasons2002** in the Review folder. Then convert the **Seasons** database to Access 97 file format, saving the converted file as **Seasons97** in the Review folder. Using Windows Explorer or My Computer, view the contents of your Review folder, and note the file sizes of the three versions of the **Seasons** database. Describe the results.

15. Exit Access.

CASE PROBLEMS

Case 1. Lim's Video Photography Several years ago, Youngho Lim left his position at a commercial photographer's studio and started his own business, Lim's Video Photography, located in San Francisco, California. Youngho quickly established a reputation as one of the area's best videographers, specializing in digital video photography. Youngho offers customers the option of storing edited videos on CD or DVD. His video shoots include weddings and other special events, as well as recording personal and commercial inventories for insurance purposes.

As his business continues to grow, Youngho relies on Access to keep track of information about clients, contracts, and so on. Youngho recently created an Access database named **Videos** to store data about his clients. You'll help Youngho complete and maintain the **Videos** database. Complete the following:

1. Make sure your Data Disk is in the disk drive.

2. Start Access and open the **Videos** database, which is located in the Cases folder on your Data Disk.

3. Open the **Client** table, print the table datasheet, and then close the table.

4. Use the Simple Query Wizard to create a query that includes the ClientName, Phone, and City fields (in that order) from the **Client** table. Name the query **Client List**. Print the query results, and then close the query.

Explore 5. Use the AutoForm: Tabular Wizard to create a form for the **Contract** table. Print the form, save it as **Contract Info**, and then close it.

Explore 6. Use the AutoReport: Columnar Wizard to create a report based on the **Contract** table. Maximize the Report window and change the Zoom setting to Fit. Use the Two Pages button on the Print Preview toolbar to view the first two pages of the report in Print Preview. Print the first page of the report, and then close and save it as **Contracts**.

7. Set the option for compacting the **Videos** database on close.

Explore 8. Convert the **Videos** database to Access 2002 file format, saving the converted file as **Videos2002** in the Cases folder. Then convert the **Videos** database to Access 97 file format, saving the converted file as **Videos97** in the Cases folder. Using Windows Explorer or My Computer, view the contents of your Cases folder, and note the file sizes of the three versions of the **Videos** database. Describe the results.

9. Exit Access.

Case 2. DineAtHome.course.com After working as both a concierge in a local hotel and a manager of several restaurants, Claire Picard founded DineAtHome.course.com in Naples, Florida. Her idea for this e-commerce company was a simple one: to provide people with an easy-to-use, online service that would allow them to order meals from one or more area restaurants and have the meals delivered to their homes. DineAtHome acts as a sort of broker between restaurants and customers. The participating restaurants offer everything from simple fare to gourmet feasts. Claire's staff performs a variety of services, from simply picking up and delivering the meals to providing linens and table service for more formal occasions.

Claire created the **Meals** database in Access to maintain information about participating restaurants and their menu offerings. She needs your help in working with this database. Complete the following:

1. Make sure your Data Disk is in the disk drive.

2. Start Access and open the **Meals** database, which is located in the Cases folder on your Data Disk.

Explore 3. Open the **Restaurant** table, print the table datasheet in landscape orientation, and then close the table.

4. Use the Simple Query Wizard to create a query that includes the RestaurantName, OwnerFirstName, OwnerLastName, and City fields (in that order) from the **Restaurant** table. Name the query **Owner List**.

Explore 5. Sort the query results in descending order by the City field. (*Hint*: Use a toolbar button.)

Explore 6. Use the "Ask a Question" box to ask the following question: "How do I select multiple records?" Click the topic "Select fields and records," and then click the topic "Select fields and records in a datasheet." Read the displayed information, and then close the Help window. Select the four records with "Marco Island" as the value in the City field, and then print just the selected records. (*Hint*: Use the Selected Record(s) option in the Print dialog box to print them.) Close the query, and save your changes to the design.

Explore 7. Use the AutoForm: Columnar Wizard to create a form for the **Restaurant** table. Use context-sensitive Help to find out how to move to a particular record and display it in the form. Click the What's This? command from the Help menu, and then use the Help pointer to click the number 1 in the Specific Record box at the bottom of the form. Read the displayed information. Click to close the Help box, use the Specific Record box to move to record 11 (for The Gazebo), and then print the form for the current record only. (*Hint*: Use the Selected Record(s) option in the Print dialog box to print the current record.) Save the form as **Restaurant Info**, and then close the form.

8. Use the AutoReport: Columnar Wizard to create a report based on the **Restaurant** table. Maximize the Report window and change the Zoom setting to Fit.

Explore 9. Use the View menu to view all eight pages of the report at the same time in Print Preview.

10. Print just the first page of the report, and then close and save the report as **Restaurants**.

11. Set the option for compacting the **Meals** database on close.

Explore 12. Convert the **Meals** database to Access 2002 file format, saving the converted file as **Meals2002** in the Cases folder. Then convert the **Meals** database to Access 97 file format, saving the converted file as **Meals97** in the Cases folder. Using Windows Explorer or My Computer, view the contents of your Cases folder, and note the file sizes of the three versions of the **Meals** database. Describe the results.

13. Exit Access.

Case 3. Redwood Zoo The Redwood Zoo is a small zoo located in the picturesque city of Gig Harbor, Washington, on the shores of Puget Sound. The zoo is ideally situated, with the natural beauty of the site providing the perfect backdrop for the zoo's varied exhibits. Although there are larger zoos in the greater Seattle area, the Redwood Zoo is considered to have some of the best exhibits of marine animals. The newly constructed polar bear habitat is a particular favorite among patrons.

Michael Rosenfeld is the director of fundraising activities for the Redwood Zoo. The zoo relies heavily on donations to fund both ongoing exhibits and temporary displays, especially those involving exotic animals. Michael created an Access database named **Redwood** to keep track of information about donors, their pledges, and the status of funds. You'll help Michael maintain the **Redwood** database. Complete the following:

1. Make sure your Data Disk is in the disk drive.

2. Start Access and open the **Redwood** database, which is located in the Cases folder on your Data Disk.

3. Open the **Donor** table, print the table datasheet, and then close the table.

Explore 4. Use the Simple Query Wizard to create a query that includes all the fields in the **Donor** table *except* the MI field. (*Hint*: Use the >> and < buttons to select the necessary fields.) Name the query **Donors**.

Explore 5. Sort the query results in descending order by the Class field. (*Hint*: Use a toolbar button.) Print the query results, and then close and save the query.

Explore 6. Use the AutoForm: Columnar Wizard to create a form for the **Fund** table. Use context-sensitive Help to find out how to move to a particular record and display it in the form. Click the What's This? command from the Help menu, and then use the Help pointer to click the number 1 in the Specific Record box at the bottom of the form. Read the displayed information. Click to close the Help box, use the Specific Record box to move to record 7 (Polar Bear Park), and then print the form for the current record only. (*Hint*: Use the Selected Record(s) option in the Print dialog box to print the current record.) Save the form as **Fund Info**, and then close it.

7. Use the AutoReport: Columnar Wizard to create a report based on the **Donor** table. Maximize the Report window and change the Zoom setting to Fit.

Explore 8. Use the View menu to view all seven pages of the report at the same time in Print Preview.

9. Print just the first page of the report, and then close and save the report as **Donors**.

10. Set the option for compacting the **Redwood** database on close.

Explore 11. Convert the **Redwood** database to Access 2002 file format, saving the converted file as **Redwood2002** in the Cases folder. Then convert the **Redwood** database to Access 97 file format, saving the converted file as **Redwood97** in the Cases folder. Using Windows Explorer or My Computer, view the contents of your Cases folder, and note the file sizes of the three versions of the **Redwood** database. Describe the results.

12. Exit Access.

Case 4. Mountain River Adventures Several years ago, Connor and Siobhan Dempsey moved to Boulder, Colorado, drawn by their love of the mountains and their interest in outdoor activities of all kinds. This interest led them to form the Mountain River Adventures center. The center began as a whitewater rafting tour provider, but quickly grew to encompass other activities, such as canoeing, hiking, camping, fishing, and rock climbing.

From the beginning, Connor and Siobhan have used computers to help them manage all aspects of their business. They recently installed Access and created a database named **Trips** to store information about clients, equipment, and the types of guided tours they provide. You'll work with the **Trips** database to manage this information. Complete the following:

1. Make sure your Data Disk is in the disk drive.

2. Start Access and open the **Trips** database, which is located in the Cases folder on your Data Disk.

3. Open the **Client** table.

Explore 4. Print the **Client** table datasheet in landscape orientation, and then close the table.

5. Use the Simple Query Wizard to create a query that includes the ClientName, City, State/Prov, and Phone fields (in that order) from the **Client** table. Name the query **Client Info**.

Explore 6. Sort the query results in descending order by State/Prov. (*Hint*: Use a toolbar button.)

7. Print the query results, and then close and save the query.

Explore 8. Use the AutoForm: Columnar Wizard to create a form for the **Client** table. Use context-sensitive Help to find out how to move to a particular record and display it in the form. Click the What's This? command from the Help menu, and then use the Help pointer to click the number 1 in the Specific Record box at the bottom of the form. Read the displayed information. Click to close the Help box, use the Specific Record box to move to record 18, and then print the form for the current record only. (*Hint*: Use the Selected Record(s) option in the Print dialog box to print the current record.) Save the form as **Client Info**, and then close it.

Explore 9. Use the AutoReport: Tabular Wizard to create a report based on the **Client** table. Maximize the Report window and change the Zoom setting to Fit. Use the Two Pages button on the Print Preview toolbar to view both pages of the report in Print Preview. Print the first page of the report in landscape orientation, and then close and save the report as **Clients**.

10. Set the option for compacting the **Trips** database on close.

Explore 11. Convert the **Trips** database to Access 2002 file format, saving the converted file as **Trips2002** in the Cases folder. Then convert the **Trips** database to Access 97 file format, saving the converted file as **Trips97** in the Cases folder. Using Windows Explorer or My Computer, view the contents of your Cases folder, and note the file sizes of the three versions of the **Trips** database. Describe the results.

12. Exit Access.

LAB ASSIGNMENTS

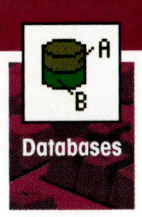

These Lab Assignments are designed to accompany the interactive Course Lab called Databases. To start the Databases Lab, click the Start button on the Windows taskbar, point to Programs, point to Course Labs, point to New Perspectives Course Labs, and then click Databases. If you do not see Course Labs on your Programs menu, see your instructor or technical support person.

Databases This Databases Lab demonstrates the essential concepts of file and database management systems. You will use the Lab to search, sort, and report the data contained in a file of classic books.

1. Click the Steps button to review basic database terminology and to learn how to manipulate the classic books database. As you proceed through the Steps, answer all of the Quick Check questions that appear. After you complete the Steps, you will see a Quick Check summary report. Follow the instructions on the screen to print this report.

2. Click the Explore button. Make sure you can apply basic database terminology to describe the classic books database by answering the following questions:
    a. How many records does the file contain?
    b. How many fields does each record contain?

c. What are the contents of the Catalog # field for the book written by Margaret Mitchell?
d. What are the contents of the Title field for the record with Thoreau in the Author field?
e. Which field has been used to sort the records?

3. In Explore, manipulate the database as necessary to answer the following questions:
   a. When the books are sorted by title, what is the first record in the file?
   b. Use the Search button to search for all the books in the West location. How many do you find?
   c. Use the Search button to search for all the books in the Main location that are checked in. What do you find?

4. Use the Report button to print out a report that groups the books by Status and sorts them by Title. On your report, circle the four field names. Draw a box around the summary statistics showing which books are currently checked in and which books are currently checked out.

INTERNET ASSIGNMENTS

Student Union

The purpose of the Internet Assignments is to challenge you to find information on the Internet that you can use to create effective documents. The actual assignments are updated and maintained on the Course Technology Web site. Log on to the Internet and use your Web browser to go to the Student Union on the New Perspectives Series site at **www.course.com/NewPerspectives/studentunion**. Click the Online Companions link, and then click the link for this text.

QUICK CHECK ANSWERS

Session 1.1
1. field
2. common field
3. primary key; foreign key
4. records; fields
5. current record symbol
6. Use the horizontal and vertical scroll bars to view fields or records not currently visible in the datasheet; use the navigation buttons to move vertically through the records.

Session 1.2
1. query
2. primary key
3. AutoForm Wizard
4. The form displays each field name to the left of its field value, which appears in a box; the widths of the boxes represent the size of the fields.
5. Print Preview
6. Compacting

TUTORIAL 2

OBJECTIVES

In this tutorial you will:

- Learn the guidelines for designing databases and setting field properties
- Create a new database
- Create and save a table
- Define fields and specify a table's primary key
- Add records to a table
- Modify the structure of a table
- Delete, move, and add fields
- Change field properties
- Copy records and import tables from another Access database
- Delete and change records

CREATING AND MAINTAINING A DATABASE

Creating the Northeast Database, and Creating, Modifying, and Updating the Position Table

CASE

Northeast Seasonal Jobs International (NSJI)

The Seasonal database contains two tables—the Employer table and the NAICS table. These tables store data about NSJI's employer customers and the NAICS codes for pertinent job positions, respectively. Elsa Jensen also wants to track information about each position that is available at each employer's place of business. This information includes the position title and wage. Elsa asks you to create a third table, named Position, in which to store the position data.

Because this is your first time creating a new table, Elsa suggests that you first create a new database, named "Northeast," and then create the new Position table in this database. This will keep the Seasonal database intact. Once the Position table is completed, you then can import the Employer and NAICS tables from the Seasonal database into your new Northeast database.

Some of the position data Elsa needs is already stored in another NSJI database. After creating the Position table and adding some records to it, you'll copy the records from the other database into the Position table. Then you'll maintain the Position table by modifying it and updating it to meet Elsa's specific data requirements.

SESSION 2.1

In this session, you will learn the guidelines for designing databases and setting field properties. You'll also learn how to create a new database, create a table, define the fields for a table, select the primary key for a table, and save the table structure.

Guidelines for Designing Databases

A database management system can be a useful tool, but only if you first carefully design the database so that it meets the needs of its users. In database design, you determine the fields, tables, and relationships needed to satisfy the data and processing requirements. When you design a database, you should follow these guidelines:

- **Identify all the fields needed to produce the required information.** For example, Elsa needs information about employers, NAICS codes, and positions. Figure 2-1 shows the fields that satisfy these information requirements.

Figure 2-1 ELSA'S DATA REQUIREMENTS

EmployerID	ContactFirstName
PositionID	ContactLastName
PositionTitle	Position
EmployerName	Wage
Address	Hours/Week
City	NAICSCode
State/Prov	NAICSDesc
PostalCode	StartDate
Country	EndDate
Phone	ReferredBy
Openings	WebSite

- **Group related fields into tables.** For example, Elsa grouped the fields relating to employers into the Employer table and the fields related to NAICS codes into the NAICS table. The other fields are grouped logically into the Position table, which you will create, as shown in Figure 2-2.

Figure 2-2 ELSA'S FIELDS GROUPED INTO TABLES

Employer table	NAICS table	Position table
EmployerID	NAICSCode	PositionID
EmployerName	NAICSDesc	PositionTitle
Address		Wage
City		Hours/Week
State/Prov		Openings
PostalCode		ReferredBy
Country		StartDate
ContactFirstName		EndDate
ContactLastName		
Position		
Phone		
WebSite		

- **Determine each table's primary key.** Recall that a primary key uniquely identifies each record in a table. Although a primary key is not mandatory in Access, it's usually a good idea to include one in each table. Without a primary key, selecting the exact record that you want can be a problem. For some tables, one of the fields, such as a Social Security or credit card number, naturally serves the function of a primary key. For other tables, two or more fields might be needed to function as the primary key. In these cases, the primary key is referred to as a **composite key**. For example, a school grade table would use a combination of student number and course code to serve as the primary key. For a third category of tables, no single field or combination of fields can uniquely identify a record in a table. In these cases, you need to add a field whose sole purpose is to serve as the table's primary key.

  For Elsa's tables, EmployerID is the primary key for the Employer table, NAICSCode is the primary key for the NAICS table, and PositionID will be the primary key for the Position table.

- **Include a common field in related tables.** You use the common field to connect one table logically with another table. For example, Elsa's Employer and Position tables will include the EmployerID field as a common field. Recall that when you include the primary key from one table as a field in a second table to form a relationship, the field is called a foreign key in the second table; therefore, the EmployerID field will be a foreign key in the Position table. With this common field, Elsa can find all positions available at a particular employer; she can use the EmployerID value for an employer and search the Position table for all records with that EmployerID value. Likewise, she can determine which employer has a particular position available by searching the Employer table to find the one record with the same EmployerID value as the corresponding value in the Position table.

- **Avoid data redundancy.** Data redundancy occurs when you store the same data in more than one place. With the exception of common fields to connect tables, you should avoid redundancy because it wastes storage space and can cause inconsistencies, if, for instance, you type a field value one way in one table and a different way in the same table or in a second table. Figure 2-3, which contains portions of potential data to be stored in the Employer and Position tables, shows an example of incorrect database design that has data redundancy in the Position table; the EmployerName field is redundant, and one value was entered incorrectly, in three different ways.

Figure 2-3   INCORRECT DATABASE DESIGN WITH DATA REDUNDANCY

Employer table

EmployerID	EmployerName	Address	Phone
10122	BeanTown Tours	105 State Street, Boston, MA 02109	617-451-1970
10125	Boston Harbor Excursions	75 Atlantic Avenue, Boston, MA 02110	617-235-1800
10126	BaySide Inn & Country Club	354 Oceanside Drive, Brewster, MA 02631	508-283-5775
10190	The Briar Rose Inn	105 Queen Street, Charlottetown PE C1A 8R4	902-626-1595
10191	Windsor Alpine Tours	14 Longmeadow Road, Laconia, NH 03246	603-266-9233
10198	Trudel Spa & Resort	40 Rue Rivard, North Hatley QC J0B 2C0	819-842-7783

Position table

PositionID	EmployerID	EmployerName	PositionTitle	Hours/Week
2040	10126	DaySide Inn & Country Club	Waiter/Waitress	32
2045	10122	BeanTown Tours	Tour Guide	24
2053	10190	The Briar Rose Inn	Host/Hostess	24
2066	10198	Trudel Spa & Resort	Lifeguard	32
2073	10126	Baside Inn & Country Club	Pro Shop Clerk	24
2078	10191	Windsor Alpine Tours	Ski Patrol	30
2079	10191	Windsor Alpine Tours	Day Care	35
2082	10125	Boston Harbor Excursions	Reservationist	40
2111	10126	BaySide Inn Club	Kitchen Help	32

inconsistent data   *data redundancy*

- **Determine the properties of each field.** You need to identify the **properties**, or characteristics, of each field so that the DBMS knows how to store, display, and process the field values. These properties include the field's name, maximum number of characters or digits, description, valid values, and other field characteristics. You will learn more about field properties later in this tutorial.

The Position table you need to create will contain the fields shown in Figure 2-2, plus the EmployerID field as a foreign key. Before you create the new Northeast database and the Position table, you first need to learn some guidelines for setting field properties.

Guidelines for Setting Field Properties

As just noted, the last step of database design is to determine which values to assign to the properties, such as the name and data type, of each field. When you select or enter a value for a property, you **set** the property. Access has rules for naming fields, choosing data types, and setting other properties for fields.

Naming Fields and Objects

You must name each field, table, and other object in an Access database. Access then stores these items in the database, using the names you supply. It's best to choose a field or object name that describes the purpose or contents of the field or object, so that later you can easily remember what the name represents. For example, the three tables in the Northeast database will be named Employer, NAICS, and Position, because these names suggest their contents.

The following rules apply to naming fields and objects:

- A name can be up to 64 characters long.
- A name can contain letters, numbers, spaces, and special characters, except for a period (.), exclamation mark (!), accent grave (`), and square brackets ([ ]).
- A name cannot start with a space.
- A table or query name must be unique within a database. A field name must be unique within a table, but it can be used again in another table.

In addition, experienced users of databases follow these conventions for naming fields and objects:

- Capitalize the first letter of each word in the name.
- Avoid extremely long names because they are difficult to remember and reference.
- Use standard abbreviations, such as Num for Number, Amt for Amount, and Qty for Quantity.
- Do not use spaces in field names because these names will appear in column headings on datasheets and on labels in forms and reports. By not using spaces, you'll be able to show more fields in these objects at one time.

Assigning Field Data Types

You must assign a data type for each field. The **data type** determines what field values you can enter for the field and what other properties the field will have. For example, the Position table will include a StartDate field, which will store date values, so you will assign the date/time data type to this field. Then Access will allow you to enter and manipulate only dates or times as values in the StartDate field.

Figure 2-4 lists the 10 data types available in Access, describes the field values allowed for each data type, explains when you should use each data type, and indicates the field size of each data type.

Figure 2-4 DATA TYPES FOR FIELDS

DATA TYPE	DESCRIPTION	FIELD SIZE
Text	Allows field values containing letters, digits, spaces, and special characters. Use for names, addresses, descriptions, and fields containing digits that are not used in calculations.	0 to 255 characters; 50 characters default
Memo	Allows field values containing letters, digits, spaces, and special characters. Use for long comments and explanations.	1 to 65,535 characters; exact size is determined by entry
Number	Allows positive and negative numbers as field values. Numbers can contain digits, a decimal point, commas, a plus sign, and a minus sign. Use for fields that you will use in calculations, except calculations involving money.	1 to 15 digits
Date/Time	Allows field values containing valid dates and times from January 1, 100 to December 31, 9999. Dates can be entered in mm/dd/yy (month, day, year) format, several other date formats, or a variety of time formats, such as 10:35 PM. You can perform calculations on dates and times, and you can sort them. For example, you can determine the number of days between two dates.	8 bytes
Currency	Allows field values similar to those for the number data type. Unlike calculations with number data type decimal values, calculations performed using the currency data type are not subject to round-off error.	Accurate to 15 digits on the left side of the decimal separator and to 4 digits on the right side

Figure 2-4	DATA TYPES FOR FIELDS, CONTINUED	
DATA TYPE	**DESCRIPTION**	**FIELD SIZE**
AutoNumber	Consists of integers with values controlled by Access. Access automatically inserts a value in the field as each new record is created. You can specify sequential numbering or random numbering, which guarantees a unique field value, so that such a field can serve as a table's primary key.	9 digits
Yes/No	Limits field values to yes and no, on and off, or true and false. Use for fields that indicate the presence or absence of a condition, such as whether an order has been filled or whether an employee is eligible for the company dental plan.	1 character
OLE Object	Allows field values that are created in other programs as objects, such as photographs, video images, graphics, drawings, sound recordings, voice-mail messages, spreadsheets, and word-processing documents. These objects can be linked or embedded.	1 gigabyte maximum; exact size depends on object size
Hyperlink	Consists of text used as a hyperlink address. A hyperlink address can have up to three parts: the text that appears in a field or control; the path to a file or page; and a location within the file or page. Hyperlinks help you to connect your application easily to the Internet or an intranet.	Up to 64,000 characters total for the three parts of a hyperlink data type
Lookup Wizard	Creates a field that lets you look up a value in another table or in a predefined list of values.	Same size as the primary key field used to perform the lookup

Setting Field Sizes

The **Field Size** property defines a field value's maximum storage size for text, number, and AutoNumber fields only. The other data types have no Field Size property because their storage size is either a fixed, predetermined amount or is determined automatically by the field value itself, as shown in Figure 2-4. A text field has a default field size of 50 characters; you can also set its field size by entering a number from 0 to 255. For example, the PositionTitle and ReferredBy fields in the Position table will be text fields with a size of 30 each.

When you use the number data type to define a field, you should set the field's Field Size property based on the largest value that you expect to store in that field. Access processes smaller data sizes faster using less memory, so you can optimize your database's performance and its storage space by selecting the correct field size for each field. For example, it would be wasteful to use the Long Integer setting when defining a field that will store only whole numbers ranging from 0 to 255, because the Long Integer setting will use four bytes of storage space. A better choice would be the Byte setting, which uses one byte of storage space to store the same values. Field Size property settings for number fields are as follows:

- **Byte:** Stores whole numbers (numbers with no fractions) from 0 to 255 in one byte
- **Integer:** Stores whole numbers from –32,768 to 32,767 in two bytes
- **Long Integer** (default): Stores whole numbers from –2,147,483,648 to 2,147,483,647 in four bytes
- **Single:** Stores positive and negative numbers to precisely seven decimal places and uses four bytes
- **Double:** Stores positive and negative numbers to precisely 15 decimal places and uses eight bytes
- **Replication ID:** Establishes a unique identifier for replication of tables, records, and other objects and uses 16 bytes
- **Decimal:** Stores positive and negative numbers to precisely 28 decimal places and uses 12 bytes

Elsa documented the design for the new Position table by listing each field's name, data type, size (if applicable), and description, as shown in Figure 2-5. Note that Elsa assigned the text data type to the PositionID, PositionTitle, EmployerID, and ReferredBy fields; the currency data type to the Wage field; the number data type to the Hours/Week and Openings fields; and the date/time data type to the StartDate and EndDate fields.

Figure 2-5   **DESIGN FOR THE POSITION TABLE**

Field Name	Data Type	Field Size	Description
PositionID	Text	4	Primary key
PositionTitle	Text	30	
EmployerID	Text	5	Foreign key
Wage	Currency		Rate per hour
Hours/Week	Number	Integer	Work hours per week
Openings	Number	Integer	Number of openings
ReferredBy	Text	30	
StartDate	Date/Time		Month and day
EndDate	Date/Time		Month and day

With Elsa's design in place, you're ready to create the new Northeast database and the Position table.

Creating a New Database

Access provides two ways for you to create a new database: using a Database Wizard or creating a blank database. When you use a Wizard, the Wizard guides you through the database creation process and provides the necessary tables, forms, and reports for the type of database you choose—all in one operation. Using a Database Wizard is an easy way to start creating a database, but only if your data requirements closely match one of the supplied templates. When you choose to create a blank database, you need to add all the tables, forms, reports, and other objects after you create the database file. Creating a blank database provides the most flexibility, allowing you to define objects in the way that you want, but it does require that you define each object separately. Whichever method you choose, you can always modify or add to your database after you create it.

The following steps outline the process for creating a new database using a Database Wizard:

1. If necessary, click the New button on the Database toolbar to display the Task Pane.

2. In the "New from template" section of the Task Pane, click General Templates. The Templates dialog box opens.

3. Click the Databases tab, and then choose the Database Wizard that most closely matches the type of database you want to create. Click the OK button.

4. In the File New Database dialog box, choose the location in which to save the new database, specify its name, and then click the Create button.

5. Complete each of the Wizard dialog boxes, clicking the Next button to move through them after making your selections.

6. Click the Finish button when you have completed all the Wizard dialog boxes.

None of the Database Wizards matches the requirements of the new Northeast database, so you'll use the Blank Database option to create it.

To create the Northeast database:

1. Place your Data Disk in the appropriate disk drive, and then start Access.

2. In the New section of the Task Pane, click **Blank Database**. The File New Database dialog box opens. This dialog box is similar to the Open dialog box.

3. Click the **Save in** list arrow, and then click the drive that contains your Data Disk.

4. Click **Tutorial** in the list box, and then click the **Open** button.

5. In the File name text box, double-click the text **db1** to select it, and then type **Northeast**.

   TROUBLE? Your File name text box might contain an entry other than "db1." Just select whatever text is in this text box, and continue with the steps.

6. Click the **Create** button. Access creates the Northeast database in the Tutorial folder on your Data Disk, and then displays the Database window for the new database with the Tables object selected.

Now you can create the Position table in the Northeast database.

Creating a Table

Creating a table consists of naming the fields and defining the properties for the fields, specifying a primary key (and a foreign key, if applicable) for the table, and then saving the table structure. You will use Elsa's design (Figure 2-5) as a guide for creating the Position table in the Northeast database.

To begin creating the Position table:

1. Click the **New** button in the Database window. The New Table dialog box opens. See Figure 2-6.

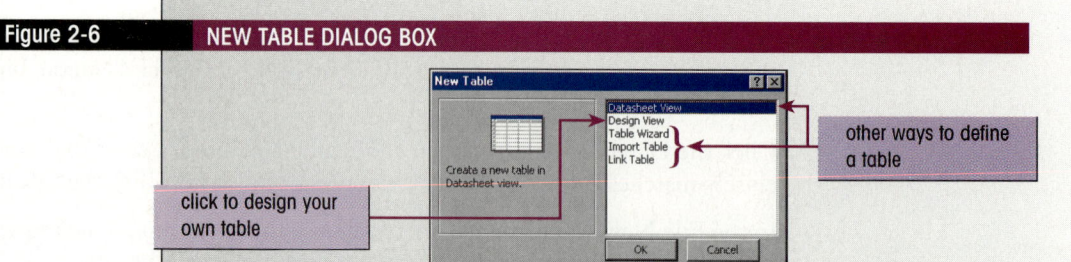

Figure 2-6   NEW TABLE DIALOG BOX

click to design your own table

other ways to define a table

TROUBLE? If the Task Pane opens and displays "New File" at the top, you clicked the New button on the Database toolbar instead of the New button in the Database window. Click the Close button to close the Task Pane, and then repeat Step 1.

TUTORIAL 2 CREATING AND MAINTAINING A DATABASE   AC 2.09

In Access, you can create a table from entered data (Datasheet View), define your own table (Design View), use a Wizard to automate the table creation process (Table Wizard), or use a Wizard to import or link data from another database or other data source (Import Table or Link Table). For the Position table, you will define your own table.

2. Click **Design View** in the list box, and then click the **OK** button. The Table window opens in Design view. (Note that you can also double-click the "Create table in Design view" option in the Database window to open the Table window in Design view.) See Figure 2-7.

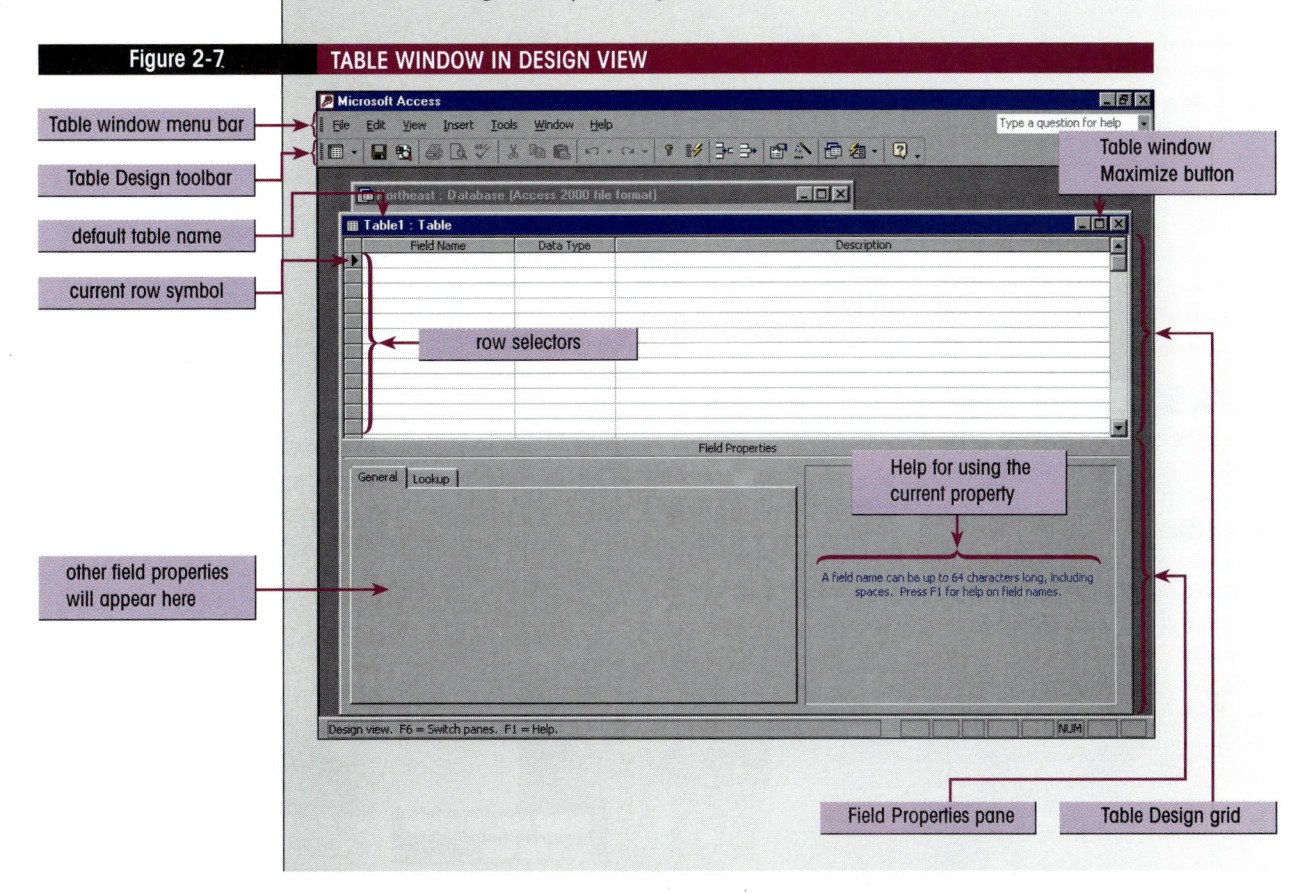

Figure 2-7   **TABLE WINDOW IN DESIGN VIEW**

- Table window menu bar
- Table Design toolbar
- default table name
- current row symbol
- row selectors
- Table window Maximize button
- Help for using the current property
- other field properties will appear here
- Field Properties pane
- Table Design grid

You use Design view to define or modify a table structure or the properties of the fields in a table. If you create a table without using a Wizard, you enter the fields and their properties for your table directly in the Table window in Design view.

Defining Fields

Initially, the default table name, Table1, appears on the Table window title bar, the current row symbol is positioned in the first row selector of the Table Design grid, and the insertion point is located in the first row's Field Name box. The purpose or characteristics of the current property (Field Name, in this case) appear in the right side of the Field Properties pane. You can display more complete information about the current property by pressing the F1 key.

You enter values for the Field Name, Data Type, and Description field properties in the Table Design grid. You select values for all other field properties, most of which are optional, in the Field Properties pane. These other properties will appear when you move to the first row's Data Type text box.

REFERENCE WINDOW

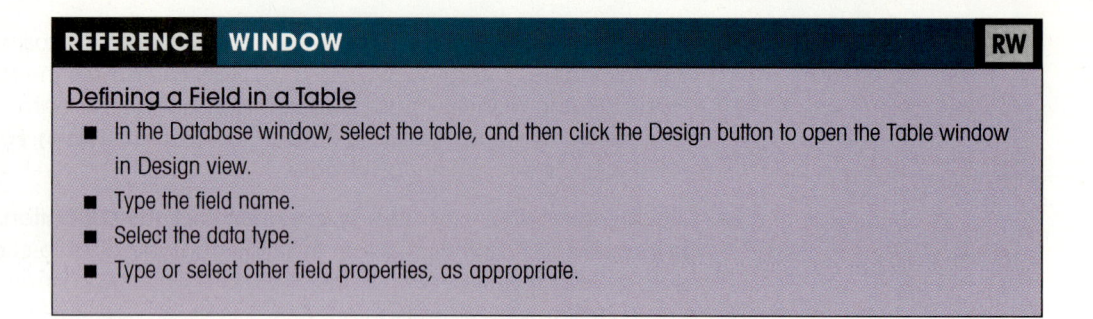

Defining a Field in a Table
- In the Database window, select the table, and then click the Design button to open the Table window in Design view.
- Type the field name.
- Select the data type.
- Type or select other field properties, as appropriate.

The first field you need to define is PositionID.

To define the PositionID field:

1. Type **PositionID** in the first row's Field Name text box, and then press the **Tab** key (or press the **Enter** key) to advance to the Data Type text box. The default data type, Text, appears highlighted in the Data Type text box, which now also contains a list arrow, and field properties for a text field appear in the Field Properties pane. See Figure 2-8.

Figure 2-8 TABLE WINDOW AFTER ENTERING THE FIRST FIELD NAME

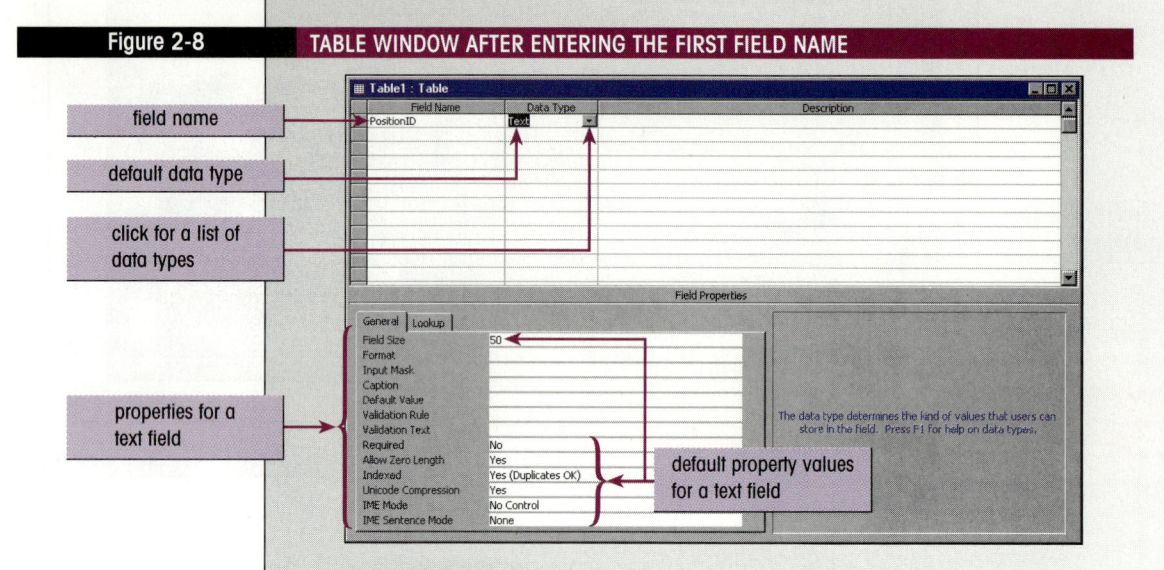

- field name
- default data type
- click for a list of data types
- properties for a text field
- default property values for a text field

Notice that the right side of the Field Properties pane now provides an explanation for the current property, Data Type.

TROUBLE? If you make a typing error, you can correct it by clicking the mouse to position the insertion point, and then using either the Backspace key to delete characters to the left of the insertion point or the Delete key to delete characters to the right of the insertion point. Then type the correct text.

Because the PositionID numbers will not be used in calculations, you will assign the text data type (as opposed to the number data type) to the PositionID field.

2. Press the **Tab** key to accept Text as the data type and to advance to the Description text box.

Next you'll enter the Description property value as "Primary key." You can use the Description property to enter an optional description for a field to explain its purpose or usage. A field's Description property can be up to 255 characters long, and its value appears on the status bar when you view the table datasheet.

3. Type **Primary key** in the Description text box.

Notice the Field Size property for the text field. The default setting of "50" is displayed. You need to change this number to "4" because all PositionID values at NSJI contain only 4 digits. (Refer to the Access Help system for a complete description of all the properties available for the different data types.)

4. Double-click the number **50** in the Field Size property box to select it, and then type **4**. The definition of the first field is completed. See Figure 2-9.

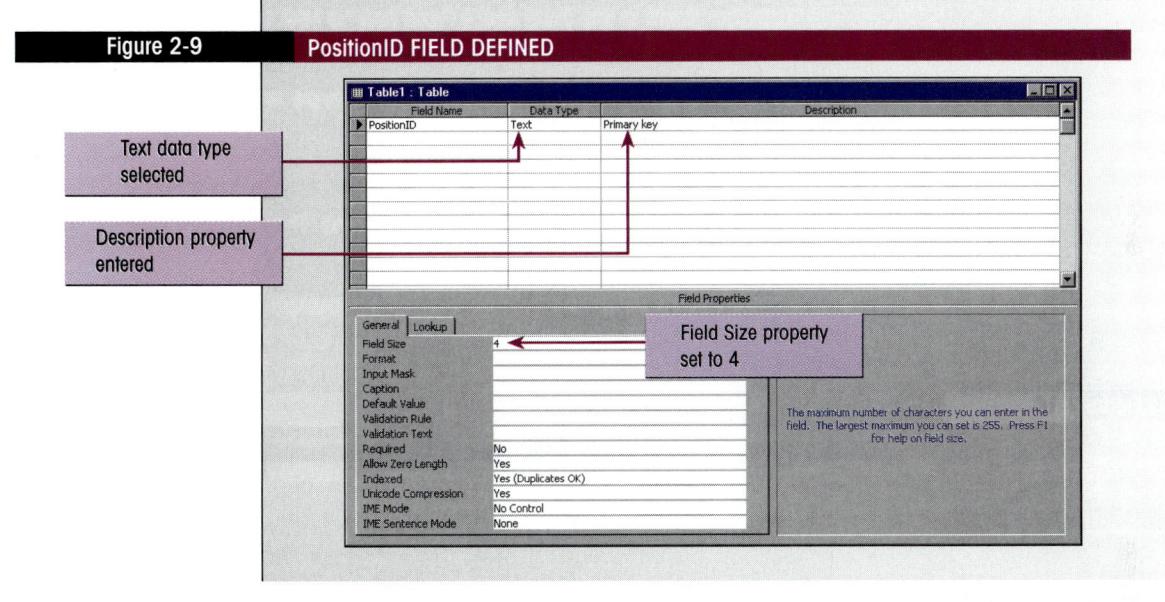

Figure 2-9   PositionID FIELD DEFINED

- Text data type selected
- Description property entered
- Field Size property set to 4

Elsa's Position table design shows PositionTitle as the second field. You will define PositionTitle as a text field with a Field Size of 30, which is a sufficient length for any title values that will be entered.

To define the PositionTitle field:

1. Place the insertion point in the second row's Field Name text box, type **PositionTitle** in the text box, and then press the **Tab** key to advance to the Data Type text box.

2. Press the **Tab** key to accept Text as the field's data type.

According to Elsa's design (Figure 2-5), you do not need to enter a description for this field. If you've assigned a descriptive field name and the field does not fulfill a special function (such as primary key), you usually do not enter a value for the optional Description property. PositionTitle is a field that does not require a value for its Description property.

Next, you'll change the Field Size property to 30. Note that when defining the fields in a table, you can move between the Table Design grid and the Field Properties pane of the Table window by pressing the F6 key.

3. Press the **F6** key to move to the Field Properties pane. The current entry for the Field Size property, 50, is highlighted.

4. Type **30** to set the Field Size property. You have completed the definition of the second field.

The third field in the Position table is the EmployerID field. Recall that this field will serve as the foreign key in the Position table, allowing you to relate data from the Position table to data in the Employer table. The field must be defined in the same way in both tables—that is, a text field with a field size of 5.

To define the EmployerID field:

1. Place the insertion point in the third row's Field Name text box, type **EmployerID** in the text box, and then press the **Tab** key to advance to the Data Type text box.

2. Press the **Tab** key to accept Text as the field's data type and to advance to the Description text box.

3. Type **Foreign key** in the Description text box.

4. Press the **F6** key to move to the Field Properties pane. The current entry for the Field Size property, 50, is highlighted.

5. Type **5** to set the Field Size property. You have completed the definition of the third field. See Figure 2-10.

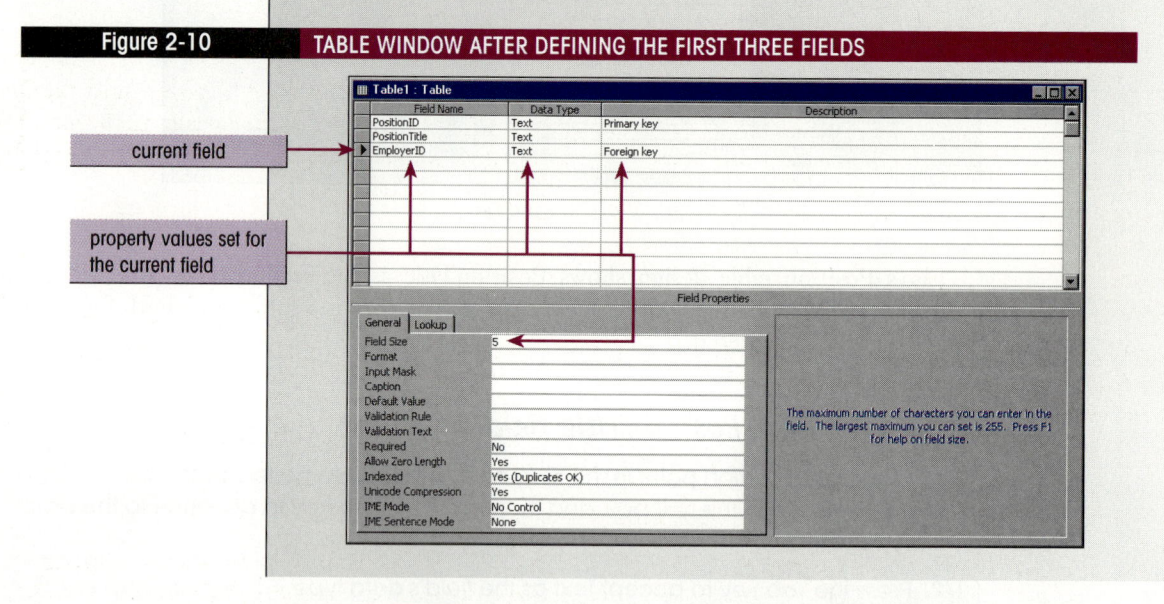

Figure 2-10 TABLE WINDOW AFTER DEFINING THE FIRST THREE FIELDS

- current field
- property values set for the current field

The fourth field is the Wage field, which will display values in the currency format.

To define the Wage field:

1. Place the insertion point in the fourth row's Field Name text box, type **Wage** in the text box, and then press the **Tab** key to advance to the Data Type text box.

2. Click the **Data Type** list arrow, click **Currency** in the list box, and then press the **Tab** key to advance to the Description text box.

3. Type **Rate per hour** in the Description text box.

Elsa wants the Wage field values to be displayed with two decimal places, and she does not want any value to be displayed by default for new records. So, you need to set the Decimal Places and Default Value properties accordingly.

4. Click the **Decimal Places** text box to position the insertion point there. A list arrow appears on the right side of the Decimal Places text box.

When you position the insertion point or select text in many Access text boxes, Access displays a list arrow, which you can click to display a list box with options. You can display the list arrow and the list box simultaneously if you click the text box near its right side.

5. Click the **Decimal Places** list arrow, and then click **2** in the list box to specify two decimal places for the Wage field values.

Next, notice the Default Value property, which specifies the value that will be automatically entered into the field when you add a new record. Currently this property has a setting of 0. Elsa wants the Wage field to be empty (that is, to contain *no* default value) when a new record is added. Therefore, you need to change the Default Value property to the setting "Null." Setting the Default Value property to "Null" tells Access to display no value in the Wage field, by default.

6. Select **0** in the Default Value text box either by dragging the pointer or double-clicking the mouse, and then type **Null**.

The next two fields in the Position table—Hours/Week and Openings—are number fields with a field size of Integer. Also, for each of these fields, Elsa wants the values displayed with no decimal places, and she does not want a default value displayed for the fields when new records are added. You'll define these two fields next.

To define the Hours/Week and Openings fields:

1. Position the insertion point in the fifth row's Field Name text box, type **Hours/Week** in the text box, and then press the **Tab** key to advance to the Data Type text box.

2. Click the **Data Type** list arrow, click **Number** in the list box, and then press the **Tab** key to advance to the Description text box.

3. Type **Work hours per week** in the Description text box.

4. Click the right side of the **Field Size** text box, and then click **Integer** to choose this setting. Recall that the Integer field size stores whole numbers in two bytes.

5. Click the right side of the **Decimal Places** text box, and then click **0** to specify no decimal places.

6. Select the value **0** in the Default Value text box, and then type **Null**.

7. Repeat Steps 1 through 6 to define the **Openings** field as the sixth field in the Position table. For the Description, enter the text **Number of openings**.

According to Elsa's design (Figure 2-5), the final three fields to be defined in the Position table are ReferredBy, a text field, and StartDate and EndDate, both date/time fields. You'll define these three fields next.

To define the ReferredBy, StartDate, and EndDate fields:

1. Position the insertion point in the seventh row's Field Name text box, type **ReferredBy** in the text box, press the **Tab** key to advance to the Data Type text box, and then press the **Tab** key again to accept the default Text data type.

2. Change the default Field Size of 50 to **30** for the ReferredBy field.

3. Position the insertion point in the eighth row's Field Name text box, type **StartDate**, and then press the **Tab** key to advance to the Data Type text box.

4. Click the **Data Type** list arrow, click **Date/Time** to select this type, press the **Tab** key, and then type **Month and day** in the Description text box.

    Elsa wants the values in the StartDate field to be displayed in a format showing only the month and day, as in the following example: 03/11. You use the Format property to control the display of a field value.

5. In the Field Properties pane, click the right side of the **Format** text box to display the list of predefined formats. As noted in the right side of the Field Properties pane, you can either choose a predefined format or enter a custom format.

    TROUBLE? If you see a list arrow instead of a list of predefined formats, click the list arrow to display the list.

    None of the predefined formats matches the layout Elsa wants for the StartDate values. Therefore, you need to create a custom date format. Figure 2-11 shows some of the symbols available for custom date and time formats. (A complete description of all the custom formats is available in Help.)

Figure 2-11   SYMBOLS FOR SOME CUSTOM DATE FORMATS

SYMBOL	DESCRIPTION
/	date separator
d	day of the month in one or two numeric digits, as needed (1 to 31)
dd	day of the month in two numeric digits (01 to 31)
ddd	first three letters of the weekday (Sun to Sat)
dddd	full name of the weekday (Sunday to Saturday)
w	day of the week (1 to 7)
ww	week of the year (1 to 53)
m	month of the year in one or two numeric digits, as needed (1 to 12)
mm	month of the year in two numeric digits (01 to 12)
mmm	first three letters of the month (Jan to Dec)
mmmm	full name of the month (January to December)
yy	last two digits of the year (01 to 99)
yyyy	full year (0100 to 9999)

Elsa wants the dates to be displayed with a two-digit month (mm) and a two-digit day (dd). You'll enter this custom format now.

6. Click the **Format** list arrow to close the list of predefined formats, and then type **mm/dd** in the Format text box. See Figure 2-12.

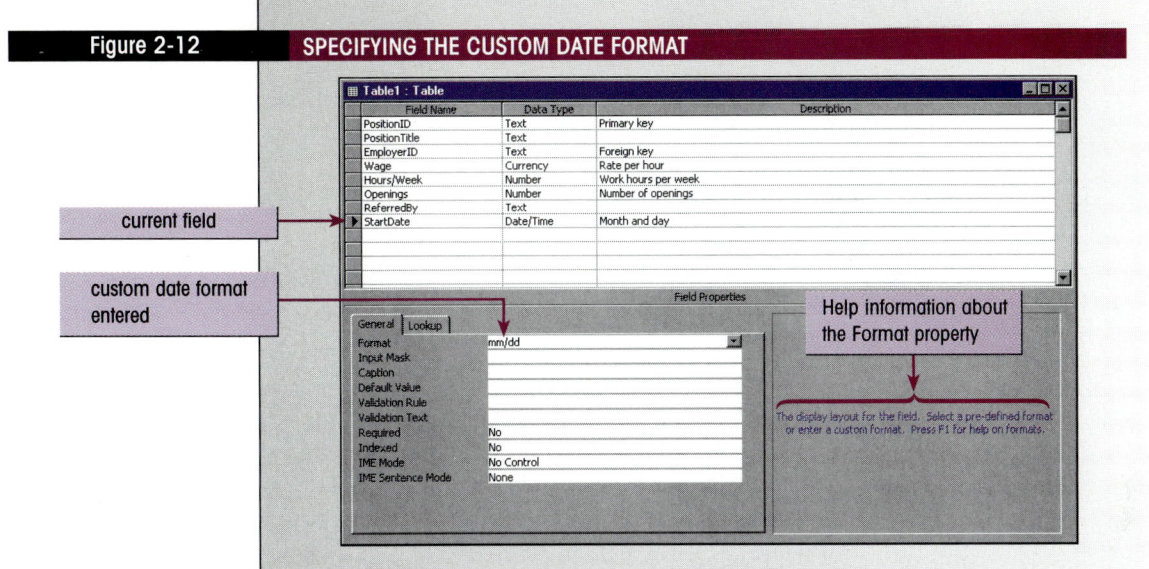

Figure 2-12 SPECIFYING THE CUSTOM DATE FORMAT

Next, you'll define the ninth and final field, EndDate. This field will have the same definition and properties as the StartDate field.

7. Place the insertion point in the ninth row's Field Name text box, type **EndDate**, and then press the **Tab** key to advance to the Data Type text box.

   You can select a value from the Data Type list box as you did for the StartDate field. Alternately, you can type the property value in the text box or type just the first character of the property value.

8. Type **d**. The value in the ninth row's Data Type text box changes to "date/Time," with the letters "ate/Time" highlighted. See Figure 2-13.

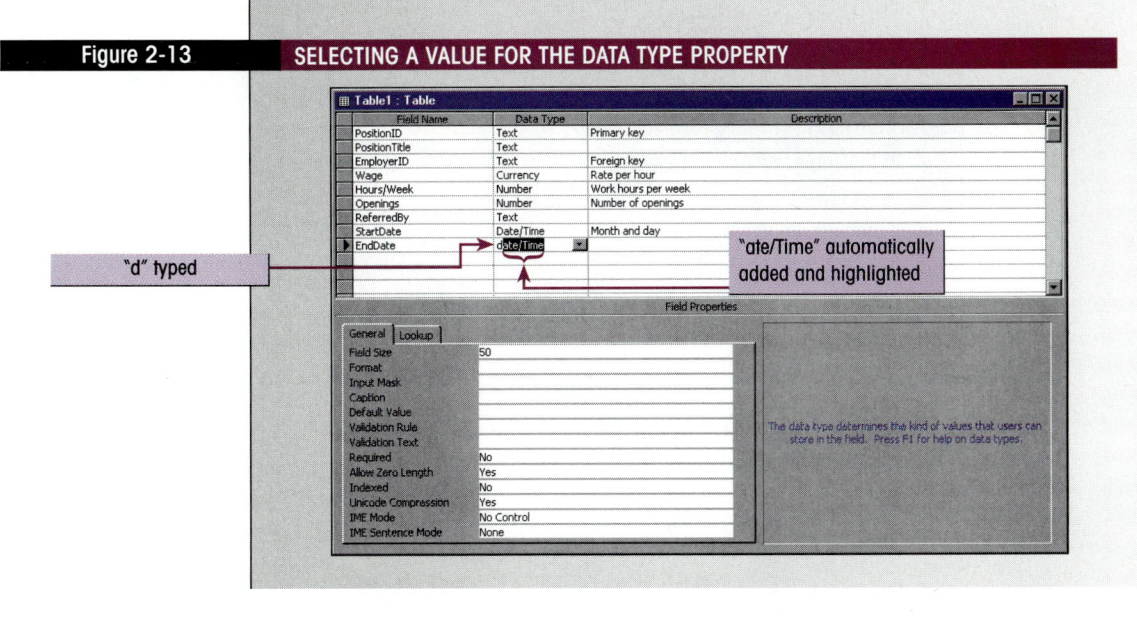

Figure 2-13 SELECTING A VALUE FOR THE DATA TYPE PROPERTY

9. Press the **Tab** key to advance to the Description text box, and then type **Month and day**. Note that Access changes the value for the Data Type property to Date/Time.

10. In the Format text box, type **mm/dd** to specify the custom date format for the EndDate field.

You've finished defining the fields for the Position table. Next, you need to specify the primary key for the table.

Specifying the Primary Key

Although Access does not require a table to have a primary key, including a primary key offers several advantages:

- A primary key uniquely identifies each record in a table.
- Access does not allow duplicate values in the primary key field. If a record already exists with a PositionID value of 1320, for example, Access prevents you from adding another record with this same value in the PositionID field. Preventing duplicate values ensures the uniqueness of the primary key field.
- When a primary key has been specified, Access forces you to enter a value for the primary key field in every record in the table. This is known as **entity integrity**. If you do not enter a value for a field, you have actually given the field what is known as a **null value**. You cannot give a null value to the primary key field because entity integrity prevents Access from accepting and processing that record.
- Access stores records on disk in the same order as you enter them but displays them in order by the field values of the primary key. If you enter records in no specific order, you are ensured that you will later be able to work with them in a more meaningful, primary key sequence.
- Access responds faster to your requests for specific records based on the primary key.

> **REFERENCE WINDOW**
>
> **Specifying a Primary Key for a Table**
> - In the Table window in Design view, click the row selector for the field you've chosen to be the primary key.
> - If the primary key will consist of two or more fields, press and hold down the Ctrl key, and then click the row selector for each additional primary key field.
> - Click the Primary Key button on the Table Design toolbar.

According to Elsa's design, you need to specify PositionID as the primary key for the Position table.

To specify PositionID as the primary key:

1. Position the pointer on the row selector for the PositionID field until the pointer changes to a ➡ shape. See Figure 2-14.

Figure 2-14   SPECIFYING PositionID AS THE PRIMARY KEY

Primary Key button

pointer

row selector

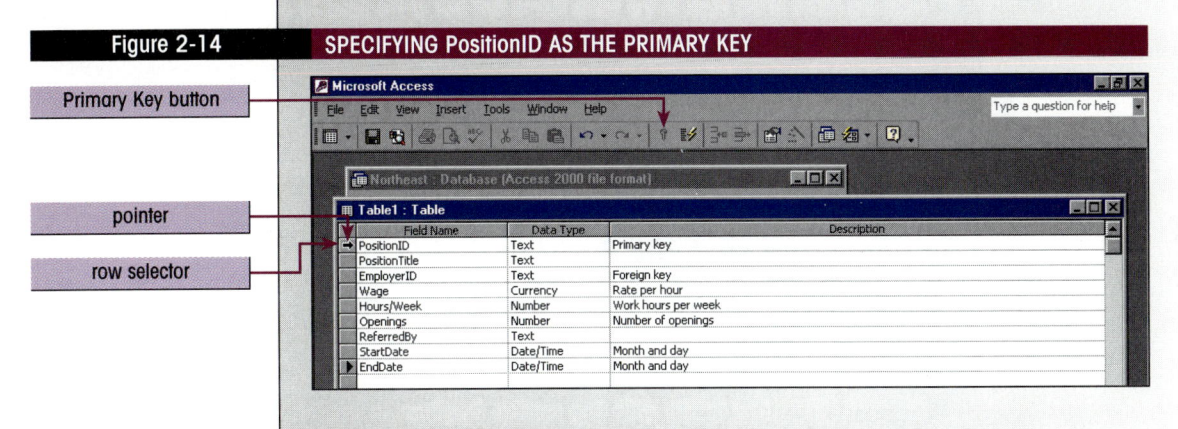

2. Click the mouse button. The entire first row of the Table Design grid is highlighted.

3. Click the **Primary Key** button on the Table Design toolbar, and then click a row other than the first to deselect the first row. A key symbol appears in the row selector for the first row, indicating that the PositionID field is the table's primary key. See Figure 2-15.

Figure 2-15   PositionID SELECTED AS THE PRIMARY KEY

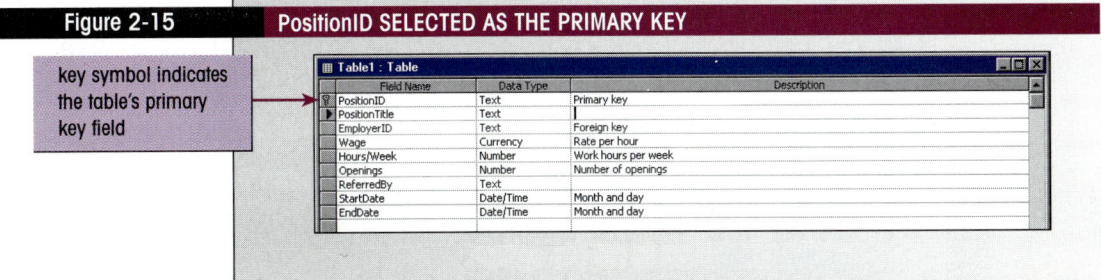

key symbol indicates the table's primary key field

TROUBLE? Your insertion point might be in a different location from the one shown in the figure, depending on where you clicked to deselect the first row.

If you specify the wrong field as the primary key, or if you later change your mind and do not want the designated primary key field to be the table's primary key, you can select the field and then click the Primary Key button on the Table Design toolbar again, which will remove the key symbol and the primary key designation from the field. Then you can choose another field to be the primary key, if necessary.

You've defined the fields for the Position table and specified its primary key, so you can now save the table structure.

Saving the Table Structure

The last step in creating a table is to name the table and save the table's structure on disk. Once the table is saved, you can use it to enter data in the table.

> **REFERENCE WINDOW**
>
> **Saving a Table Structure**
> - Click the Save button on the Table Design toolbar.
> - Type the name of the table in the Table Name text box of the Save As dialog box.
> - Click the OK button (or press the Enter key).

According to Elsa's plan, you need to save the table you've defined as "Position."

To name and save the Position table:

1. Click the **Save** button 🖫 on the Table Design toolbar. The Save As dialog box opens.

2. Type **Position** in the Table Name text box, and then press the **Enter** key. Access saves the table with the name Position in the Northeast database on your Data Disk. Notice that Position now appears instead of Table1 in the Table window title bar.

Recall that in Tutorial 1 you set the Compact on Close option for the Seasonal database so that it would be compacted automatically each time you closed it. Now you'll set this option for your new Northeast database, so that it will be compacted automatically.

To set the option for compacting the Northeast database automatically:

1. Click **Tools** on the menu bar, and then click **Options**. The Options dialog box opens.

2. Click the **General** tab in the dialog box, and then click the **Compact on Close** check box to select it.

3. Click the **OK** button to set the option.

The Position table is now complete. In Session 2.2, you'll continue to work with the Position table by entering records in it, modifying its structure, and maintaining data in the table. You will also import two tables, Employer and NAICS, from the Seasonal database into the Northeast database.

Session 2.1 Quick Check

1. What guidelines should you follow when designing a database?
2. What is the purpose of the Data Type property for a field?
3. For which three types of fields can you assign a field size?

4. In Design view, which key do you press to move between the Table Design grid and the Field Properties pane?

5. You use the _____ property to control the display of a field value.

6. A(n) _____ value, which results when you do not enter a value for a field, is not permitted for a primary key.

SESSION 2.2

In this session, you will add records to a table; modify the structure of an existing table by deleting, moving, and adding fields and changing field properties; copy records from another Access database; import tables from another Access database; and update an existing database by deleting and changing records.

Adding Records to a Table

You can add records to an Access table in several ways. A table datasheet provides a simple way for you to add records. As you learned in Tutorial 1, a datasheet shows a table's contents in rows and columns. Each row is a separate record in the table, and each column contains the field values for one field in the table. If you are currently working in Design view, you first must change from Design view to Datasheet view in order to view the table's datasheet.

Elsa asks you to add the two records shown in Figure 2-16 to the Position table. These two records contain data for positions that have recently become available at two employers.

Figure 2-16   RECORDS TO BE ADDED TO THE POSITION TABLE

PositionID	PositionTitle	EmployerID	Wage	Hours/Week	Openings	ReferredBy	StartDate	EndDate
2021	Waiter/Waitress	10155	9.50	30	1	Sue Brown	6/30	9/15
2017	Tour Guide	10149	15.00	20	1	Ed Curran	9/21	11/1

To add the records in the Position table datasheet:

1. If you took a break after the previous session, make sure that Access is running and that the Position table of the Northeast database is open in Design view. To open the table in Design view from the Database window, right-click the **Position** table, and then click **Design View** on the shortcut menu.

   Access displays the fields you defined for the Position table in Design view. Now you need to switch to Datasheet view so that you can enter the two records for Elsa.

2. Click the **View** button for Datasheet view on the Table Design toolbar. The Table window opens in Datasheet view. See Figure 2-17.

ACCESS   **AC 2.20**   TUTORIAL 2   CREATING AND MAINTAINING A DATABASE

Figure 2-17   **TABLE WINDOW IN DATASHEET VIEW**

Callouts: current record symbol; field names; Description property for the current field; Table window

The table's nine field names appear at the top of the datasheet. Some of the field names might not be visible. The current record symbol in the first row's record selector identifies the currently selected record, which contains no data until you enter the first record. The insertion point is located in the first row's PositionID field, whose Description property appears on the status bar.

3. Type **2021**, which is the first record's PositionID field value, and then press the **Tab** key. Each time you press the Tab key, the insertion point moves to the right to the next field in the record. See Figure 2-18.

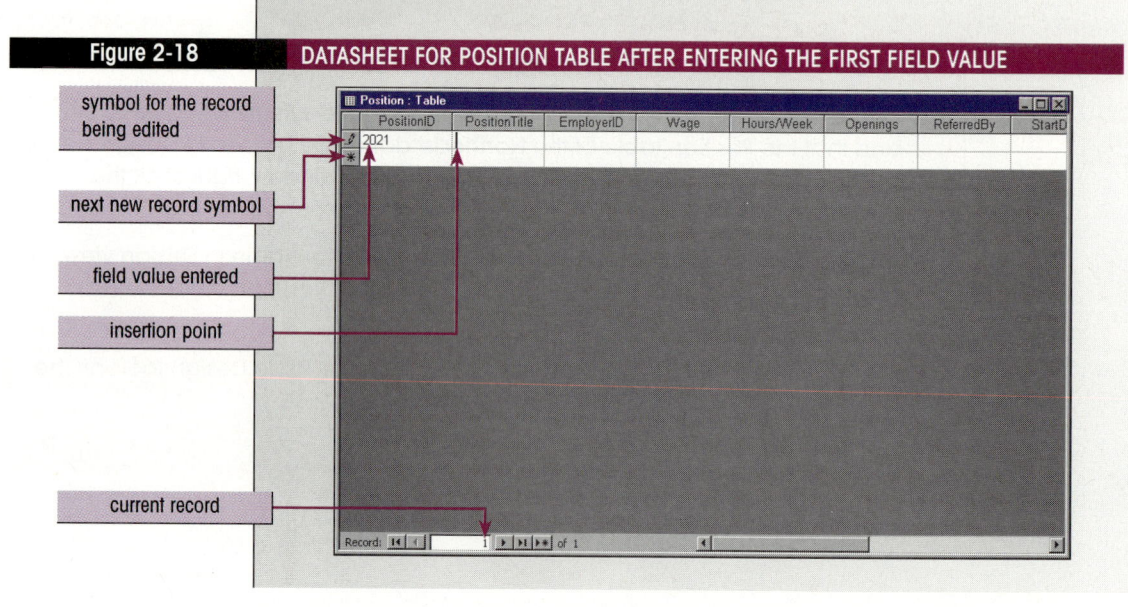

Figure 2-18   **DATASHEET FOR POSITION TABLE AFTER ENTERING THE FIRST FIELD VALUE**

Callouts: symbol for the record being edited; next new record symbol; field value entered; insertion point; current record

TROUBLE? If you make a mistake when typing a value, use the Backspace key to delete characters to the left of the insertion point or the Delete key to delete characters to the right of the insertion point. Then type the correct value. If you want to correct a value by replacing it entirely, double-click the value to select it, and then type the correct value.

The pencil symbol in the first row's record selector indicates that the record is being edited. The star symbol in the second row's record selector identifies the second row as the next one available for a new record. Notice that all the fields are initially empty; this occurs because you set the Default Value property for the fields (as appropriate) to Null.

4. Type **Waiter/Waitress** in the PositionTitle field, and then press the **Tab** key. The insertion point moves to the EmployerID field.

5. Type **10155** and then press the **Tab** key. The insertion point moves to the right side of the Wage field.

Recall that the PositionID, PositionTitle, and EmployerID fields are all text fields and that the Wage field is a currency field. Field values for text fields are left-aligned in their boxes, and field values for number, date/time, and currency fields are right-aligned in their boxes.

6. Type **9.5** and then press the **Tab** key. Access displays the field value with a dollar sign and two decimal places ($9.50), as specified by the currency format. You do not need to type the dollar sign, commas, or decimal point (for whole dollar amounts) because Access adds these symbols automatically for you.

7. In the Hours/Week field, type **30**, press the **Tab** key, type **1** in the Openings field, and then press the **Tab** key.

8. Type **Sue Brown** in the ReferredBy field, and then press the **Tab** key. Depending on your monitor's resolution and size, the display of the datasheet might shift so that the next field, StartDate, is completely visible.

9. Type **6/30** in the StartDate field, and then press the **Tab** key. Access displays the value as 06/30, as specified by the custom date format (mm/dd) you set for this field. The insertion point moves to the final field in the table, EndDate.

10. Type **9/15** in the EndDate field, and then press the **Tab** key. Access displays the value as 09/15, shifts the display of the datasheet back to the left, stores the first completed record in the Position table, removes the pencil symbol from the first row's record selector, advances the insertion point to the second row's PositionID text box, and places the current record symbol in the second row's record selector.

Now you can enter the values for the second record.

11. Refer to Figure 2-16, and repeat Steps 3 through 10 to add the second record to the table. Access saves the record in the Position table, and moves the insertion point to the beginning of the third row. See Figure 2-19.

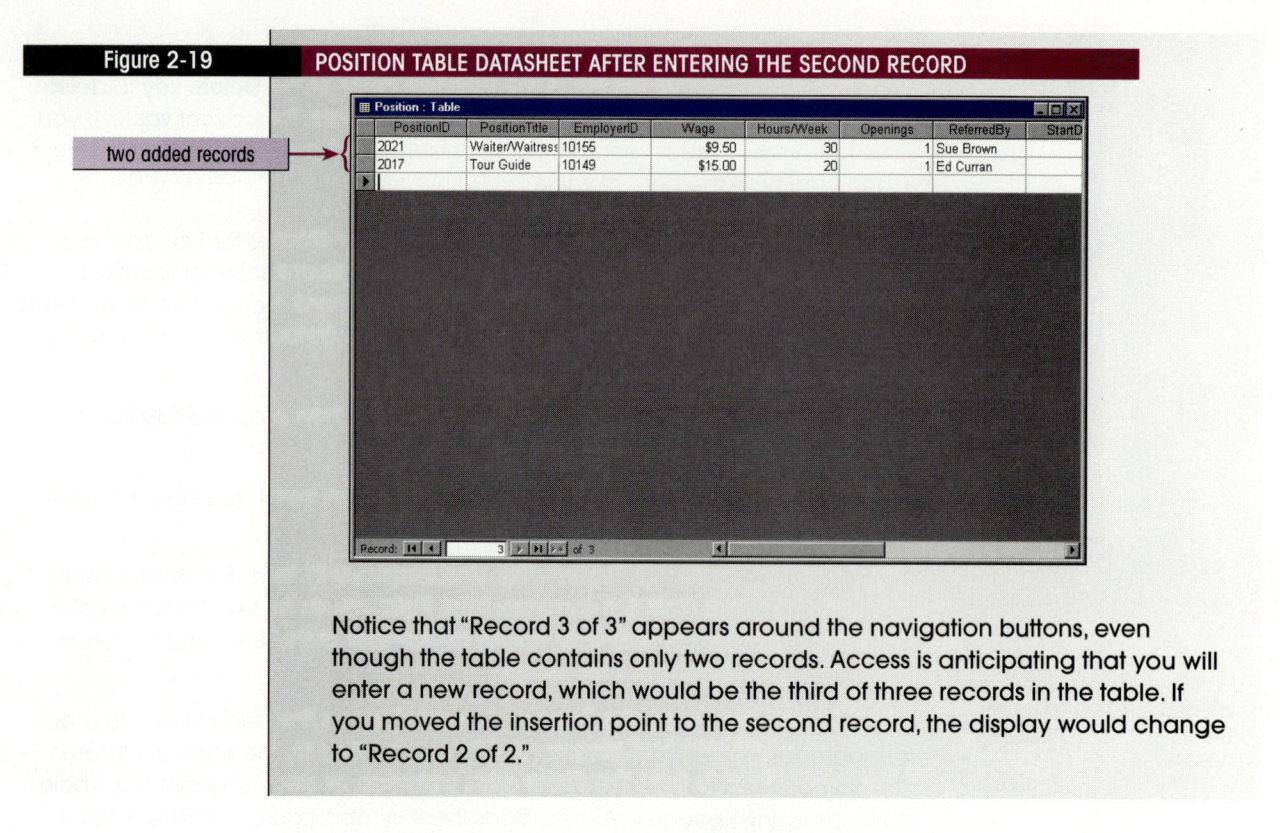

Figure 2-19   **POSITION TABLE DATASHEET AFTER ENTERING THE SECOND RECORD**

two added records

PositionID	PositionTitle	EmployerID	Wage	Hours/Week	Openings	ReferredBy	StartD
2021	Waiter/Waitress	10155	$9.50	30	1	Sue Brown	
2017	Tour Guide	10149	$15.00	20	1	Ed Curran	

Notice that "Record 3 of 3" appears around the navigation buttons, even though the table contains only two records. Access is anticipating that you will enter a new record, which would be the third of three records in the table. If you moved the insertion point to the second record, the display would change to "Record 2 of 2."

Notice that the two records are currently listed in the order in which you entered them. However, once you close the table or change to another view, and then redisplay the table datasheet, the records will be listed in primary key order by the values in the PositionID field.

Modifying the Structure of an Access Table

Even a well-designed table might need to be modified. For example, the government at all levels and competitors place demands on a company to track more data and to modify the data it already tracks. Access allows you to modify a table's structure in Design view: you can add and delete fields, change the order of fields, and change the properties of the fields.

After holding a meeting with her staff members and reviewing the structure of the Position table and the format of the field values in the datasheet, Elsa has several changes she wants you to make to the table. First, she has decided that it's not necessary to keep track of the name of the person who originally requested a particular position, so she wants you to delete the ReferredBy field. Also, she thinks that the Wage field should remain a currency field, but she wants the dollar signs removed from the displayed field values in the datasheet. She also wants the Openings field moved to the end of the table. Finally, she wants you to add a new yes/no field, named Experience, to the table to indicate whether the available position requires that potential recruits have prior experience in that type of work. The Experience field will be inserted between the Hours/Week and StartDate fields. Figure 2-20 shows Elsa's modified design for the Position table.

Figure 2-20 — MODIFIED DESIGN FOR THE POSITION TABLE

Field Name	Data Type	Field Size	Description
PositionID	Text	4	Primary key
PositionTitle	Text	30	
EmployerID	Text	5	Foreign key
Wage	Currency		Rate per hour
Hours/Week	Number	Integer	Work hours per week
Experience	Yes/No		Experience required
StartDate	Date/Time		Month and day
EndDate	Date/Time		Month and day
Openings	Number	Integer	Number of openings

You'll begin modifying the table by deleting the ReferredBy field.

Deleting a Field

After you've defined a table structure and added records to the table, you can delete a field from the table structure. When you delete a field, you also delete all the values for the field from the table. Therefore, you should make sure that you need to delete a field and that you delete the correct field.

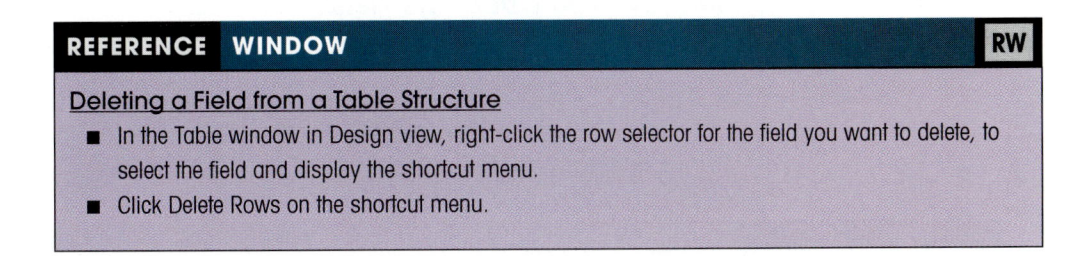

REFERENCE WINDOW

Deleting a Field from a Table Structure
- In the Table window in Design view, right-click the row selector for the field you want to delete, to select the field and display the shortcut menu.
- Click Delete Rows on the shortcut menu.

You need to delete the ReferredBy field from the Position table structure.

To delete the ReferredBy field:

1. Click the **View** button for Design view on the Table Datasheet toolbar. The Table window for the Position table opens in Design view.

2. Position the pointer on the row selector for the ReferredBy field until the pointer changes to a ➡ shape.

3. Right-click to select the entire row for the ReferredBy field and display the shortcut menu, and then click **Delete Rows**.

    A dialog box opens asking you to confirm the deletion.

4. Click the **Yes** button to close the dialog box and to delete the field and its values from the table. See Figure 2-21.

Figure 2-21   **TABLE STRUCTURE AFTER DELETING ReferredBy FIELD**

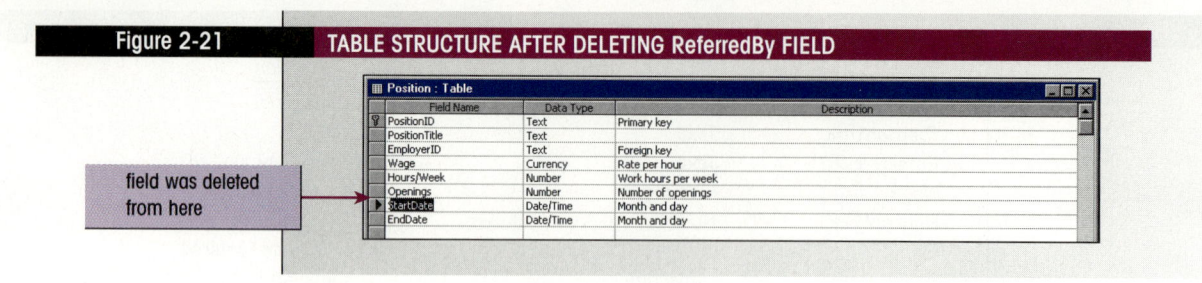

field was deleted from here

You have deleted the ReferredBy field in the Table window, but the change doesn't take place in the table on disk until you save the table structure. Because you have other modifications to make to the table, you'll wait until you finish them all before saving the modified table structure to disk.

Moving a Field

To move a field, you use the mouse to drag it to a new location in the Table window in Design view. Your next modification to the Position table structure is to move the Openings field to the end of the table, as Elsa requested.

To move the Openings field:

1. Click the **row selector** for the Openings field to select the entire row.

2. Place the pointer in the row selector for the Openings field, click the pointer, and then drag the pointer to the row selector below the EndDate row selector. See Figure 2-22.

Figure 2-22   **MOVING A FIELD IN THE TABLE STRUCTURE**

selected field

position the move pointer in this row selector

move pointer

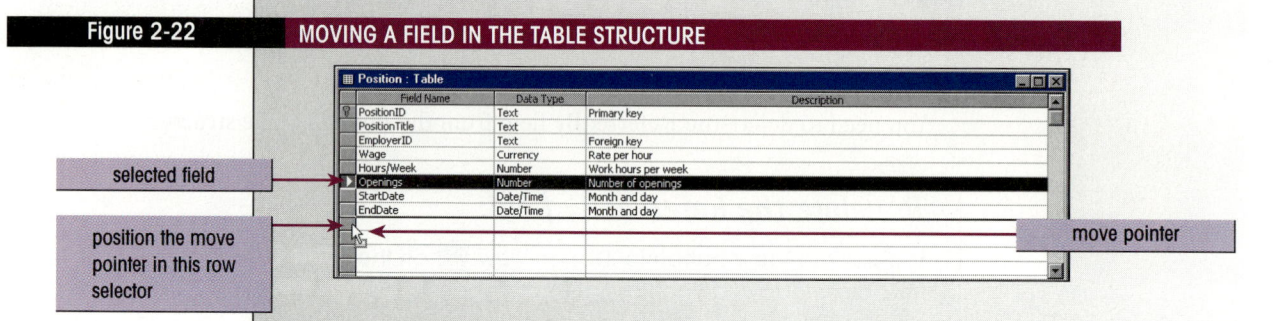

3. Release the mouse button. Access moves the Openings field below the EndDate field in the table structure.

   TROUBLE? If the Openings field did not move, repeat Steps 1 through 3, making sure you firmly hold down the mouse button during the drag operation.

Adding a Field

Next, you need to add the Experience field to the table structure between the Hours/Week and StartDate fields. To add a new field between existing fields, you must insert a row. You begin by selecting the field that will be below the new field you want to insert.

TUTORIAL 2 CREATING AND MAINTAINING A DATABASE   AC 2.25

> **REFERENCE WINDOW**
>
> **Adding a Field Between Two Existing Fields**
> - In the Table window in Design view, right-click the row selector for the row above which you want to add a new field, to select the field and display the shortcut menu.
> - Click Insert Rows on the shortcut menu.
> - Define the new field by entering the field name, data type, description (optional), and any property specifications.

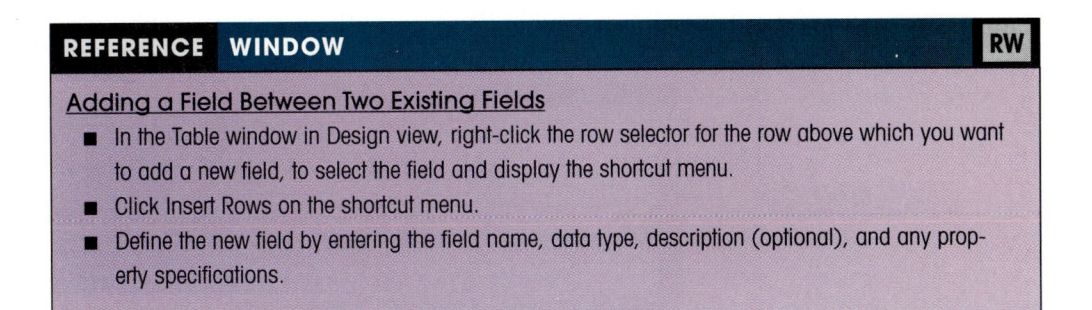

To add the Experience field to the Position table:

1. Right-click the **row selector** for the StartDate field to select this field and display the shortcut menu, and then click **Insert Rows**. Access adds a new, blank row between the Hours/Week and StartDate fields. See Figure 2-23.

Figure 2-23   AFTER INSERTING A ROW IN THE TABLE STRUCTURE

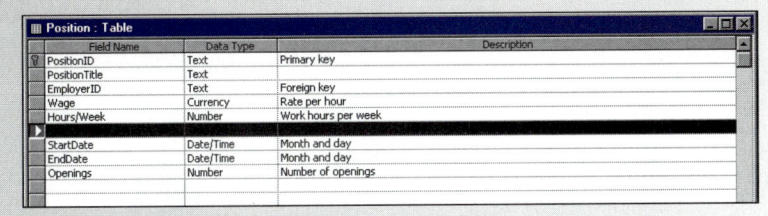

Field Name	Data Type	Description
PositionID	Text	Primary key
PositionTitle	Text	
EmployerID	Text	Foreign key
Wage	Currency	Rate per hour
Hours/Week	Number	Work hours per week
StartDate	Date/Time	Month and day
EndDate	Date/Time	Month and day
Openings	Number	Number of openings

   You'll define the Experience field in the new row of the Position table. Access will add this new field to the Position table structure between the Hours/Week and StartDate fields.

2. Click the **Field Name** text box for the new row, type **Experience**, and then press the **Tab** key.

   The Experience field will be a yes/no field that will specify whether prior work experience is required for the position.

3. Type **y**. Access completes the data type as "yes/No."

4. Press the **Tab** key to select the yes/no data type and to move to the Description text box.

   Notice that Access changes the value in the Data Type text box from "yes/No" to "Yes/No."

5. Type **Experience required** in the Description text box.

   Elsa wants the Experience field to have a Default Value property value of "No," so you need to set this property.

6. In the Field Properties pane, click the **Default Value** text box, type **no**, and then click somewhere outside of the Default Value text box to deselect the value. Notice that Access changes the Default Value property value from "no" to "No." See Figure 2-24.

Figure 2-24 EXPERIENCE FIELD ADDED TO THE POSITION TABLE

new field

Default Value property set to "No"

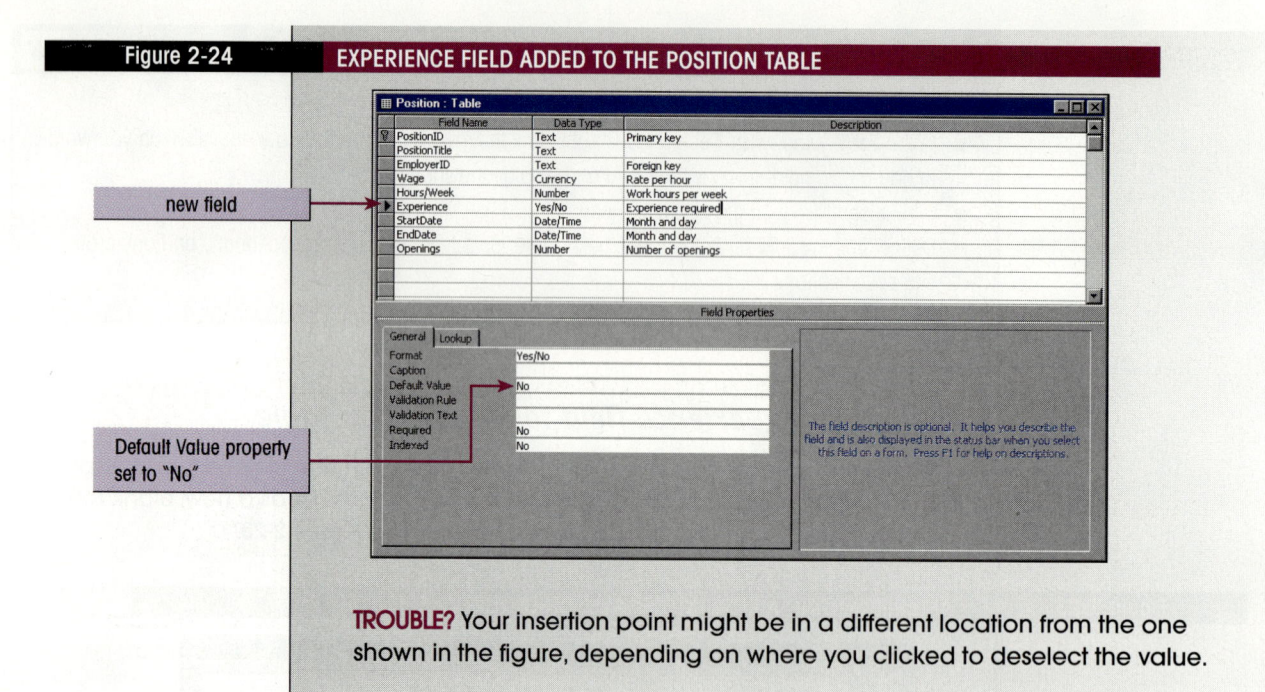

TROUBLE? Your insertion point might be in a different location from the one shown in the figure, depending on where you clicked to deselect the value.

You've completed adding the Experience field to the Position table in Design view. As with the other changes you've made in Design view, however, the Experience field is not added to the Position table in the Northeast database until you save the changes to the table structure.

Changing Field Properties

Elsa's last modification to the table structure is to remove the dollar signs from the Wage field values displayed in the datasheet—repeated dollar signs are unnecessary and they clutter the datasheet. As you learned earlier when defining the StartDate and EndDate fields, you use the Format property to control the display of a field value.

To change the Format property of the Wage field:

1. Click the **Description** text box for the Wage field. The Wage field is now the current field.

2. Click the right side of the **Format** text box to display the Format list box. See Figure 2-25.

Figure 2-25 FORMAT LIST BOX FOR THE WAGE FIELD

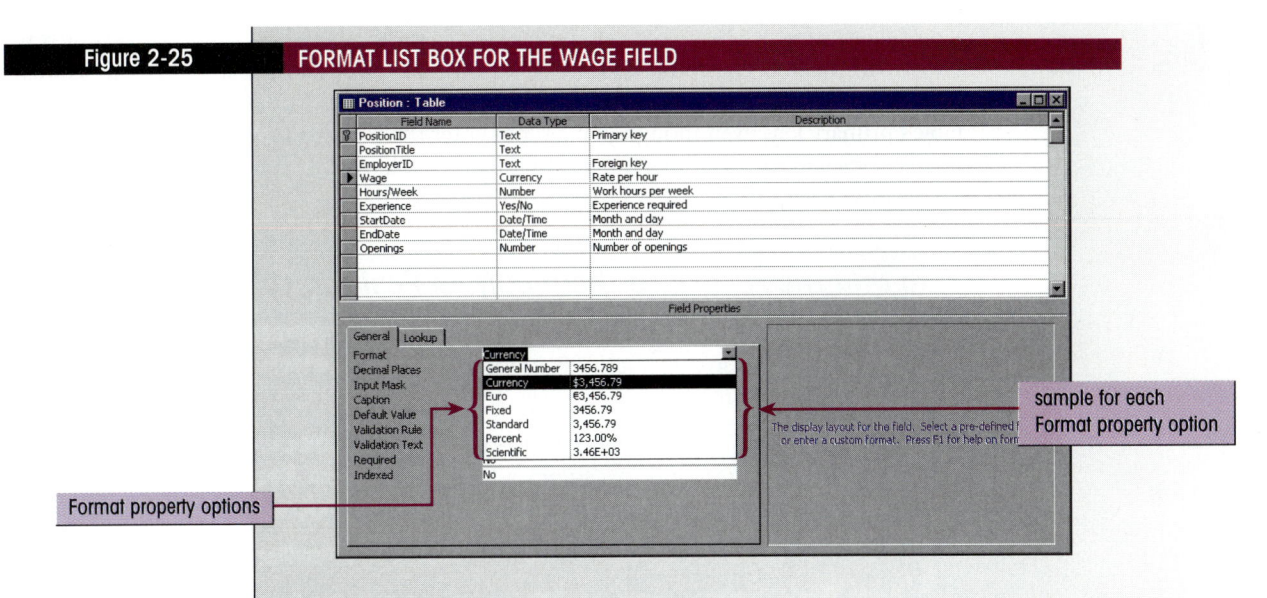

To the right of each Format property option is a field value whose appearance represents a sample of the option. The Standard option specifies the format Elsa wants for the Wage field.

3. Click **Standard** in the Format list box to accept this option for the Format property.

Elsa wants you to add a third record to the Position table datasheet. Before you can add the record, you must save the modified table structure, and then switch to the Position table datasheet.

To save the modified table structure, and then switch to the datasheet:

1. Click the **Save** button on the Table Design toolbar. The modified table structure for the Position table is stored in the Northeast database. Note that if you forget to save the modified structure and try to close the table or switch to another view, Access will prompt you to save the table before you can continue.

2. Click the **View** button for Datasheet view on the Table Design toolbar. The Position table datasheet opens. See Figure 2-26.

Figure 2-26 DATASHEET FOR THE MODIFIED POSITION TABLE

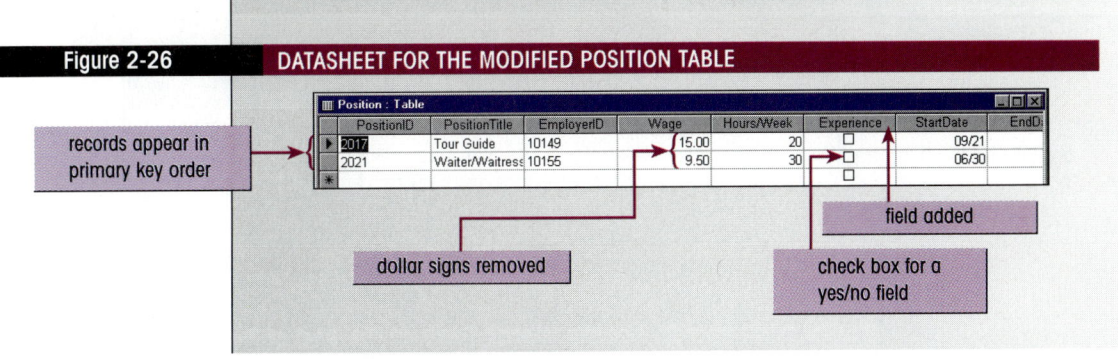

Notice that the ReferredBy field no longer appears in the datasheet, the Openings field is now the rightmost column (you might need to scroll the datasheet to see it), the Wage field values do not contain dollar signs, and the Experience field appears between the Hours/Week and StartDate fields. The Experience column contains check boxes to represent the yes/no field values. Empty check boxes signify "No," which is the default value you assigned to the Experience field. A check mark in the check box indicates a "Yes" value. Also notice that the records appear in ascending order based on the value in the PositionID field, the Position table's primary key, even though you did not enter the records in this order.

Elsa asks you to add a third record to the table. This record is for a position that requires prior work experience.

To add the record to the modified Position table:

1. Click the **New Record** button on the Table Datasheet toolbar. The insertion point moves to the PositionID field for the third row, which is the next row available for a new record.

2. Type **2020**. The pencil symbol appears in the row selector for the third row, and the star appears in the row selector for the fourth row. Recall that these symbols represent a record being edited and the next available record, respectively.

3. Press the **Tab** key. The insertion point moves to the PositionTitle field.

4. Type **Host/Hostess**, press the **Tab** key to move to the EmployerID field, type **10163**, and then press the **Tab** key. The Wage field is now the current field.

5. Type **18.5** and then press the **Tab** key. Access displays the value as "18.50" (with no dollar sign).

6. Type **32** in the Hours/Week field, and then press the **Tab** key. The Experience field is now the current field.

   Recall that the default value for this field is "No," which means the check box is initially empty. For yes/no fields with check boxes, you press the Tab key to leave the check box unchecked; you press the spacebar or click the check box to add or remove a check mark in the check box. Because this position requires experience, you need to insert a check mark in the check box.

7. Press the **spacebar**. A check mark appears in the check box.

8. Press the **Tab** key, type **6/15** in the StartDate field, press the **Tab** key, and then type **10/1** in the EndDate field.

9. Press the **Tab** key, type **1** in the Openings field, and then press the **Tab** key. Access saves the record in the Position table and moves the insertion point to the beginning of the fourth row. See Figure 2-27.

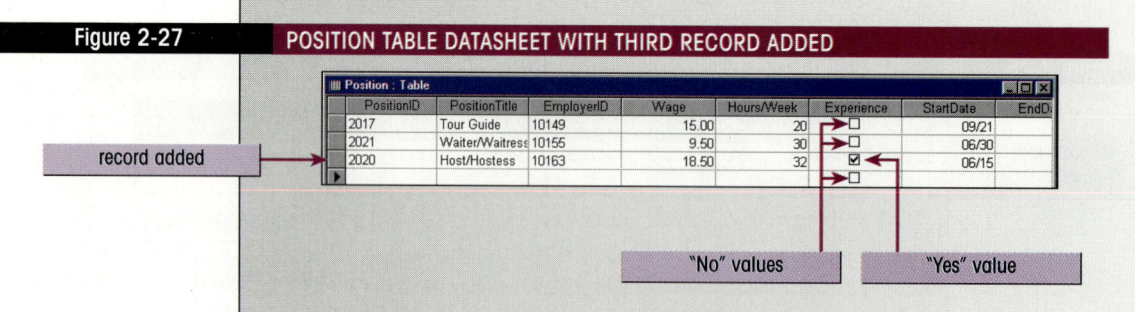

Figure 2-27 **POSITION TABLE DATASHEET WITH THIRD RECORD ADDED**

PositionID	PositionTitle	EmployerID	Wage	Hours/Week	Experience	StartDate	EndD
2017	Tour Guide	10149	15.00	20	☐	09/21	
2021	Waiter/Waitress	10155	9.50	30	☐	06/30	
2020	Host/Hostess	10163	18.50	32	☑	06/15	

record added ← (points to 2020 row)

"No" values — "Yes" value

As you add records, Access places them at the end of the datasheet. If you switch to Design view and then return to the datasheet, or if you close the table and then open the datasheet, Access will display the records in primary key sequence.

For many of the fields, the columns are wider than necessary for the field values. You can resize the datasheet columns so that they are only as wide as needed to display the longest value in the column, including the field name. Resizing datasheet columns to their best fit improves the display of the datasheet and allows you to view more fields at the same time.

To resize the Position datasheet columns to their best fit:

1. Place the pointer on the line between the PositionID and PositionTitle field names until the pointer changes to a ↔ shape.

2. Double-click the pointer. The PositionID column is resized so that it is only as wide as the longest value in the column (the field name, in this case).

3. Double-click the ↔ pointer on the line to the right of each remaining field name to resize all the columns in the datasheet to their best fit. See Figure 2-28.

Figure 2-28   DATASHEET AFTER RESIZING ALL COLUMNS TO THEIR BEST FIT

PositionID	PositionTitle	EmployerID	Wage	Hours/Week	Experience	StartDate	EndDate	Openings
2017	Tour Guide	10149	15.00	20	☐	09/21	11/01	1
2020	Host/Hostess	10163	18.50	32	☑	06/15	10/01	1
2021	Waiter/Waitress	10155	9.50	30	☐	06/30	09/15	1
					☐			

Notice that all nine fields in the Position table are now visible in the datasheet.

You have modified the Position table structure and added one record. Next you need to obtain the rest of the records for this table from another database, and then import the two tables from the Seasonal database (Employer and NAICS) into your Northeast database.

Obtaining Data from Another Access Database

Sometimes the data you need for your database might already exist in another Access database. You can save time in obtaining this data by copying and pasting records from one database table into another or by importing an entire table from one database into another.

Copying Records from Another Access Database

You can copy and paste records from a table in the same database or in a different database only if the tables have the same structure—that is, the tables contain the same fields in the same order. Elsa's NEJobs database in the Tutorial folder on your Data Disk has a table named Available Positions that has the same table structure as the Position table. The records in the Available Positions table are the records Elsa wants you to copy into the Position table.

Other programs, such as Microsoft Word and Microsoft Excel, allow you to have two or more documents open at a time. However, you can have only one Access database open at a time. Therefore, you need to close the Northeast database, open the Available Positions table in the NEJobs database, select and copy the table records, close the NEJobs database, reopen the Position table in the Northeast database, and then paste the copied records. (*Note*: If you have a database open and then open a second database, Access will automatically close the first database for you.)

To copy the records from the Available Positions table:

1. Click the **Close** button ⊠ on the Table window title bar to close the Position table. A message box opens asking if you want to save the changes to the layout of the Position table. This box appears because you resized the datasheet columns to their best fit.

2. Click the **Yes** button in the message box.

3. Click ⊠ on the Database window title bar to close the Northeast database.

4. Click the **Open** button on the Database toolbar to display the Open dialog box.

5. If necessary, display the list of files on your Data Disk, and then open the **Tutorial** folder.

6. Open the database file named **NEJobs**. The Database window opens. Notice that the NEJobs database contains only one table, the Available Positions table. This table contains the records you need to copy.

7. Click **Available Positions** in the Tables list box (if necessary), and then click the **Open** button in the Database window. The datasheet for the Available Positions table opens. See Figure 2-29. Note that this table contains a total of 62 records.

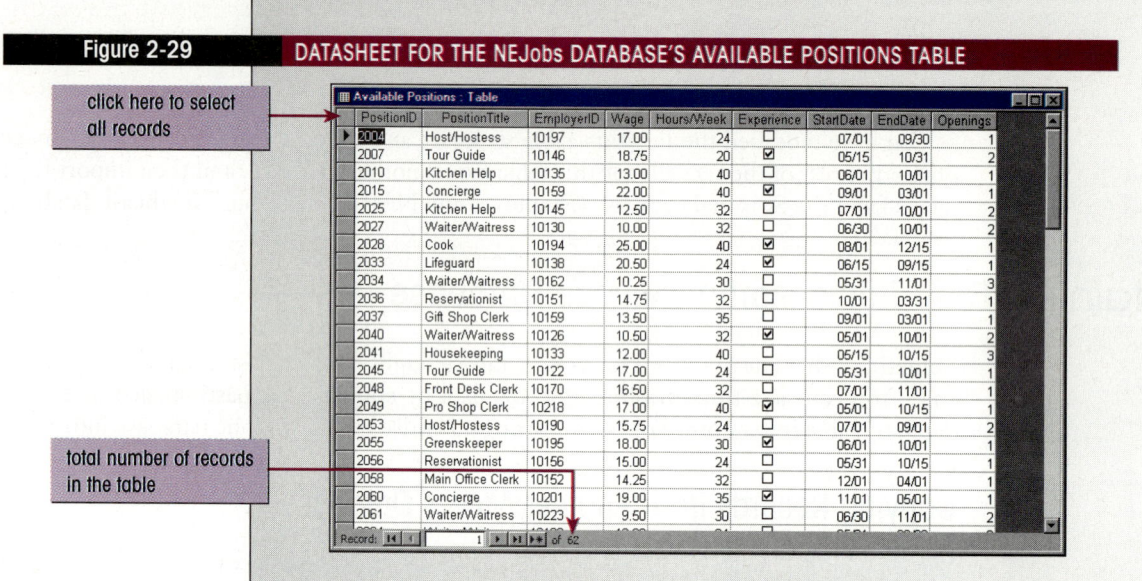

Figure 2-29 DATASHEET FOR THE NEJobs DATABASE'S AVAILABLE POSITIONS TABLE

click here to select all records

total number of records in the table

Elsa wants you to copy all the records in the Available Positions table. You can select all records by clicking the row selector for the field name row.

8. Click the **row selector** for the field name row (see Figure 2-29). All the records in the table are now highlighted, which means that Access has selected all of them.

9. Click the **Copy** button on the Table Datasheet toolbar. All the records are copied to the Windows Clipboard.

   TROUBLE? If a Clipboard panel opens in the Task Pane, click its Close button to close it, and then continue with Step 10.

10. Click ⊠ on the Table window title bar. A dialog box opens asking if you want to save the data you copied to the Windows Clipboard.

TUTORIAL 2 CREATING AND MAINTAINING A DATABASE   AC 2.31   ACCESS

11. Click the **Yes** button in the dialog box. The dialog box closes, and then the table closes.

12. Click **X** on the Database window title bar to close the NEJobs database.

To finish copying and pasting the records, you must open the Position table and paste the copied records into the table.

To paste the copied records into the Position table:

1. Click **File** on the menu bar, and then click **Northeast** in the list of recently opened databases. The Database window opens, showing the tables for the Northeast database.

2. In the Tables list box, click **Position** (if necessary), and then click the **Open** button in the Database window. The datasheet for the Position table opens.

   You must paste the records at the end of the table.

3. Click the **row selector** for row four, which is the next row available for a new record.

4. Click the **Paste** button on the Table Datasheet toolbar. A dialog box opens asking if you are sure you want to paste the records (62 in all).

5. Click the **Yes** button. All the records are pasted from the Windows Clipboard, and the pasted records remain highlighted. See Figure 2-30. Notice that the table now contains a total of 65 records—the three original records plus the 62 copied records.

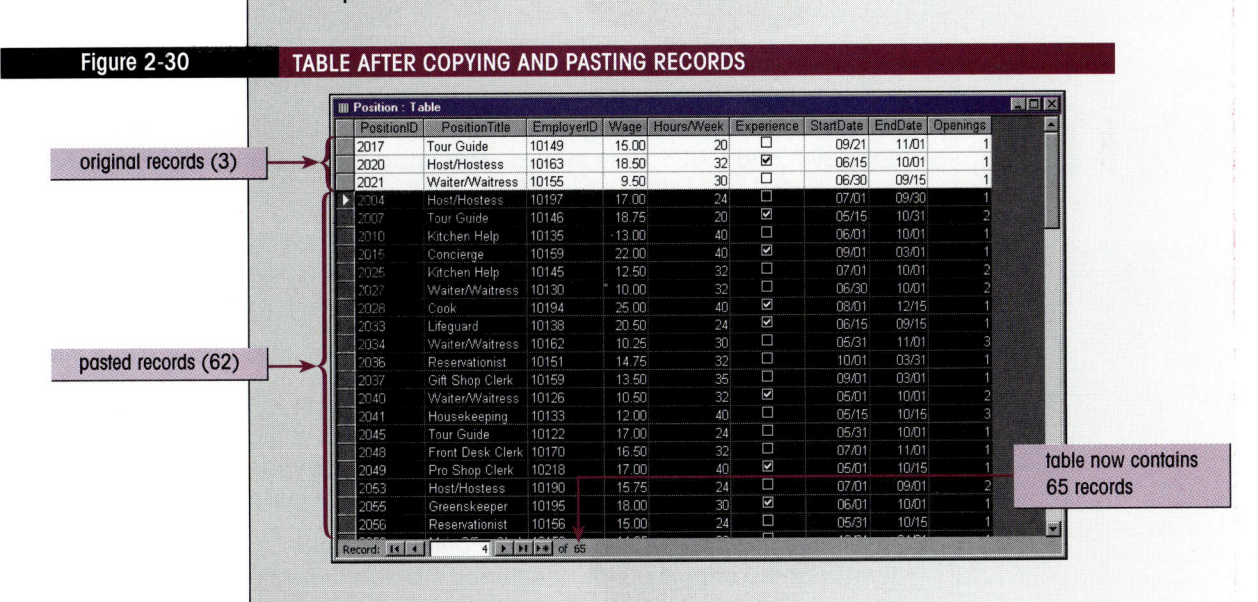

Figure 2-30 TABLE AFTER COPYING AND PASTING RECORDS

PositionID	PositionTitle	EmployerID	Wage	Hours/Week	Experience	StartDate	EndDate	Openings
2017	Tour Guide	10149	15.00	20	☐	09/21	11/01	1
2020	Host/Hostess	10163	18.50	32	☑	06/15	10/01	1
2021	Waiter/Waitress	10155	9.50	30	☐	06/30	09/15	1
2004	Host/Hostess	10197	17.00	24	☐	07/01	09/30	1
2007	Tour Guide	10146	18.75	20	☑	05/15	10/31	2
2010	Kitchen Help	10135	13.00	40	☐	06/01	10/01	1
2015	Concierge	10159	22.00	40	☑	09/01	03/01	1
2025	Kitchen Help	10145	12.50	32	☐	07/01	10/01	2
2027	Waiter/Waitress	10130	10.00	32	☐	06/30	10/01	2
2028	Cook	10194	25.00	40	☑	08/01	12/15	1
2033	Lifeguard	10138	20.50	24	☑	06/15	09/15	1
2034	Waiter/Waitress	10162	10.25	30	☐	05/31	11/01	3
2036	Reservationist	10151	14.75	32	☐	10/01	03/31	1
2037	Gift Shop Clerk	10159	13.50	35	☐	09/01	03/01	1
2040	Waiter/Waitress	10126	10.50	32	☑	05/01	10/01	2
2041	Housekeeping	10133	12.00	40	☐	05/15	10/15	3
2045	Tour Guide	10122	17.00	24	☐	05/31	10/01	1
2048	Front Desk Clerk	10170	16.50	32	☐	07/01	11/01	1
2049	Pro Shop Clerk	10218	17.00	40	☑	05/01	10/15	1
2053	Host/Hostess	10190	15.75	24	☐	07/01	09/01	2
2055	Greenskeeper	10195	18.00	30	☑	06/01	10/01	1
2056	Reservationist	10156	15.00	24	☐	05/31	10/15	1

- original records (3)
- pasted records (62)
- table now contains 65 records

Record: 4 of 65

6. Click the **Close** button **X** on the Table window title bar to close the Position table.

Importing a Table from Another Access Database

When you import a table from one Access database to another, you place a copy of the table—including its structure, field definitions, and field values—in the database into which you import it. There are two ways to import a table from another Access database into your current database: using the Get External Data option on the File menu, or using the Import Table Wizard, which is available in the New Table dialog box. You'll use both methods to import the two tables from the Seasonal database into your Northeast database.

To import the Employer and NAICS tables:

1. Make sure the Northeast Database window is open on your screen.

2. Click **File** on the menu bar, position the pointer on the double-arrow at the bottom of the File menu to display the full menu (if necessary), point to **Get External Data**, and then click **Import**. The Import dialog box opens. This dialog box is similar to the Open dialog box.

3. Display the list of files in your Tutorial folder, click **Seasonal**, and then click the **Import** button. The Import Objects dialog box opens. See Figure 2-31.

Figure 2-31   IMPORT OBJECTS DIALOG BOX

table objects in the Seasonal database → Employer, NAICS

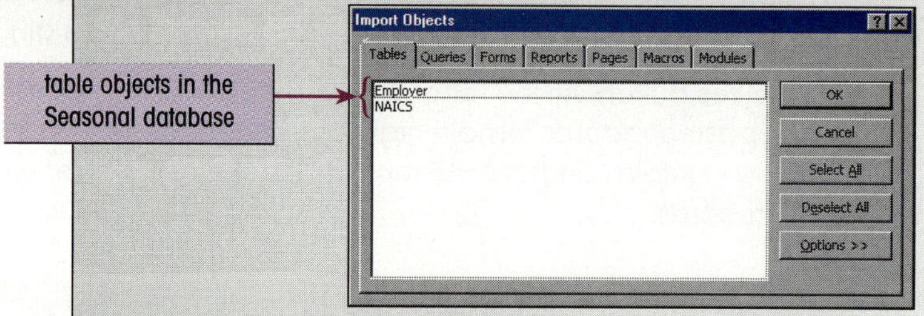

The Tables tab of the dialog box lists both tables in the Seasonal database—Employer and NAICS. Note that you can import other objects as well (queries, forms, reports, and so on).

4. Click **Employer** in the list of tables, and then click the **OK** button. The Import Objects dialog box closes, and the Employer table is now listed in the Northeast Database window.

   Now you'll use the Import Table Wizard to import the NAICS table. (Note that you could also use the Select All button in the Import Objects dialog box to import all the objects listed on the current tab at the same time.)

5. Click the **New** button in the Database window, click **Import Table** in the New Table dialog box, and then click the **OK** button. The Import dialog box opens.

6. If necessary, display the list of files in your Tutorial folder, click **Seasonal**, and then click the **Import** button. The Import Objects dialog box opens, again displaying the tables in the Seasonal database.

7. Click **NAICS** in the list of tables, and then click the **OK** button to import the NAICS table into the Northeast database.

TUTORIAL 2 CREATING AND MAINTAINING A DATABASE   AC 2.33

Now that you have all the records in the Position table and all three tables in the Northeast database, Elsa examines the records to make sure they are correct. She finds one record in the Position table that she wants you to delete and another record that needs changes to its field values.

Updating a Database

Updating, or **maintaining**, a database is the process of adding, changing, and deleting records in database tables to keep them current and accurate. You've already added records to the Position table. Now Elsa wants you to delete and change records.

Deleting Records

To delete a record, you need to select the record in Datasheet view, and then delete it using the Delete Record button on the Table Datasheet toolbar or the Delete Record option on the shortcut menu.

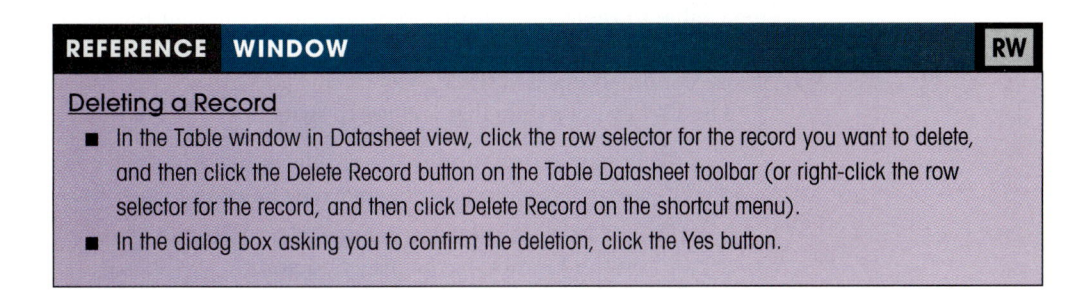

REFERENCE WINDOW

Deleting a Record
- In the Table window in Datasheet view, click the row selector for the record you want to delete, and then click the Delete Record button on the Table Datasheet toolbar (or right-click the row selector for the record, and then click Delete Record on the shortcut menu).
- In the dialog box asking you to confirm the deletion, click the Yes button.

Elsa asks you to delete the record whose PositionID is 2015 because this record was entered in error; the position for this record does not exist. The fourth record in the table has a PositionID value of 2015. This record is the one you need to delete.

To delete the record:

1. Open the Position table in Datasheet view.

2. Right-click the **row selector** for row four. Access selects the fourth record and displays the shortcut menu. See Figure 2-32.

Figure 2-32   DELETING A RECORD

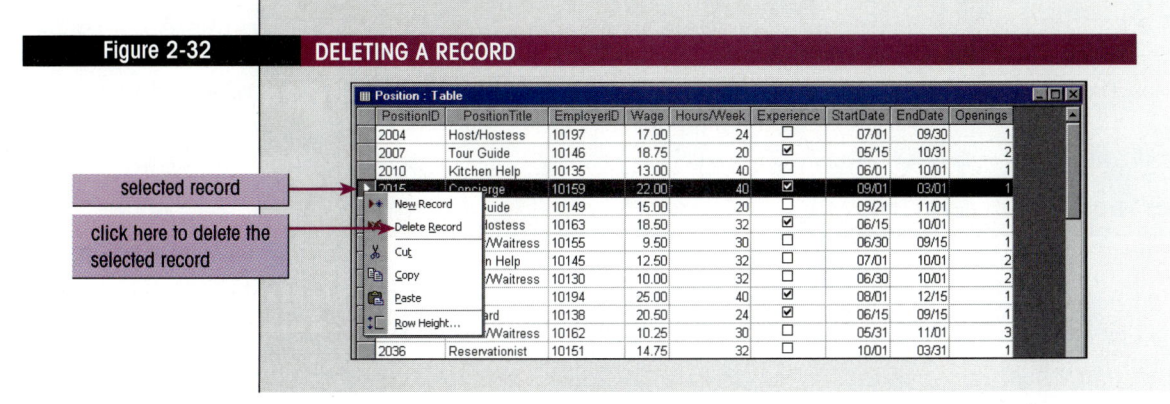

3. Click **Delete Record** on the shortcut menu. Access deletes the record and opens a dialog box asking you to confirm the deletion. Because the deletion of a record is permanent and cannot be undone, Access prompts you to make sure that you want to delete the record.

   TROUBLE? If you selected the wrong record for deletion, click the No button. Access ends the deletion process and continues to display the selected record. Repeat Steps 2 and 3 to delete the correct record.

4. Click the **Yes** button to confirm the deletion and close the dialog box.

Elsa's final update to the Position table involves changes to field values in one of the records.

Changing Records

To change the field values in a record, you first must make the record the current record. Then you position the insertion point in the field value to make minor changes or select the field value to replace it entirely. In Tutorial 1, you used the mouse with the scroll bars and the navigation buttons to navigate through the records in a datasheet. You can also use keystroke combinations and the F2 key to navigate a datasheet and to select field values.

The **F2 key** is a toggle that you use to switch between navigation mode and editing mode:

- In **navigation mode**, Access selects an entire field value. If you type while you are in navigation mode, your typed entry replaces the highlighted field value.
- In **editing mode**, you can insert or delete characters in a field value based on the location of the insertion point.

Figure 2-33 shows some of the navigation mode and editing mode keystroke techniques.

Figure 2-33 NAVIGATION MODE AND EDITING MODE KEYSTROKE TECHNIQUES

PRESS	TO MOVE THE SELECTION IN NAVIGATION MODE	TO MOVE THE INSERTION POINT IN EDITING MODE
←	Left one field value at a time	Left one character at a time
→	Right one field value at a time	Right one character at a time
Home	Left to the first field value in the record	To the left of the first character in the field value
End	Right to the last field value in the record	To the right of the last character in the field value
↑ or ↓	Up or down one record at a time	Up or down one record at a time and switch to navigation mode
Tab or Enter	Right one field value at a time	Right one field value at a time and switch to navigation mode
Ctrl + Home	To the first field value in the first record	To the left of the first character in the field value
Ctrl + End	To the last field value in the last record	To the right of the last character in the field value

The record Elsa wants you to change has a PositionID field value of 2125. Some of the values were entered incorrectly for this record, and you need to enter the correct values.

To modify the record:

1. Make sure the PositionID field value for the fourth record is still highlighted, indicating that the table is in navigation mode.

2. Press **Ctrl + End**. Access displays records from the end of the table and selects the last field value in the last record. This field value is for the Openings field.

3. Press the **Home** key. The first field value in the last record is now selected. This field value is for the PositionID field.

4. Press the ↑ key. The PositionID field value for the previous record (PositionID 2125) is selected. This record is the one you need to change.

   Elsa wants you to change these field values in the record: PositionID to 2124, EmployerID to 10163, Wage to 14.50, Experience to "Yes" (checked), and EndDate to 10/15.

5. Type **2124**, press the **Tab** key twice, type **10163**, press the **Tab** key, type **14.5**, press the **Tab** key twice, press the **spacebar** to insert a check mark in the Experience check box, press the **Tab** key twice, and then type **10/15**. The changes to the record are complete. See Figure 2-34.

Figure 2-34   **TABLE AFTER CHANGING FIELD VALUES IN A RECORD**

field values changed

PositionID	Position	EmployerID	Wage	Hours	Experience	StartDate	EndDate	Openings
2115	Gift Shop Clerk	10154	13.00	25	☐	05/01	09/30	1
2117	Housekeeping	10220	13.50	30	☐	06/30	09/30	3
2118	Greenskeeper	10218	17.00	32	☐	05/01	11/01	1
2120	Lifeguard	10154	19.00	32	☑	06/15	09/30	2
2122	Kitchen Help	10151	13.00	35	☐	09/01	03/31	3
2123	Main Office Clerk	10170	14.50	32	☐	07/01	11/15	1
2124	Kitchen Help	10163	14.50	40	☑	06/01	10/15	2
2127	Waiter/Waitress	10185	10.50	40	☐	12/01	05/01	1

Record: 63 of 64

You've completed all of Elsa's updates to the Position table. Now you can exit Access.

6. Click the **Close** button ⊠ on the Access window title bar to close the Position table and the Northeast database, and to exit Access.

Elsa and her staff members approve of the revised table structure for the Position table. They are confident that the table will allow them to easily track position data for NSJI's employer customers.

Session 2.2 QUICK CHECK

1. What does a pencil symbol in a datasheet's row selector represent? A star symbol?
2. What is the effect of deleting a field from a table structure?
3. How do you insert a field between existing fields in a table structure?
4. A field with the _____ data type can appear in the table datasheet as a check box.
5. Describe the two ways in which you can display the Import dialog box, so that you can import a table from one Access database to another.
6. In Datasheet view, what is the difference between navigation mode and editing mode?

REVIEW ASSIGNMENTS

Elsa needs a database to track data about the students recruited by NSJI and about the recruiters who find jobs for the students. She asks you to create the database by completing the following:

1. Make sure your Data Disk is in the appropriate disk drive, and then start Access.
2. Create a new, blank database named **Recruits** and save it in the Review folder on your Data Disk.

Explore

3. Use the Table Wizard to create a new table named **Recruiter** in the **Recruits** database, as follows:
   a. Base the new table on the Employees sample table, which is one of the sample tables in the Business category.
   b. Add the following fields to your table (in the order shown): SocialSecurityNumber, Salary, FirstName, MiddleName, and LastName.
   c. Click SocialSecurityNumber in the "Fields in my new table" list, and then use the Rename Field button to change the name of this field to SSN. Click the Next button.
   d. Name the new table **Recruiter**, and choose the option for setting the primary key yourself. Click the Next button.
   e. Specify SSN as the primary key field and accept the default data type. Click the Next button.
   f. In the final Table Wizard dialog box, click the Finish button to display the table in Datasheet view. (*Note:* The field names appear with spaces between words; this is how the Table Wizard is set up to format these field names when they appear in Datasheet view.)
4. Add the recruiter records shown in Figure 2-35 to the **Recruiter** table. (*Note:* You do not have to type the dashes in the SSN field values or commas in the Salary field values; the Table Wizard formatted these fields so that these symbols are entered automatically for you.)

Figure 2-35

SSN	Salary	First Name	Middle Name	Last Name
892-77-1201	40,000	Kate	Teresa	Foster
901-63-1554	38,500	Paul	Michael	Kirnicki
893-91-0178	40,000	Ryan	James	DuBrava

5. Make the following changes to the structure of the **Recruiter** table:
   a. Move the Salary field so that it appears after the LastName field.
   b. Add a new field between the LastName and Salary fields, using the following properties:
      Field Name: BonusQuota
      Data Type: Number
      Description: Number of recruited students needed to receive bonus
      Field Size: Byte
      Decimal Places: 0
   c. Change the format of the Salary field so that commas are displayed, dollar signs are not displayed, and no decimal places are displayed in the field values.
   d. Save the revised table structure.
6. Use the **Recruiter** datasheet to update the database as follows:
   a. Enter these BonusQuota values for the three records: 60 for Kate Foster; 60 for Ryan DuBrava; and 50 for Paul Kirnicki.
   b. Add a record to the **Recruiter** datasheet with the following field values:
      SSN: 899-40-2937
      First Name: Sonia
      Middle Name: Lee
      Last Name: Xu
      BonusQuota: 50
      Salary: 39,250

7. Close the **Recruiter** table, and then set the option for compacting the **Recruits** database on close.
8. Elsa created a database with her name as the database name. The **Recruiter Employees** table in that database has the same format as the **Recruiter** table you created. Copy all the records from the **Recruiter Employees** table in the **Elsa** database (located in the Review folder on your Data Disk) to the end of the **Recruiter** table in the **Recruits** database.

Explore

9. Because you added a number of records to the database, its size has increased. Compact the database manually using the Compact and Repair Database option.
10. Delete the MiddleName field from the **Recruiter** table structure, and then save the table structure.
11. Resize all columns in the datasheet for the **Recruiter** table to their best fit.
12. Print the **Recruiter** table datasheet, and then save and close the table.
13. Create a table named **Student** using the Import Table Wizard. The table you need to import is named **Student**, which is one of the tables in the **Elsa** database located in the Review folder on your Data Disk.
14. Make the following modifications to the structure of the **Student** table in the **Recruits** database:
    a. Enter the following Description property values:
       StudentID: Primary key
       SSN: Foreign key value of the recruiter for this student
    b. Change the Field Size property for both the FirstName field and the LastName field to 15.
    c. Move the BirthDate field so that it appears between the Nation and Gender fields.
    d. Change the format of the BirthDate field so that it displays only two digits for the year instead of four.
    e. Save the table structure changes. (Answer "Yes" to any warning messages about property changes and lost data.)
15. Switch to Datasheet view, and then resize all columns in the datasheet to fit the data.
16. Delete the record with the StudentID DRI9901 from the **Student** table.
17. Save, print, and then close the **Student** datasheet.
18. Close the **Recruits** database, and then exit Access.

CASE PROBLEMS

Case 1. Lim's Video Photography Youngho Lim uses the **Videos** database to maintain information about the clients, contracts, and events for his video photography business. Youngho asks you to help him maintain the database by completing the following:

1. Make sure your Data Disk is in the appropriate disk drive.
2. Start Access and open the **Videos** database located in the Cases folder on your Data Disk.

Explore

3. Use Design view to create a table using the table design shown in Figure 2-36.

Figure 2-36

Field Name	Data Type	Description	Field Size	Other Properties
Shoot#	Number	Primary key	Long Integer	Decimal Places: 0 Default Value: Null
ShootType	Text		2	
ShootTime	Date/Time			Format: Medium Time
Duration	Number	# of hours	Single	Default Value: Null
Contact	Text	Person who booked shoot	30	
Location	Text		30	
ShootDate	Date/Time			Format: mm/dd/yyyy
Contract#	Number	Foreign key	Integer	Decimal Places: 0 Default Value: Null

4. Specify Shoot# as the primary key, and then save the table as **Shoot**.
5. Add the records shown in Figure 2-37 to the **Shoot** table.

Figure 2-37

Shoot#	ShootType	ShootTime	Duration	Contact	Location	ShootDate	Contract#
927032	AP	4:00 PM	3.5	Ellen Quirk	Elm Lodge	9/27/2003	2412
103031	HP	9:00 AM	3.5	Tom Bradbury	Client's home	10/30/2003	2611

6. Youngho created a database named **Events** that contains a table with shoot data named **Shoot Events**. The **Shoot** table you created has the same format as the **Shoot Events** table. Copy all the records from the **Shoot Events** table in the **Events** database (located in the Cases folder on your Data Disk) to the end of the **Shoot** table in the **Videos** database.
7. Modify the structure of the **Shoot** table by completing the following:
    a. Delete the Contact field.
    b. Move the ShootDate field so that it appears between the ShootType and ShootTime fields.
8. Switch to Datasheet view and resize all columns in the datasheet for the **Shoot** table to their best fit.
9. Use the **Shoot** datasheet to update the database as follows:
    a. For Shoot# 421032, change the ShootTime value to 7:00 PM, and change the Location value to Le Bistro.
    b. Add a record to the **Shoot** datasheet with the following field values:
       Shoot#:   913032
       ShootType: SE
       ShootDate: 9/13/2003
       ShootTime: 1:00 PM
       Duration: 2.5
       Location: High School football field
       Contract#:   2501
10. Switch to Design view, and then switch back to Datasheet view so that the records appear in primary key sequence by Shoot#. Resize any datasheet columns to their best fit, as necessary.
11. Print the **Shoot** table datasheet, and then save and close the table.

Explore 12. Create a table named **ShootDesc**, based on the data shown in Figure 2-38 and according to the following steps:

Figure 2-38

ShootType	ShootDesc
AP	Anniversary Party
BM	Bar/Bat Mitzvah
BP	Birthday Party
CP	Insurance Commercial Property
DR	Dance Recital
GR	Graduation
HP	Insurance Home Property
LS	Legal Services
RC	Religious Ceremony
SE	Sports Event
WE	Wedding

a. Select the Datasheet View option in the New Table dialog box.
b. Enter the 11 records shown in Figure 2-38. (Do *not* enter the field names at this point.)
c. Switch to Design view, supply the table name, and then answer "No" if asked if you want to create a primary key.

d. Type the following field names and set the following properties for the two text fields:

ShootType
Description: Primary key
Field Size: 2

ShootDesc
Description: Description of shoot
Field Size: 30

e. Specify the primary key, save the table structure changes, and then switch back to Datasheet view. If you receive any warning messages, answer "Yes" to continue.

f. Resize both datasheet columns to their best fit; then save, print, and close the datasheet.

13. Close the **Videos** database, and then exit Access.

Case 2. DineAtHome.course.com Claire Picard uses the **Meals** database to track information about local restaurants and orders placed at the restaurants by the customers of her e-commerce business. You'll help her maintain this database by completing the following:

1. Make sure your Data Disk is in the appropriate disk drive.
2. Start Access and open the **Meals** database located in the Cases folder on your Data Disk.
3. Use Design view to create a table using the table design shown in Figure 2-39.

Figure 2-39

Field Name	Data Type	Description	Field Size	Other Properties
Order#	Number	Primary key	Long Integer	Decimal Places: 0 Default Value: Null
Restaurant#	Number	Foreign key	Long Integer	Decimal Places: 0
OrderAmt	Currency	Total amount of order		Format: Fixed

4. Specify Order# as the primary key, and then save the table as **Order**.
5. Add the records shown in Figure 2-40 to the **Order** table.

Figure 2-40

Order#	Restaurant#	OrderAmt
3117	131	155.35
3123	115	45.42
3020	120	85.50

Explore

6. Modify the structure of the **Order** table by adding a new field between the Restaurant# and OrderAmt fields, with the following properties:

Field Name: OrderDate
Data Type: Date/Time
Format: Long Date

7. Use the revised **Order** datasheet to update the database as follows:

a. Enter the following OrderDate values for the three records: 1/15/03 for Order# 3020, 4/2/03 for Order# 3117, and 5/1/03 for Order# 3123.

b. Add a new record to the **Order** datasheet with the following field values:
Order#:   3045
Restaurant#:   108
OrderDate: 3/16/03
OrderAmt: 50.25

8. Claire created a database named **Customer** that contains a table with order data named **Order Records**. The **Order** table you created has the same format as the **Order Records** table. Copy all the records from the **Order Records** table in the **Customer** database (located in the Cases folder on your Data Disk) to the end of the **Order** table in the **Meals** database.

9. Resize all columns in the datasheet for the **Order** table to their best fit.
10. For Order# 3039, change the OrderAmt value to 87.30.
11. Delete the record for Order# 3068.
12. Print the **Order** table datasheet, and then save and close the table.
13. Close the **Meals** database, and then exit Access.

Case 3. **Redwood Zoo**   Michael Rosenfeld continues to track information about donors, their pledges, and the status of funds to benefit the Redwood Zoo. Help him maintain the **Redwood** database by completing the following:

1. Make sure your Data Disk is in the appropriate disk drive.
2. Start Access and open the **Redwood** database located in the Cases folder on your Data Disk.
3. Create a table named **Pledge** using the Import Table Wizard. The table you need to import is named **Pledge Records**, which is located in the **Pledge** database in the Cases folder on your Data Disk.

Explore
4. After importing the **Pledge Records** table, use the shortcut menu to rename the table to **Pledge** in the Database window.

Explore
5. Modify the structure of the **Pledge** table by completing the following:
   a. Enter the following Description property values:
      Pledge#:   Primary key
      DonorID: Foreign key
      FundCode: Foreign key
   b. Change the format of the PledgeDate field to mm/dd/yyyy.
   c. Change the Data Type of the TotalPledged field to Currency with the Standard format.
   d. Specify a Default Value of B for the PaymentMethod field.
   e. Specify a Default Value of F for the PaymentSchedule field.
   f. Save the modified table structure.

6. Switch to Datasheet view, and then resize all columns in the datasheet to their best fit.
7. Use the **Pledge** datasheet to update the database as follows:
   a. Add a new record to the **Pledge** table with the following field values:
      Pledge#:   2695
      DonorID: 59045
      FundCode: P15
      PledgeDate: 7/11/2003
      TotalPledged: 1000
      PaymentMethod: B
      PaymentSchedule: M
   b. Change the TotalPledged value for Pledge# 2499 to 150.
   c. Change the FundCode value for Pledge# 2332 to B03.
8. Print the **Pledge** table datasheet, and then save and close the table.
9. Close the **Redwood** database, and then exit Access.

Case 4. **Mountain River Adventures**   Connor and Siobhan Dempsey use the **Trips** database to track the data about the guided tours they provide. You'll help them maintain this database by completing the following:

1. Make sure your Data Disk is in the appropriate disk drive.
2. Start Access and open the **Trips** database located in the Cases folder on your Data Disk.

Explore
3. Use the Import Spreadsheet Wizard to create a new table named **Rafting Trip**. The data you need to import is contained in the **Rafting** workbook, which is a Microsoft Excel file located in the Cases folder on your Data Disk.
   a. Select the Import Table option in the New Table dialog box.
   b. Change the entry in the Files of type list box to display the list of Excel workbook files in the Cases folder.

c. Select the **Rafting** file and then click the Import button.

d. In the Import Spreadsheet Wizard dialog boxes, choose the Sheet1 worksheet; choose the option for using column headings as field names; select the option for choosing your own primary key; specify Trip# as the primary key; and enter the table name (**Rafting Trip**). Otherwise, accept the Wizard's choices for all other options for the imported data.

4. Open the **Rafting Trip** table and resize all datasheet columns to their best fit.

5. Modify the structure of the **Rafting Trip** table by completing the following:

    a. For the Trip# field, enter a Description property of "Primary key", change the Field Size to Long Integer, and set the Decimal Places property to 0.

    b. For the River field, change the Field Size to 45.

    c. For the TripDistance field, enter a Description property of "Distance in miles", change the Field Size to Integer, and set the Decimal Places property to 0.

    d. For the TripDays field, enter a Description property of "Number of days for the trip", and change the Field Size to Single.

    e. For the Fee/Person field, change the Data Type to Currency and set the Format property to Fixed.

    f. Save the table structure. If you receive any warning messages about lost data or integrity rules, click the Yes button.

6. Use the **Rafting Trip** datasheet to update the database as follows:

    a. For Trip# 3142, change the TripDistance value to 20.

    b. Add a new record to the **Rafting Trip** table with the following field values:

Trip#:	3675
River:	Colorado River (Grand Canyon)
TripDistance:	110
TripDays:	2.5
Fee/Person:	215

    c. Delete the record for Trip# 3423.

7. Print the **Rafting Trip** table datasheet, and then close the table.

8. Use Design view to create a new table named **Booking** using the table design shown in Figure 2-41.

Figure 2-41

Field Name	Data Type	Description	Field Size	Other Properties
Booking#	Number	Primary key	Long Integer	Decimal Places: 0 Default Value: Null
Client#	Number	Foreign key	Integer	Decimal Places: 0
TripDate	Date/Time			Format: Short Date
Trip#	Number	Foreign key	Long Integer	Decimal Places: 0
People	Number	Number of people in the group	Byte	Decimal Places: 0

9. Specify Booking# as the primary key, and then save the table as **Booking**.

10. Add the records shown in Figure 2-42 to the **Booking** table.

Figure 2-42

Booking#	Client#	TripDate	Trip#	People
410	330	6/5/03	3529	4
403	315	7/1/03	3107	7
411	311	7/5/03	3222	5

11. Connor created a database named **Groups** that contains a table with booking data named **Group Info**. The **Booking** table you created has the same format as the **Group Info** table. Copy all the records from the **Group Info** table in the **Groups** database (located in the Cases folder on your Data Disk) to the end of the **Booking** table in the **Trips** database.
12. Resize all columns in the **Booking** datasheet to their best fit.
13. Print the **Booking** datasheet, and then save and close the table.
14. Close the **Trips** database, and then exit Access.

INTERNET ASSIGNMENTS

Student Union

The purpose of the Internet Assignments is to challenge you to find information on the Internet that you can use to create effective documents. The actual assignments are updated and maintained on the Course Technology Web site. Log on to the Internet and use your Web browser to go to the Student Union on the New Perspectives Series site at **www.course.com/NewPerspectives/studentunion**. Click the Online Companions link, and then click the link for this text.

QUICK CHECK ANSWERS

Session 2.1

1. Identify all the fields needed to produce the required information, group related fields into tables, determine each table's primary key, include a common field in related tables, avoid data redundancy, and determine the properties of each field.
2. The Data Type property determines what field values you can enter for the field and what other properties the field will have.
3. text, number, and AutoNumber fields
4. F6
5. Format
6. null

Session 2.2

1. the record being edited; the next row available for a new record
2. The field and all its values are removed from the table.
3. In Design view, right-click the row selector for the row above which you want to insert the field, click Insert Rows on the shortcut menu, and then define the new field.
4. yes/no
5. Make sure the database into which you want to import a table is open, click the File menu, point to Get External Data, and then click Import; or, click the New button in the Database window, click Import Table in the New Table dialog box, and then click the OK button.
6. In navigation mode, the entire field value is selected, and anything you type replaces the field value; in editing mode, you can insert or delete characters in a field value based on the location of the insertion point.

TUTORIAL 3

OBJECTIVES

In this tutorial you will:

- Learn how to use the Query window in Design view
- Create, run, and save queries
- Update data using a query
- Define a relationship between two tables
- Sort data in a query
- Filter data in a query
- Specify an exact match condition in a query
- Change a datasheet's appearance
- Use a comparison operator to match a range of values
- Use the And and Or logical operators
- Use multiple undo and redo
- Perform calculations in a query using calculated fields, aggregate functions, and record group calculations

QUERYING A DATABASE

Retrieving Information About Employers and Their Positions

CASE

Northeast Seasonal Jobs International (NSJI)

At a recent company meeting, Elsa Jensen and other NSJI employees discussed the importance of regularly monitoring the business activity of the company's employer clients. For example, Zack Ward and his marketing staff track employer activity to develop new strategies for promoting NSJI's services. Matt Griffin, the manager of recruitment, needs to track information about available positions, so that he can find student recruits to fill those positions. In addition, Elsa is interested in analyzing other aspects of the business, such as the wage amounts paid for different positions at different employers. All of these informational needs can be satisfied by queries that retrieve information from the Northeast database.

SESSION 3.1

In this session, you will use the Query window in Design view to create, run, and save queries; update data using a query; define a one-to-many relationship between two tables; sort data with a toolbar button and in Design view; and filter data in a query datasheet.

Introduction to Queries

As you learned in Tutorial 1, a query is a question you ask about data stored in a database. For example, Zack might create a query to find records in the Employer table for only those employers located in a specific state or province. When you create a query, you tell Access which fields you need and what criteria Access should use to select the records.

Access provides powerful query capabilities that allow you to:

- display selected fields and records from a table
- sort records
- perform calculations
- generate data for forms, reports, and other queries
- update data in the tables in a database
- find and display data from two or more tables

Most questions about data are generalized queries in which you specify the fields and records you want Access to select. These common requests for information, such as "Which employers are located in Quebec?" or "How many waiter/waitress positions are available?" are called **select queries**. The answer to a select query is returned in the form of a datasheet. The result of a query is also referred to as a **recordset**, because the query produces a set of records that answers your question.

More specialized, technical queries, such as finding duplicate records in a table, are best formulated using a Query Wizard. A Query Wizard prompts you for information by asking a series of questions and then creates the appropriate query based on your answers. In Tutorial 1, you used the Simple Query Wizard to display only some of the fields in the Employer table; Access provides other Query Wizards for more complex queries. For common, informational queries, it is easier for you to design your own query than to use a Query Wizard.

Zack wants you to create a query to display the employer ID, employer name, city, contact first name, contact last name, and Web site information for each record in the Employer table. He needs this information for a market analysis his staff is completing on NSJI's employer clients. You'll open the Query window to create the query for Zack.

Query Window

You use the Query window in Design view to create a query. In Design view, you specify the data you want to view by constructing a query by example. When you use **query by example** (**QBE**), you give Access an example of the information you are requesting. Access then retrieves the information that precisely matches your example.

For Zack's query, you need to display data from the Employer table. You'll begin by starting Access, opening the Northeast database, and displaying the Query window in Design view.

To start Access, open the Northeast database, and open the Query window in Design view:

1. Place your Data Disk in the appropriate disk drive.

2. Start Access and open the **Northeast** database located in the Tutorial folder on your Data Disk. The Northeast database is displayed in the Database window.

3. Click **Queries** in the Objects bar of the Database window, and then click the **New** button. The New Query dialog box opens. See Figure 3-1.

| Figure 3-1 | NEW QUERY DIALOG BOX |

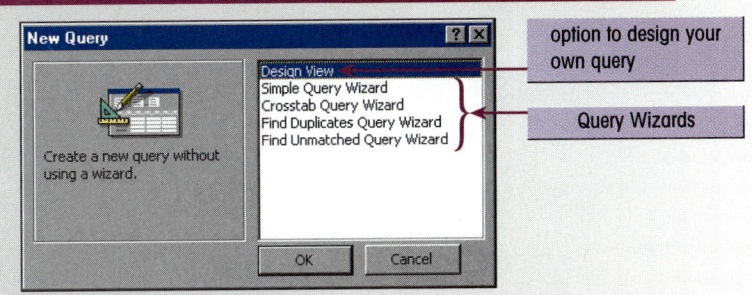

You'll design your own query instead of using a Query Wizard.

4. If necessary, click **Design View** in the list box.

5. Click the **OK** button. Access opens the Show Table dialog box on top of the Query window. (Note that you could also have double-clicked the "Create query in Design view" option in the Database window.) Notice that the title bar of the Query window shows that you are creating a select query.

The query you are creating will retrieve data from the Employer table, so you need to add this table to the Select Query window.

6. Click **Employer** in the Tables list box (if necessary), click the **Add** button, and then click the **Close** button. Access places the Employer table's field list in the Select Query window and closes the Show Table dialog box.

To display more of the fields you'll be using for creating queries, you'll maximize the Select Query window.

7. Click the **Maximize** button □ on the Select Query window title bar. See Figure 3-2.

Figure 3-2 SELECT QUERY IN DESIGN VIEW

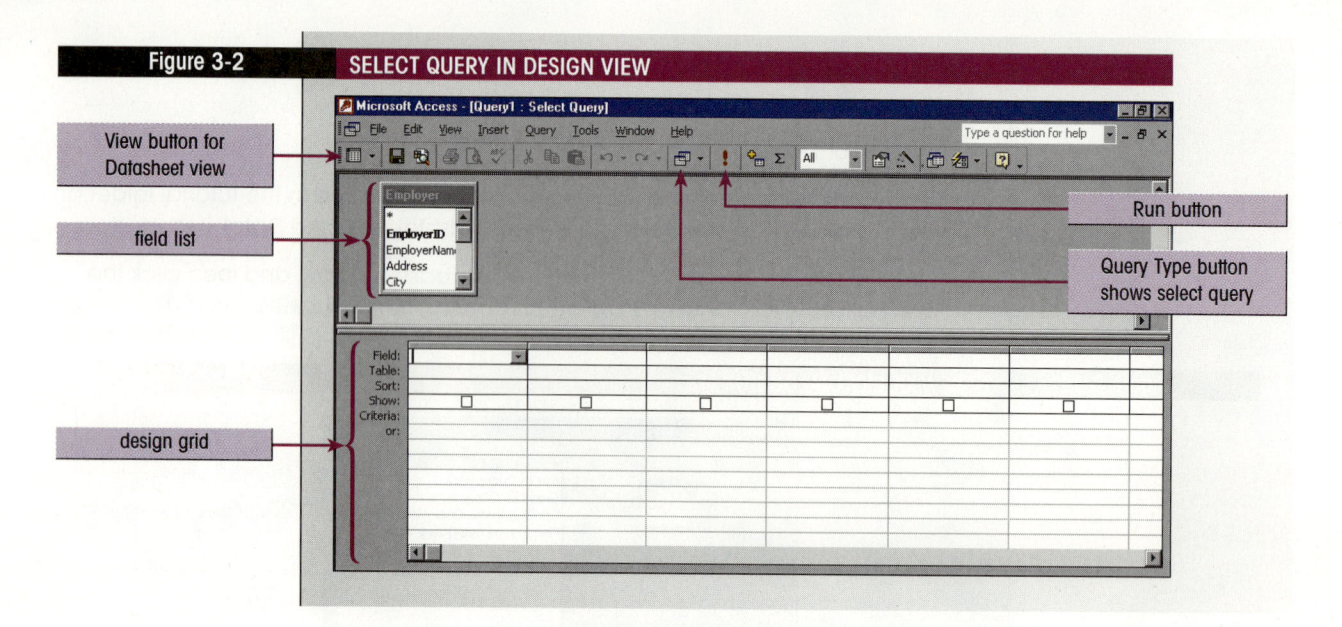

Labels on figure: View button for Datasheet view; field list; design grid; Run button; Query Type button shows select query

In Design view, the Select Query window contains the standard title bar, the menu bar, the status bar, and the Query Design toolbar. On the toolbar, the Query Type button shows a select query; the icon on this button changes according to the type of query you are creating. The title bar on the Select Query window displays the query type (Select Query) and the default query name (Query1). You'll change the default query name to a more meaningful one later when you save the query.

The Select Query window in Design view contains a field list and the design grid. The **field list** contains the fields for the table you are querying. The table name appears at the top of the list box, and the fields are listed in the order in which they appear in the table. You can scroll the field list to see more fields; or, you can expand the field list to display all the fields and the complete field names by resizing the field list box.

In the **design grid**, you include the fields and record selection criteria for the information you want to see. Each column in the design grid contains specifications about a field you will use in the query. You can choose a single field for your query by dragging its name from the field list to the design grid in the lower portion of the window. Alternatively, you can double-click a field name to place it in the next available design grid column.

When you are constructing a query, you can see the query results at any time by clicking the View button or the Run button on the Query Design toolbar. In response, Access displays the datasheet, which contains the set of fields and records that results from answering, or **running**, the query. The order of the fields in the datasheet is the same as the order of the fields in the design grid. Although the datasheet looks just like a table datasheet and appears in Datasheet view, a query datasheet is temporary, and its contents are based on the criteria you establish in the design grid. In contrast, a table datasheet shows the permanent data in a table. However, you can update data while viewing a query datasheet, just as you can when working in a table datasheet or form.

If the query you are creating includes every field from the specified table, you can use one of the following three methods to transfer all the fields from the field list to the design grid:

- Click and drag each field individually from the field list to the design grid. Use this method if you want the fields in your query to appear in an order that is different from the order in the field list.

- Double-click the asterisk in the field list. Access places the table name followed by a period and an asterisk (as in "Employer.*") in the design grid, which signifies that the order of the fields will be the same in the query as it is in the field list. Use this method if you don't need to sort the query or specify conditions for the records you want to select. The advantage of using this method is that you do not need to change the query if you add or delete fields from the underlying table structure. Such changes are reflected automatically in the query.

- Double-click the field list title bar to highlight all the fields, and then click and drag one of the highlighted fields to the design grid. Access places each field in a separate column and arranges the fields in the order in which they appear in the field list. Use this method when you need to sort your query or include record selection criteria.

Now you'll create and run Zack's query to display selected fields from the Employer table.

Creating and Running a Query

The default table datasheet displays all the fields in the table, in the same order as they appear in the table. In contrast, a query datasheet can display selected fields from a table, and the order of the fields can be different from that of the table.

Zack wants the Employer table's EmployerID, EmployerName, City, ContactFirstName, ContactLastName, and WebSite fields to appear in the query results. You'll add each of these fields to the design grid.

To select the fields for the query, and then run the query:

1. Drag **EmployerID** from the Employer field list to the design grid's first column Field text box, and then release the mouse button. See Figure 3-3.

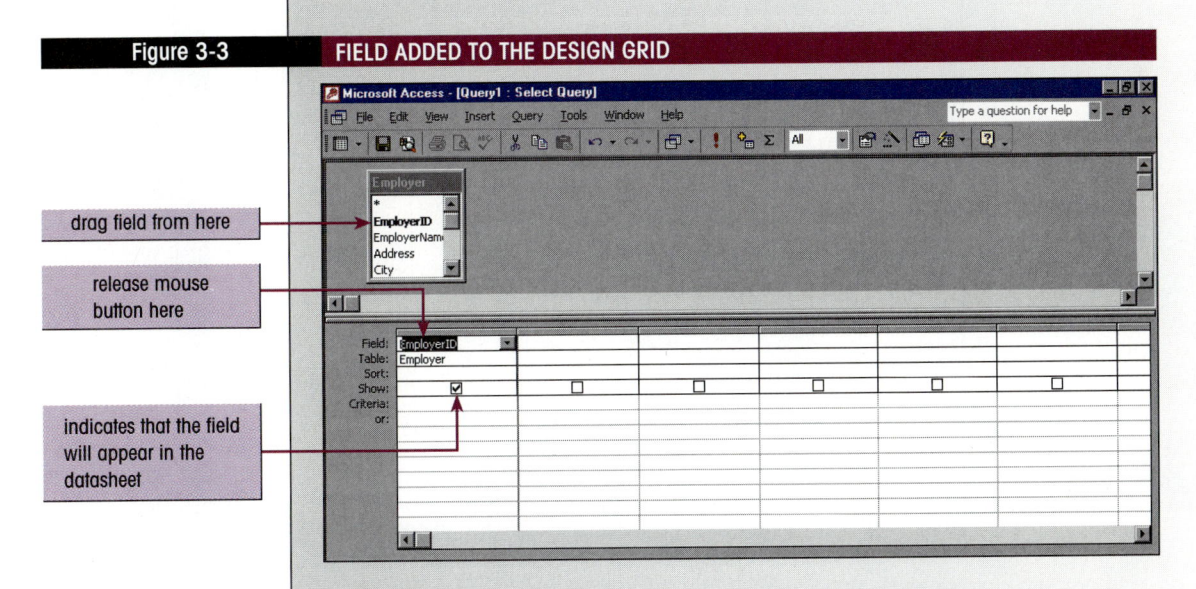

Figure 3-3 FIELD ADDED TO THE DESIGN GRID

- drag field from here
- release mouse button here
- indicates that the field will appear in the datasheet

In the design grid's first column, the field name EmployerID appears in the Field text box, the table name Employer appears in the Table text box, and the check mark in the Show check box indicates that the field will be displayed in the datasheet when you run the query. Sometimes you might not want to display a field and its values in the query results. For example, if you are creating a query to show all employers located in Massachusetts, and you assign the name "Employers in Massachusetts" to the query, you do not need to include the State/Prov field value for each record in the query results—every State/Prov field value would be "MA" for Massachusetts. Even if you choose not to include a field in the display of the query results, you can still use the field as part of the query to select specific records or to specify a particular sequence for the records in the datasheet.

2. Double-click **EmployerName** in the Employer field list. Access adds this field to the second column of the design grid.

3. Scrolling the Employer field list as necessary, repeat Step 2 for the **City**, **ContactFirstName**, **ContactLastName**, and **WebSite** fields to add these fields to the design grid in that order.

   TROUBLE? If you double-click the wrong field and accidentally add it to the design grid, you can remove the field from the grid. Select the field's column by clicking the pointer ↓ on the bar above the Field text box for the field you want to delete, and then press the Delete key (or click Edit on the menu bar, and then click Delete Columns).

   Having selected the fields for Zack's query, you now can run the query.

4. Click the **Run** button on the Query Design toolbar. Access runs the query and displays the results in Datasheet view. See Figure 3-4.

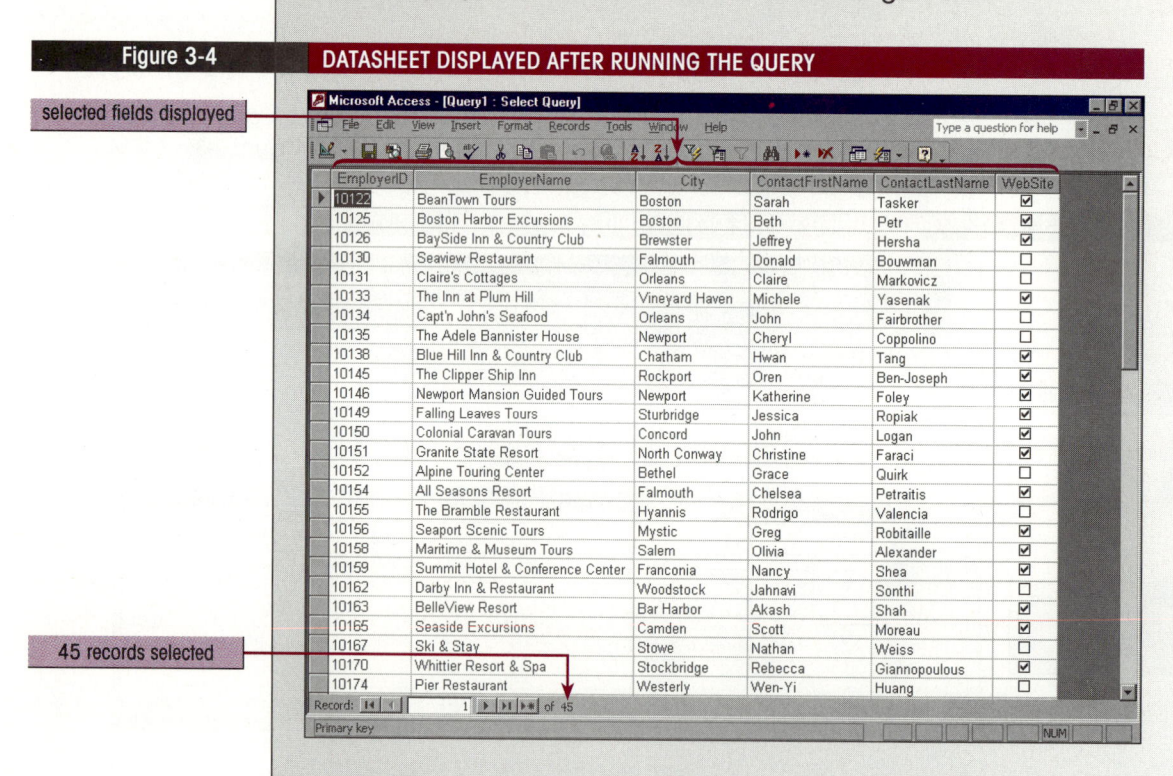

Figure 3-4 DATASHEET DISPLAYED AFTER RUNNING THE QUERY

selected fields displayed

EmployerID	EmployerName	City	ContactFirstName	ContactLastName	WebSite
10122	BeanTown Tours	Boston	Sarah	Tasker	☑
10125	Boston Harbor Excursions	Boston	Beth	Petr	☑
10126	BaySide Inn & Country Club	Brewster	Jeffrey	Hersha	☑
10130	Seaview Restaurant	Falmouth	Donald	Bouwman	☐
10131	Claire's Cottages	Orleans	Claire	Markovicz	☐
10133	The Inn at Plum Hill	Vineyard Haven	Michele	Yasenak	☑
10134	Capt'n John's Seafood	Orleans	John	Fairbrother	☐
10135	The Adele Bannister House	Newport	Cheryl	Coppolino	☐
10138	Blue Hill Inn & Country Club	Chatham	Hwan	Tang	☑
10145	The Clipper Ship Inn	Rockport	Oren	Ben-Joseph	☑
10146	Newport Mansion Guided Tours	Newport	Katherine	Foley	☑
10149	Falling Leaves Tours	Sturbridge	Jessica	Ropiak	☑
10150	Colonial Caravan Tours	Concord	John	Logan	☑
10151	Granite State Resort	North Conway	Christine	Faraci	☑
10152	Alpine Touring Center	Bethel	Grace	Quirk	☐
10154	All Seasons Resort	Falmouth	Chelsea	Petraitis	☑
10155	The Bramble Restaurant	Hyannis	Rodrigo	Valencia	☐
10156	Seaport Scenic Tours	Mystic	Greg	Robitaille	☑
10158	Maritime & Museum Tours	Salem	Olivia	Alexander	☑
10159	Summit Hotel & Conference Center	Franconia	Nancy	Shea	☑
10162	Darby Inn & Restaurant	Woodstock	Jahnavi	Sonthi	☐
10163	BelleView Resort	Bar Harbor	Akash	Shah	☑
10165	Seaside Excursions	Camden	Scott	Moreau	☑
10167	Ski & Stay	Stowe	Nathan	Weiss	☐
10170	Whittier Resort & Spa	Stockbridge	Rebecca	Giannopoulous	☑
10174	Pier Restaurant	Westerly	Wen-Yi	Huang	☐

45 records selected

Record: 1 of 45

The six fields you added to the design grid appear in the datasheet, and the records are displayed in primary key sequence by EmployerID. Access selected a total of 45 records for display in the datasheet.

> Zack asks you to save the query as "Employer Analysis" so that he can easily retrieve the same data again.
>
> 5. Click the **Save** button on the Query Datasheet toolbar. The Save As dialog box opens.
>
> 6. Type **Employer Analysis** in the Query Name text box, and then press the **Enter** key. Access saves the query with the specified name in the Northeast database on your Data Disk and displays the name in the title bar.

When viewing the results of the query, Zack noticed a couple of changes that need to be made to the data in the Employer table. The Adele Bannister House recently developed a Web site, so the WebSite field for this record needs to be updated. In addition, the contact information has changed for the Alpine Touring Center.

Updating Data Using a Query

Although a query datasheet is temporary and its contents are based on the criteria in the query design grid, you can update the data in a table using a query datasheet. In this case, Zack has changes he wants you to make to records in the Employer table. Instead of making the changes in the table datasheet, you can make them in the Employer Analysis query datasheet. The underlying Employer table will be updated with the changes you make.

> ### To update data using the Employer Analysis query datasheet:
>
> 1. For the record with EmployerID 10135 (The Adele Bannister House), click the check box in the WebSite field to place a check mark in it.
>
> 2. For the record with EmployerID 10152 (Alpine Touring Center), change the ContactFirstName field value to **Mary** and change the ContactLastName field value to **Grant**.
>
> 3. Click the **Close Window** button on the menu bar to close the query. Note that the Employer Analysis query appears in the list of queries.
>
> 4. Click the **Restore Window** button on the menu bar to return the Database window to its original size.
>
>   Now you will check the Employer table to verify that the changes you made in the query datasheet were also made to the Employer table records.
>
> 5. Click **Tables** in the Objects bar of the Database window, click **Employer** in the list of tables, and then click the **Open** button. The Employer table datasheet opens.
>
> 6. For the record with EmployerID 10135, scroll the datasheet to the right to verify that the WebSite field contains a check mark. For the record with EmployerID 10152, scroll to the right to see the new contact information (Mary Grant).
>
> 7. Click the **Close** button on the Employer table window to close it.

Matt also wants to view specific information in the Northeast database. However, he needs to see data from both the Employer table and the Position table at the same time. To view data from two tables at the same time, you need to define a relationship between the tables.

Defining Table Relationships

One of the most powerful features of a relational database management system is its ability to define relationships between tables. You use a common field to relate one table to another. The process of relating tables is often called performing a **join**. When you join tables that have a common field, you can extract data from them as if they were one larger table. For example, you can join the Employer and Position tables by using the EmployerID field in both tables as the common field. Then you can use a query, a form, or a report to extract selected data from each table, even though the data is contained in two separate tables, as shown in Figure 3-5. In the Positions query shown in Figure 3-5, the PositionID, PositionTitle, and Wage columns are fields from the Position table, and the EmployerName and State/Prov columns are fields from the Employer table. The joining of records is based on the common field of EmployerID. The Employer and Position tables have a type of relationship called a one-to-many relationship.

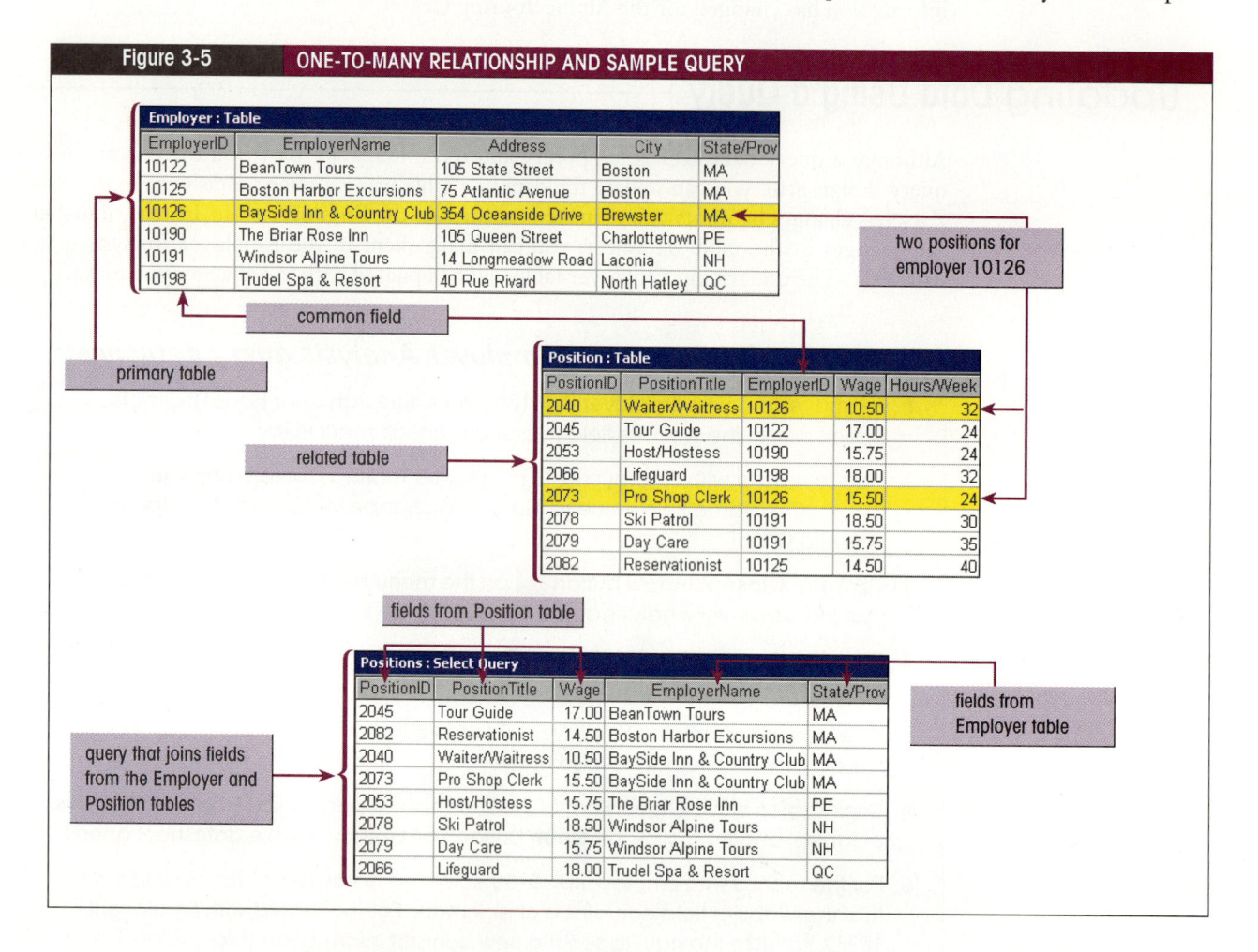

Figure 3-5   ONE-TO-MANY RELATIONSHIP AND SAMPLE QUERY

Employer : Table

EmployerID	EmployerName	Address	City	State/Prov
10122	BeanTown Tours	105 State Street	Boston	MA
10125	Boston Harbor Excursions	75 Atlantic Avenue	Boston	MA
10126	BaySide Inn & Country Club	354 Oceanside Drive	Brewster	MA
10190	The Briar Rose Inn	105 Queen Street	Charlottetown	PE
10191	Windsor Alpine Tours	14 Longmeadow Road	Laconia	NH
10198	Trudel Spa & Resort	40 Rue Rivard	North Hatley	QC

- primary table
- common field
- two positions for employer 10126

Position : Table

PositionID	PositionTitle	EmployerID	Wage	Hours/Week
2040	Waiter/Waitress	10126	10.50	32
2045	Tour Guide	10122	17.00	24
2053	Host/Hostess	10190	15.75	24
2066	Lifeguard	10198	18.00	32
2073	Pro Shop Clerk	10126	15.50	24
2078	Ski Patrol	10191	18.50	30
2079	Day Care	10191	15.75	35
2082	Reservationist	10125	14.50	40

- related table
- fields from Position table

Positions : Select Query

PositionID	PositionTitle	Wage	EmployerName	State/Prov
2045	Tour Guide	17.00	BeanTown Tours	MA
2082	Reservationist	14.50	Boston Harbor Excursions	MA
2040	Waiter/Waitress	10.50	BaySide Inn & Country Club	MA
2073	Pro Shop Clerk	15.50	BaySide Inn & Country Club	MA
2053	Host/Hostess	15.75	The Briar Rose Inn	PE
2078	Ski Patrol	18.50	Windsor Alpine Tours	NH
2079	Day Care	15.75	Windsor Alpine Tours	NH
2066	Lifeguard	18.00	Trudel Spa & Resort	QC

- query that joins fields from the Employer and Position tables
- fields from Employer table

One-to-Many Relationships

A **one-to-many relationship** exists between two tables when one record in the first table matches zero, one, or many records in the second table, and when one record in the second table matches exactly one record in the first table. For example, as shown in Figure 3-5, employers 10126 and 10191 each have two available positions, and employers 10122, 10125, 10190, and 10198 each have one available position. Every position has a single matching employer.

Access refers to the two tables that form a relationship as the primary table and the related table. The **primary table** is the "one" table in a one-to-many relationship; in Figure 3-5, the Employer table is the primary table because there is only one employer for each available position. The **related table** is the "many" table; in Figure 3-5, the Position table is the related table because there can be many positions offered by each employer.

Because related data is stored in two tables, inconsistencies between the tables can occur. Consider the following scenarios:

- Matt adds a position record to the Position table for a new employer, Glen Cove Inn, using EmployerID 10132. Matt did not first add the new employer's information to the Employer table, so this position does not have a matching record in the Employer table. The data is inconsistent, and the position record is considered to be an **orphaned** record.
- Matt changes the EmployerID in the Employer table for BaySide Inn & Country Club from 10126 to 10128. Two orphaned records for employer 10126 now exist in the Position table, and the database is inconsistent.
- Matt deletes the record for Boston Harbor Excursions, employer 10125, in the Employer table because this employer is no longer an NSJI client. The database is again inconsistent; one record for employer 10125 in the Position table has no matching record in the Employer table.

You can avoid these problems by specifying referential integrity between tables when you define their relationships.

Referential Integrity

Referential integrity is a set of rules that Access enforces to maintain consistency between related tables when you update data in a database. Specifically, the referential integrity rules are as follows:

- When you add a record to a related table, a matching record must already exist in the primary table, thereby preventing the possibility of orphaned records.
- If you attempt to change the value of the primary key in the primary table, Access prevents this change if matching records exist in a related table. However, if you choose the **cascade updates** option, Access permits the change in value to the primary key and changes the appropriate foreign key values in the related table, thereby eliminating the possibility of inconsistent data.
- When you delete a record in the primary table, Access prevents the deletion if matching records exist in a related table. However, if you choose the **cascade deletes** option, Access deletes the record in the primary table and also deletes all records in related tables that have matching foreign key values.

Now you'll define a one-to-many relationship between the Employer and Position tables so that you can use fields from both tables to create a query that will retrieve the information Matt needs. You will also define a one-to-many relationship between the NAICS (primary) table and the Employer (related) table.

Defining a Relationship Between Two Tables

When two tables have a common field, you can define a relationship between them in the Relationships window. The **Relationships window** illustrates the relationships among a database's tables. In this window, you can view or change existing relationships, define new relationships between tables, and rearrange the layout of the tables in the window.

You need to open the Relationships window and define the relationship between the Employer and Position tables. You'll define a one-to-many relationship between the two tables, with Employer as the primary table and Position as the related table, and with EmployerID as the common field (the primary key in the Employer table and a foreign key in the Position table). You'll also define a one-to-many relationship between the NAICS and Employer tables, with NAICS as the primary table and Employer as the related table, and with NAICSCode as the common field (the primary key in the NAICS table and a foreign key in the Employer table).

To define the one-to-many relationship between the Employer and Position tables:

1. Click the **Relationships** button on the Database toolbar. The Show Table dialog box opens on top of the Relationships window. See Figure 3-6.

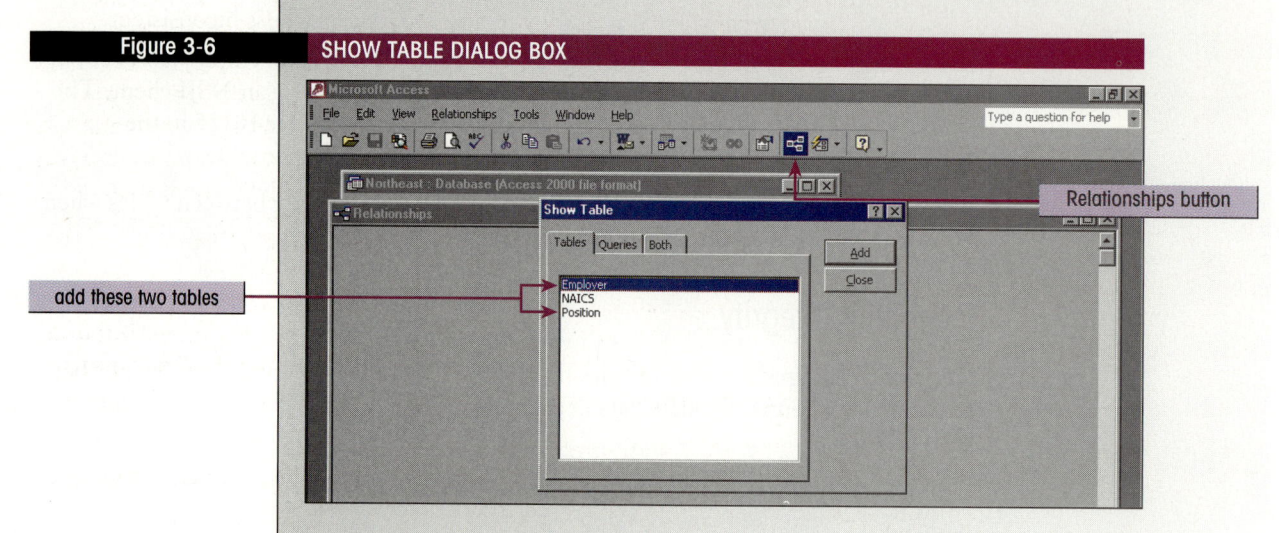

Figure 3-6   SHOW TABLE DIALOG BOX

add these two tables

Relationships button

You must add each table participating in a relationship to the Relationships window.

2. Click **Employer** (if necessary), and then click the **Add** button. The Employer field list is added to the Relationships window.

3. Click **Position**, and then click the **Add** button. The Position field list is added to the Relationships window.

4. Click the **Close** button in the Show Table dialog box to close it and reveal the entire Relationships window.

To form the relationship between the two tables, you drag the common field of EmployerID from the primary table to the related table. Then Access opens the Edit Relationships dialog box, in which you select the relationship options for the two tables.

5. Click **EmployerID** in the Employer field list, and drag it to **EmployerID** in the Position field list. When you release the mouse button, the Edit Relationships dialog box opens. See Figure 3-7.

Figure 3-7 EDIT RELATIONSHIPS DIALOG BOX

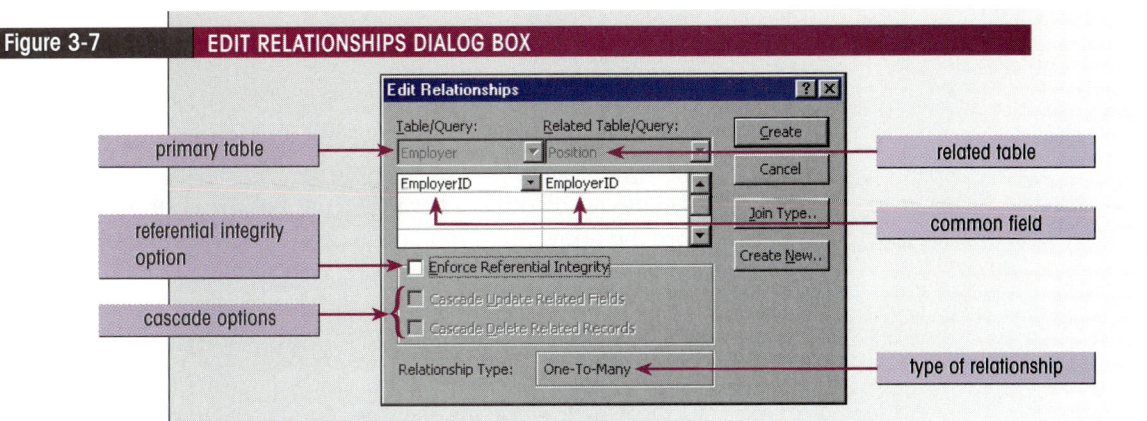

- primary table
- related table
- referential integrity option
- common field
- cascade options
- type of relationship

The primary table, related table, and common field appear at the top of the dialog box. The type of relationship, One-To-Many, appears at the bottom of the dialog box. When you click the Enforce Referential Integrity check box, the two cascade options become available. If you select the Cascade Update Related Fields option, Access will change the appropriate foreign key values in the related table when you change a primary key value in the primary table. If you select the Cascade Delete Related Records option, when you delete a record in the primary table, Access will delete all records in the related table that have a matching foreign key value.

6. Click the **Enforce Referential Integrity** check box, click the **Cascade Update Related Fields** check box, and then click the **Cascade Delete Related Records** check box. **Note:** You should select this option with caution because you might inadvertently delete records you do not want deleted.

7. Click the **Create** button to define the one-to-many relationship between the two tables and to close the dialog box. The completed relationship appears in the Relationships window. See Figure 3-8.

Figure 3-8 DEFINED RELATIONSHIP IN THE RELATIONSHIPS WINDOW

- "one" side of the relationship
- "many" side of the relationship
- join line

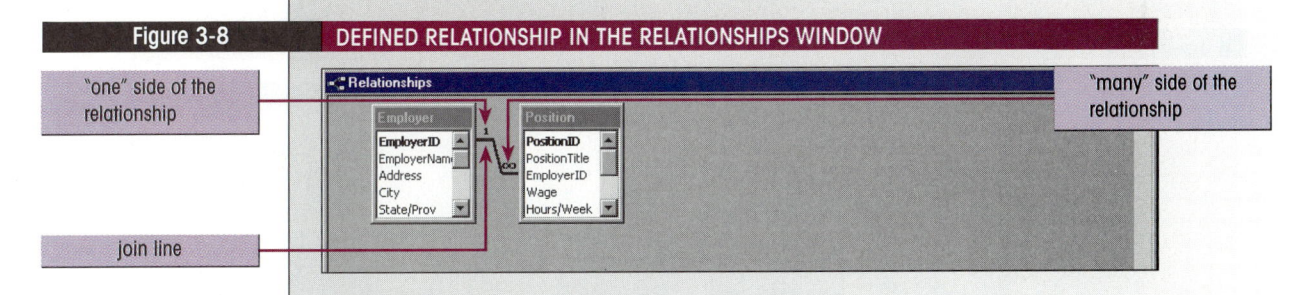

The **join line** connects the EmployerID fields, which are common to the two tables. The common field joins the two tables, which have a one-to-many relationship. The "one" side of the relationship has the digit 1 at its end, and the "many" side of the relationship has the infinity symbol ∞ at its end. The two tables are still separate tables, but you can use the data in them as if they were one table.

Now you need to define the one-to-many relationship between the NAICS and Employer tables. In this relationship, NAICS is the primary ("one") table because there is only one code for each employer. Employer is the related ("many") table because there are multiple employers with the same NAICS code.

To define the one-to-many relationship between the NAICS and Employer tables:

1. Click the **Show Table** button on the Relationship toolbar. The Show Table dialog box opens on top of the Relationships window.

2. Click **NAICS** in the list of tables, click the **Add** button, and then click the **Close** button to close the Show Table dialog box. The NAICS field list appears in the Relationships window to the right of the Position field list. To make it easier to define the relationship, you'll move the NAICS field list below the Employer and Position field lists.

3. Click the NAICS field list title bar and drag the list until it is below the Position table (see Figure 3-9), and then release the mouse button.

4. Scroll the Employer field list until the NAICSCode field is visible. Because the NAICS table is the primary table in this relationship, you need to drag the NAICSCode field from the NAICS field list to the Employer field list. Notice that the NAICSCode field in the NAICS table appears in a bold font; this indicates that the field is the table's primary key. On the other hand, the NAICSCode field in the Employer table is not bold, which is a reminder that this field is the foreign key in this table.

5. Click and drag the **NAICSCode** field in the NAICS field list to the **NAICSCode** field in the Employer field list. When you release the mouse button, the Edit Relationships dialog box opens.

6. Click the **Enforce Referential Integrity** check box, click the **Cascade Update Related Fields** check box, and then click the **Cascade Delete Related Records** check box. You now have selected all the necessary relationship options.

7. Click the **Create** button to define the one-to-many relationship between the two tables and close the dialog box. The completed relationship appears in the Relationships window. See Figure 3-9.

Figure 3-9   BOTH RELATIONSHIPS DEFINED

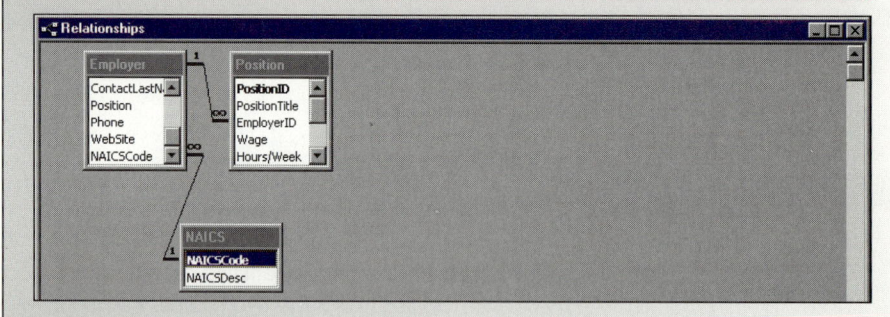

With both relationships defined, you have connected the data among the three tables in the Northeast database.

8. Click the **Save** button on the Relationship toolbar to save the layout in the Relationships window.

9. Click the **Close** button on the Relationships window title bar. The Relationships window closes, and you return to the Database window.

Creating a Multi-table Query

Now that you have joined the Employer and Position tables, you can create a query to produce the information Matt wants. To help him determine his recruiting needs, Matt wants a query that displays the EmployerName, City, and State/Prov fields from the Employer table and the Openings, PositionTitle, StartDate, and EndDate fields from the Position table.

To create, run, and save the query using the Employer and Position tables:

1. Click **Queries** in the Objects bar of the Database window, and then double-click **Create query in Design view**. The Show Table dialog box opens on top of the Query window in Design view.

   You need to add the Employer and Position tables to the Query window.

2. Click **Employer** in the Tables list box (if necessary), click the **Add** button, click **Position**, click the **Add** button, and then click the **Close** button. The Employer and Position field lists appear in the Query window, and the Show Table dialog box closes. Note that the one-to-many relationship that exists between the two tables is shown in the Query window. Also, notice that the join line is thick at both ends; this signifies that you selected the option to enforce referential integrity. If you had not selected this option, the join line would be thin at both ends and neither the "1" nor the infinity symbol would appear, even though there is a one-to-many relationship between the two tables.

   You need to place the EmployerName, City, and State/Prov fields from the Employer field list into the design grid, and then place the Openings, PositionTitle, StartDate, and EndDate fields from the Position field list into the design grid.

3. Double-click **EmployerName** in the Employer field list to place EmployerName in the design grid's first column Field text box.

4. Repeat Step 3 to add the **City** and **State/Prov** fields from the Employer table, so that these fields are placed in the second and third columns of the design grid.

5. Repeat Step 3 to add the **Openings**, **PositionTitle**, **StartDate**, and **EndDate** fields (in that order) from the Position table, so that these fields are placed in the fourth through seventh columns of the design grid.

   The query specifications are completed, so you now can run the query.

6. Click the **Run** button on the Query Design toolbar. Access runs the query and displays the results in the datasheet.

7. Click the **Maximize** button on the Query window title bar. See Figure 3-10.

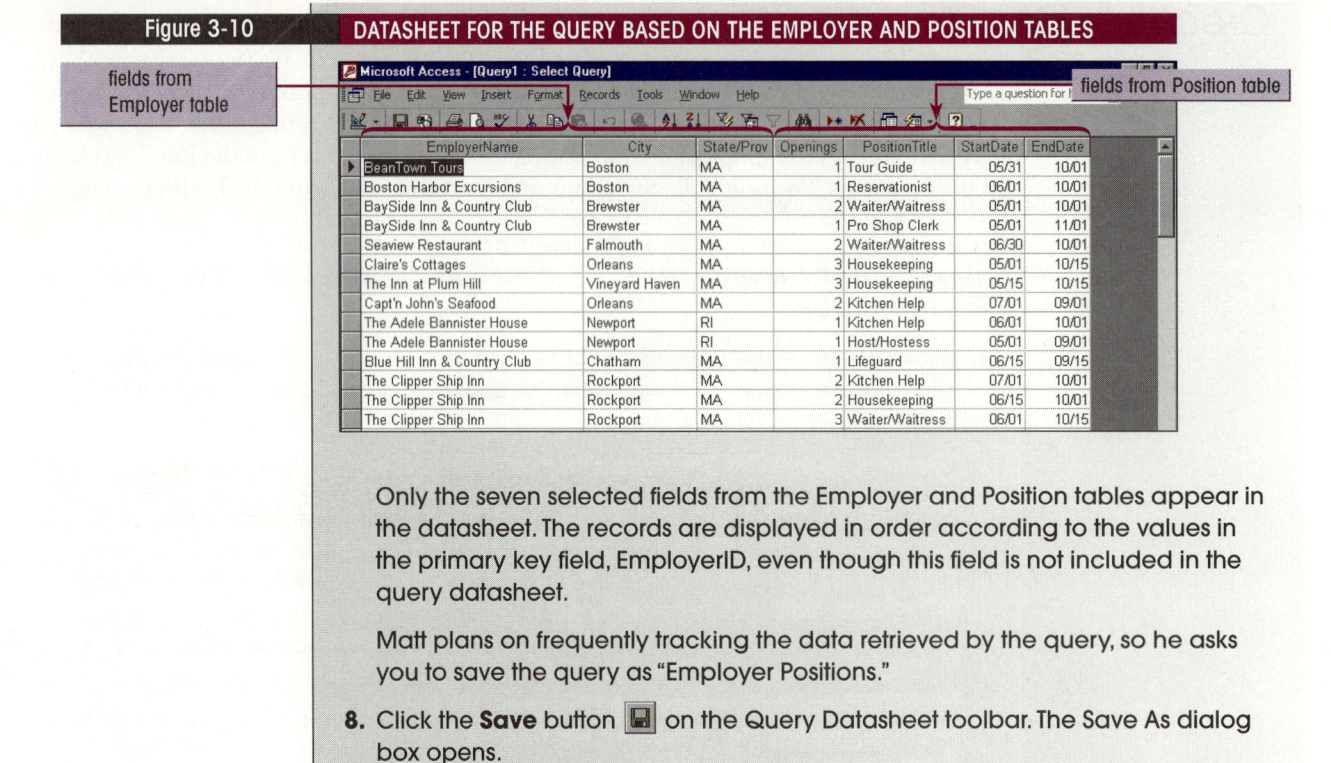

Figure 3-10 DATASHEET FOR THE QUERY BASED ON THE EMPLOYER AND POSITION TABLES

fields from Employer table → EmployerName, City, State/Prov
fields from Position table → Openings, PositionTitle, StartDate, EndDate

EmployerName	City	State/Prov	Openings	PositionTitle	StartDate	EndDate
BeanTown Tours	Boston	MA	1	Tour Guide	05/31	10/01
Boston Harbor Excursions	Boston	MA	1	Reservationist	06/01	10/01
BaySide Inn & Country Club	Brewster	MA	2	Waiter/Waitress	05/01	10/01
BaySide Inn & Country Club	Brewster	MA	1	Pro Shop Clerk	05/01	11/01
Seaview Restaurant	Falmouth	MA	2	Waiter/Waitress	06/30	10/01
Claire's Cottages	Orleans	MA	3	Housekeeping	05/01	10/15
The Inn at Plum Hill	Vineyard Haven	MA	3	Housekeeping	05/15	10/15
Capt'n John's Seafood	Orleans	MA	2	Kitchen Help	07/01	09/01
The Adele Bannister House	Newport	RI	1	Kitchen Help	06/01	10/01
The Adele Bannister House	Newport	RI	1	Host/Hostess	05/01	09/01
Blue Hill Inn & Country Club	Chatham	MA	1	Lifeguard	06/15	09/15
The Clipper Ship Inn	Rockport	MA	2	Kitchen Help	07/01	10/01
The Clipper Ship Inn	Rockport	MA	2	Housekeeping	06/15	10/01
The Clipper Ship Inn	Rockport	MA	3	Waiter/Waitress	06/01	10/15

Only the seven selected fields from the Employer and Position tables appear in the datasheet. The records are displayed in order according to the values in the primary key field, EmployerID, even though this field is not included in the query datasheet.

Matt plans on frequently tracking the data retrieved by the query, so he asks you to save the query as "Employer Positions."

8. Click the **Save** button on the Query Datasheet toolbar. The Save As dialog box opens.

9. Type **Employer Positions** in the Query Name text box, and then press the **Enter** key. Access saves the query with the specified name and displays the name in the title bar.

Matt decides he wants the records displayed in alphabetical order by employer name. Because the query displays data in order by the field value of EmployerID, which is the primary key for the Employer table, you need to sort the records by EmployerName to display the data in the order Matt wants.

Sorting Data in a Query

Sorting is the process of rearranging records in a specified order or sequence. Sometimes you might need to sort data before displaying or printing it to meet a specific request. For example, Matt might want to review position information arranged by the StartDate field because he needs to know which positions are available earliest in the year. On the other hand, Elsa might want to view position information arranged by the Openings field for each employer, because she monitors employer activity for NSJI.

When you sort data in a query, you do not change the sequence of the records in the underlying tables. Only the records in the query datasheet are rearranged according to your specifications.

To sort records, you must select the **sort key**, which is the field used to determine the order of records in the datasheet. In this case, Matt wants the data sorted by the employer name, so you need to specify the EmployerName field as the sort key. Sort keys can be text, number, date/time, currency, AutoNumber, yes/no, or Lookup Wizard fields, but not memo, OLE object, or hyperlink fields. You sort records in either ascending (increasing) or descending (decreasing) order. Figure 3-11 shows the results of each type of sort for different data types.

Figure 3-11 SORTING RESULTS FOR DIFFERENT DATA TYPES

DATA TYPE	ASCENDING SORT RESULTS	DESCENDING SORT RESULTS
Text	A to Z	Z to A
Number	lowest to highest numeric value	highest to lowest numeric value
Date/Time	oldest to most recent date	most recent to oldest date
Currency	lowest to highest numeric value	highest to lowest numeric value
AutoNumber	lowest to highest numeric value	highest to lowest numeric value
Yes/No	yes (check mark in check box) then no values	no then yes values

Access provides several methods for sorting data in a table or query datasheet and in a form. One method, clicking a toolbar sort button, lets you sort the displayed records quickly.

Using a Toolbar Button to Sort Data

The **Sort Ascending** and **Sort Descending** buttons on the toolbar allow you to sort records immediately, based on the values in the selected field. First you select the column on which you want to base the sort, and then you click the appropriate sort button on the toolbar to rearrange the records in either ascending or descending order. Unless you save the datasheet or form after you've sorted the records, the rearrangement of records is temporary.

Recall that in Tutorial 1 you used the Sort Ascending button to sort query results by the State/Prov field. You'll use this same button to sort the Employer Positions query results by the EmployerName field.

To sort the records using a toolbar sort button:

1. Click any visible EmployerName field value to establish the field as the current field (if necessary).

2. Click the **Sort Ascending** button on the Query Datasheet toolbar. The records are rearranged in ascending order by employer name. See Figure 3-12.

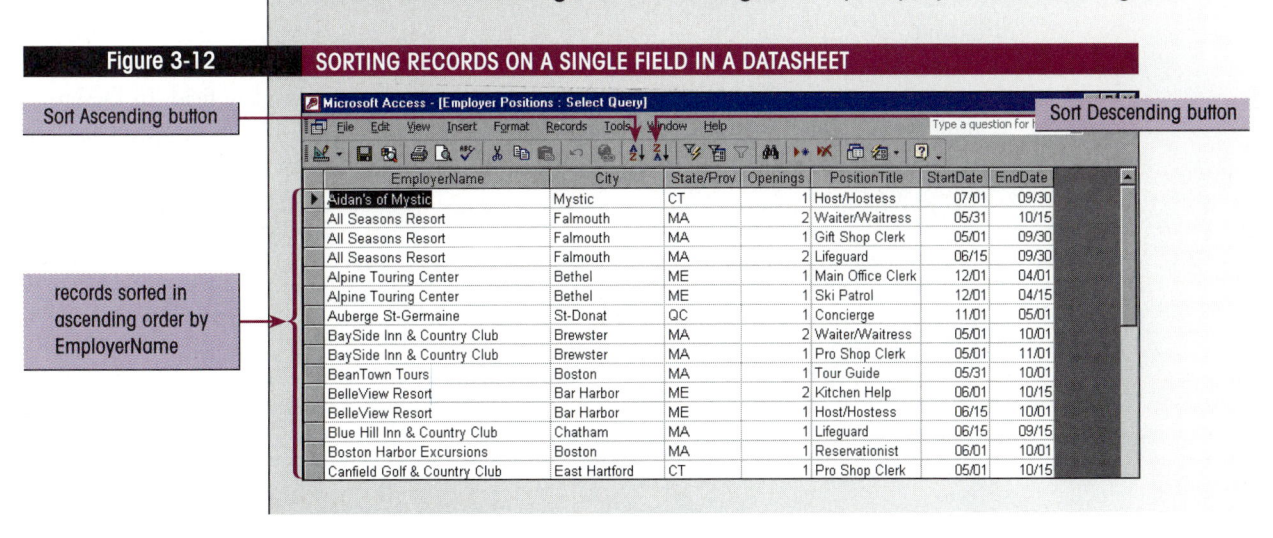

Figure 3-12 SORTING RECORDS ON A SINGLE FIELD IN A DATASHEET

Sort Ascending button

Sort Descending button

records sorted in ascending order by EmployerName

EmployerName	City	State/Prov	Openings	PositionTitle	StartDate	EndDate
Aidan's of Mystic	Mystic	CT	1	Host/Hostess	07/01	09/30
All Seasons Resort	Falmouth	MA	2	Waiter/Waitress	05/31	10/15
All Seasons Resort	Falmouth	MA	1	Gift Shop Clerk	05/01	09/30
All Seasons Resort	Falmouth	MA	2	Lifeguard	06/15	09/30
Alpine Touring Center	Bethel	ME	1	Main Office Clerk	12/01	04/01
Alpine Touring Center	Bethel	ME	1	Ski Patrol	12/01	04/15
Auberge St-Germaine	St-Donat	QC	1	Concierge	11/01	05/01
BaySide Inn & Country Club	Brewster	MA	2	Waiter/Waitress	05/01	10/01
BaySide Inn & Country Club	Brewster	MA	1	Pro Shop Clerk	05/01	11/01
BeanTown Tours	Boston	MA	1	Tour Guide	05/31	10/01
BelleView Resort	Bar Harbor	ME	2	Kitchen Help	06/01	10/15
BelleView Resort	Bar Harbor	ME	1	Host/Hostess	06/15	10/01
Blue Hill Inn & Country Club	Chatham	MA	1	Lifeguard	06/15	09/15
Boston Harbor Excursions	Boston	MA	1	Reservationist	06/01	10/01
Canfield Golf & Country Club	East Hartford	CT	1	Pro Shop Clerk	05/01	10/15

After viewing the query results, Matt decides that he'd prefer to see the records arranged by the value in the PositionTitle field, so that he can identify the types of positions he needs to fill. He also wants to display the records in descending order according to the value of the Openings field, so that he can easily see how many openings there are for each position. To do this you need to sort using two fields.

Sorting Multiple Fields in Design View

Sort keys can be unique or nonunique. A sort key is **unique** if the value of the sort key field for each record is different. The EmployerID field in the Employer table is an example of a unique sort key because each employer record has a different value in this field. A sort key is **nonunique** if more than one record can have the same value for the sort key field. For example, the PositionTitle field in the Position table is a nonunique sort key because more than one record can have the same PositionTitle value.

When the sort key is nonunique, records with the same sort key value are grouped together, but they are not in a specific order within the group. To arrange these grouped records in a specific order, you can specify a **secondary sort key**, which is a second sort key field. The first sort key field is called the **primary sort key**. Note that the primary sort key is *not* the same as a table's primary key field. A table has at most one primary key, which must be unique, whereas any field in a table can serve as a primary sort key.

Access lets you select up to 10 different sort keys. When you use the toolbar sort buttons, the sort key fields must be in adjacent columns in the datasheet. You highlight the adjacent columns, and Access sorts first by the first column and then by each other highlighted column in order from left to right.

Matt wants the records sorted first by the PositionTitle field and then by the Openings field. The two fields are adjacent, but not in the correct left-to-right order, so you cannot use the toolbar buttons to sort them. You could move the Openings field to the right of the PositionTitle field in the query datasheet. However, you can specify only one type of sort—either ascending or descending—for selected columns in the query datasheet. This is not what Matt wants; he wants the PositionTitle field values to be sorted in ascending alphabetical order and the Openings field values to be sorted in descending order.

In this case, you need to specify the sort keys for the query in Design view. Any time you want to sort on multiple fields that are nonadjacent or in the wrong order, but do not want to rearrange the columns in the query datasheet to accomplish the sort, you must specify the sort keys in Design view.

In the Query window in Design view, Access first uses the sort key that is leftmost in the design grid. Therefore, you must arrange the fields you want to sort from left to right in the design grid, with the primary sort key being the leftmost sort key field. In Design view, multiple sort fields do not have to be adjacent to each other, as they do in Datasheet view; however, they must be in the correct left-to-right order.

> **REFERENCE WINDOW**   RW
>
> **Sorting a Query Datasheet**
> - In the query datasheet, select the column or adjacent columns on which you want to sort.
> - Click the Sort Ascending button or the Sort Descending button on the Query Datasheet toolbar.
>
> or
>
> - In Design view, position the fields serving as sort keys from left (primary sort key) to right, and then select the sort order for each sort key.

To achieve the results Matt wants, you need to switch to Design view, move the Openings field to the right of the EndDate field, and then specify the sort order for the two fields.

To select the two sort keys in Design view:

1. Click the **View** button for Design view on the Query Datasheet toolbar to open the query in Design view.

   First, you'll move the Openings field to the right of the EndDate field. Remember, in Design view, the sort fields do not have to be adjacent, and non-sort key fields can appear between sort key fields. So, you will move the Openings field to the end of the query design, following the EndDate field.

2. If necessary, click the right arrow in the design grid's horizontal scroll bar a few times to scroll to the right so that both the Openings and EndDate fields are completely visible.

3. Position the pointer in the Openings field selector until the pointer changes to a ↓ shape, and then click to select the field. See Figure 3-13.

Figure 3-13   **SELECTED OPENINGS FIELD**

Field:	State/Prov	Openings	PositionTitle	StartDate	EndDate	
Table:	Employer	Position	Position	Position	Position	
Sort:						
Show:	☑	☑	☑	☑	☑	☐
Criteria:						
or:						

entire column is selected

Openings field selector

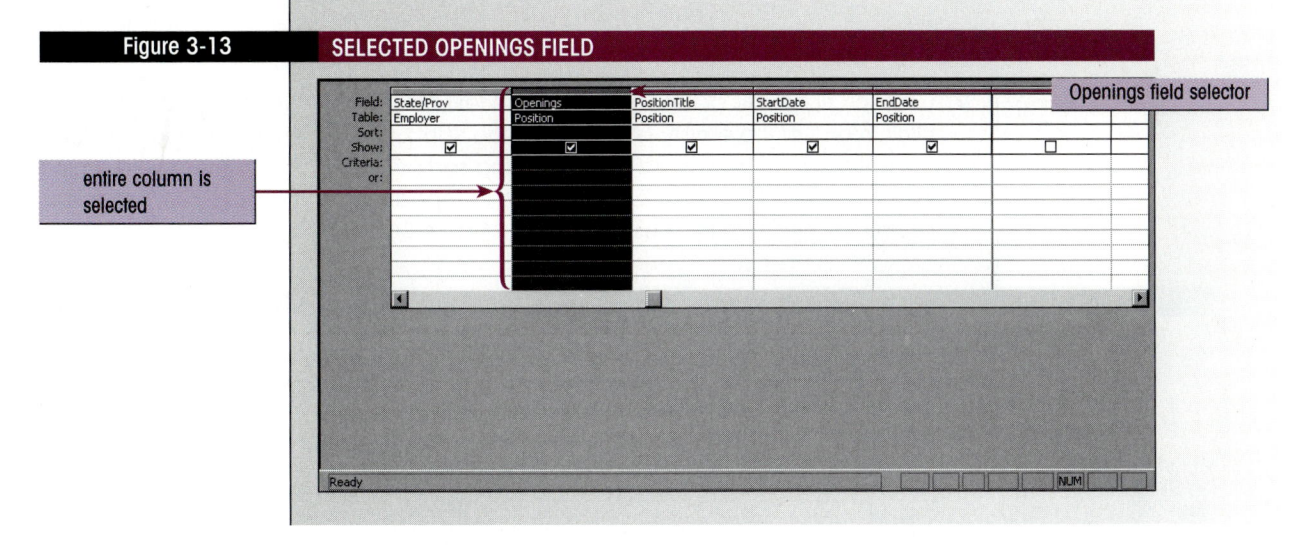

4. Position the pointer in the Openings field selector, and then click and drag the pointer to the right until the vertical line on the right of the EndDate field is highlighted. See Figure 3-14.

Figure 3-14 DRAGGING THE FIELD IN THE DESIGN GRID

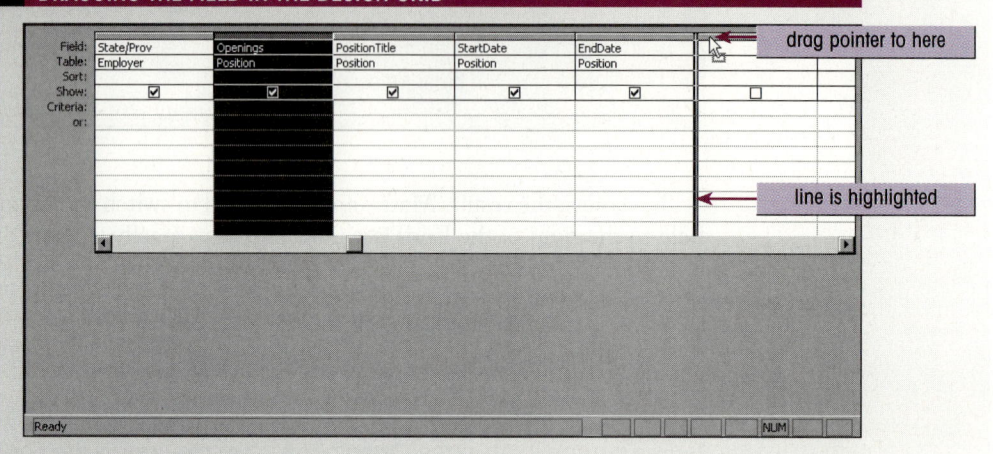

drag pointer to here

line is highlighted

5. Release the mouse button. The Openings field moves to the right of the EndDate field.

The fields are now in the correct order for the sort. Next, you need to specify an ascending sort order for the PositionTitle field and a descending sort order for the Openings field.

6. Click the right side of the **PositionTitle Sort** text box to display the list arrow and the sort options, and then click **Ascending**. You've selected an ascending sort order for the PositionTitle field, which will be the primary sort key. The PositionTitle field is a text field, and an ascending sort order will display the field values in alphabetical order.

7. Click the right side of the **Openings Sort** text box, click **Descending**, and then click in one of the empty text boxes to the right of the Openings field to deselect the setting. You've selected a descending sort order for the Openings field, which will be the secondary sort key, because it appears to the right of the primary sort key (PositionTitle) in the design grid. See Figure 3-15.

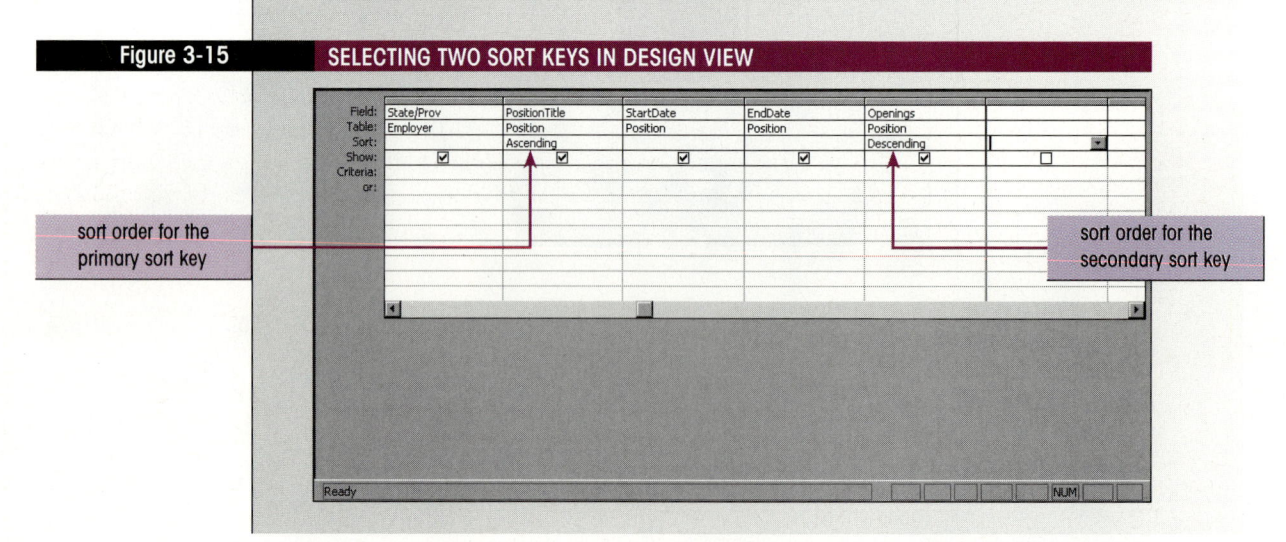

Figure 3-15 SELECTING TWO SORT KEYS IN DESIGN VIEW

sort order for the primary sort key

sort order for the secondary sort key

You have finished your query changes, so now you can run the query and then save the modified query with the same query name.

8. Click the **Run** button on the Query Design toolbar. Access runs the query and displays the query datasheet. The records appear in ascending order, based on the values of the PositionTitle field. Within groups of records with the same PositionTitle field value, the records appear in descending order by the values of the Openings field. See Figure 3-16.

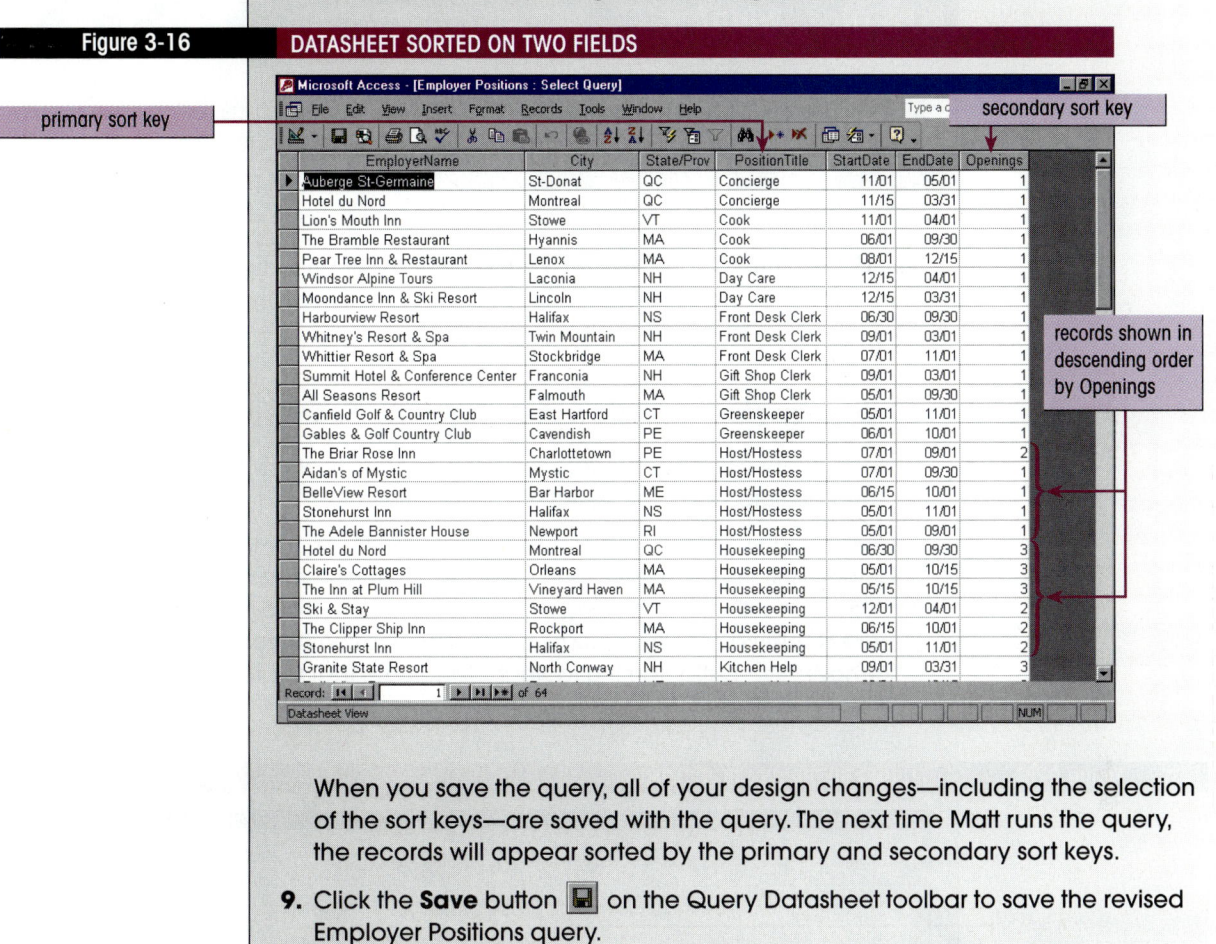

Figure 3-16   DATASHEET SORTED ON TWO FIELDS

primary sort key
secondary sort key
records shown in descending order by Openings

EmployerName	City	State/Prov	PositionTitle	StartDate	EndDate	Openings
Auberge St-Germaine	St-Donat	QC	Concierge	11/01	05/01	1
Hotel du Nord	Montreal	QC	Concierge	11/15	03/31	1
Lion's Mouth Inn	Stowe	VT	Cook	11/01	04/01	1
The Bramble Restaurant	Hyannis	MA	Cook	06/01	09/30	1
Pear Tree Inn & Restaurant	Lenox	MA	Cook	08/01	12/15	1
Windsor Alpine Tours	Laconia	NH	Day Care	12/15	04/01	1
Moondance Inn & Ski Resort	Lincoln	NH	Day Care	12/15	03/31	1
Harbourview Resort	Halifax	NS	Front Desk Clerk	06/30	09/30	1
Whitney's Resort & Spa	Twin Mountain	NH	Front Desk Clerk	09/01	03/01	1
Whittier Resort & Spa	Stockbridge	MA	Front Desk Clerk	07/01	11/01	1
Summit Hotel & Conference Center	Franconia	NH	Gift Shop Clerk	09/01	03/01	1
All Seasons Resort	Falmouth	MA	Gift Shop Clerk	05/01	09/30	1
Canfield Golf & Country Club	East Hartford	CT	Greenskeeper	05/01	11/01	1
Gables & Golf Country Club	Cavendish	PE	Greenskeeper	06/01	10/01	1
The Briar Rose Inn	Charlottetown	PE	Host/Hostess	07/01	09/01	2
Aidan's of Mystic	Mystic	CT	Host/Hostess	07/01	09/30	1
BelleView Resort	Bar Harbor	ME	Host/Hostess	06/15	10/01	1
Stonehurst Inn	Halifax	NS	Host/Hostess	05/01	11/01	1
The Adele Bannister House	Newport	RI	Host/Hostess	05/01	09/01	1
Hotel du Nord	Montreal	QC	Housekeeping	06/30	09/30	3
Claire's Cottages	Orleans	MA	Housekeeping	05/01	10/15	3
The Inn at Plum Hill	Vineyard Haven	MA	Housekeeping	05/15	10/15	3
Ski & Stay	Stowe	VT	Housekeeping	12/01	04/01	2
The Clipper Ship Inn	Rockport	MA	Housekeeping	06/15	10/01	2
Stonehurst Inn	Halifax	NS	Housekeeping	05/01	11/01	2
Granite State Resort	North Conway	NH	Kitchen Help	09/01	03/31	3

When you save the query, all of your design changes—including the selection of the sort keys—are saved with the query. The next time Matt runs the query, the records will appear sorted by the primary and secondary sort keys.

9. Click the **Save** button on the Query Datasheet toolbar to save the revised Employer Positions query.

Matt wants to concentrate on the positions in the datasheet with a start date sometime in May, to see how many recruits he will need to fill these positions. Selecting only the records with a StartDate field value in May is a temporary change that Matt wants in the datasheet, so you do not need to switch to Design view and change the query. Instead, you can apply a filter.

Filtering Data

A **filter** is a set of restrictions you place on the records in an open datasheet or form to *temporarily* isolate a subset of the records. A filter lets you view different subsets of displayed records so that you can focus on only the data you need. Unless you save a query or form with a filter applied, an applied filter is not available the next time you run the query or open the form.

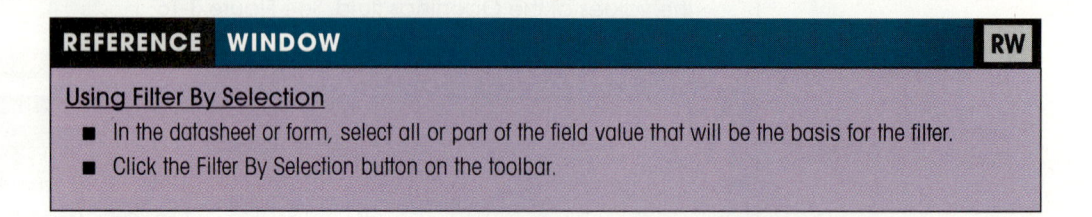

The simplest technique for filtering records is Filter By Selection. **Filter By Selection** lets you select all or part of a field value in a datasheet or form, and then display only those records that contain the selected value in the field. Another technique for filtering records is to use **Filter By Form**, which changes your datasheet to display empty fields. Then you can select a value from the list arrow that appears when you click any blank field to apply a filter that selects only those records containing that value.

REFERENCE WINDOW

Using Filter By Selection
- In the datasheet or form, select all or part of the field value that will be the basis for the filter.
- Click the Filter By Selection button on the toolbar.

For Matt's request, you need to select just the beginning digits "05" in the StartDate field, to view all the records with a May start date, and then use Filter By Selection to display only those query records with this same partial value.

To display the records using Filter By Selection:

1. In the query datasheet, locate the first occurrence of a May date in the StartDate field, and then select **05** in that field value.

2. Click the **Filter By Selection** button on the Query Datasheet toolbar. Access displays the filtered results. Only the 17 query records that have a StartDate field value with the beginning digits "05" appear in the datasheet. The status bar's display (FLTR), the area next to the navigation buttons, and the selected Remove Filter button on the toolbar all indicate that the records have been filtered. See Figure 3-17.

Figure 3-17   **USING FILTER BY SELECTION**

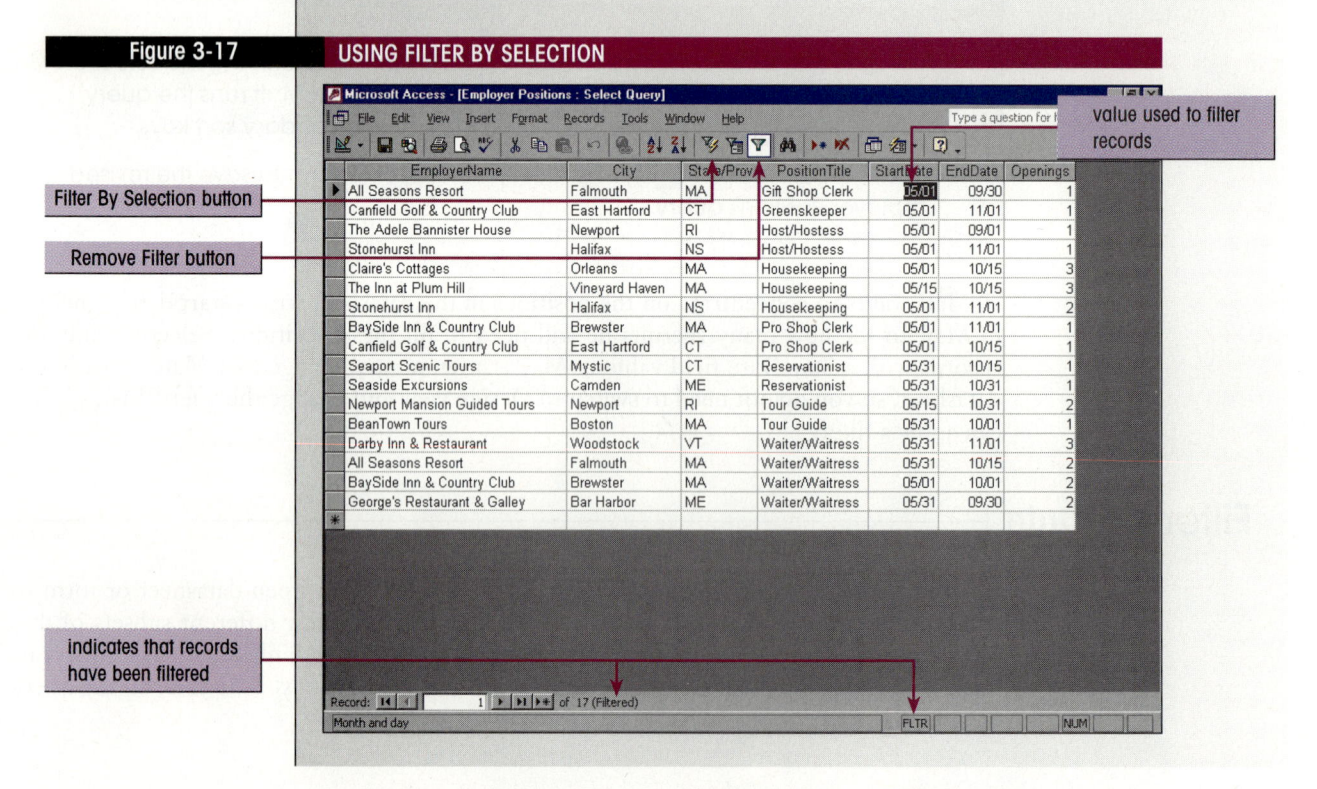

TUTORIAL 3 QUERYING A DATABASE   AC 3.21   ACCESS

> **TROUBLE?** If you are unable to select only the digits "05" in the StartDate field because the entire field value (including a four-digit year) is displayed when you click in the field, your Windows date settings might be affecting the display of the field values. In this case, you can either read through the remaining steps on this page without completing them, or ask your instructor for assistance.
>
> Next, Matt wants to view only those records with a StartDate value of 05/01, because he needs to fill those positions before the other May positions. So, you need to filter by the complete field value of 05/01.
>
> 3. Click in any StartDate field value of **05/01**, and then click . The filtered display now shows only the 9 records with a value of 05/01 in the StartDate field.
>
>   Now you can redisplay all the query records by clicking the Remove Filter button; this button works as a toggle to switch between the filtered and nonfiltered displays.
>
> 4. Click the **Remove Filter** button on the Query Datasheet toolbar. Access redisplays all the records in the query datasheet.
>
> 5. Click the **Save** button on the Query Datasheet toolbar, and then click the **Close Window** button on the menu bar to save and close the query and return to the Database window.
>
> 6. Click the **Restore Window** button on the menu bar to return the Database window to its original size.

The queries you've created will help NSJI employees retrieve just the information they want to view. In the next session, you'll continue to create queries to meet their information needs.

Session 3.1 QUICK CHECK

1. What is a select query?
2. Describe the field list and the design grid in the Query window in Design view.
3. How are a table datasheet and a query datasheet similar? How are they different?
4. The _____ is the "one" table in a one-to-many relationship, and the _____ is the "many" table in the relationship.
5. _____ is a set of rules that Access enforces to maintain consistency between related tables when you update data in a database.
6. For a date/time field, how do the records appear when sorted in ascending order?
7. When must you define multiple sort keys in Design view instead of in the query datasheet?
8. A(n) _____ is a set of restrictions you place on the records in an open datasheet or form to isolate a subset of records temporarily.

SESSION 3.2

In this session, you will specify an exact match condition in a query, change a datasheet's appearance, use a comparison operator to match a range of values, use the And and Or logical operators to define multiple selection criteria for queries, use multiple undo and redo, and perform calculations in queries.

Defining Record Selection Criteria for Queries

Matt wants to display employer and position information for all positions with a start date of 07/01, so that he can plan his recruitment efforts accordingly. For this request, you could create a query to select the correct fields and all records in the Employer and Position tables, select a StartDate field value of 07/01 in the query datasheet, and then click the Filter By Selection button to filter the query results to display only those positions starting on July 1. However, a faster way of displaying the data Matt needs is to create a query that displays the selected fields and only those records in the Employer and Position tables that satisfy a condition.

Just as you can display selected fields from a database in a query datasheet, you can display selected records. To tell Access which records you want to select, you must specify a condition as part of the query. A **condition** is a criterion, or rule, that determines which records are selected. To define a condition for a field, you place the condition in the field's Criteria text box in the design grid.

A condition usually consists of an operator, often a comparison operator, and a value. A **comparison operator** asks Access to compare the value in a database field to the condition value and to select all the records for which the relationship is true. For example, the condition >15.00 for the Wage field selects all records in the Position table having Wage field values greater than 15.00. Figure 3-18 shows the Access comparison operators.

Figure 3-18   ACCESS COMPARISON OPERATORS

OPERATOR	MEANING	EXAMPLE
=	equal to (optional; default operator)	="Hall"
<	less than	<#1/1/99#
<=	less than or equal to	<=100
>	greater than	>"C400"
>=	greater than or equal to	>=18.75
<>	not equal to	<>"Hall"
Between ... And...	between two values (inclusive)	Between 50 And 325
In ( )	in a list of values	In ("Hall", "Seeger")
Like	matches a pattern that includes wildcards	Like "706*"

Specifying an Exact Match

For Matt's request, you need to create a query that will display only those records in the Position table with the value 07/01 in the StartDate field. This type of condition is called an **exact match** because the value in the specified field must match the condition exactly in order for the record to be included in the query results. You'll use the Simple Query Wizard to create the query, and then you'll specify the exact match condition.

To create the query using the Simple Query Wizard:

1. If you took a break after the previous session, make sure that Access is running, the Northeast database is open, and the Queries object is selected in the Database window.

2. Double-click **Create query by using wizard**. Access opens the first Simple Query Wizard dialog box, in which you select the tables (or queries) and fields for the query.

3. Click the **Tables/Queries** list arrow, and then click **Table: Position**. The fields in the Position table appear in the Available Fields list box. Except for the PositionID and EmployerID fields, you will include all fields from the Position table in the query.

4. Click the >> button. All the fields from the Available Fields list box move to the Selected Fields list box.

5. Scroll up and click **PositionID** in the Selected Fields list box, click the < button to move the PositionID field back to the Available Fields list box, click **EmployerID** in the Selected Fields list box, and then click the < button to move the EmployerID field back to the Available Fields list box.

   Matt also wants certain information from the Employer table included in the query results. Because he wants the fields from the Employer table to appear in the query datasheet to the right of the fields from the Position table fields, you need to click the last field in the Selected Fields list box so that the new Employer fields will be inserted below it in the list.

6. Click **Openings** in the Selected Fields list box.

7. Click the **Tables/Queries** list arrow, and then click **Table: Employer**. The fields in the Employer table now appear in the Available Fields list box. Notice that the fields you selected from the Position table remain in the Selected Fields list box.

8. Click **EmployerName** in the Available Fields list box, and then click the > button to move EmployerName to the Selected Fields list box, below the Openings field.

9. Repeat Step 8 to move the **State/Prov**, **ContactFirstName**, **ContactLastName**, and **Phone** fields into the Selected Fields list box. (Note that you can also double-click a field to move it from the Available Fields list box to the Selected Fields list box.)

10. Click the **Next** button to open the second Simple Query Wizard dialog box, in which you choose whether the query will display records from the selected tables or a summary of those records. Summary options show calculations such as average, minimum, maximum, and so on. Matt wants to view the details for the records, not a summary.

11. Make sure the **Detail (shows every field of every record)** option button is selected, and then click the **Next** button to open the last Simple Query Wizard dialog box, in which you choose a name for the query and complete the Wizard. You need to enter a condition for the query, so you'll want to modify the query's design.

12. Type **July 1 Positions**, click the **Modify the query design** option button, and then click the **Finish** button. Access saves the query as July 1 Positions and opens the query in Design view. See Figure 3-19.

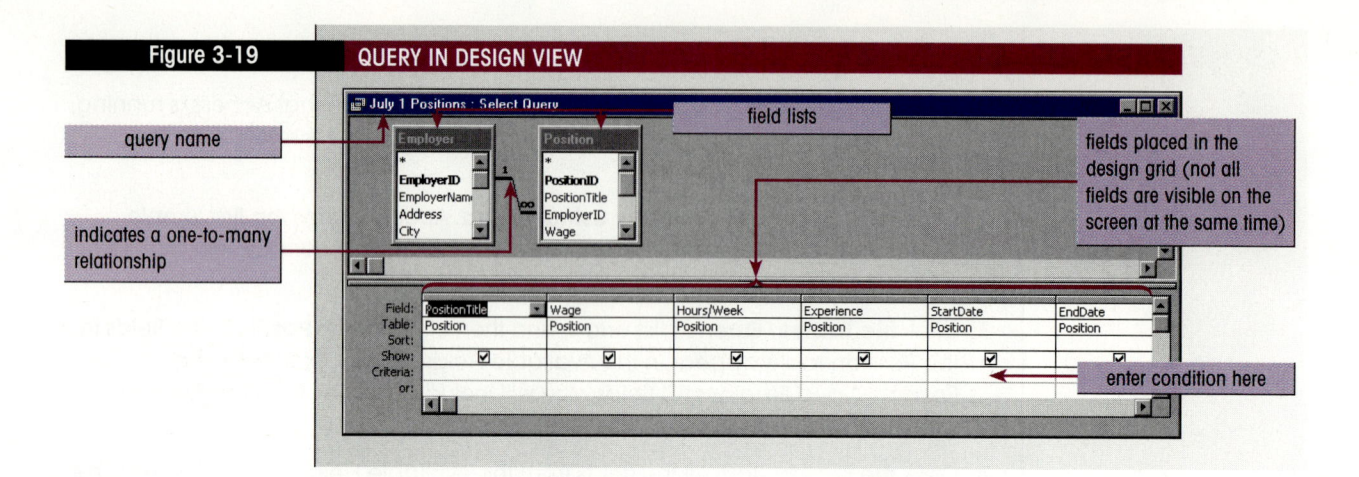

Figure 3-19 QUERY IN DESIGN VIEW

- query name
- field lists
- fields placed in the design grid (not all fields are visible on the screen at the same time)
- indicates a one-to-many relationship
- enter condition here

The field lists for the Employer and Position tables appear in the top portion of the window, and the join line indicating a one-to-many relationship connects the two tables. The selected fields appear in the design grid. Not all of the fields are visible in the grid; to see the other selected fields, you need to scroll to the right using the horizontal scroll bar.

To display the information Matt wants, you need to enter the condition for the StartDate field in its Criteria text box. Matt wants to display only those records with a start date of 07/01.

To enter the exact match condition, and then run the query:

1. Click the **StartDate Criteria** text box, type **7/01**, and then press the **Enter** key. The condition changes to #7/01/2003#.

   TROUBLE? If your date is displayed with a two-digit year, or if it shows a different year, don't worry. You can customize Windows to display different date formats.

   Access automatically placed number signs (#) before and after the condition. You must place date and time values inside number signs when using these values as selection criteria. If you omit the number signs, however, Access will include them automatically.

2. Click the **Run** button on the Query Design toolbar. Access runs the query and displays the selected field values for only those records with a StartDate field value of 07/01. A total of 9 records are selected and displayed in the datasheet. See Figure 3-20.

   TROUBLE? If your query does not produce the results shown in Figure 3-20, you probably need to specify the year "01" as part of the StartDate criteria. To do so, return to the query in Design view, enter the criteria "7/01/01" for the StartDate, and then repeat Step 2.

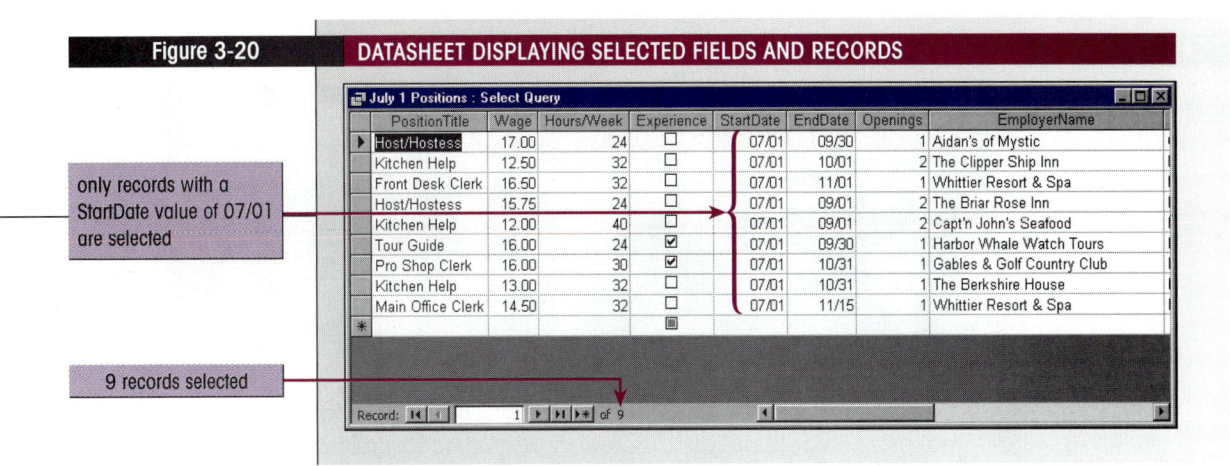

Figure 3-20   DATASHEET DISPLAYING SELECTED FIELDS AND RECORDS

only records with a StartDate value of 07/01 are selected

9 records selected

PositionTitle	Wage	Hours/Week	Experience	StartDate	EndDate	Openings	EmployerName
Host/Hostess	17.00	24	☐	07/01	09/30	1	Aidan's of Mystic
Kitchen Help	12.50	32	☐	07/01	10/01	2	The Clipper Ship Inn
Front Desk Clerk	16.50	32	☐	07/01	11/01	1	Whittier Resort & Spa
Host/Hostess	15.75	24	☐	07/01	09/01	2	The Briar Rose Inn
Kitchen Help	12.00	40	☐	07/01	09/01	2	Capt'n John's Seafood
Tour Guide	16.00	24	☑	07/01	09/30	1	Harbor Whale Watch Tours
Pro Shop Clerk	16.00	30	☑	07/01	10/31	1	Gables & Golf Country Club
Kitchen Help	13.00	32	☐	07/01	10/31	1	The Berkshire House
Main Office Clerk	14.50	32	☐	07/01	11/15	1	Whittier Resort & Spa

Matt would like to see more fields and records on the screen at one time. He asks you to maximize the datasheet, change the datasheet's font size, and resize all the columns to their best fit.

Changing a Datasheet's Appearance

You can change the characteristics of a datasheet, including the font type and size of text in the datasheet, to improve its appearance or readability. As you learned in Tutorial 2, you can also resize the datasheet columns to view more columns on the screen at the same time.

You'll maximize the datasheet, change the font size from the default 10 points to 8, and then resize the datasheet columns.

To change the font size and resize columns in the datasheet:

1. Click the **Maximize** button on the Query window title bar.

2. Click **Format** on the menu bar, and then click **Font** to open the Font dialog box.

3. Scroll the Size list box, click **8**, and then click the **OK** button. The font size for the entire datasheet changes to 8.

   Next you need to resize the columns to their best fit, so that each column is just wide enough to fit the longest value in the column. Instead of resizing each column individually, as you did in Tutorial 2, you'll select all the columns and resize them at the same time.

4. Position the pointer in the PositionTitle field selector. When the pointer changes to a ↓ shape, click to select the entire column.

5. Click the right arrow on the horizontal scroll bar until the Phone field is fully visible, and then position the pointer in the Phone field selector until the pointer changes to a ↓ shape.

6. Press and hold the **Shift** key, and then click the mouse button. All the columns are selected. Now you can resize all of them at once.

7. Position the pointer at the right edge of the Phone field selector until the pointer changes to a ↔ shape. See Figure 3-21.

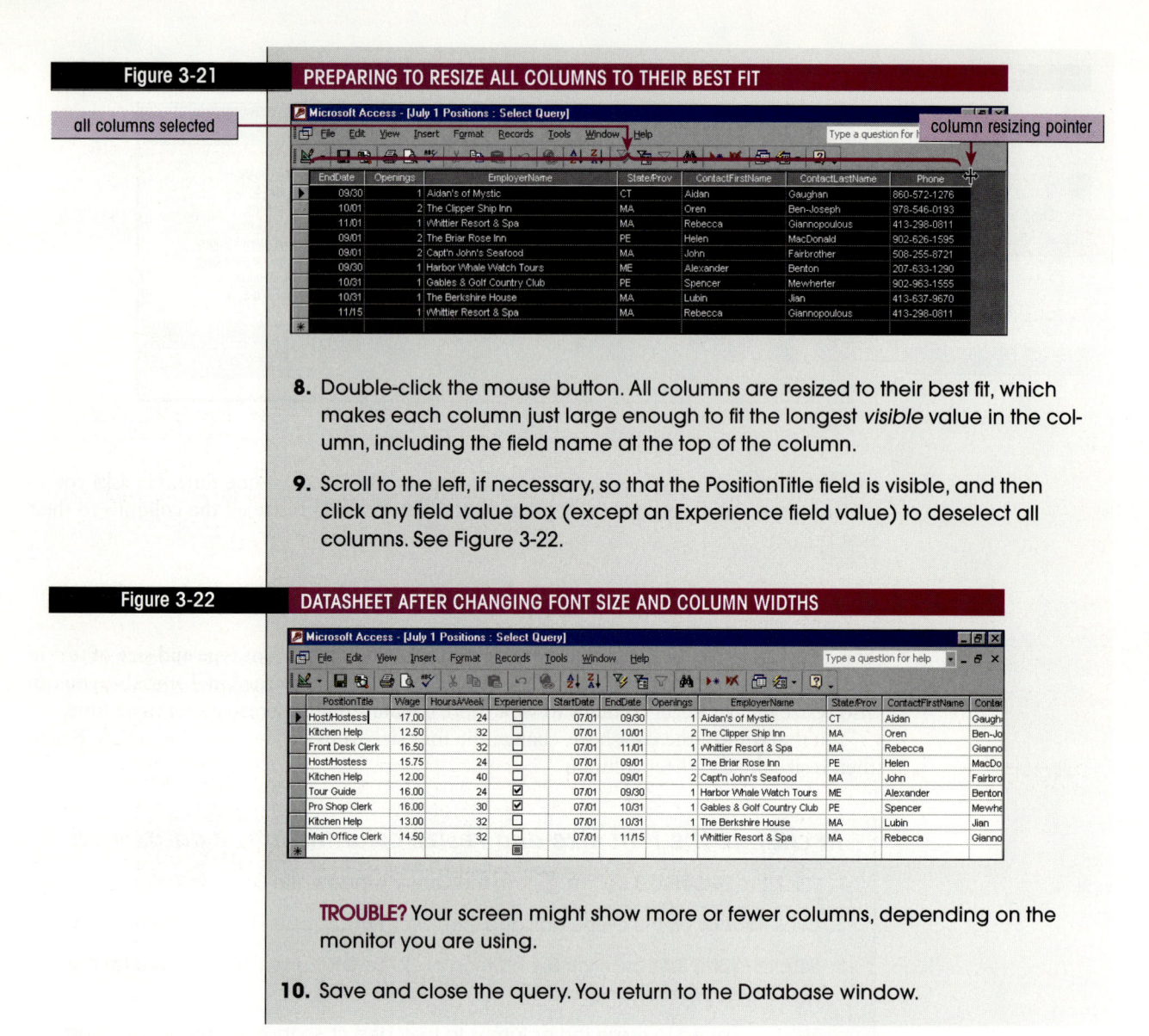

Figure 3-21 — PREPARING TO RESIZE ALL COLUMNS TO THEIR BEST FIT

all columns selected

column resizing pointer

8. Double-click the mouse button. All columns are resized to their best fit, which makes each column just large enough to fit the longest *visible* value in the column, including the field name at the top of the column.

9. Scroll to the left, if necessary, so that the PositionTitle field is visible, and then click any field value box (except an Experience field value) to deselect all columns. See Figure 3-22.

Figure 3-22 — DATASHEET AFTER CHANGING FONT SIZE AND COLUMN WIDTHS

TROUBLE? Your screen might show more or fewer columns, depending on the monitor you are using.

10. Save and close the query. You return to the Database window.

After viewing the query results, Matt decides that he would like to see the same fields, but only for those records whose Wage field value is equal to or greater than 17.00. He needs this information when he recruits students who will require a higher wage per hour for the available positions. To create the query needed to produce these results, you need to use a comparison operator to match a range of values—in this case, any Wage value greater than or equal to 17.00.

Using a Comparison Operator to Match a Range of Values

Once you create and save a query, you can click the Open button to run it again, or you can click the Design button to change its design. Because the design of the query you need to create next is similar to the July 1 Positions query, you will change its design, run the query to test it, and then save the query with a new name, which keeps the July 1 Positions query intact.

To change the July 1 Positions query design to create a new query:

1. Click the **July 1 Positions** query in the Database window (if necessary), and then click the **Design** button to open the July 1 Positions query in Design view.

2. Click the **Wage Criteria** text box, type **>=17**, and then press the **Tab** key three times. See Figure 3-23.

Figure 3-23   CHANGING A QUERY'S DESIGN TO CREATE A NEW QUERY

Field:	PositionTitle	Wage	Hours/Week	Experience	StartDate	EndDate	Openi
Table:	Position	Position	Position	Position	Position	Position	Positio
Sort:							
Show:	☑	☑	☑	☑	☑	☑	
Criteria:		>=17			#7/1/2003#		
or:							

new condition → (points to >=17)
condition to delete → (points to #7/1/2003#)

Matt's new condition specifies that a record will be selected only if its Wage field value is 17.00 or higher. Before you run the query, you need to delete the condition for the StartDate field.

3. With the StartDate field condition highlighted, press the **Delete** key. Now there is no condition for the StartDate field.

4. Click the **Run** button ❗ on the Query Design toolbar. Access runs the query and displays the selected fields for only those records with a Wage field value greater than or equal to 17.00. A total of 19 records are selected. See Figure 3-24.

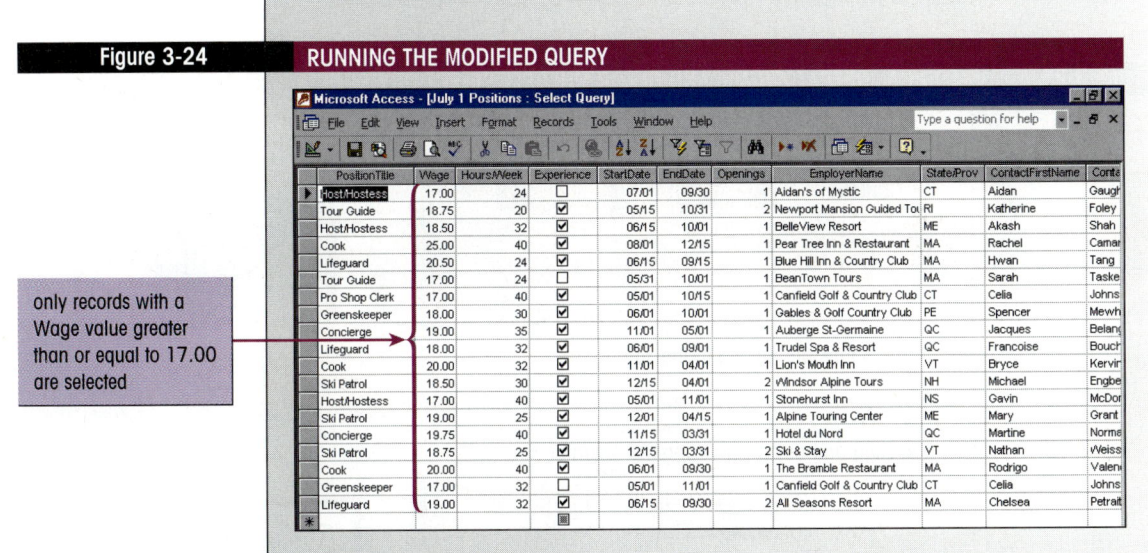

Figure 3-24   RUNNING THE MODIFIED QUERY

PositionTitle	Wage	Hours/Week	Experience	StartDate	EndDate	Openings	EmployerName	State/Prov	ContactFirstName	Cont
Host/Hostess	17.00	24	☐	07/01	09/30	1	Aidan's of Mystic	CT	Aidan	Gaugh
Tour Guide	18.75	20	☑	05/15	10/31	2	Newport Mansion Guided Tou	RI	Katherine	Foley
Host/Hostess	18.50	32	☑	06/15	10/01	1	BelleView Resort	ME	Akash	Shah
Cook	25.00	40	☑	08/01	12/15	1	Pear Tree Inn & Restaurant	MA	Rachel	Camar
Lifeguard	20.50	24	☑	06/15	09/15	1	Blue Hill Inn & Country Club	MA	Hwan	Tang
Tour Guide	17.00	24	☐	05/31	10/01	1	BeanTown Tours	MA	Sarah	Taske
Pro Shop Clerk	17.00	40	☑	05/01	10/15	1	Canfield Golf & Country Club	CT	Celia	Johns
Greenskeeper	18.00	30	☑	06/01	10/01	1	Gables & Golf Country Club	PE	Spencer	Mewh
Concierge	19.00	35	☑	11/01	05/01	1	Auberge St-Germaine	QC	Jacques	Belan
Lifeguard	18.00	32	☑	06/01	09/01	1	Trudel Spa & Resort	QC	Francoise	Bouch
Cook	20.00	32	☑	11/01	04/01	1	Lion's Mouth Inn	VT	Bryce	Kervin
Ski Patrol	18.50	30	☑	12/15	04/01	2	Windsor Alpine Tours	NH	Michael	Engbe
Host/Hostess	17.00	40	☑	05/01	11/01	1	Stonehurst Inn	NS	Gavin	McDor
Ski Patrol	19.00	25	☑	12/01	04/15	1	Alpine Touring Center	ME	Mary	Grant
Concierge	19.75	40	☑	11/15	03/31	1	Hotel du Nord	QC	Martine	Norme
Ski Patrol	18.75	25	☑	12/15	03/31	2	Ski & Stay	VT	Nathan	Weiss
Cook	20.00	40	☑	06/01	09/30	1	The Bramble Restaurant	MA	Rodrigo	Valen
Greenskeeper	17.00	32	☐	05/01	11/01	1	Canfield Golf & Country Club	CT	Celia	Johns
Lifeguard	19.00	32	☑	06/15	09/30	2	All Seasons Resort	MA	Chelsea	Petrat

only records with a Wage value greater than or equal to 17.00 are selected

So that Matt can display this information again, as necessary, you'll save the query as High Wage Amounts.

5. Click **File** on the menu bar, click the double-arrow at the bottom of the menu to display the full menu (if necessary), and then click **Save As** to open the Save As dialog box.

6. In the text box for the new query name, type **High Wage Amounts**. Notice that the As text box specifies that you are saving the data as a query.

> **7.** Click the **OK** button to save the query using the new name. The new query name appears in the title bar.
>
> **8.** Close the Query window and return to the Database window.

Elsa asks Matt for a list of the positions with a start date of 07/01 for only the employers in Prince Edward Island. She wants to increase NSJI's business activity throughout eastern Canada (Prince Edward Island in particular), especially in the latter half of the year. To produce this data, you need to create a query containing two conditions—one for the position's start date and another to specify only the employers in Prince Edward Island (PE).

Defining Multiple Selection Criteria for Queries

Multiple conditions require you to use **logical operators** to combine two or more conditions. When you want a record selected only if two or more conditions are met, you need to use the **And logical operator**. In this case, Elsa wants to see only those records with a StartDate field value of 07/01 *and* a State/Prov field value of PE. If you place conditions in separate fields in the *same* Criteria row of the design grid, all conditions in that row must be met in order for a record to be included in the query results. However, if you place conditions in *different* Criteria rows, a record will be selected if at least one of the conditions is met. If none of the conditions is met, Access does not select the record. When you place conditions in different Criteria rows, you are using the **Or logical operator**. Figure 3-25 illustrates the difference between the And and Or logical operators.

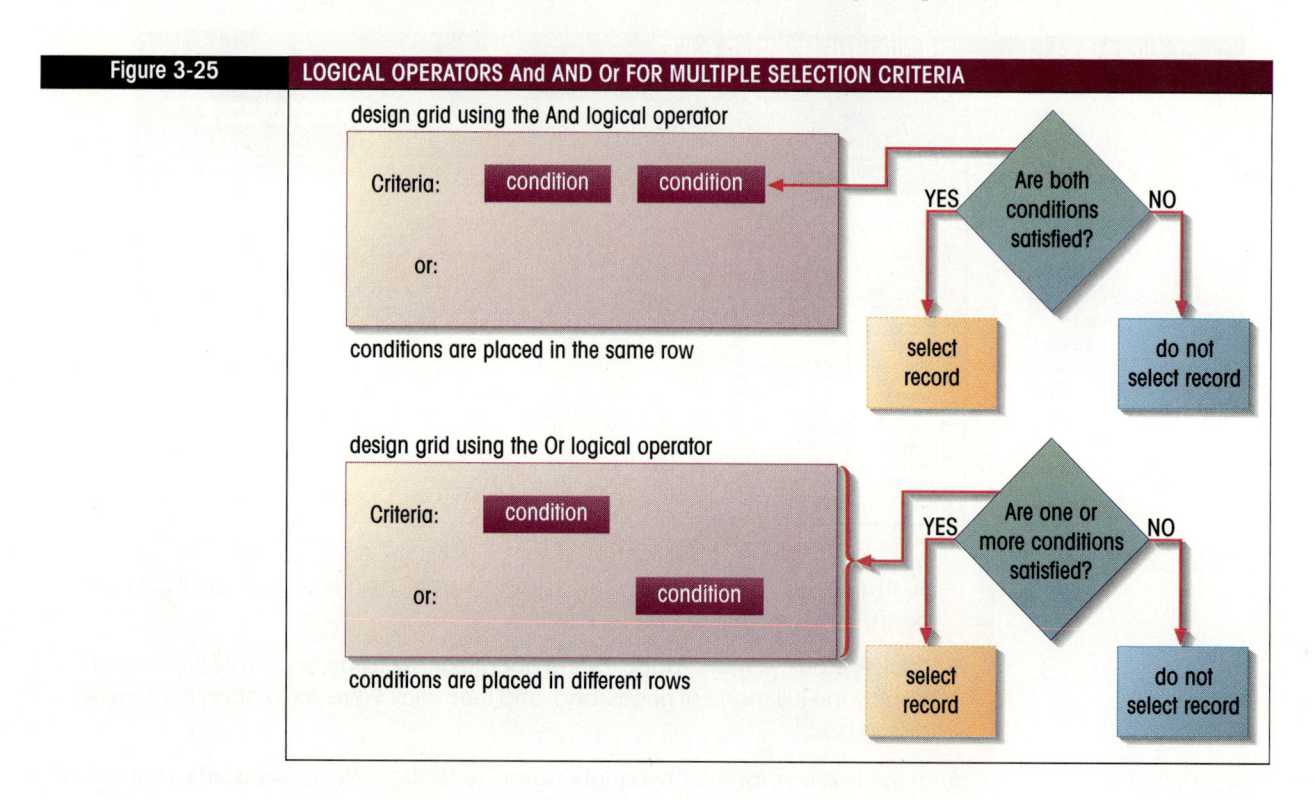

Figure 3-25   LOGICAL OPERATORS And AND Or FOR MULTIPLE SELECTION CRITERIA

The And Logical Operator

To create Elsa's query, you need to modify the existing July 1 Positions query to show only the records for employers located in Prince Edward Island and offering positions starting on 07/01. For the modified query, you must add a second condition in the same Criteria row. The existing condition for the StartDate field finds records for positions that start on July 1; the new condition "PE" in the State/Prov field will find records for employers in Prince Edward Island. Because the conditions appear in the same Criteria row, the query will select records only if both conditions are met.

After modifying the query, you'll save it and then rename it as "PE July 1 Positions," overwriting the July 1 Positions query, which Matt no longer needs.

To modify the July 1 Positions query and use the And logical operator:

1. With the Queries object selected in the Database window, click **July 1 Positions** (if necessary), and then click the **Design** button to open the query in Design view.

2. Scroll the design grid to the right, click the **State/Prov Criteria** text box, type **PE**, and then press the ↓ key. See Figure 3-26.

Figure 3-26 QUERY TO FIND POSITIONS IN PE THAT START ON 07/01

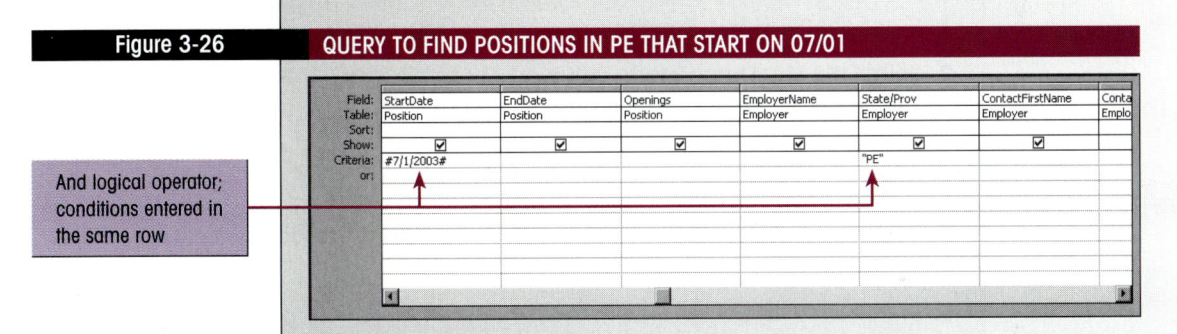

And logical operator; conditions entered in the same row

Notice that Access added quotation marks around the entry "PE"; you can type the quotation marks when you enter the condition, but if you forget to do so, Access will add them for you automatically.

The condition for the StartDate field is already entered, so you can run the query.

3. Run the query. Access displays in the datasheet only those records that meet both conditions: a StartDate field value of 07/01 and a State/Prov field value of PE. Two records are selected. See Figure 3-27.

Figure 3-27 RESULTS OF QUERY USING THE AND LOGICAL OPERATOR

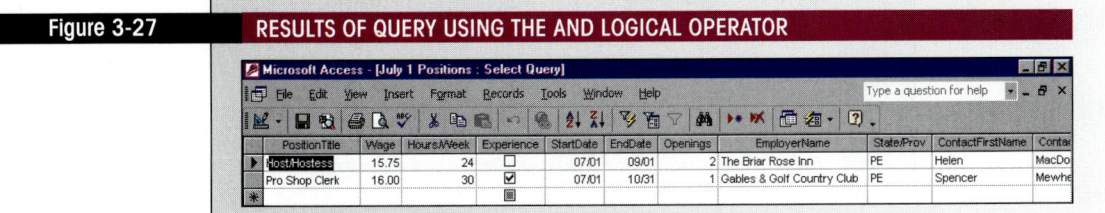

Now you can save the changes to the query and rename it.

4. Save and close the query. You return to the Database window.

5. Right-click **July 1 Positions** in the Queries list box, and then click **Rename** on the shortcut menu.

6. Click to position the insertion point to the left of the word "July," type **PE**, press the **spacebar**, and then press the **Enter** key. The query name is now PE July 1 Positions.

Using Multiple Undo and Redo

In previous versions of Access, you could not undo certain actions. Now Access allows you to undo and redo multiple actions when you are working in Design view for tables, queries, forms, reports, and so on. For example, when working in the Query window in Design view, if you specify multiple selection criteria for a query, you can use the multiple undo feature to remove the criteria—even after you run and save the query.

To see how this feature works, you will reopen the PE July 1 Positions query in Design view, delete the two criteria, and then reinsert them using multiple undo.

To modify the PE July 1 Positions query and use the multiple undo feature:

1. Open the **PE July 1 Positions** query in Design view.

2. Select the StartDate Criteria value, **#7/1/2003#**, and then press the **Delete** key. The StartDate Criteria text box is now empty.

3. Press the **Tab** key four times to move to and select **"PE"**, the State/Prov Criteria value, and then press the **Delete** key.

4. Run the query. Notice that the results display all records for the fields specified in the query design grid.

5. Switch back to Design view.

   Now you will use multiple undo to reverse the edits you made and reinsert the two conditions.

6. Click the **list arrow** for the Undo button on the Query Design toolbar. A menu appears listing the actions you can undo. See Figure 3-28.

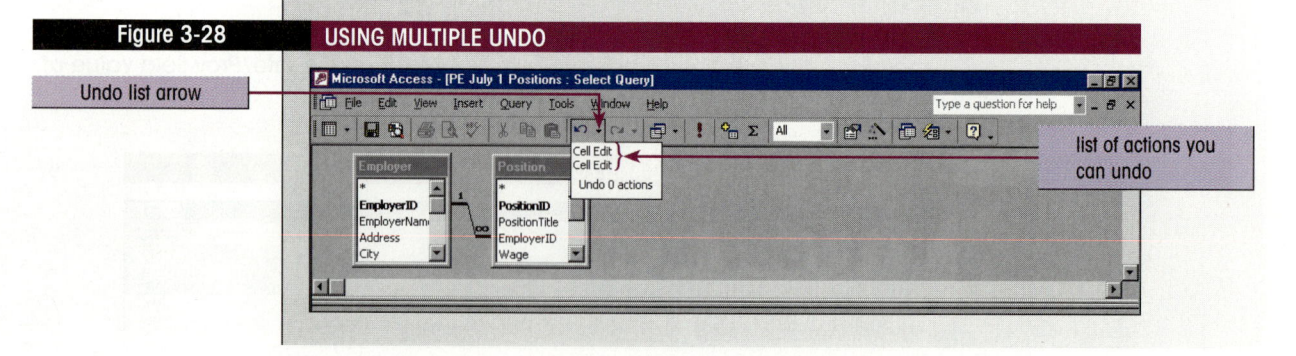

Figure 3-28   USING MULTIPLE UNDO

Undo list arrow

list of actions you can undo

Two items, both named "Cell Edit," are listed in the Undo list box. These items represent the two changes you made to the query design—first deleting the StartDate condition and then deleting the State/Prov condition. If you select an action that is below other items in the list, you will undo all the actions above the one you select, in addition to the one you select. Currently no actions are selected, so the list box indicates "Undo 0 actions."

7. Position the pointer over the second occurrence of **Cell Edit** in the list. Notice that both undo actions are highlighted, and the list box indicates that you can undo two actions.

8. Click the second occurrence of **Cell Edit**. Both actions are "undone," and the two conditions are redisplayed in the query design grid. The multiple undo feature makes it easy for you to test different criteria for a query and, when necessary, to undo your actions based on the query results.

   Notice that the Redo button and list arrow are now available. You can redo the actions you've just undone.

9. Click the **list arrow** for the Redo button on the Query Design toolbar. The Redo list box indicates that you can redo the two cell edits.

10. Click the **list arrow** for the Redo button again to close the Redo list box without selecting any option.

11. Close the query. Click the **No** button in the message box that opens, asking if you want to save your changes. You return to the Database window.

Matt has another request for information. He knows that it can be difficult to find student recruits for positions that offer fewer than 30 hours of work per week or that require prior work experience. So that his staff can focus on such positions, Matt wants to see a list of those positions that provide less than 30 hours of work or that require experience. To create this query, you need to use the Or logical operator.

The Or Logical Operator

For Matt's request, you need a query that selects a record when either one of two conditions is satisfied or when both conditions are satisfied. That is, a record is selected if the Hours/Week field value is less than 30 *or* if the Experience field value is "Yes" (checked). You will enter the condition for the Hours/Week field in one Criteria row and the condition for the Experience field in another Criteria row, thereby using the Or logical operator.

To display the information Matt wants to view, you'll create a new query containing the EmployerName and City fields from the Employer table and the PositionTitle, Hours/Week, and Experience fields from the Position table. Then you'll specify the conditions using the Or logical operator.

To create the query and use the Or logical operator:

1. In the Database window, double-click **Create query in Design view**. The Show Table dialog box opens on top of the Query window in Design view.

2. Click **Employer** in the Tables list box (if necessary), click the **Add** button, click **Position**, click the **Add** button, and then click the **Close** button. The Employer and Position field lists appear in the Query window and the Show Table dialog box closes.

3. Double-click **EmployerName** in the Employer field list to add the EmployerName field to the design grid's first column Field text box.

4. Repeat Step 3 to add the **City** field from the Employer table, and then add the **PositionTitle**, **Hours/Week**, and **Experience** fields from the Position table.

   Now you need to specify the first condition, <30, in the Hours/Week field.

5. Click the **Hours/Week Criteria** text box, type **<30** and then press the **Tab** key.

   Because you want records selected if either of the conditions for the Hours/Week or Experience fields is satisfied, you must enter the condition for the Experience field in the "or" row of the design grid.

6. Press the ↓ key, and then type **Yes** in the "or" text box for Experience. See Figure 3-29.

Figure 3-29   QUERY WINDOW WITH THE OR LOGICAL OPERATOR

Field:	EmployerName	City	PositionTitle	Hours/Week	Experience		
Table:	Employer	Employer	Position	Position	Position		
Sort:							
Show:	☑	☑	☑	☑	☑	☐	
Criteria:				<30			
or:					Yes		

Or logical operator; conditions entered in different rows

7. Run the query. Access displays only those records that meet either condition: an Hours/Week field value less than 30 or an Experience field value of "Yes" (checked). A total of 35 records are selected.

   Matt wants the list displayed in alphabetical order by EmployerName. The first record's EmployerName field is highlighted, indicating the current field.

8. Click the **Sort Ascending** button on the Query Datasheet toolbar.

9. Resize all datasheet columns to their best fit. Scroll through the entire datasheet to make sure that all values are completely displayed. Deselect all columns when you are finished resizing them, and then return to the top of the datasheet. See Figure 3-30.

TUTORIAL 3 QUERYING A DATABASE   AC 3.33

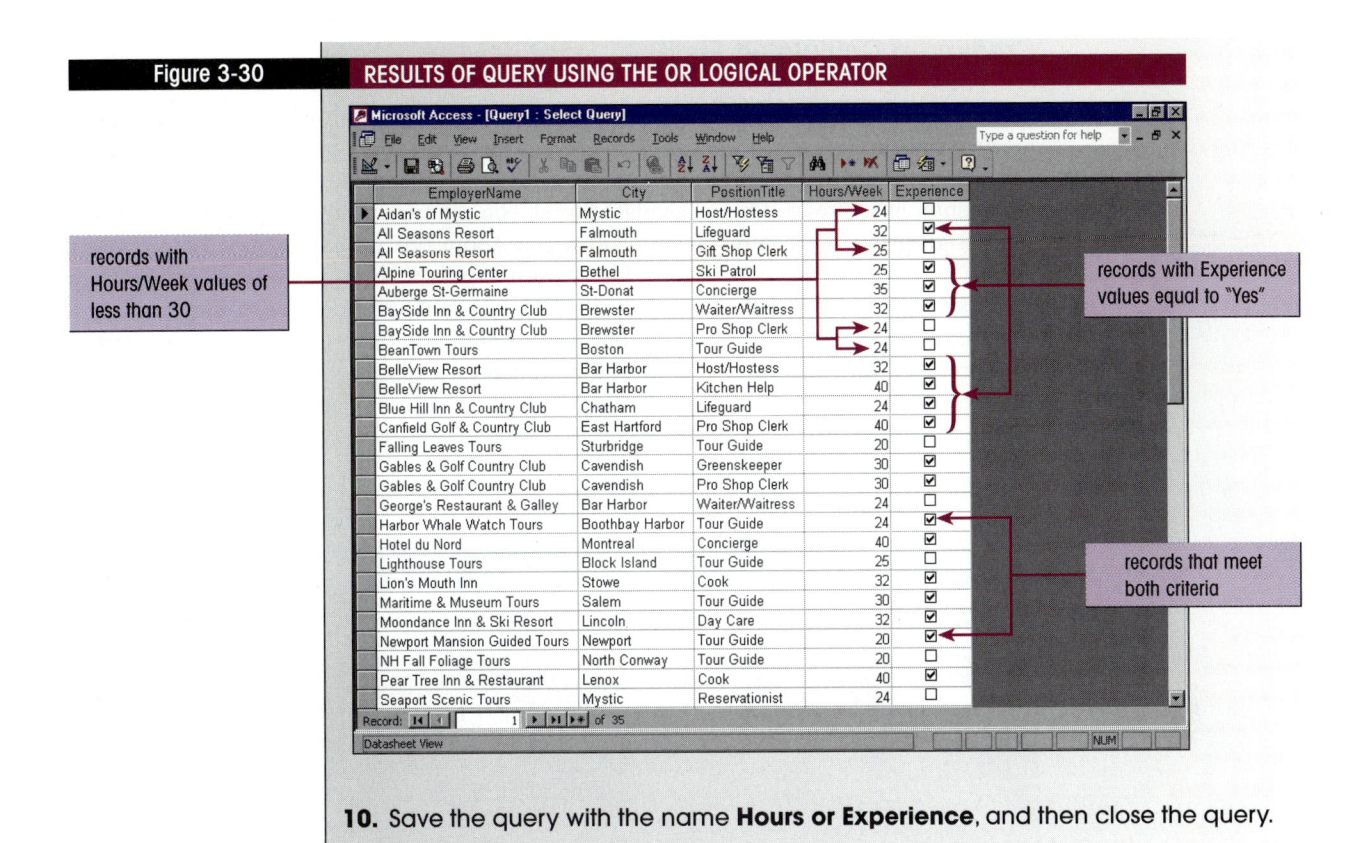

Figure 3-30   RESULTS OF QUERY USING THE OR LOGICAL OPERATOR

EmployerName	City	PositionTitle	Hours/Week	Experience
Aidan's of Mystic	Mystic	Host/Hostess	24	☐
All Seasons Resort	Falmouth	Lifeguard	32	☑
All Seasons Resort	Falmouth	Gift Shop Clerk	25	☐
Alpine Touring Center	Bethel	Ski Patrol	25	☑
Auberge St-Germaine	St-Donat	Concierge	35	☑
BaySide Inn & Country Club	Brewster	Waiter/Waitress	32	☑
BaySide Inn & Country Club	Brewster	Pro Shop Clerk	24	☐
BeanTown Tours	Boston	Tour Guide	24	☐
BelleView Resort	Bar Harbor	Host/Hostess	32	☑
BelleView Resort	Bar Harbor	Kitchen Help	40	☑
Blue Hill Inn & Country Club	Chatham	Lifeguard	24	☑
Canfield Golf & Country Club	East Hartford	Pro Shop Clerk	40	☑
Falling Leaves Tours	Sturbridge	Tour Guide	20	☐
Gables & Golf Country Club	Cavendish	Greenskeeper	30	☑
Gables & Golf Country Club	Cavendish	Pro Shop Clerk	30	☑
George's Restaurant & Galley	Bar Harbor	Waiter/Waitress	24	☐
Harbor Whale Watch Tours	Boothbay Harbor	Tour Guide	24	☑
Hotel du Nord	Montreal	Concierge	40	☑
Lighthouse Tours	Block Island	Tour Guide	25	☐
Lion's Mouth Inn	Stowe	Cook	32	☑
Maritime & Museum Tours	Salem	Tour Guide	30	☑
Moondance Inn & Ski Resort	Lincoln	Day Care	32	☑
Newport Mansion Guided Tours	Newport	Tour Guide	20	☑
NH Fall Foliage Tours	North Conway	Tour Guide	20	☐
Pear Tree Inn & Restaurant	Lenox	Cook	40	☑
Seaport Scenic Tours	Mystic	Reservationist	24	☐

records with Hours/Week values of less than 30

records with Experience values equal to "Yes"

records that meet both criteria

10. Save the query with the name **Hours or Experience**, and then close the query.

Next, Elsa wants to use the Northeast database to perform calculations. She is considering offering a 2% bonus per week to the student recruits in higher paid positions, based on employer recommendation, and she wants to know exactly what these bonuses would be.

Performing Calculations

In addition to using queries to retrieve, sort, and filter data in a database, you can use a query to perform calculations. To perform a calculation, you define an **expression** containing a combination of database fields, constants, and operators. For numeric expressions, the data types of the database fields must be number, currency, or date/time; the constants are numbers such as .02 (for the 2% bonus); and the operators can be arithmetic operators (+ – * /) or other specialized operators. In complex expressions, you can enclose calculations in parentheses to indicate which one should be performed first. In expressions without parentheses, Access calculates in the following order of precedence: multiplication and division before addition and subtraction. When operators have equal precedence, Access calculates them in order from left to right.

To perform a calculation in a query, you add a calculated field to the query. A **calculated field** is a field that displays the results of an expression. A calculated field appears in a query datasheet or in a form or report; however, it does not exist in a database. When you run a query that contains a calculated field, Access evaluates the expression defined by the calculated field and displays the resulting value in the datasheet, form, or report.

Creating a Calculated Field

To produce the information Elsa wants, you need to open the High Wage Amounts query and create a calculated field that will multiply each Wage field value by each Hours/Week value, and then multiply that amount by .02 to determine the 2% weekly bonus Elsa is considering.

To enter an expression for a calculated field, you can type it directly in a Field text box in the design grid. Alternately, you can open the Zoom box or Expression Builder and use either one to enter the expression. The **Zoom box** is a large text box for entering text, expressions, or other values. **Expression Builder** is an Access tool that contains an expression box for entering the expression, buttons for common operators, and one or more lists of expression elements, such as table and field names. Unlike a Field text box, which is too small to show an entire expression at one time, the Zoom box and Expression Builder are large enough to display lengthy expressions. In most cases, Expression Builder provides the easiest way to enter expressions.

REFERENCE WINDOW

Using Expression Builder
- Open the query in Design view.
- In the design grid, position the insertion point in the Field text box of the field for which you want to create an expression.
- Click the Build button on the Query Design toolbar.
- Use the expression elements and common operators to build the expression, or type the expression directly.
- Click the OK button.

You'll begin by copying, pasting, and renaming the High Wage Amounts query, keeping the original query intact. You'll name the new query "High Wages with Bonus." Then you'll modify this query in Design view to show only the information Elsa wants to view.

To copy the High Wage Amounts query and paste the copy with a new name:

1. Right-click the **High Wage Amounts** query in the list of queries, and then click **Copy** on the shortcut menu.

2. Right-click an empty area of the Database window, and then click **Paste** on the shortcut menu. The Paste As dialog box opens.

3. Type **High Wages with Bonus** in the Query Name text box, and then press the **Enter** key. The new query appears in the query list, along with the original High Wage Amounts query.

Now you're ready to modify the High Wages with Bonus query to create the calculated field for Elsa.

To modify the High Wages with Bonus query:

1. Open the **High Wages with Bonus** query in Design view.

   Elsa wants to see only the EmployerName, PositionTitle, and Wage fields in the query results. First, you'll delete the unnecessary fields, and then you'll move the EmployerName field so that it appears first in the query results.

2. Scroll the design grid to the right until the Hours/Week and EmployerName fields are visible at the same time.

3. Position the pointer on the Hours/Week field until the pointer changes to a ⬇ shape, click and hold down the mouse button, drag the mouse to the right to highlight the Hours/Week, Experience, StartDate, EndDate, and Openings fields, and then release the mouse button.

4. Press the **Delete** key to delete the five selected fields.

5. Repeat Steps 3 and 4 to delete the State/Prov, ContactFirstName, ContactLastName, and Phone fields from the query design grid.

   Next you'll move the EmployerName field to the left of the PositionTitle field so that the Wage values will appear next to the calculated field values in the query results.

6. Scroll the design grid back to the left (if necessary), select the **EmployerName** field, and then use the pointer ▨ to drag the field to the left of the PositionTitle field. See Figure 3-31.

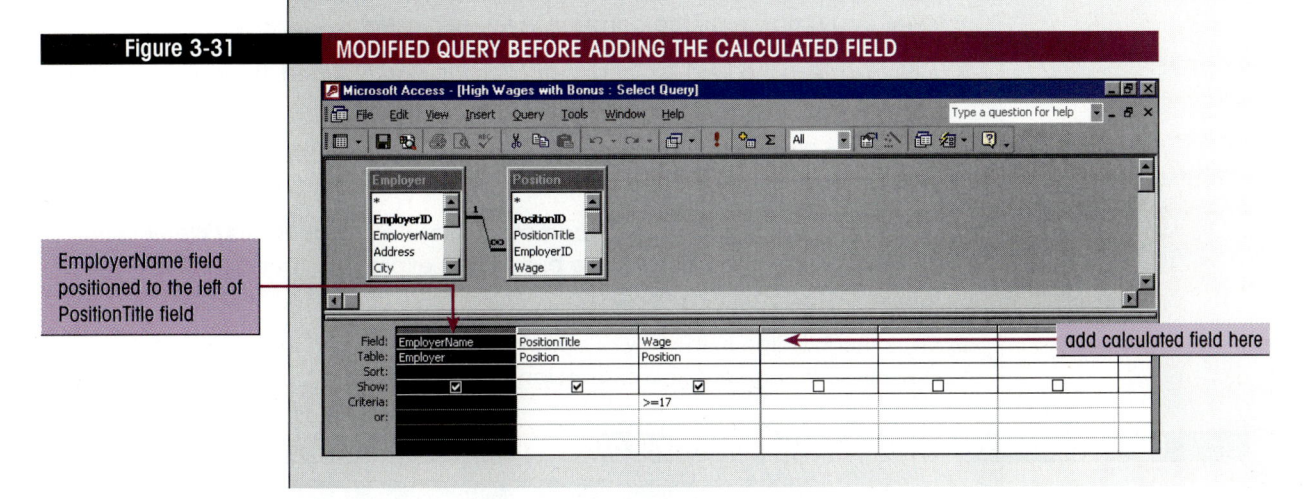

Figure 3-31 MODIFIED QUERY BEFORE ADDING THE CALCULATED FIELD

EmployerName field positioned to the left of PositionTitle field

add calculated field here

Now you're ready to use Expression Builder to enter the calculated field in the High Wages with Bonus query.

To add the calculated field to the High Wages with Bonus query:

1. Position the insertion point in the Field text box to the right of the Wage field, and then click the **Build** button on the Query Design toolbar. The Expression Builder dialog box opens. See Figure 3-32.

Figure 3-32 INITIAL EXPRESSION BUILDER DIALOG BOX

expression box
common operators
expression elements

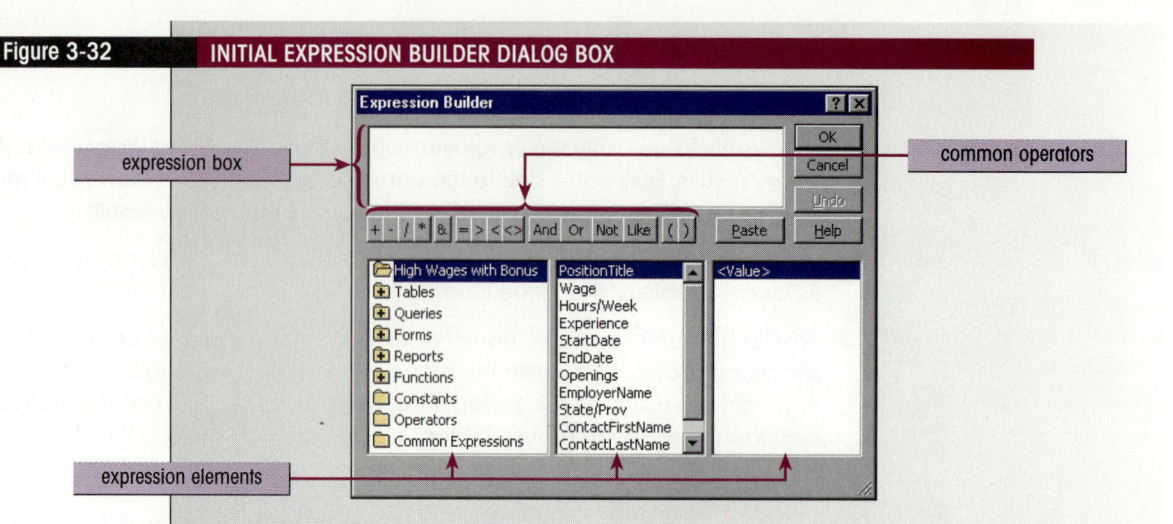

You use the common operators and expression elements to help you build an expression. Note that the High Wages with Bonus query is already selected in the list box on the lower left; the fields included in the original version of the query are listed in the center box.

The expression for the calculated field will multiply the Wage field values by the Hours/Week field values, and then multiply that amount by the numeric constant .02 (which represents a 2% bonus). To include a field in the expression, you select the field and then click the Paste button. To include a numeric constant, you simply type the constant in the expression.

2. Click **Wage** in the field list, and then click the **Paste** button. [Wage] appears in the expression box.

   To include the multiplication operator in the expression, you click the asterisk (*) button.

3. Click the * button in the row of common operators, click **Hours/Week** in the field list, and then click the **Paste** button. The expression multiplies the Wage values by the Hours/Week values.

4. Click the * button in the row of common operators, and then type **.02**. You have finished entering the expression. See Figure 3-33.

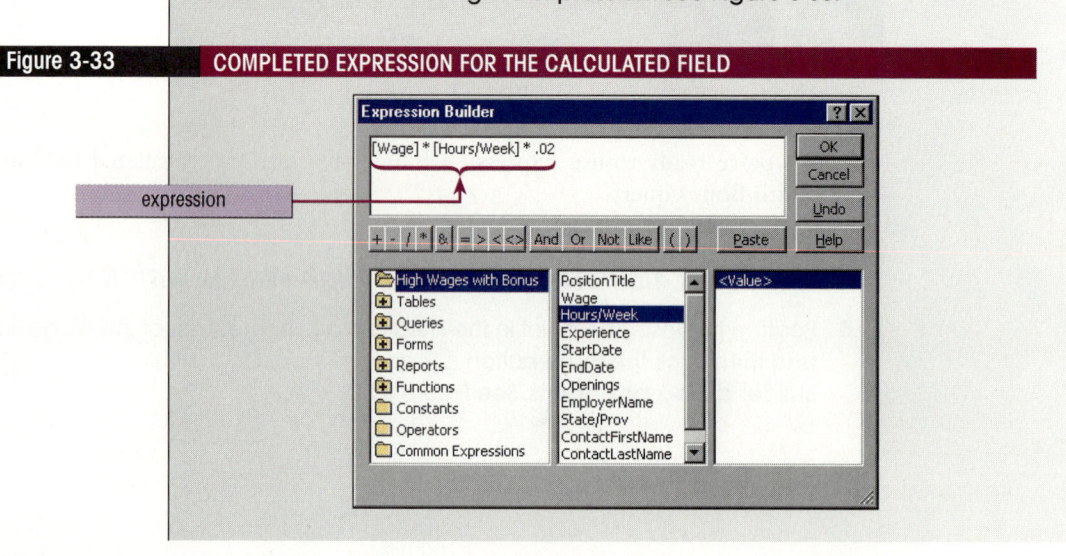

Figure 3-33 COMPLETED EXPRESSION FOR THE CALCULATED FIELD

expression: [Wage] * [Hours/Week] * .02

Note that you also could have typed the expression directly into the expression box, instead of clicking the field names and the operator.

5. Click the **OK** button. Access closes the Expression Builder dialog box and adds the expression to the design grid in the Field text box for the calculated field.

   Next, you need to specify a name for the calculated field as it will appear in the query results.

6. Press the **Home** key to position the insertion point to the left of the expression.

   You'll enter the name WeeklyBonus, which is descriptive of the field's contents; then you'll run the query.

7. Type **WeeklyBonus**:. *Make sure you include the colon following the field name.* The colon is needed to separate the field name from its expression.

8. Run the query. Access displays the query datasheet, which contains the three specified fields and the calculated field with the name "WeeklyBonus." Resize all datasheet columns to their best fit. See Figure 3-34.

Figure 3-34   DATASHEET DISPLAYING THE CALCULATED FIELD

EmployerName	PositionTitle	Wage	WeeklyBonus
Aidan's of Mystic	Host/Hostess	17.00	8.16
Newport Mansion Guided Tours	Tour Guide	18.75	7.5
BelleView Resort	Host/Hostess	18.50	11.84
Pear Tree Inn & Restaurant	Cook	25.00	20
Blue Hill Inn & Country Club	Lifeguard	20.50	9.84
BeanTown Tours	Tour Guide	17.00	8.16
Canfield Golf & Country Club	Pro Shop Clerk	17.00	13.6
Gables & Golf Country Club	Greenskeeper	18.00	10.8
Auberge St-Germaine	Concierge	19.00	13.3
Trudel Spa & Resort	Lifeguard	18.00	11.52
Lion's Mouth Inn	Cook	20.00	12.8
Windsor Alpine Tours	Ski Patrol	18.50	11.1
Stonehurst Inn	Host/Hostess	17.00	13.6
Alpine Touring Center	Ski Patrol	19.00	9.5
Hotel du Nord	Concierge	19.75	15.8
Ski & Stay	Ski Patrol	18.75	9.375
The Bramble Restaurant	Cook	20.00	16
Canfield Golf & Country Club	Greenskeeper	17.00	10.88
All Seasons Resort	Lifeguard	19.00	12.16

specified name for the calculated field

calculated field values

Notice the WeeklyBonus value for Ski & Stay; the value appears with three decimal places (9.375). Currency values should have only two decimal places, so you need to format the WeeklyBonus calculated field so that all values appear in the Fixed format with two decimal places.

To format the calculated field:

1. Switch to Design view.

2. Right-click the **WeeklyBonus** calculated field in the design grid to open the shortcut menu, and then click **Properties**. The property sheet for the selected field opens. The property sheet for a field provides options for changing the display of field values in the datasheet.

3. Click the right side of the **Format** text box to display the list of formats, and then click **Fixed**.

4. Click the right side of the **Decimal Places** text box, and then click **2**.

5. Click in the **Description** text box to deselect the Decimal Places setting. See Figure 3-35.

Figure 3-35   PROPERTY SHEET SETTINGS TO FORMAT THE CALCULATED FIELD

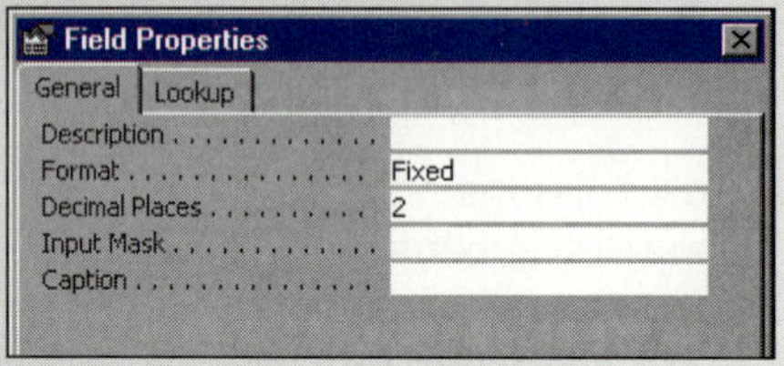

```
Field Properties
General | Lookup
Description . . . . . . . . . . . .
Format . . . . . . . . . . . . . .   Fixed
Decimal Places . . . . . . . . .   2
Input Mask . . . . . . . . . . . .
Caption . . . . . . . . . . . . . .
```

Now that you have formatted the calculated field, you can run the query.

6. Close the Field Properties window, and then save and run the query. The value for Ski & Stay now correctly appears as 9.38.

7. Close the query.

Elsa prepares a report on a regular basis that includes a summary of information about the wages paid to student recruits. She lists the minimum hourly wage paid, the average wage amount, and the maximum hourly wage paid. She asks you to create a query to determine these statistics from data in the Position table.

Using Aggregate Functions

You can calculate statistical information, such as totals and averages, on the records selected by a query. To do this, you use the Access aggregate functions. **Aggregate functions** perform arithmetic operations on selected records in a database. Figure 3-36 lists the most frequently used aggregate functions. Aggregate functions operate on the records that meet a query's selection criteria. You specify an aggregate function for a specific field, and the appropriate operation applies to that field's values for the selected records.

Figure 3-36   FREQUENTLY USED AGGREGATE FUNCTIONS

AGGREGATE FUNCTION	DETERMINES	DATA TYPES SUPPORTED
Avg	Average of the field values for the selected records	AutoNumber, Currency, Date/Time, Number
Count	Number of records selected	AutoNumber, Currency, Date/Time, Memo, Number, OLE Object, Text, Yes/No
Max	Highest field value for the selected records	AutoNumber, Currency, Date/Time, Number, Text
Min	Lowest field value for the selected records	AutoNumber, Currency, Date/Time, Number, Text
Sum	Total of the field values for the selected records	AutoNumber, Currency, Date/Time, Number

To display the minimum, average, and maximum of all the wage amounts in the Position table, you will use the Min, Avg, and Max aggregate functions for the Wage field.

To calculate the minimum, average, and maximum of all wage amounts:

1. Double-click **Create query in Design view**, click **Position**, click the **Add** button, and then click the **Close** button. The Position field list is added to the Query window and the Show Table dialog box closes.

   To perform the three calculations on the Wage field, you need to add the field to the design grid three times.

2. Double-click **Wage** in the Position field list three times to add three copies of the field to the design grid.

   You need to select an aggregate function for each Wage field. When you click the Totals button on the Query Design toolbar, a row labeled "Total" is added to the design grid. The Total row provides a list of the aggregate functions that you can select.

3. Click the **Totals** button ∑ on the Query Design toolbar. A new row labeled "Total" appears between the Table and Sort rows in the design grid. See Figure 3-37.

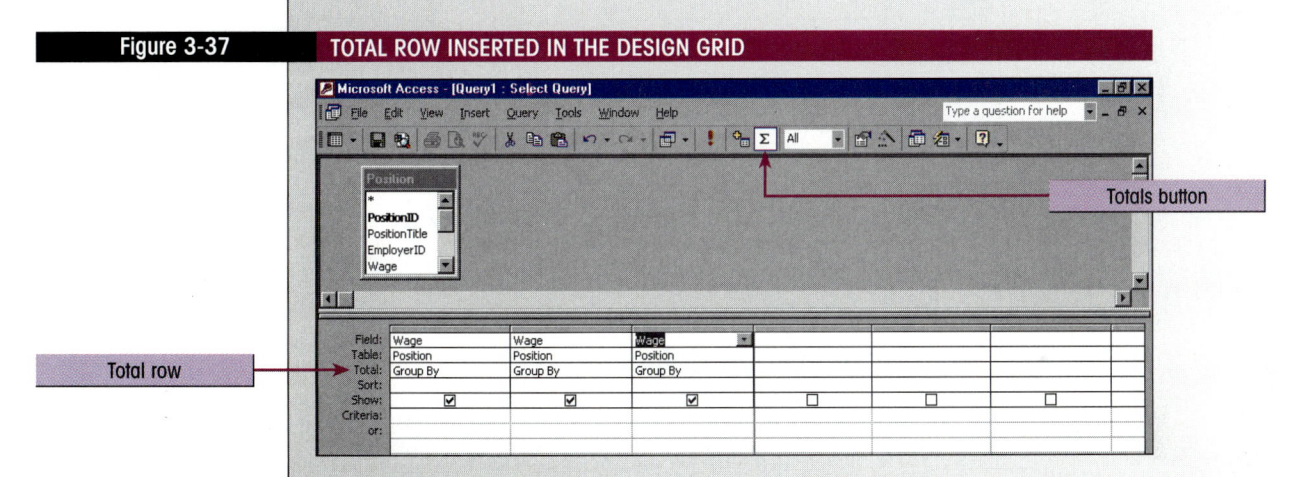

| Figure 3-37 | **TOTAL ROW INSERTED IN THE DESIGN GRID** |

   In the Total row, you specify the aggregate function you want to use for a field.

4. Click the right side of the first column's **Total** text box, and then click **Min**. This field will calculate the minimum amount of all the Wage field values.

   When you run the query, Access automatically will assign a datasheet column name of "MinOfWage" for this field. You can change the datasheet column name to a more descriptive or readable name by entering the name you want in the Field text box. However, you must also keep the field name Wage in the Field text box, because it identifies the field whose values will be calculated. The Field text box will contain the datasheet column name you specify followed by the field name (Wage) with a colon separating the two names.

5. Position the insertion point to the left of Wage in the first column's Field text box, and then type **MinimumWage**:. Be sure that you type the colon.

6. Click the right side of the second column's **Total** text box, and then click **Avg**. This field will calculate the average of all the Wage field values.

7. Position the insertion point to the left of Wage in the second column's Field text box, and then type **AverageWage**:.

8. Click the right side of the third column's **Total** text box, and then click **Max**. This field will calculate the maximum amount of all the Wage field values.

9. Position the insertion point to the left of Wage in the third column's Field text box, and then type **MaximumWage:**.

   The query design is completed, so you can run the query.

10. Run the query. Access displays one record containing the three aggregate function values. The single row of summary statistics represents calculations based on the 64 records selected by the query.

    You need to resize the three columns to their best fit to see the column names.

11. Resize all columns to their best fit, and then position the insertion point in the field value in the first column. See Figure 3-38.

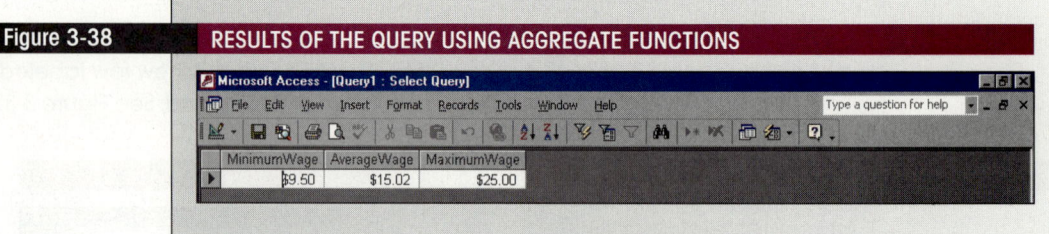

Figure 3-38   RESULTS OF THE QUERY USING AGGREGATE FUNCTIONS

MinimumWage	AverageWage	MaximumWage
$9.50	$15.02	$25.00

12. Save the query as **Wage Statistics**, and then close the query.

Elsa also wants her report to include the same wage statistics (minimum, average, and maximum) for each type of position. She asks you to display the wage statistics for each different PositionTitle value in the Position table.

Using Record Group Calculations

In addition to calculating statistical information on all or selected records in selected tables, you can calculate statistics for groups of records. For example, you can determine the number of employers in each state or province, or the average wage amount by position.

To create a query for Elsa's latest request, you can modify the current query by adding the PositionTitle field and assigning the Group By operator to it. The **Group By operator** divides the selected records into groups based on the values in the specified field. Those records with the same value for the field are grouped together, and the datasheet displays one record for each group. Aggregate functions, which appear in the other columns of the design grid, provide statistical information for each group.

You need to modify the current query to add the Group By operator for the PositionTitle field. This will display the statistical information grouped by position for the 64 selected records in the query. As you did earlier, you will copy the Wage Statistics query and paste it with a new name, keeping the original query intact, to create the new query.

To copy and paste the query, and then add the PositionTitle field with the Group By operator:

1. Right-click the **Wage Statistics** query in the list of queries, and then click **Copy** on the shortcut menu.

2. Right-click an empty area of the Database window, and then click **Paste** on the shortcut menu.

3. Type **Wage Statistics by Position** in the Query Name text box, and then press the **Enter** key.

   Now you're ready to modify the query design.

4. Open the **Wage Statistics by Position** query in Design view.

5. Double-click **PositionTitle** in the Position field list to add the field to the design grid. Group By, which is the default option in the Total row, appears for the PositionTitle field.

   You've completed the query changes, so you can run the query.

6. Run the query. Access displays 16 records—one for each PositionTitle group. Each record contains the three aggregate function values and the PositionTitle field value for the group. Again, the summary statistics represent calculations based on the 64 records selected by the query. See Figure 3-39.

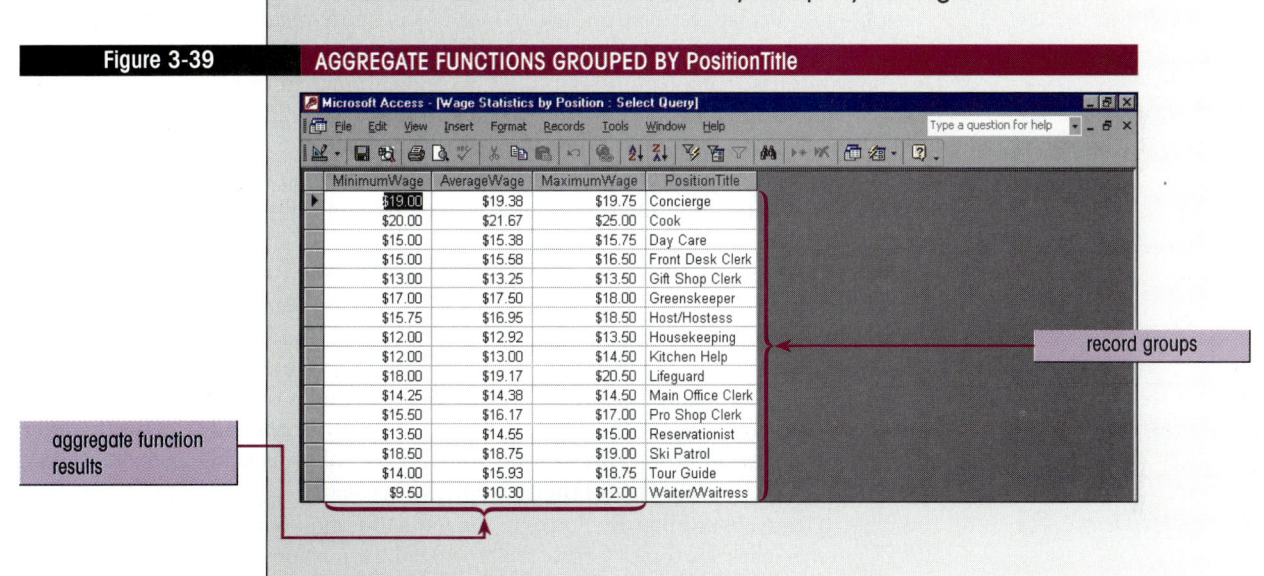

Figure 3-39   **AGGREGATE FUNCTIONS GROUPED BY PositionTitle**

MinimumWage	AverageWage	MaximumWage	PositionTitle
$19.00	$19.38	$19.75	Concierge
$20.00	$21.67	$25.00	Cook
$15.00	$15.38	$15.75	Day Care
$15.00	$15.58	$16.50	Front Desk Clerk
$13.00	$13.25	$13.50	Gift Shop Clerk
$17.00	$17.50	$18.00	Greenskeeper
$15.75	$16.95	$18.50	Host/Hostess
$12.00	$12.92	$13.50	Housekeeping
$12.00	$13.00	$14.50	Kitchen Help
$18.00	$19.17	$20.50	Lifeguard
$14.25	$14.38	$14.50	Main Office Clerk
$15.50	$16.17	$17.00	Pro Shop Clerk
$13.50	$14.55	$15.00	Reservationist
$18.50	$18.75	$19.00	Ski Patrol
$14.00	$15.93	$18.75	Tour Guide
$9.50	$10.30	$12.00	Waiter/Waitress

aggregate function results

record groups

7. Save and close the query, and then click the **Close** button ⊠ on the Access window title bar to close the Northeast database and to exit Access.

   TROUBLE? If a dialog box opens and asks if you want to empty the Clipboard, click the Yes button.

The queries you've created and saved will help Elsa, Zack, Matt, and other employees to monitor and analyze the business activity of NSJI's employer customers. Now any NSJI staff member can run the queries at any time, modify them as needed, or use them as the basis for designing new queries to meet additional information requirements.

Session 3.2 QUICK CHECK

1. A(n) _____ is a criterion, or rule, that determines which records are selected for a query datasheet.
2. In the design grid, where do you place the conditions for two different fields when you use the And logical operator? The Or logical operator?

3. To perform a calculation in a query, you define a(n) _____ containing a combination of database fields, constants, and operators.
4. How does a calculated field differ from a table field?
5. What is an aggregate function?
6. The _____ operator divides selected records into groups based on the values in a field.

REVIEW ASSIGNMENTS

Elsa needs information from the **Recruits** database, and she asks you to query the database by completing the following:

1. Make sure your Data Disk is in the appropriate disk drive, start Access, and then open the **Recruits** database located in the Review folder on your Data Disk.

2. Create a select query based on the **Student** table. Display the StudentID, FirstName, and LastName fields in the query results; sort in ascending order based on the LastName field values; and select only those records whose Nation value equals Ireland. (*Hint*: Do not display the Nation field values in the query results.) Save the query as **Students from Ireland**, run the query, and then print the query datasheet.

3. Use the **Students from Ireland** datasheet to update the **Student** table by changing the FirstName field value for StudentID OMA9956 to Richard. Print the query datasheet, and then close the query.

4. Define a one-to-many relationship between the primary **Recruiter** table and the related **Student** table. Select the referential integrity option and both cascade options for the relationship.

5. Use Design view to create a select query based on the **Recruiter** and **Student** tables. Select the fields FirstName (from the **Student** table), LastName (from the **Student** table), City, Nation, BonusQuota, Salary, and SSN (from the **Student** table), in that order. Sort in ascending order based on the Nation field values. Select only those records whose SSN equals "977071798." (*Hint*: Do not type the dashes for the SSN criterion, and do not display the SSN field values in the query results.) Save the query as **Wolfe Recruits**, and then run the query. Resize all columns in the datasheet to fit the data. Print the datasheet, and then save the query.

Explore 6. Use Help to learn about Filter By Form. In the Ask a Question box, type, "How do I create a filter?" and then click the topic "Create a filter." Read the portions of the topic pertaining to Filter By Selection and Filter By Form, and then close the Microsoft Access Help window.

Explore 7. Use the Filter By Form button on the Query Datasheet toolbar to filter the records in the **Wolfe Recruits** datasheet that have a Nation field value of "Spain," and then apply the filter. Print the query datasheet.

Explore 8. Remove the filter to display all records, and then save and close the query.

Explore 9. Use Design view to create a query based on the **Recruiter** table that shows all recruiters with a BonusQuota field value between 40 and 50, and whose Salary field value is greater than 35000. (*Hint*: Refer to Figure 3-18 to determine the correct comparison operator to use.) Display all fields except SSN from the **Recruiter** table. Save the query as **Bonus Info**, and then run the query.

Explore 10. Switch to Design view for the **Bonus Info** query. Create a calculated field named RaiseAmt that displays the net amount of a 3% raise to the Salary values. Display the results in descending order by RaiseAmt. Save the query as **Salaries with Raises**, run the query, resize all columns in the datasheet to fit the data, print the query datasheet, and then save and close the query.

11. In the Database window, copy the **Students from Ireland** query, and then paste it with the new name **Students from Holland Plus Younger Students**. Open the new query in Design view. Modify the query to display only those records with a Nation field value of Holland or with a BirthDate field value greater than 1/1/84. Also, modify the query to include the Nation field values in the query results. Save and run the query. Resize all columns in the datasheet to fit the data, print the query datasheet, and then save and close the query.

12. Create a new query based on the **Recruiter** table. Use the Min, Max, and Avg aggregate functions to find the lowest, highest, and average values in the Salary field. Name the three aggregate fields LowestSalary, HighestSalary, and AverageSalary, respectively. Save the query as **Salary Statistics**, and then run the query. Resize all columns in the datasheet to fit the data, print the query datasheet, and then save and close the query.
13. Open the **Salary Statistics** query in Design view. Modify the query so that the records are grouped by the BonusQuota field. Save the query as **Salary Statistics by BonusQuota**, run the query, print the query datasheet, and then close the query.
14. Close the **Recruits** database, and then exit Access.

CASE PROBLEMS

Case 1. Lim's Video Photography Youngho Lim wants to view specific information about his clients and video shoot events. He asks you to query the **Videos** database by completing the following:
1. Make sure your Data Disk is in the appropriate disk drive, start Access, and then open the **Videos** database located in the Cases folder on your Data Disk.

Explore
2. Define the necessary one-to-many relationships between the database tables, as follows: between the primary **Client** table and the related **Contract** table, between the primary **Contract** table and the related **Shoot** table, and between the primary **ShootDesc** table and the related **Shoot** table. (*Hint*: Add all four tables to the Relationships window, and then define the three relationships.) Select the referential integrity option and both cascade options for each relationship.
3. Create a select query based on the **Client** and **Contract** tables. Display the ClientName, City, ContractDate, and ContractAmt fields, in that order. Sort in ascending order based on the ClientName field values. Run the query, save the query as **Client Contracts**, and then print the datasheet.
4. Use Filter By Selection to display only those records with a City field value of Oakland in the **Client Contracts** datasheet. Print the datasheet and then remove the filter. Save and close the query.
5. Open the **Client Contracts** query in Design view. Modify the query to display only those records with a ContractAmt value greater than or equal to 600. Run the query, save the query as **Contract Amounts**, and then print the datasheet.
6. Switch to Design view for the **Contract Amounts** query. Modify the query to display only those records with a ContractAmt value greater than or equal to 600 and with a City value of San Francisco. Also modify the query so that the City field values are not displayed in the query results. Run the query, save it as **SF Contract Amounts**, print the datasheet, and then close the query.
7. Close the **Videos** database, and then exit Access.

Case 2. DineAtHome.course.com Claire Picard is completing an analysis of the orders placed at restaurants that use her company's services. To help her find the information she needs, you'll query the **Meals** database by completing the following:
1. Make sure your Data Disk is in the appropriate disk drive, start Access, and then open the **Meals** database located in the Cases folder on your Data Disk.
2. Define a one-to-many relationship between the primary **Restaurant** table and the related **Order** table. Select the referential integrity option and both cascade options for the relationship.
3. Use Design view to create a select query based on the **Restaurant** and **Order** tables. Display the fields RestaurantName, City, OrderAmt, and OrderDate, in that order. Sort in descending order based on the OrderAmt field values. Select only those records whose OrderAmt is greater than 150. Save the query as **Large Orders**, and then run the query.
4. Use the **Large Orders** datasheet to update the **Order** table by changing the OrderAmt value for the first record in the datasheet to 240.25. Print the datasheet, and then close the query.

5. Use Design view to create a select query based on the **Restaurant** and **Order** tables. For all orders placed on 03/21/2003, display the Order#, OrderAmt, OrderDate, and RestaurantName fields. Save the query as **March 21 Orders**, and then run the query. Switch to Design view, modify the query so that the OrderDate values do not appear in the query results, and then save the modified query. Run the query, print the query results, and then close the query.

6. Use Design view to create a select query based on the **Restaurant** table. For all restaurants that have a Website and are located in Naples, display the RestaurantName, OwnerFirstName, OwnerLastName, and Phone fields. Save the query as **Naples Restaurants with Websites**, run the query, print the query results, and then close the query.

7. Use Design view to create a select query based on the **Restaurant** and **Order** tables. For all orders placed on 03/14/2003 or 03/15/2003, display the fields OrderDate, OrderAmt, RestaurantName, and Restaurant# (from the **Restaurant** table). Display the results in ascending order by OrderDate and then in descending order by OrderAmt. Save the query as **Selected Dates**, run the query, print the query datasheet, and then close the query.

Explore

8. Use the **Order** table to display the highest, lowest, total, average, and count of the OrderAmt field for all orders. Then do the following:
    a. Specify column names of HighestOrder, LowestOrder, TotalOrders, AverageOrder, and #Orders. Use the property sheet for each column (except #Orders) to format the results as Fixed with two decimal places. Save the query as **Order Statistics**, and then run the query. Resize all datasheet columns to their best fit, save the query, and then print the query results.
    b. Change the query to display the same statistics grouped by RestaurantName. (*Hint*: Use the Show Table button on the Query Design toolbar to add the **Restaurant** table to the query.) Save the query as **Order Statistics by Restaurant**. Run the query, print the query results, and then close the query.

9. Close the **Meals** database, and then exit Access.

Case 3. Redwood Zoo Michael Rosenfeld wants to find specific information about the donors and their pledge amounts for the Redwood Zoo. You'll help them find the information in the **Redwood** database by completing the following:

1. Make sure your Data Disk is in the appropriate disk drive, start Access, and then open the **Redwood** database located in the Cases folder on your Data Disk.

Explore

2. Define the necessary one-to-many relationships between the database tables, as follows: between the primary **Donor** table and the related **Pledge** table, and between the primary **Fund** table and the related **Pledge** table. (*Hint*: Add all three tables to the Relationships window, and then define the two relationships.) Select the referential integrity option and both cascade options for each relationship.

3. Use Design view to create a select query that, for all pledges with a TotalPledged field value of greater than 200, displays the DonorID (from the **Donor** table), FirstName, LastName, Pledge#, TotalPledged, and FundName fields. Sort the query in ascending order by TotalPledged. Save the query as **Large Pledges**, and then run the query.

4. Use the **Large Pledges** datasheet to update the **Pledge** table by changing the TotalPledged field value for Pledge# 2976 to 750. Print the query datasheet, and then close the query.

5. Use Design view to create a select query that, for all donors who pledged less than $150 or who donated to the Whale Watchers fund, displays the Pledge#, PledgeDate, TotalPledged, FirstName, and LastName fields. Save the revised query as **Pledged or Whale Watchers**, run the query, and then print the query datasheet. Change the query to select all donors who pledged less than $150 and who donated to the Whale Watchers fund. Save the revised query as **Pledged and Whale Watchers**, and then run the query. Close the query.

Explore

6. Use Design view to create a select query that displays the DonorID (from the **Donor** table), TotalPledged, PaymentMethod, PledgeDate, and FundName fields. Save the query as **Pledges after Costs**. Create a calculated field named Overhead that displays the results of multiplying the TotalPledged field values by 15% (to account for overhead costs). Save the query, and then create a second calculated field named NetPledge that displays the results of subtracting the Overhead field values from the TotalPledged field values.

Format the calculated fields as Fixed. Display the results in ascending order by TotalPledged. Save the modified query, and then run the query. Resize all datasheet columns to their best fit, print the query results, and then save and close the query.

Explore 7. Use the **Pledge** table to display the sum, average, and count of the TotalPledged field for all pledges. Then do the following:
   a. Specify column names of TotalPledge, AveragePledge, and #Pledges.
   b. Change properties so that the values in the TotalPledge and AveragePledge columns display two decimal places and the Fixed format.
   c. Save the query as **Pledge Statistics**, run the query, resize all datasheet columns to their best fit, and then print the query datasheet. Save the query.
   d. Change the query to display the sum, average, and count of the TotalPledged field for all pledges by FundName. (*Hint*: Use the Show Table button on the Query Design toolbar to add the **Fund** table to the query.) Save the query as **Pledge Statistics by Fund**, run the query, print the query datasheet, and then close the query.

8. Close the **Redwood** database, and then exit Access.

Case 4. Mountain River Adventures Connor and Siobhan Dempsey want to analyze data about their clients and the rafting trips they take. Help them query the **Trips** database by completing the following:

1. Make sure your Data Disk is in the appropriate disk drive, start Access, and then open the **Trips** database located in the Cases folder on your Data Disk.

Explore 2. Define the necessary one-to-many relationships between the database tables, as follows: between the primary **Client** table and the related **Booking** table, and between the primary **Rafting Trip** table and the related **Booking** table. (*Hint*: Add all three tables to the Relationships window, and then define the two relationships.) Select the referential integrity option and both cascade options for each relationship.

3. For all clients, display the ClientName, City, State/Prov, Booking#, and TripDate fields. Save the query as **Client Trip Dates**, and then run the query. Resize all datasheet columns to their best fit. In Datasheet view, sort the query results in ascending order by the TripDate field. Print the query datasheet, and then save and close the query.

4. For all clients from Colorado (CO), display the ClientName, City, State/Prov, Trip#, People, and TripDate fields. Sort the query in ascending order by City. Save the query as **Colorado Clients**, and then run the query. Modify the query to remove the display of the State/Prov field values from the query results. Save the modified query, run the query, print the query datasheet, and then close the query.

Explore 5. For all clients who are not from Colorado or who are taking a rafting trip in the month of July 2003, display the ClientName, City, State/Prov, Booking#, TripDate, and Trip# fields. (*Hint*: Refer to Figure 3-18 to determine the correct comparison operators to use.) Sort the query in descending order by TripDate. Save the query as **Out of State or July**, run the query, and then print the query datasheet. Change the query to select all clients who are not from Colorado and who are taking a rafting trip in the month of July 2003. Sort the query in ascending order by State/Prov. Save the query as **Out of State and July**, run the query, print the query datasheet, and then close the query.

6. For all bookings, display the Booking#, TripDate, Trip# (from the **Booking** table), River, People, and Fee/Person fields. Save the query as **Trip Cost**. Then create a calculated field named TripCost that displays the results of multiplying the People field values by the Fee/Person field values. Display the results in descending order by TripCost. Run the query, resize all datasheet columns to their best fit, print the query datasheet, and then save and close the query.

Explore 7. Use the **Rafting Trip** table to determine the minimum, average, and maximum Fee/Person for all trips. Use the Ask a Question box to ask the question, "What is a caption?" and then locate and click the topic "Change a field name in a query." Read the displayed information, and then click and read the subtopic "Change a field's caption."

Close the Help window. Set the Caption property of the three fields to Lowest Fee, Average Fee, and Highest Fee, respectively. Also set the properties so that the results of the three fields are displayed as Fixed with two decimal places. Save the query as **Fee Statistics**, run the query, resize all datasheet columns to their best fit, print the query datasheet, and then save the query again. Revise the query to show the fee statistics grouped by People. (*Hint*: Use the Show Table button on the Query Design toolbar to display the Show Table dialog box.) Save the revised query as **Fee Statistics by People**, run the query, print the query datasheet, and then close the query.

Explore

8. Use the Ask a Question box to ask the following question: "How do I create a Top Values query?" Click the topic "Show only the high or low values in a query." Read the displayed information, and then close the Help window. Open the **Trip Cost** query in Design view, and then modify the query to display only the top five values for the TripCost field. Save the query as **Top Trip Cost**, run the query, print the query datasheet, and then close the query.

9. Close the **Trips** database, and then exit Access.

INTERNET ASSIGNMENTS

Student Union

The purpose of the Internet Assignments is to challenge you to find information on the Internet that you can use to create effective documents. The actual assignments are updated and maintained on the Course Technology Web site. Log on to the Internet and use your Web browser to go to the Student Union on the New Perspectives Series site at **www.course.com/NewPerspectives/studentunion**. Click the Online Companions link, and then click the link for this text.

QUICK CHECK ANSWERS

Session 3.1

1. a general query in which you specify the fields and records you want Access to select
2. The field list contains the table name at the top of the list box and the table's fields listed in the order in which they appear in the table; the design grid displays columns that contain specifications about a field you will use in the query.
3. A table datasheet and a query datasheet look the same, appearing in Datasheet view, and can be used to update data in a database. A table datasheet shows the permanent data in a table, whereas a query datasheet is temporary and its contents are based on the criteria you establish in the design grid.
4. primary table; related table
5. Referential integrity
6. oldest to most recent date
7. when you want to perform different types of sorts (both ascending and descending, for example) on multiple fields, and when you want to sort on multiple fields that are nonadjacent or in the wrong order, but you do not want to rearrange the columns in the query datasheet to accomplish the sort
8. filter

Session 3.2

1. condition
2. in the same Criteria row; in different Criteria rows
3. expression
4. A calculated field appears in a query datasheet, form, or report but does not exist in a database, as does a table field.
5. a function that performs an arithmetic operation on selected records in a database
6. Group By

TUTORIAL 4

OBJECTIVES

In this tutorial you will:

- Create a form using the Form Wizard
- Change a form's AutoFormat
- Find data using a form
- Preview and print selected form records
- Maintain table data using a form
- Check the spelling of table data using a form
- Create a form with a main form and a subform
- Create a report using the Report Wizard
- Insert a picture in a report
- Preview and print a report

CREATING FORMS AND REPORTS

Creating a Position Data Form, an Employer Positions Form, and an Employers and Positions Report

CASE

Northeast Seasonal Jobs International (NSJI)

Elsa Jensen wants to continue enhancing the Northeast database to make it easier for NSJI employees to find and maintain data. In particular, she wants the database to include a form based on the Position table to make it easier for employees to enter and change data about available positions. She also wants the database to include a form that shows data from both the Employer and Position tables at the same time. This form will show the position information for each employer along with the corresponding employer data, providing a complete picture of NSJI's employer clients and their available positions.

In addition, Zack Ward would like the database to include a formatted report of employer and position data so that his marketing staff members will have printed output when completing market analyses and planning strategies for selling NSJI's services to employer clients. He wants the information to be formatted attractively, perhaps by including a picture or graphic image on the report for visual interest.

SESSION 4.1

In this session, you will create a form using the Form Wizard, change a form's AutoFormat, find data using a form, preview and print selected form records, maintain table data using a form, and check the spelling of table data using a form.

Creating a Form Using the Form Wizard

As you learned in Tutorial 1, a form is an object you use to maintain, view, and print records in a database. In Access, you can design your own forms or use a Form Wizard to create them for you automatically.

Elsa asks you to create a new form that her staff can use to view and maintain data in the Position table. In Tutorial 1, you used the AutoForm Wizard to create the Employer Data form in the Seasonal database. The AutoForm Wizard creates a form automatically, using all the fields in the selected table or query. To create the form for the Position table, you'll use the Form Wizard. The **Form Wizard** allows you to choose some or all of the fields in the selected table or query, choose fields from other tables and queries, and display the selected fields in any order on the form. You can also apply an existing style to the form to format its appearance quickly.

To open the Northeast database and activate the Form Wizard:

1. Place your Data Disk in the appropriate disk drive.

2. Start Access and open the **Northeast** database located in the Tutorial folder on your Data Disk.

3. Click **Forms** in the Objects bar of the Database window.

4. Click the **New** button in the Database window. The New Form dialog box opens.

5. Click **Form Wizard**, click the list arrow for choosing a table or query, click **Position** to select this table as the source for the form, and then click the **OK** button. The first Form Wizard dialog box opens. See Figure 4-1.

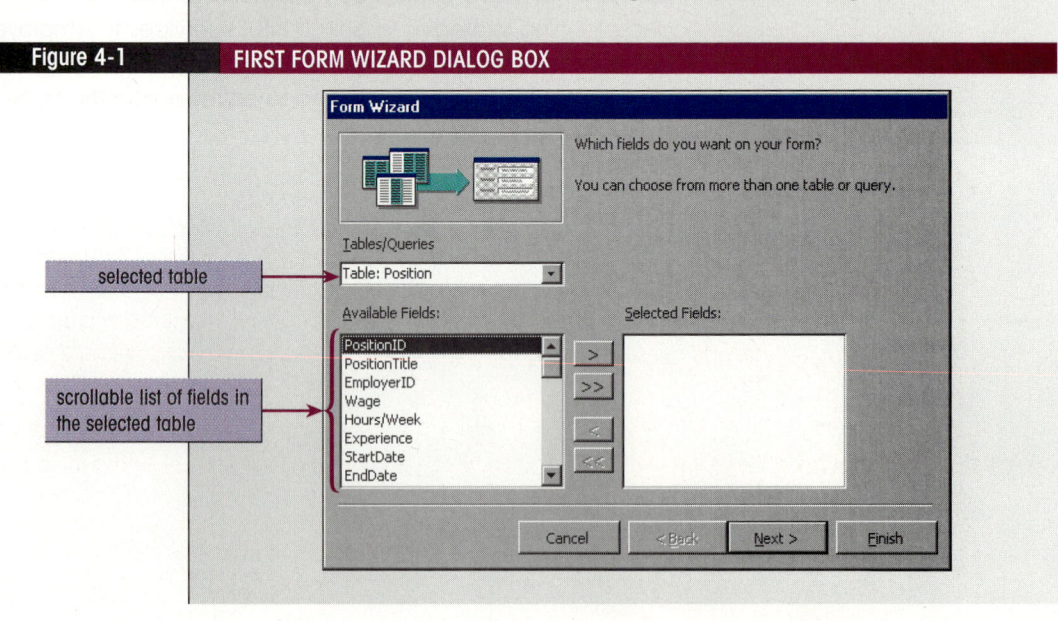

Figure 4-1 **FIRST FORM WIZARD DIALOG BOX**

TUTORIAL 4 CREATING FORMS AND REPORTS   AC 4.03   ACCESS

Elsa wants the form to display all the fields in the Position table, but in a different order. She would like the Experience field to appear at the bottom of the form so that it stands out more, making it easier to determine if a position requires prior work experience.

To finish creating the form using the Form Wizard:

1. Click **PositionID** in the Available Fields list box (if necessary), and then click the **>** button to move the field to the Selected Fields list box.

2. Repeat Step 1 to select the **PositionTitle**, **EmployerID**, **Wage**, **Hours/Week**, **StartDate**, **EndDate**, **Openings**, and **Experience** fields, in that order. Remember, you can also double-click a field to move it from the Available Fields list box to the Selected Fields list box.

3. Click the **Next** button to display the second Form Wizard dialog box, in which you select a layout for the form. See Figure 4-2.

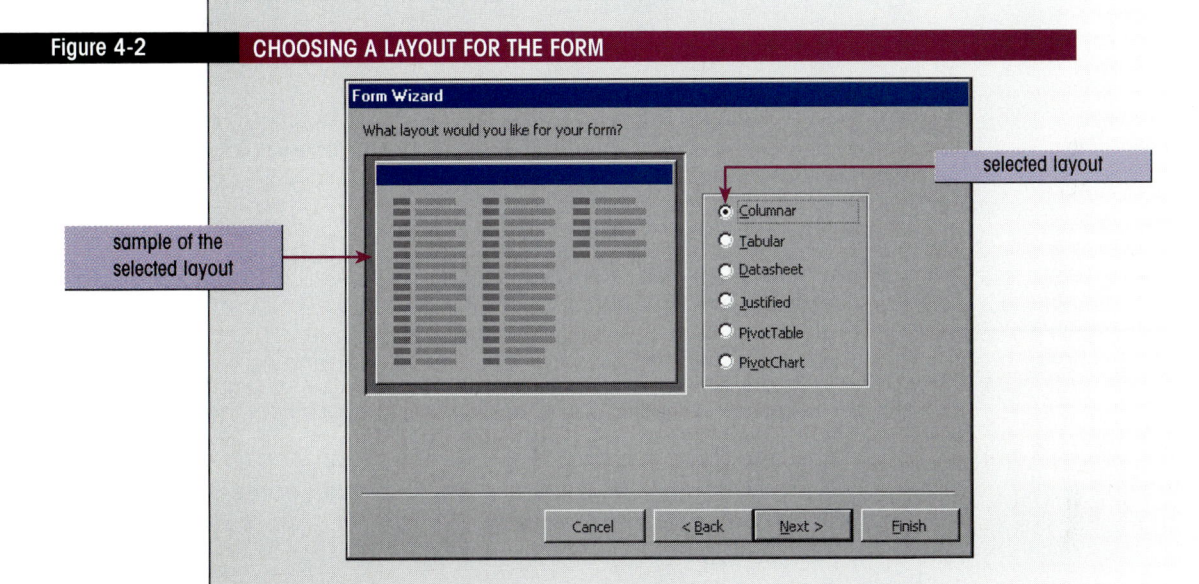

Figure 4-2   **CHOOSING A LAYOUT FOR THE FORM**

The layout choices are Columnar, Tabular, Datasheet, Justified, PivotTable, and PivotChart. A sample of the selected layout appears on the left side of the dialog box.

4. Click each of the option buttons and review the corresponding sample layout.

The Tabular and Datasheet layouts display the fields from multiple records at one time, whereas the Columnar and Justified layouts display the fields from one record at a time. The PivotTable and PivotChart layouts display summary and analytical information. Elsa thinks the Columnar layout is the appropriate arrangement for displaying and updating data in the table, so you'll choose this layout.

5. Click the **Columnar** option button (if necessary), and then click the **Next** button. Access displays the third Form Wizard dialog box, in which you choose a style for the form. See Figure 4-3.

Figure 4-3 CHOOSING A STYLE FOR THE FORM

sample of the selected style

Form Wizard styles

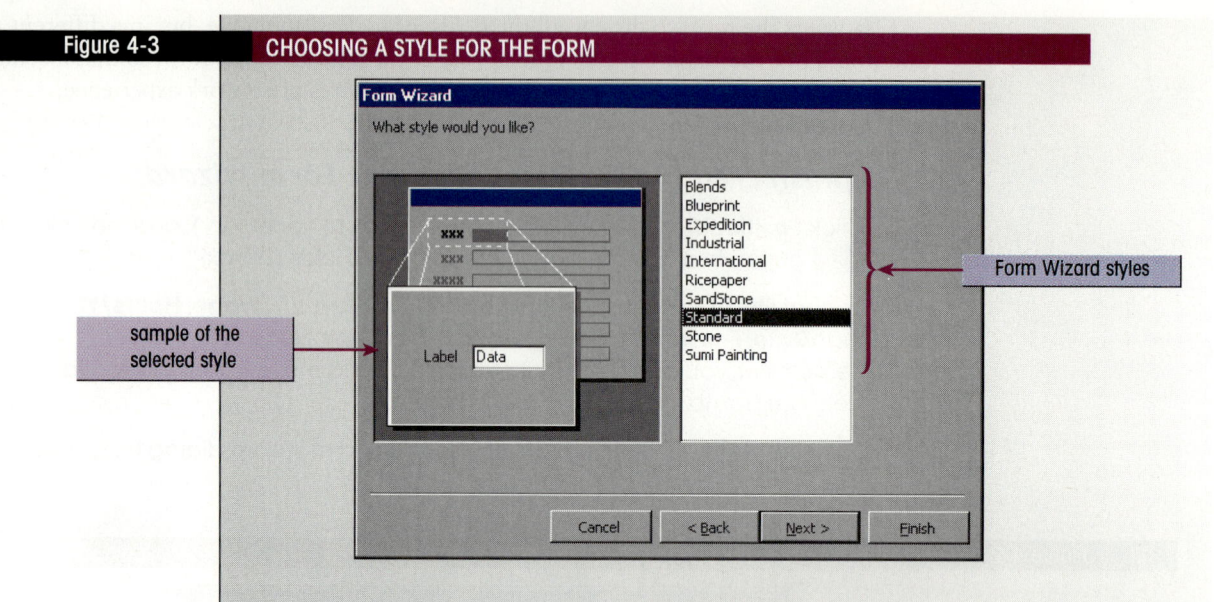

A sample of the selected style appears in the box on the left. If you choose a style, which is called an **AutoFormat**, and decide you'd prefer a different one after the form is created, you can change it.

TROUBLE? Don't worry if a different form style is selected in your dialog box instead of the one shown in Figure 4-3. The dialog box displays the most recently used style, which might be different on your computer.

6. Click each of the styles and review the corresponding sample.

   Elsa likes the Expedition style and asks you to use it for the form.

7. Click **Expedition** and then click the **Next** button. Access displays the final Form Wizard dialog box and shows the Position table's name as the default form name. "Position" is also the default title that will appear in the form's title bar. See Figure 4-4.

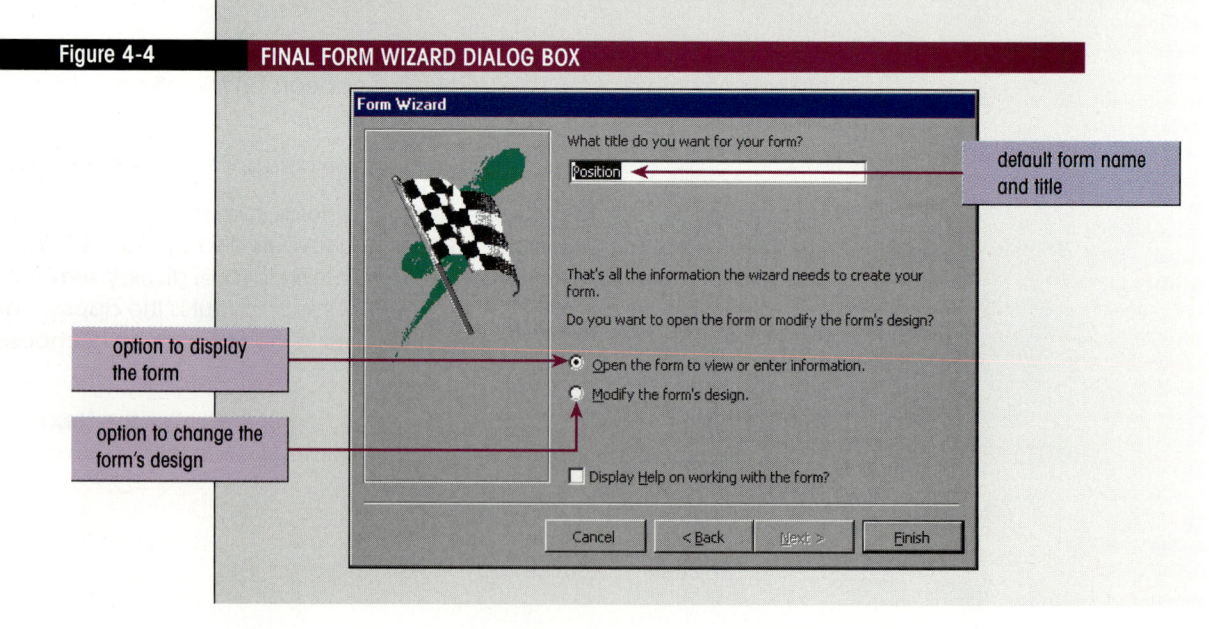

Figure 4-4 FINAL FORM WIZARD DIALOG BOX

default form name and title

option to display the form

option to change the form's design

You'll use "Position Data" as the form name and, because you don't need to change the form's design at this point, you'll display the form.

8. Click the insertion point to the right of Position in the text box, press the **spacebar**, type **Data**, and then click the **Finish** button. The completed form opens in Form view. See Figure 4-5.

Figure 4-5   COMPLETED FORM FOR THE POSITION TABLE

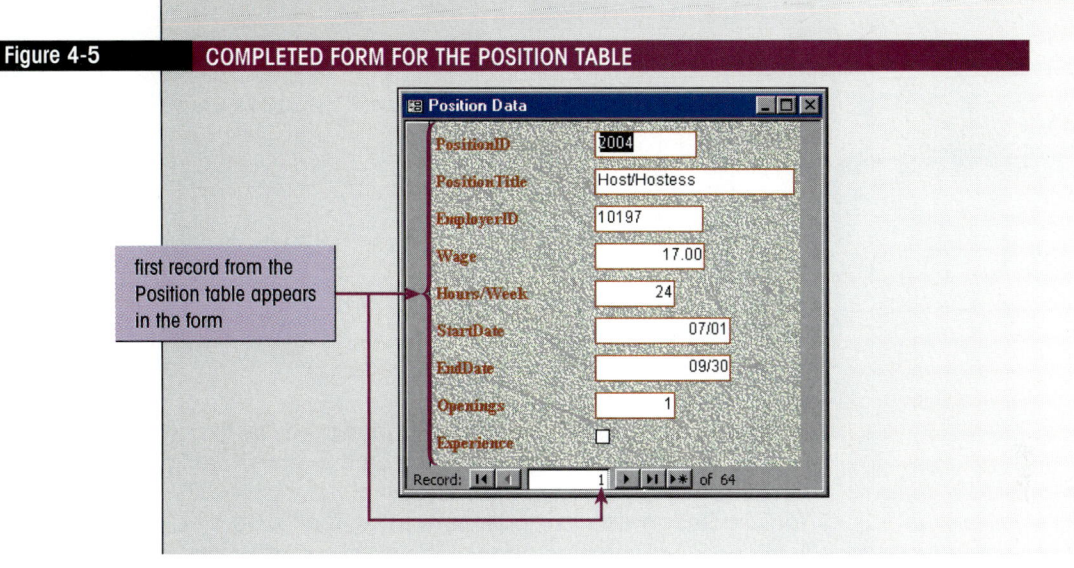

first record from the Position table appears in the form

After viewing the form, Elsa decides that she doesn't like the form's style; the background makes the field names a bit difficult to read. She asks you to change the form's style.

Changing a Form's AutoFormat

You can change a form's appearance by choosing a different AutoFormat for the form. As you learned when you created the Position Data form, an AutoFormat is a predefined style for a form (or report). The AutoFormats available for a form are the ones you saw when you selected the form's style using the Form Wizard. To change an AutoFormat, you must switch to Design view.

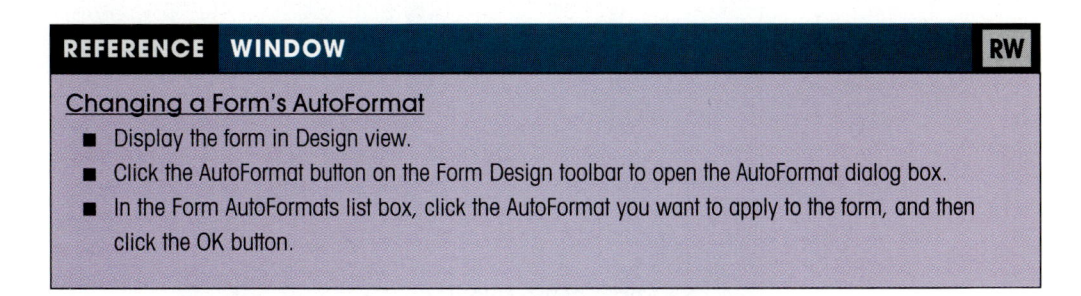

REFERENCE WINDOW   **RW**

Changing a Form's AutoFormat
- Display the form in Design view.
- Click the AutoFormat button on the Form Design toolbar to open the AutoFormat dialog box.
- In the Form AutoFormats list box, click the AutoFormat you want to apply to the form, and then click the OK button.

To change the AutoFormat for the Position Data form:

1. Click the **View** button for Design view on the Form View toolbar. The form is displayed in Design view. See Figure 4-6.

Figure 4-6 FORM DISPLAYED IN DESIGN VIEW

AutoFormat button

Form window

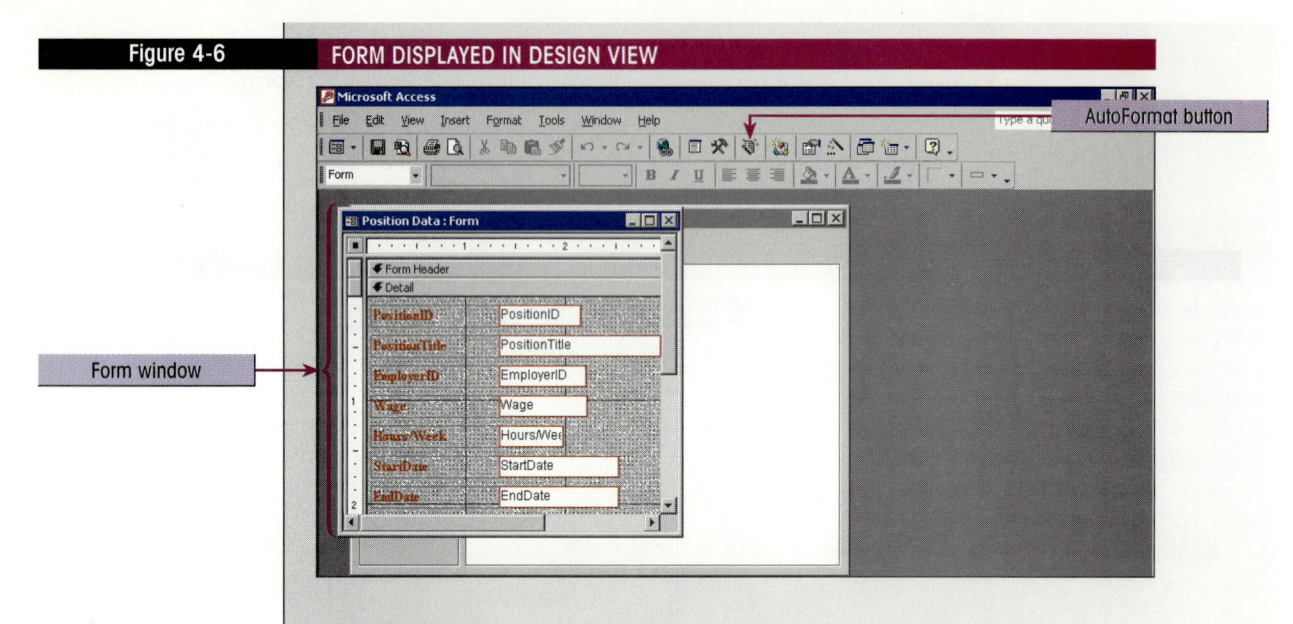

TROUBLE? If your screen displays any window other than those shown in Figure 4-6, click the Close button ✗ on the window's title bar to close it.

You use Design view to modify an existing form or to create a form from scratch. In this case, you need to change the AutoFormat for the Position Data form.

2. Click the **AutoFormat** button on the Form Design toolbar. The AutoFormat dialog box opens.

3. Click the **Options** button to display the AutoFormat options. See Figure 4-7.

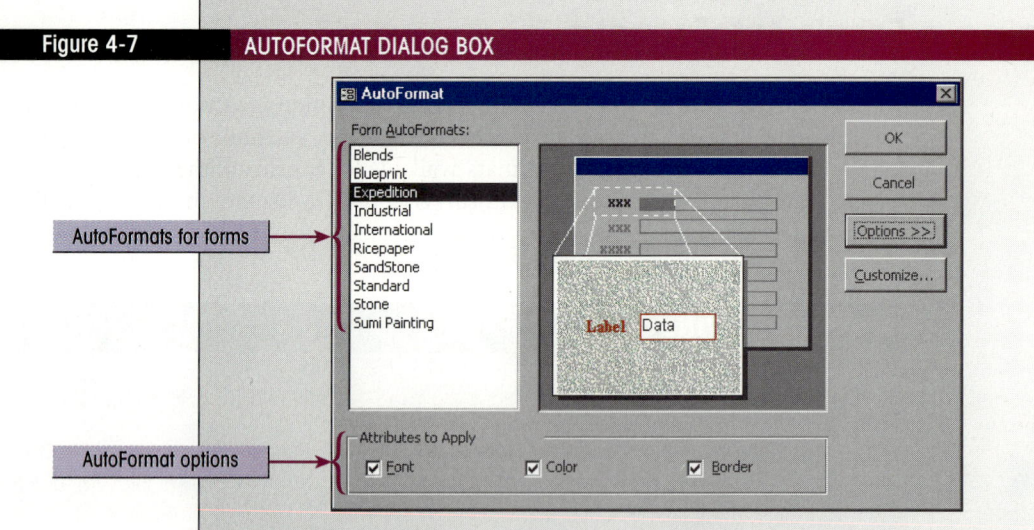

Figure 4-7 AUTOFORMAT DIALOG BOX

AutoFormats for forms

AutoFormat options

A sample of the selected AutoFormat appears to the right of the Form AutoFormats list box. The options at the bottom of the dialog box let you apply the selected AutoFormat or just its font, color, or border.

Elsa decides that she prefers the Standard AutoFormat, because its field names and field values are easy to read.

4. Click **Standard** in the Form AutoFormats list box, and then click the **OK** button. The AutoFormat dialog box closes, the Standard AutoFormat is applied to the form, and the Form window in Design view becomes the active window.

5. Click the **View** button for Form view 🔲 on the Form Design toolbar. The form is displayed in Form view with the new AutoFormat. See Figure 4-8.

Figure 4-8   FORM DISPLAYED WITH THE NEW AUTOFORMAT

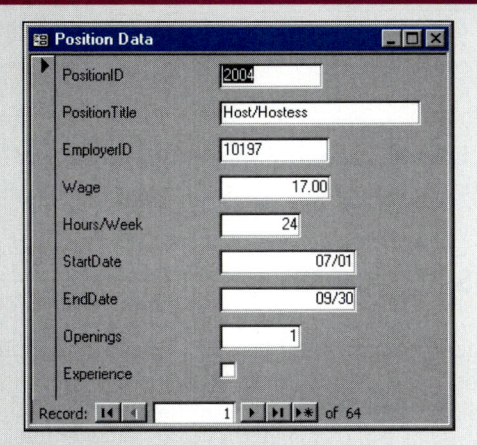

Position Data	
PositionID	2004
PositionTitle	Host/Hostess
EmployerID	10197
Wage	17.00
Hours/Week	24
StartDate	07/01
EndDate	09/30
Openings	1
Experience	☐

Record: |◄ ◄ 1 ► ►| ►* of 64

You have finished modifying the format of the form and can now save it.

6. Click the **Save** button 💾 on the Form View toolbar to save the modified form.

Elsa wants to use the Position Data form to view some data in the Position table. To view data, you need to navigate through the form. As you learned in Tutorial 1, you navigate through a form in the same way that you navigate through a table datasheet. Also, the navigation mode and editing mode keystroke techniques you used with datasheets in Tutorial 2 are the same when navigating a form.

To navigate through the Position Data form:

1. Press the **Tab** key to move to the PositionTitle field value, and then press the **End** key to move to the Experience field. Because the Experience field is a yes/no field, its value is not highlighted; instead, a dotted outline appears around the field name to indicate that it is the current field.

2. Press the **Home** key to move back to the PositionID field value. The first record in the Position table still appears in the form.

3. Press **Ctrl + End** to move to the Experience field for record 64, which is the last record in the table. The record number for the current record appears in the Specific Record box between the navigation buttons at the bottom of the form.

4. Click the **Previous Record** navigation button ◄ to move to the Experience field in record 63.

5. Press the ↑ key twice to move to the EndDate field in record 63.

6. Click the insertion point between the numbers "1" and "5" in the EndDate field value to switch to editing mode, press the **Home** key to move the insertion point to the beginning of the field value, and then press the **End** key to move the insertion point to the end of the field value.

7. Click the **First Record** navigation button to move to the EndDate field value in the first record. The entire field value is highlighted because you have switched from editing mode to navigation mode.

8. Click the **Next Record** navigation button to move to the EndDate field value in record 2, the next record.

Elsa asks you to display the records for The Clipper Ship Inn, whose EmployerID is 10145, because she wants to review the available positions for this employer.

Finding Data Using a Form

The **Find** command lets you search for data in a form or datasheet so you can display only those records you want to view. You choose a field to serve as the basis for the search by making that field the current field; then you enter the value you want Access to match in the Find and Replace dialog box. You can use the Find command by clicking the toolbar Find button or by using the Edit menu.

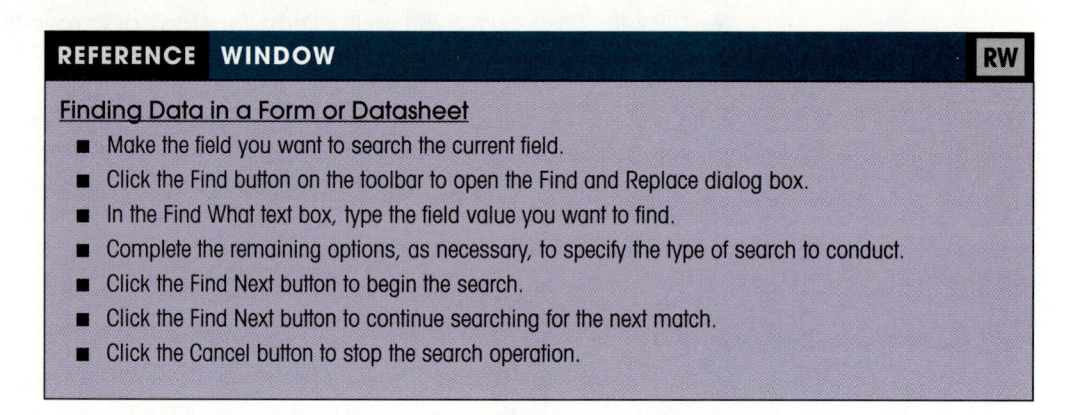

REFERENCE WINDOW

Finding Data in a Form or Datasheet
- Make the field you want to search the current field.
- Click the Find button on the toolbar to open the Find and Replace dialog box.
- In the Find What text box, type the field value you want to find.
- Complete the remaining options, as necessary, to specify the type of search to conduct.
- Click the Find Next button to begin the search.
- Click the Find Next button to continue searching for the next match.
- Click the Cancel button to stop the search operation.

You need to find all records in the Position table for The Clipper Ship Inn, whose EmployerID is 10145.

To find the records using the Position Data form:

1. Click in the **EmployerID** field value box. This is the field that you will search for matching values.

2. Click the **Find** button on the Form View toolbar. The Find and Replace dialog box opens. Note that the Look In list box shows the name of the field that Access will search (in this case, the current EmployerID field), and the Match list box indicates that Access will find values that match the entire entry in the field. You could choose to match only part of a field value or only the beginning of each field value.

3. If the Find and Replace dialog box covers the form, move the dialog box by dragging its title bar. If necessary, move the Position Data form window so that you can see both the dialog box and the form at the same time. See Figure 4-9.

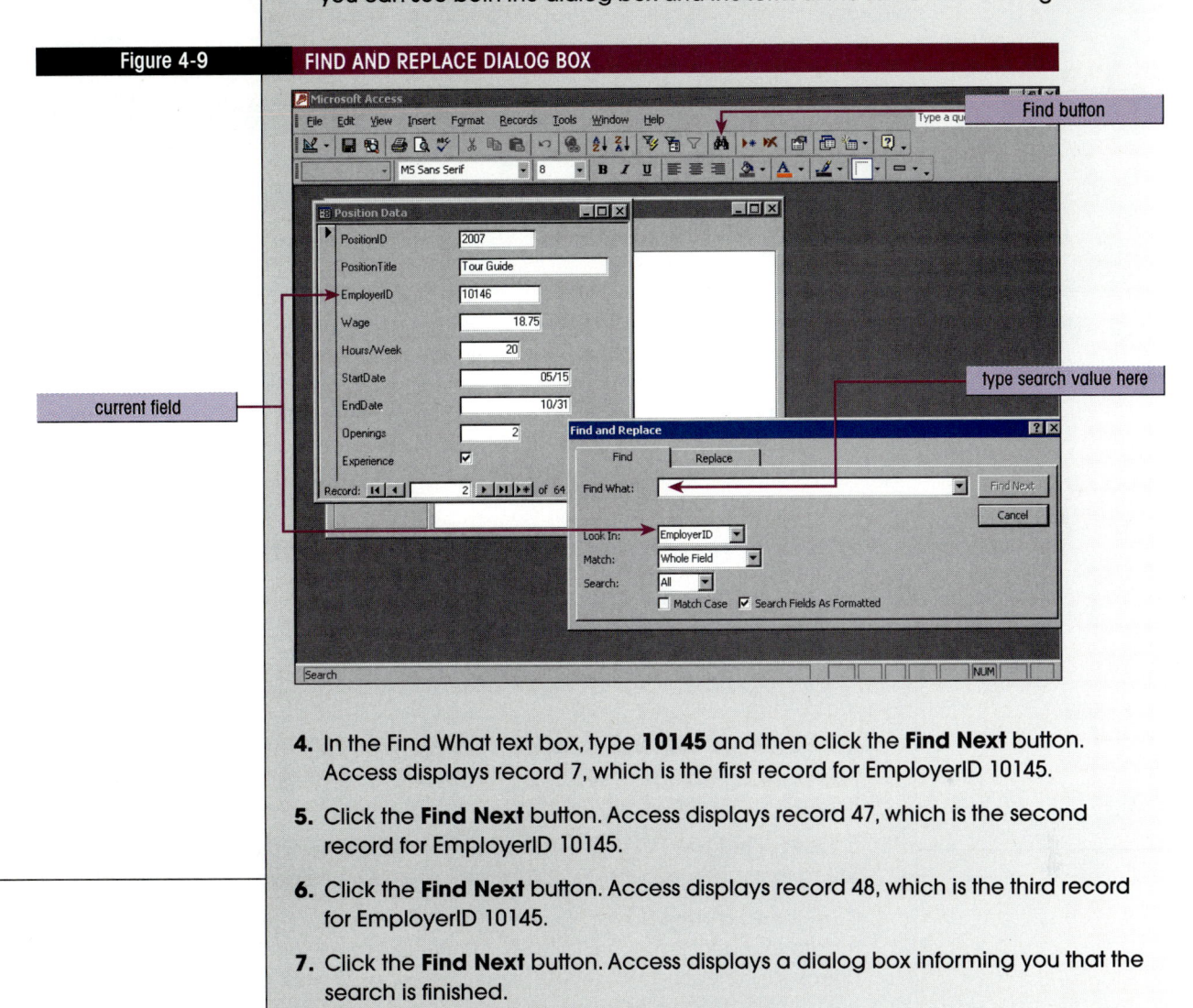

Figure 4-9   **FIND AND REPLACE DIALOG BOX**

4. In the Find What text box, type **10145** and then click the **Find Next** button. Access displays record 7, which is the first record for EmployerID 10145.

5. Click the **Find Next** button. Access displays record 47, which is the second record for EmployerID 10145.

6. Click the **Find Next** button. Access displays record 48, which is the third record for EmployerID 10145.

7. Click the **Find Next** button. Access displays a dialog box informing you that the search is finished.

8. Click the **OK** button to close the dialog box.

The search value you enter can be an exact value, such as the EmployerID 10145 you just entered, or it can include wildcard characters. A **wildcard character** is a placeholder you use when you know only part of a value or when you want to start or end with a specific character or match a certain pattern. Figure 4-10 shows the wildcard characters you can use when finding data.

Figure 4-10 WILDCARD CHARACTERS

WILDCARD CHARACTER	PURPOSE	EXAMPLE
*	Match any number of characters. It can be used as the first and/or last character in the character string.	th* finds *the, that, this, therefore,* and so on
?	Match any single alphabetic character.	a?t finds *act, aft, ant, apt,* and *art*
[ ]	Match any single character within the brackets.	a[fr]t finds *aft* and *art* but not *act, ant,* and *apt*
!	Match any character not within brackets.	a[!fr]t finds *act, ant,* and *apt* but not *aft* and *art*
-	Match any one of a range of characters. The range must be in ascending order (a to z, not z to a).	a[d-p]t finds *aft, ant,* and *apt* but not *act* and *art*
#	Match any single numeric character.	#72 finds *072, 172, 272, 372,* and so on

Elsa wants to view the position records for two employers: George's Restaurant & Galley (EmployerID 10180) and Moondance Inn & Ski Resort (EmployerID 10185). Matt Griffin, the manager of recruitment, knows of some student recruits with prior work experience who are interested in working for these employers. Elsa wants to see which positions, if any, require experience. You'll use the * wildcard character to search for these employers' positions.

To find the records using the * wildcard character:

1. Click **10145** in the Find What text box to select the entire value, and then type **1018***.

   Access will match any field value in the EmployerID field that starts with the digits 1018.

2. Click the **Find Next** button. Access displays record 64, which is the first record found for EmployerID 10185. Note that the Experience field value is unchecked, indicating that this position does not require experience.

3. Click the **Find Next** button. Access displays record 25, which is the first record found for EmployerID 10180. Again, the Experience field value is unchecked.

4. Click the **Find Next** button. Access displays record 42, which is the second record found for EmployerID 10185. In this case, the Experience field value is checked, indicating that this position requires prior work experience.

5. Click the **Find Next** button. Access displays a dialog box informing you that the search is finished.

6. Click the **OK** button to close the dialog box.

7. Click the **Cancel** button to close the Find and Replace dialog box.

Of the three positions, only one requires experience—PositionID 2089. Elsa asks you to use the form to print the data for record 42, which is for PositionID 2089, so that she can give the printout to Matt.

Previewing and Printing Selected Form Records

Access prints as many form records as can fit on a printed page. If only part of a form record fits on the bottom of a page, the remainder of the record prints on the next page. Access allows you to print all pages or a range of pages. In addition, you can print the currently selected form record.

Before printing record 42, you'll preview the form record to see how it will look when printed. Notice that the current record number (in this case, 42) appears in the Specific Record box at the bottom of the form.

To preview the form and print the data for record 42:

1. Click the **Print Preview** button on the Form View toolbar. The Print Preview window opens, showing the form records for the Position table in miniature. If you clicked the Print button now, all the records for the table would be printed, beginning with the first record.

2. Click the **Maximize** button on the form's title bar.

3. Click the **Zoom** button on the Print Preview toolbar, and then use the vertical scroll bar to view the entire page. Each record from the Position table appears in a separate form. See Figure 4-11.

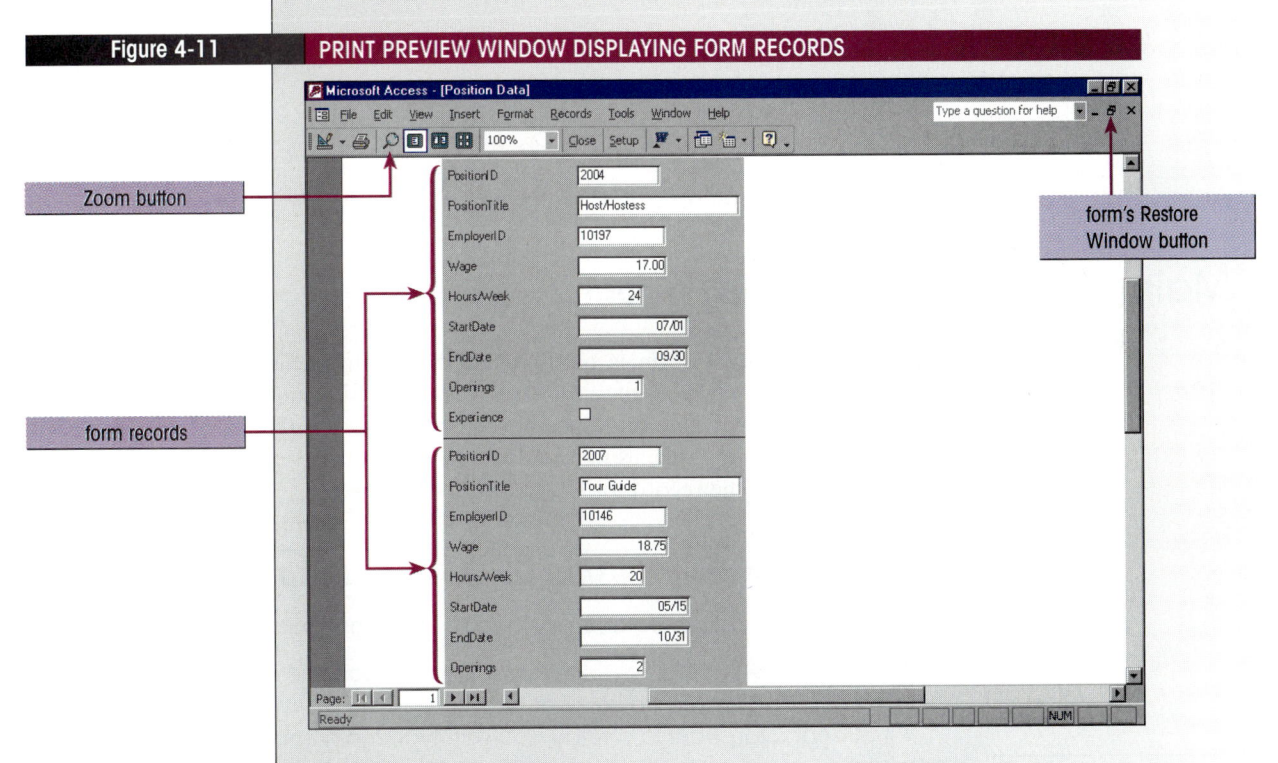

Figure 4-11 PRINT PREVIEW WINDOW DISPLAYING FORM RECORDS

[Screenshot showing Microsoft Access Print Preview window with form records. Labels point to: Zoom button, form records, and form's Restore Window button. Visible data includes PositionID 2004 (Host/Hostess, EmployerID 10197, Wage 17.00, Hours/Week 24, StartDate 07/01, EndDate 09/30, Openings 1) and PositionID 2007 (Tour Guide, EmployerID 10146, Wage 18.75, Hours/Week 20, StartDate 05/15, EndDate 10/31, Openings 2).]

4. Click the **Restore Window** button on the Print Preview menu bar, and then click the **Close** button on the Print Preview toolbar to return to the table in Form view.

The record that you need to print, PositionID 2089, appears in the form. To print selected records you need to use the Print dialog box.

> 5. Click **File** on the menu bar, and then click **Print**. The Print dialog box opens.
> 6. Click the **Selected Record(s)** option button to print the current form record (record 42).
> 7. Click the **OK** button to close the dialog box and to print the selected record.

Elsa has identified several updates, as shown in Figure 4-12, that she wants you to make to the Position table. You'll use the Position Data form to update the data in the Position table.

Figure 4-12 **UPDATES TO THE POSITION TABLE**

PositionID	Update Action
2033	Change Hours/Week to 35 Change StartDate to 6/30
2072	Delete record
2130	Add new record for PositionID 2130: PositionTitle = Housekeeping EmployerID = 10151 Wage = 12.50 Hours/Week = 30 StartDate = 6/1 EndDate = 10/15 Openings = 2 Experience = No

Maintaining Table Data Using a Form

Maintaining data using a form is often easier than using a datasheet, because you can concentrate on all the changes required to a single record at one time. You already know how to navigate a form and find specific records. Now you'll make the changes Elsa requested to the Position table, using the Position Data form.

First, you'll update the record for PositionID 2033.

> ### To change the record using the Position Data form:
>
> 1. Make sure the Position Data form is displayed in Form view.
>
>   When she reviewed the position data to identify possible corrections, Elsa noted that 10 is the record number for PositionID 2033. If you know the number of the record you want to display, you can type the number in the Specific Record box and press the Enter key to go directly to that record.
>
> 2. Select **42** in the Specific Record box, type **10**, and then press the **Enter** key. Record 10 (PositionID 2033) is now the current record.
>
>   You need to change the Hours/Week field value to 35 and the StartDate field value to 6/30 for this record.

3. Click the insertion point to the left of the number 2 in the Hours/Week field value, press the **Delete** key twice, and then type **35**. Note that the pencil symbol appears in the upper-left corner of the form, indicating that the form is in editing mode.

4. Press the **Tab** key to move to and select the StartDate field value, type **6/30**, and then press the **Enter** key. See Figure 4-13.

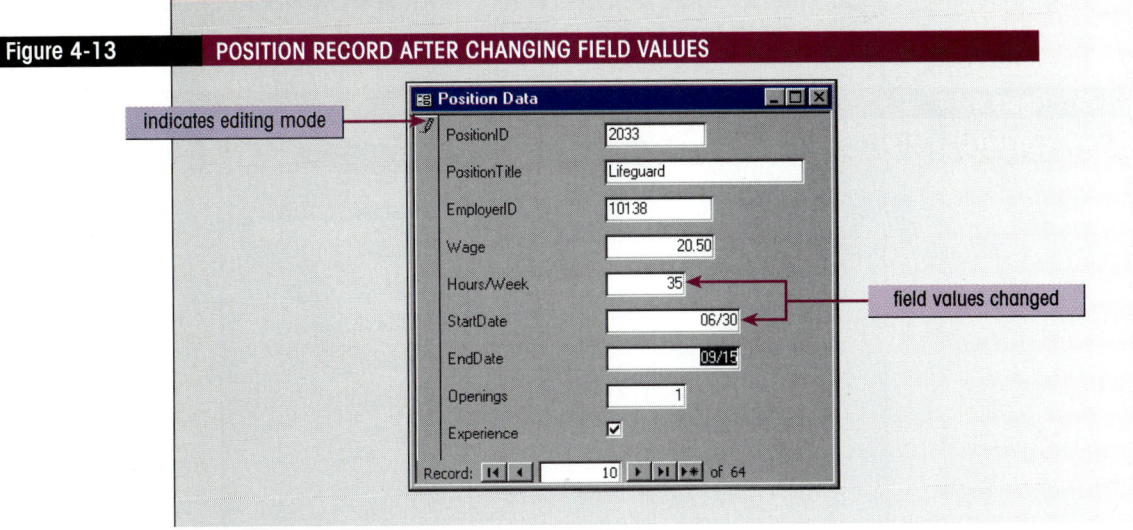

Figure 4-13   POSITION RECORD AFTER CHANGING FIELD VALUES

(Screenshot of Position Data form showing: PositionID 2033, PositionTitle Lifeguard, EmployerID 10138, Wage 20.50, Hours/Week 35, StartDate 06/30, EndDate 09/15, Openings 1, Experience checked, Record 10 of 64. Annotations: "indicates editing mode" pointing to pencil icon; "field values changed" pointing to Hours/Week and StartDate.)

You have completed the changes for PositionID 2033. Elsa's next update is to delete the record for PositionID 2072. The employer client recently informed Elsa that a full-time, permanent employee has been hired for this position, so it is no longer available for student recruits.

To delete the record using the Position Data form:

1. Click anywhere in the PositionID field value to make it the current field.

2. Click the **Find** button on the Form View toolbar. The Find and Replace dialog box opens.

3. Type **2072** in the Find What text box, click the **Find Next** button, and then click the **Cancel** button. The record for PositionID 2072 is now the current record.

4. Click the **Delete Record** button on the Form View toolbar. A dialog box opens, asking you to confirm the record deletion.

5. Click the **Yes** button. The dialog box closes, and the record for PositionID 2072 is deleted from the table.

Elsa's final maintenance change is to add a record for a new position available at the Granite State Resort.

To add the new record using the Position Data form:

1. Click the **New Record** button on the Form View toolbar. Record 64, the next record available for a new record, becomes the current record. All field value boxes are empty, and the insertion point is positioned at the beginning of the field value box for PositionID.

2. Refer to Figure 4-14 and enter the value shown for each field. Press the **Tab** key to move from field to field.

Figure 4-14   COMPLETED FORM FOR THE NEW RECORD

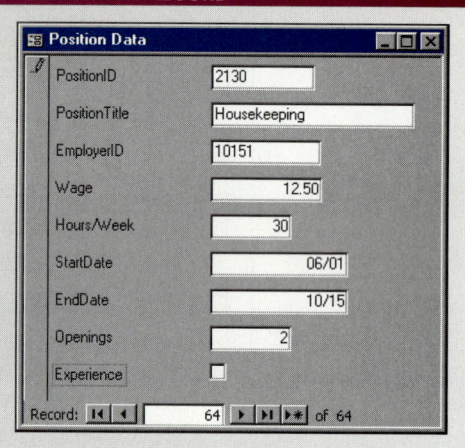

PositionID	2130
PositionTitle	Housekeeping
EmployerID	10151
Wage	12.50
Hours/Week	30
StartDate	06/01
EndDate	10/15
Openings	2
Experience	☐

Record: 64 of 64

TROUBLE? Compare your screen with Figure 4-14. If any field value is wrong, correct it now, using the methods described earlier for editing field values.

3. After entering the value for Openings, press the **Tab** key twice (if necessary). Record 65, the next record available for a new record, becomes the current record, and the record for PositionID 2130 is saved in the Position table.

You've completed Elsa's changes to the Position table, so you can close the Position Data form.

4. Click the **Close** button on the form's title bar. The form closes and you return to the Database window. Notice that the Position Data form is listed in the Forms list box.

Checking the Spelling of Table Data Using a Form

You can check the spelling of table data using a table or query datasheet or a form that displays the table data. The Spelling feature searches through the data and identifies any words that are not included in its dictionary. Sometimes the word is misspelled, and you can correct it; other words are spelled correctly, but they are not listed in the spelling dictionary.

Elsa wants to make sure that the position data contains no spelling errors. You'll use the Position Data form to check the spelling of data in the Position table.

TUTORIAL 4 CREATING FORMS AND REPORTS   AC 4.15

To check the spelling of data using the Position Data form:

1. Double-click **Position Data** to open the form in Form view. The form displays data for the first record.

2. Click the **Spelling** button on the Form View toolbar. The Spelling dialog box opens, identifying the word "Reservationist" as not in its dictionary. See Figure 4-15.

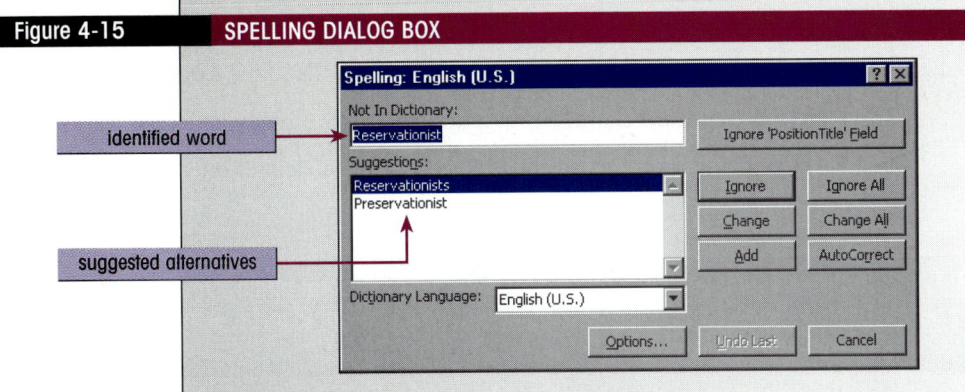

Figure 4-15   SPELLING DIALOG BOX

- identified word
- suggested alternatives

TROUBLE? If the word "Reservationist" is not identified by the Spelling feature, it was probably added to your dictionary. Just continue with the steps.

Note that the dialog box provides buttons for ignoring the word or changing it to one of the suggested alternatives, plus an option for ignoring all entries in the selected field (PositionTitle, in this case). The word is spelled correctly, so you will ignore all occurrences of this word in the Position table.

3. Click the **Ignore All** button. Next, the Spelling dialog box identifies the word "Greenskeeper" as not in its dictionary, and suggests the spelling should be two words, "Greens keeper." You'll change to the suggested spelling.

4. Click the **Change All** button. All occurrences of the word "Greenskeeper" are changed to the words "Greens keeper" in the Position table.

   A dialog box opens, informing you that the spell check is complete.

5. Click the **OK** button to close the dialog box.

6. Close the form.

You can customize how the Spelling feature works in Access by changing the settings on the Spelling tab of the Options dialog box, which you open by choosing Options from the Tools menu. For example, you can choose another language for the main dictionary, and you can create custom dictionaries to contain words or phrases specific to the type of data in your database. Adding frequently used words to a custom dictionary will prevent the Spelling feature from identifying those words as not in its dictionary, thereby speeding up the spell check process.

The Position Data form will enable Elsa and her staff to enter and maintain data easily in the Position table. In the next session, you'll create another form for working with data in both the Position and Employer tables at the same time. You'll also create a report showing data from both tables.

Session 4.1 Quick Check

1. Describe the difference between creating a form using the AutoForm Wizard and creating a form using the Form Wizard.
2. What is an AutoFormat, and how do you change one for an existing form?
3. Which table record is displayed in a form when you press Ctrl + End while you are in navigation mode?
4. You can use the Find command to search for data in a form or _____.
5. Which wildcard character matches any single alphabetic character?
6. How many form records does Access print by default on a page?

SESSION 4.2

In this session, you will create a form with a main form and a subform, modify a form in Design view, create a report using the Report Wizard, insert a picture in a report, and preview and print a report.

Elsa would like you to create a form so that she can view the data for each employer and its available positions at the same time. The type of form you need to create will include a main form and a subform.

Creating a Form with a Main Form and a Subform

To create a form based on two tables, you must first define a relationship between the two tables. In Tutorial 3, you defined a one-to-many relationship between the Employer (primary) and Position (related) tables, so you are ready to create the form based on both tables.

When you create a form containing data from two tables that have a one-to-many relationship, you actually create a main form for data from the primary table and a subform for data from the related table. Access uses the defined relationship between the tables to join the tables automatically through the common field that exists in both tables.

Elsa and her staff will use the form when contacting employers about their available positions. The main form will contain the employer ID and name, contact first and last names, and phone number for each employer. The subform will contain the position ID and title, wage, hours/week, experience, start and end dates, and number of openings for each position.

You'll use the Form Wizard to create the form.

To create the form using the Form Wizard:

1. If you took a break after the previous session, make sure that Access is running and the Northeast database is open.
2. Make sure the Forms object is selected in the Database window, and then click the **New** button. The New Form dialog box opens.

    When creating a form based on two tables, you first choose the primary table and select the fields you want to include in the main form; then you choose the related table and select fields from it for the subform.

3. Click **Form Wizard**, click the list arrow for choosing a table or query, click **Employer** to select this table as the source for the main form, and then click the **OK** button. The first Form Wizard dialog box opens, in which you select fields in the order you want them to appear on the main form.

    Elsa wants the form to include only the EmployerID, EmployerName, ContactFirstName, ContactLastName, and Phone fields from the Employer table.

4. Click **EmployerID** in the Available Fields list box (if necessary), and then click the `>` button to move the field to the Selected Fields list box.

5. Repeat Step 4 for the **EmployerName**, **ContactFirstName**, **ContactLastName**, and **Phone** fields.

    The EmployerID field will appear in the main form, so you do not have to include it in the subform. Otherwise, Elsa wants the subform to include all the fields from the Position table.

6. Click the **Tables/Queries** list arrow, and then click **Table: Position**. The fields from the Position table appear in the Available Fields list box. The quickest way to add the fields you want to include is to move all the fields to the Selected Fields list box, and then to remove the only field you don't want to include (EmployerID).

7. Click the `>>` button to move all the fields from the Position table to the Selected Fields list box.

8. Click **Position.EmployerID** in the Selected Fields list box, and then click the `<` button to move the field back to the Available Fields list box. Note that the table name (Position) is included in the field name to distinguish it from the same field (EmployerID) in the Employer table.

9. Click the **Next** button. The next Form Wizard dialog box opens. See Figure 4-16.

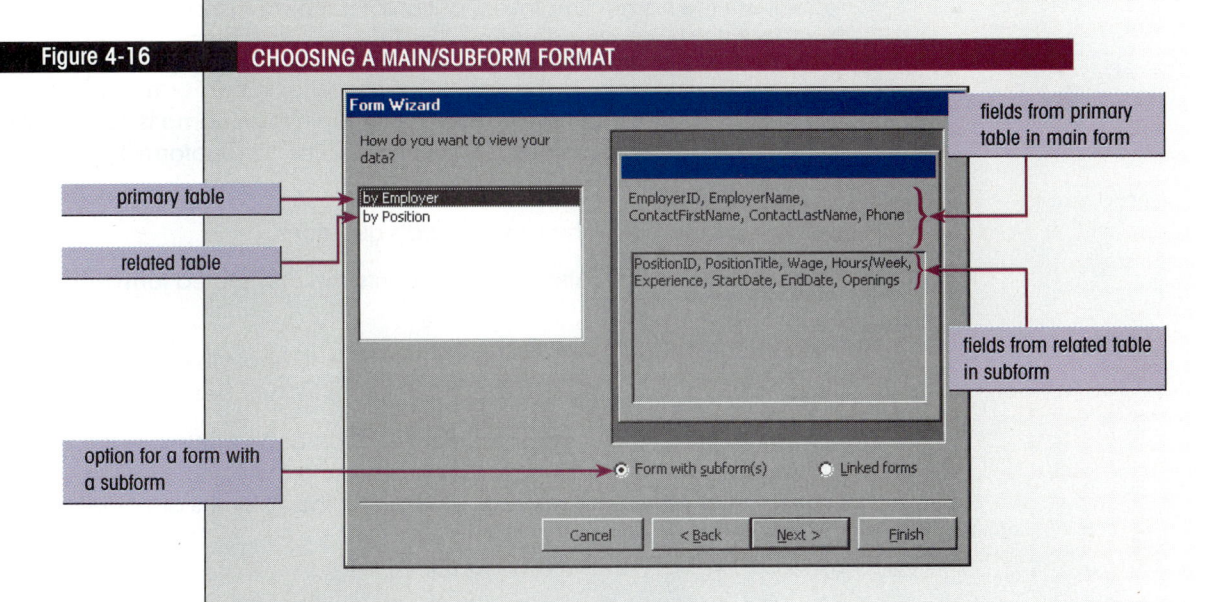

Figure 4-16   CHOOSING A MAIN/SUBFORM FORMAT

- primary table
- related table
- option for a form with a subform
- fields from primary table in main form
- fields from related table in subform

In this dialog box, the list box on the left shows the order in which you will view the selected data: first by data from the primary Employer table, and then by data from the related Position table. The form will be displayed as shown in the right side of the dialog box, with the fields from the Employer table at the top in the main form, and the fields from the Position table at the bottom in the subform. The selected option button specifies a main form with a subform. The Linked forms option creates a form structure where only the main form fields are displayed. A button with the subform's name on it appears on the main form; you can click this button to display the associated subform records.

The default options shown in Figure 4-16 are correct for creating a form with Employer data in the main form and Position data in the subform.

To finish creating the form:

1. Click the **Next** button. The next Form Wizard dialog box opens, in which you choose the subform layout.

   The Tabular layout displays subform fields as a table, whereas the Datasheet layout displays subform fields as a table datasheet. The PivotTable and PivotChart layouts display summary and analytical information. The layout choice is a matter of personal preference. You'll use the Datasheet layout.

2. Click the **Datasheet** option button (if necessary), and then click the **Next** button. The next Form Wizard dialog box opens, in which you choose the form's style.

   Elsa wants all forms in the Northeast database to have the same style, so you will choose Standard, which is the same style you applied to the Position Data form.

3. Click **Standard** (if necessary), and then click the **Next** button. The next Form Wizard dialog box opens, in which you choose names for the main form and the subform.

   You will use the name "Employer Positions" for the main form and the name "Position Subform" for the subform.

4. Click the insertion point to the right of the last letter in the Form text box, press the **spacebar**, and then type **Positions**. The main form name is now Employer Positions. Note that the default subform name, Position Subform, is the name you want, so you don't need to change it.

   You have answered all the Form Wizard's questions.

5. Click the **Finish** button. After a few moments, the completed form opens in Form view.

   Some of the columns in the subform are not wide enough to display the field names entirely. You need to resize the columns to their best fit.

6. Double-click the pointer ↔ at the right edge of each column in the subform, scrolling the subform to the right, as necessary, to display additional columns. Scroll the subform all the way back to the left. The columns are resized to their best fit. See Figure 4-17.

TUTORIAL 4 CREATING FORMS AND REPORTS   AC 4.19

Figure 4-17 **MAIN FORM WITH SUBFORM IN FORM VIEW**

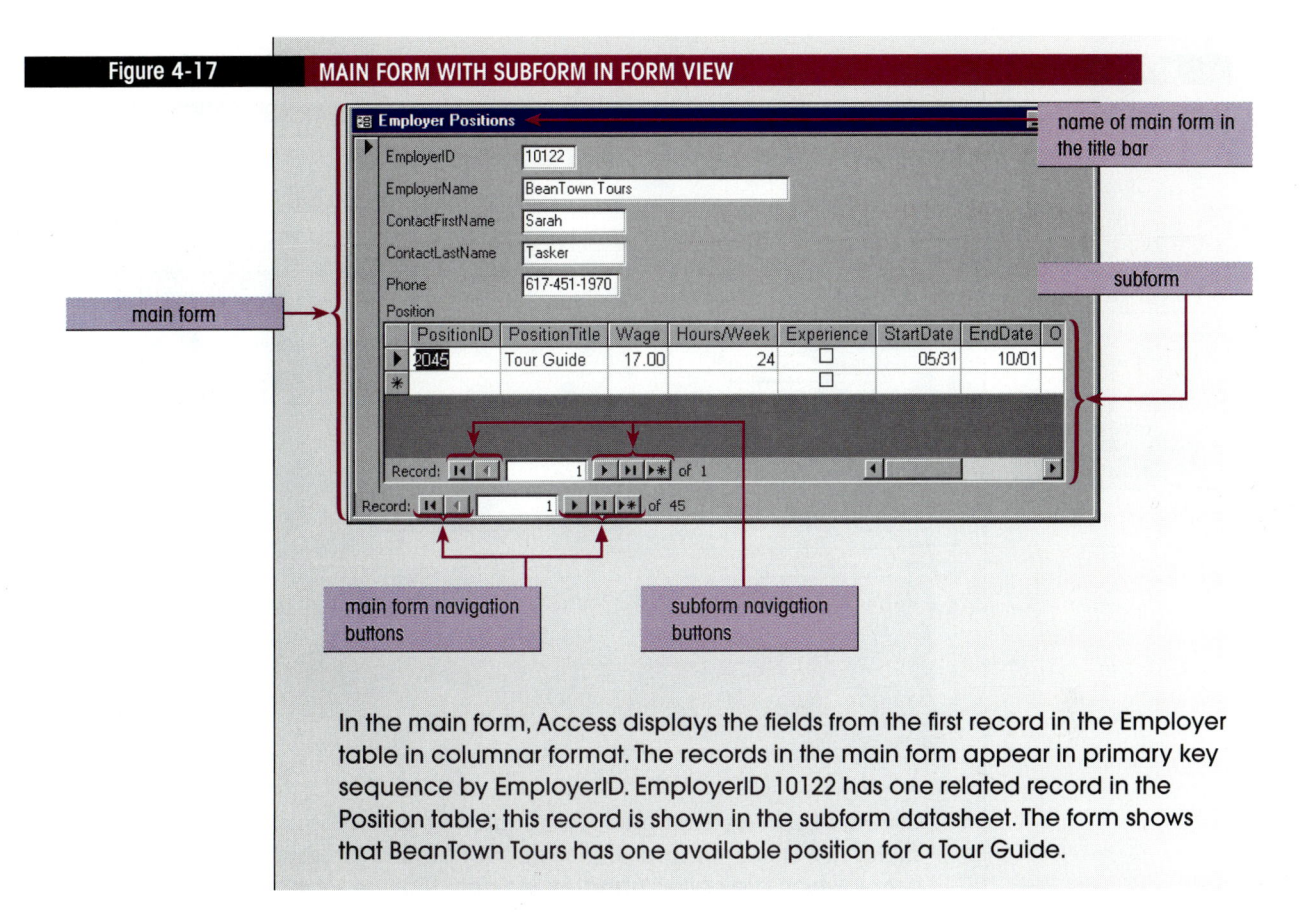

[Screenshot of the Employer Positions form showing:
- name of main form in the title bar
- main form with fields: EmployerID 10122, EmployerName BeanTown Tours, ContactFirstName Sarah, ContactLastName Tasker, Phone 617-451-1970
- Position subform with columns: PositionID 2045, PositionTitle Tour Guide, Wage 17.00, Hours/Week 24, Experience, StartDate 05/31, EndDate 10/01
- subform navigation buttons (Record 1 of 1)
- main form navigation buttons (Record 1 of 45)]

In the main form, Access displays the fields from the first record in the Employer table in columnar format. The records in the main form appear in primary key sequence by EmployerID. EmployerID 10122 has one related record in the Position table; this record is shown in the subform datasheet. The form shows that BeanTown Tours has one available position for a Tour Guide.

Notice that the subform is not wide enough to display all the fields from the Position table. Although the subform includes a horizontal scroll bar, which allows you to view the other fields, Elsa wants all the fields from the Position table to be visible in the subform at the same time. Even if you maximized the Form window, the subform would still not display all of the fields. You need to widen the main form and the subform in Design view.

Modifying a Form in Design View

Just as you use Design view to modify the format and content of tables and queries, you use Design view to modify a form. You can change the fields that are displayed on a form, and modify their size, location, format, and so on. You need to open the Employer Positions form in Design view and resize the Position subform to display all the fields at the same time.

To widen the Position subform:

1. Click the **View** button for Design view on the Form View toolbar to display the form in Design view.

2. Click the **Maximize** button to enlarge the window. See Figure 4-18.

Figure 4-18 FORM DISPLAYED IN DESIGN VIEW

Form Header bar for subform

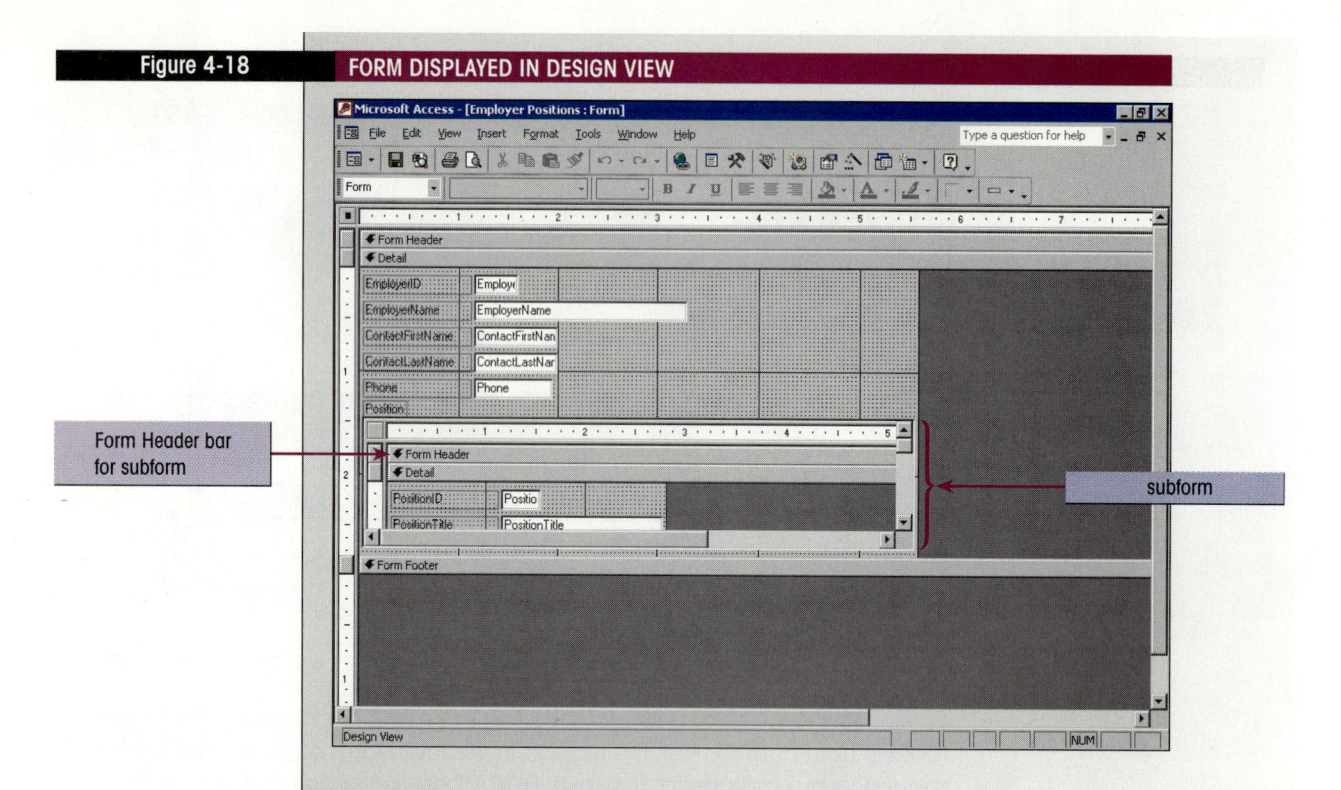

subform

3. Click the **Form Header** bar for the subform (refer to Figure 4-18) to select the subform. Notice that small boxes appear around the subform's border. These boxes, which are called **handles**, indicate that the subform is selected and can be manipulated. See Figure 4-19.

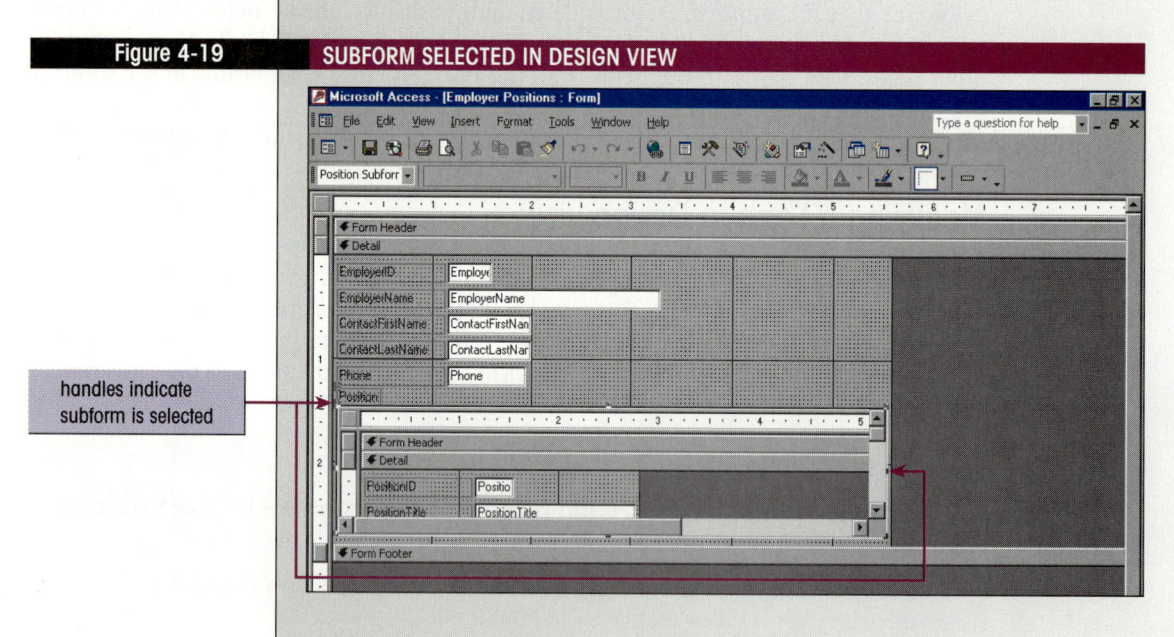

Figure 4-19 SUBFORM SELECTED IN DESIGN VIEW

handles indicate subform is selected

4. Position the pointer on the right-center sizing handle so it changes to a ↔ shape, and then click and drag the handle to the right to the **6.5**-inch mark on the horizontal ruler. See Figure 4-20.

Figure 4-20   **RESIZING THE POSITION SUBFORM**

widen the subform to this mark

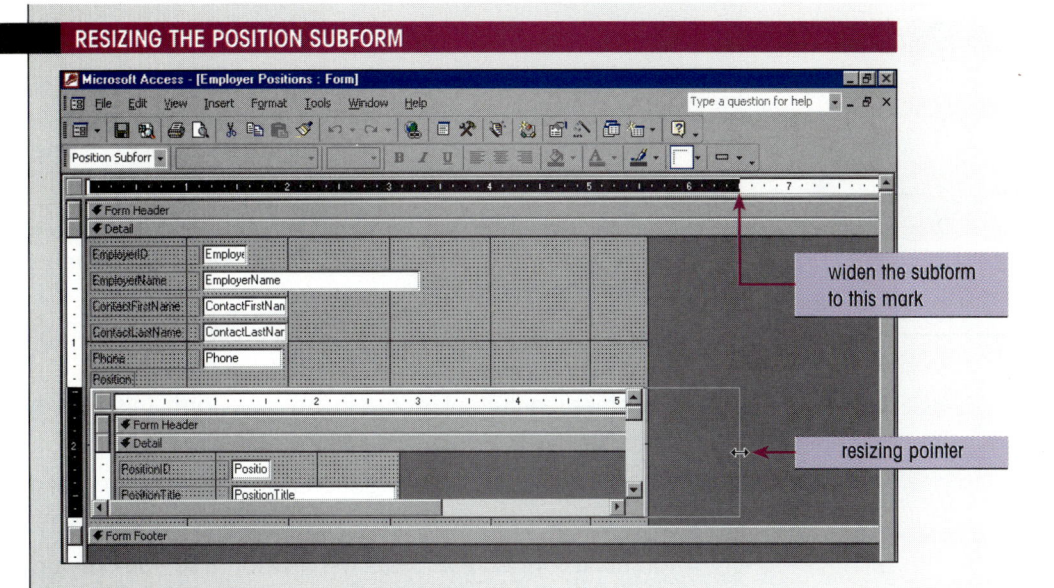

resizing pointer

5. Release the mouse button. The subform section is resized. Notice that the main form section is also resized.

6. Switch back to Form view. Notice that all the field names in the Position Subform are now visible.

7. Click the **Restore Window** button on the menu bar to restore the form to its original size. Now you need to resize the Form window in Form view so that all the fields will be displayed when the Form window is not maximized.

8. Position the pointer on the right edge of the form so it changes to a ↔ shape, and then click and drag the right edge of the form to resize it so that it matches the form shown in Figure 4-21.

Figure 4-21   **FORM WITH ALL SUBFORM FIELDS VISIBLE**

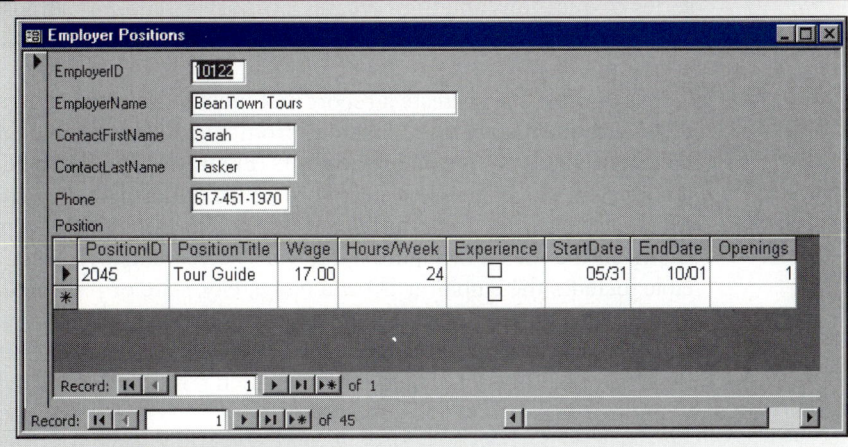

9. Save the modified form.

Two sets of navigation buttons appear at the bottom of the Form view window. You use the top set of navigation buttons to select records from the related table in the subform, and the bottom set to select records from the primary table in the main form.

You'll use the navigation buttons to view different records.

To navigate to different main form and subform records:

1. Click the **Last Record** navigation button in the main form. Record 45 in the Employer table for Lighthouse Tours becomes the current record in the main form. The subform shows that this employer has one available Tour Guide position.

2. Click the **Previous Record** navigation button in the main form. Record 44 in the Employer table for Harbor Whale Watch Tours becomes the current record in the main form.

3. Select **44** in the Specific Record box for the main form, type **32**, and then press the **Enter** key. Record 32 in the Employer table for Windsor Alpine Tours becomes the current record in the main form. This employer has two available positions.

4. Click the **Last Record** navigation button in the subform. Record 2 in the Position table becomes the current record in the subform.

   You have finished your work with the form, so you can close it.

5. Close the form. Notice that both the main form, Employer Positions, and the subform, Position Subform, appear in the Forms list box.

Zack would like a report showing data from both the Employer and Position tables so that all the pertinent information about employer clients and their positions is available in one place. To satisfy Zack's request, you'll create the report using the Report Wizard.

Creating a Report Using the Report Wizard

As you learned in Tutorial 1, a report is a formatted printout of the contents of one or more tables in a database. In Access, you can create your own reports or use the Report Wizard to create them for you. Like the Form Wizard, the **Report Wizard** asks you a series of questions and then creates a report based on your answers. Whether you use the Report Wizard or design your own report, you can change the report's design after you create it.

Zack wants you to create a report that includes selected employer data from the Employer table and all the available positions from the Position table for each employer. Zack has sketched a design of the report he wants (Figure 4-22). Like the Employer Positions form you just created, which includes a main form and a subform, the report will be based on both tables, which are joined in a one-to-many relationship through the common EmployerID field. As shown in the sketch in Figure 4-22, the selected employer data from the primary Employer table includes the employer ID and name, city, state or province, contact first and last names, and phone number. Below the data for each employer, the report will include the position ID and title, wage, hours/week, experience, start and end dates, and openings data from the related Position table. The set of field values for each position is called a **detail record**.

Figure 4-22 REPORT SKETCH FOR THE EMPLOYERS AND POSITIONS REPORT

fields from the related Position table

fields from the primary Employer table

detail records

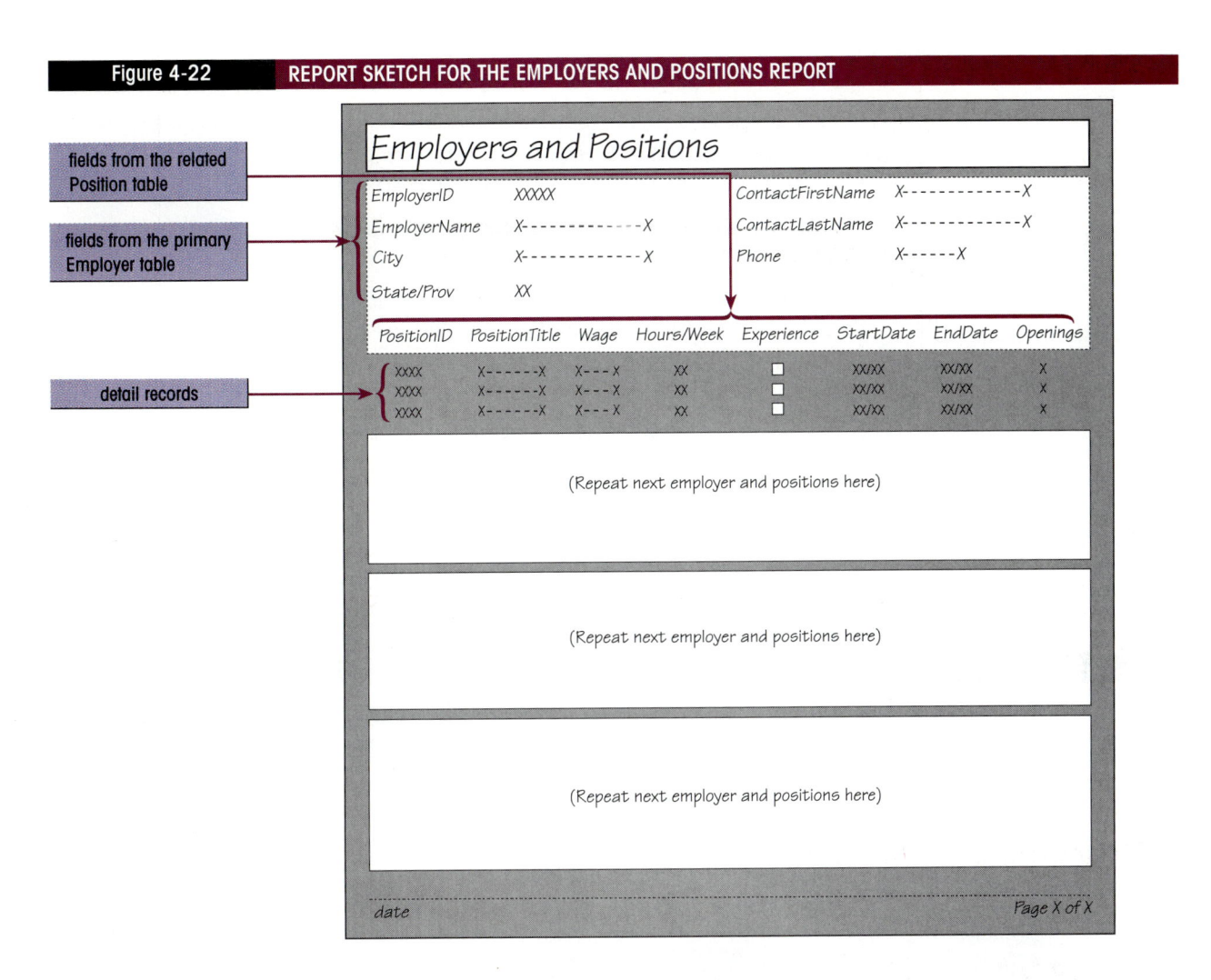

Employers and Positions

EmployerID	XXXXX	ContactFirstName	X------------X
EmployerName	X------------X	ContactLastName	X------------X
City	X------------X	Phone	X------X
State/Prov	XX		

PositionID PositionTitle Wage Hours/Week Experience StartDate EndDate Openings
XXXX   X------X   X---X   XX   ☐   XX/XX   XX/XX   X
XXXX   X------X   X---X   XX   ☐   XX/XX   XX/XX   X
XXXX   X------X   X---X   XX   ☐   XX/XX   XX/XX   X

(Repeat next employer and positions here)

(Repeat next employer and positions here)

(Repeat next employer and positions here)

date   Page X of X

You'll use the Report Wizard to create the report according to the design in Zack's sketch.

To start the Report Wizard and select the fields to include in the report:

1. Click **Reports** in the Objects bar of the Database window to display the Reports list box. You have not yet created any reports.

2. Click the **New** button in the Database window. The New Report dialog box opens.

   As was the case when you created the form with a subform, initially you can choose only one table or query to be the data source for the report. Then you can include data from other tables. You will select the primary Employer table in the New Report dialog box.

3. Click **Report Wizard**, click the list arrow for choosing a table or query, and then click **Employer**.

4. Click the **OK** button. The first Report Wizard dialog box opens.

   In the first Report Wizard dialog box, you select fields in the order you want them to appear on the report. Zack wants the EmployerID, EmployerName, City,

State/Prov, ContactFirstName, ContactLastName, and Phone fields from the Employer table to appear on the report.

5. Click **EmployerID** in the Available Fields list box (if necessary), and then click the > button. The field moves to the Selected Fields list box.

6. Repeat Step 5 to add the **EmployerName**, **City**, **State/Prov**, **ContactFirstName**, **ContactLastName**, and **Phone** fields to the report.

7. Click the **Tables/Queries** list arrow, and then click **Table: Position**. The fields from the Position table appear in the Available Fields list box.

The EmployerID field will appear on the report with the employer data, so you do not have to include it in the detail records for each position. Otherwise, Zack wants all the fields from the Position table to be included in the report.

8. Click the >> button to move all the fields from the Available Fields list box to the Selected Fields list box.

9. Click **Position.EmployerID** in the Selected Fields list box, click the < button to move the selected field back to the Available Fields list box, and then click the **Next** button. The second Report Wizard dialog box opens. See Figure 4-23.

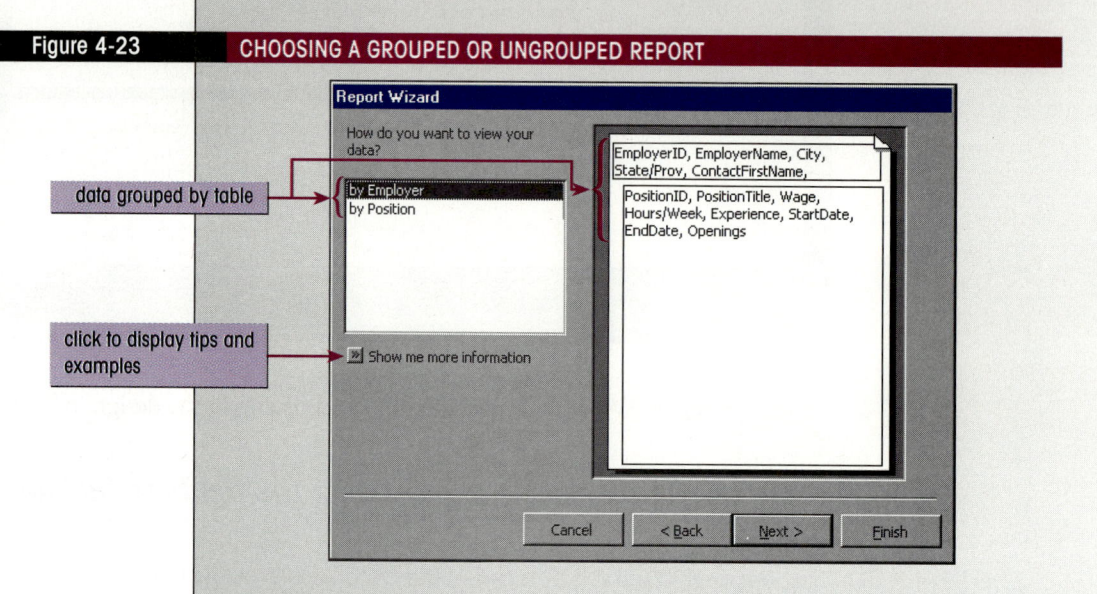

Figure 4-23 CHOOSING A GROUPED OR UNGROUPED REPORT

data grouped by table

click to display tips and examples

You can choose to arrange the selected data grouped by table, which is the default, or ungrouped. For a grouped report, the data from a record in the primary table appears as a group, followed on subsequent lines of the report by the joined records from the related table. For the report you are creating, data from a record in the Employer table appears in a group, followed by the related records for each employer from the Position table. An example of an ungrouped report would be a report of records from the Employer and Position tables in order by PositionID. Each position and its associated employer data would appear together on one or more lines of the report; the data would not be grouped by table.

You can display tips and examples for the choices in the Report Wizard dialog box by clicking the "Show me more information" button.

TUTORIAL 4 CREATING FORMS AND REPORTS   AC 4.25

To display tips about the options in the Report Wizard dialog box:

1. Click the [»] button. The Report Wizard Tips dialog box opens. Read the information shown in the dialog box.

   You can display examples of different grouping methods by clicking the [»] button ("Show me examples").

2. Click [»]. The Report Wizard Examples dialog box opens. See Figure 4-24.

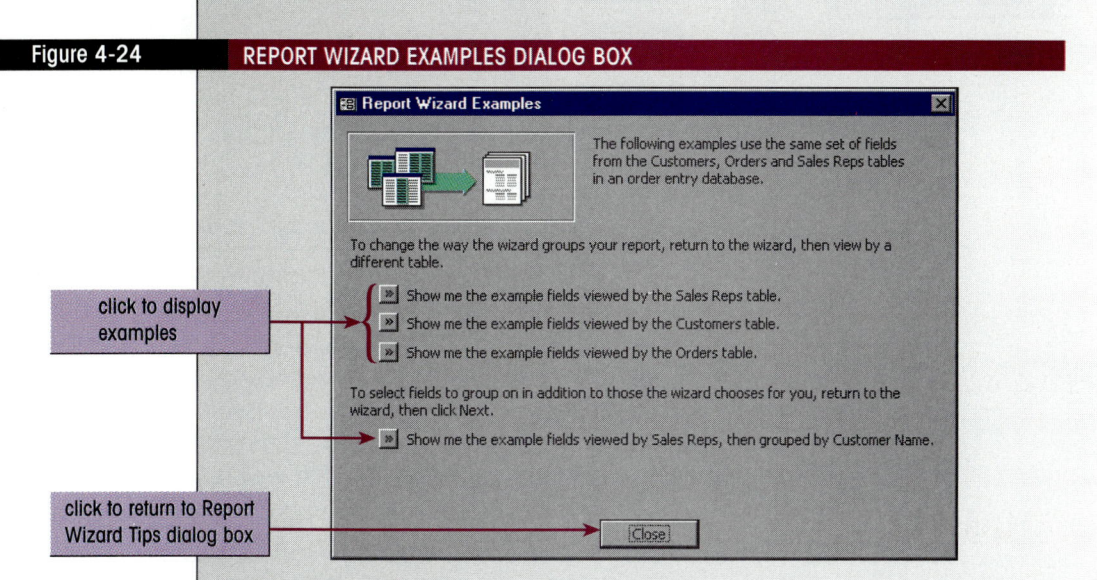

Figure 4-24   REPORT WIZARD EXAMPLES DIALOG BOX

click to display examples

click to return to Report Wizard Tips dialog box

You can display examples of different grouping methods by clicking the [»] buttons.

3. Click each [»] button in turn, review the displayed example, and then click the **Close** button to return to the Report Wizard Examples dialog box.

4. Click the **Close** button to return to the Report Wizard Tips dialog box, and then click the **Close** button to return to the second Report Wizard dialog box.

The default options shown on your screen are correct for the report Zack wants, so you can continue responding to the Report Wizard questions.

To finish creating the report using the Report Wizard:

1. Click the **Next** button. The next Report Wizard dialog box opens, in which you choose additional grouping levels.

   Two grouping levels are shown: one for an employer's data, and the other for an employer's positions. Grouping levels are useful for reports with multiple levels, such as those containing monthly, quarterly, and annual totals, or for those containing city and country groups. Zack's report contains no further grouping levels, so you can accept the default options.

2. Click the **Next** button. The next Report Wizard dialog box opens, in which you choose the sort order for the detail records. See Figure 4-25.

Figure 4-25 CHOOSING THE SORT ORDER FOR DETAIL RECORDS

options for sorting on multiple fields

click to display field list

Ascending sort order selected; click to change to Descending sort order

The records from the Position table for an employer represent the detail records for Zack's report. He wants these records to appear in increasing, or ascending, order by the value in the PositionID field. The Ascending option is already selected by default. To change to descending order, you simply click this button, which acts as a toggle between the two sort orders. Also, notice that you can sort on multiple fields, as you can with queries.

3. Click the **1** list arrow, click **PositionID**, and then click the **Next** button. The next Report Wizard dialog box opens, in which you choose a layout and page orientation for the report. See Figure 4-26.

Figure 4-26 CHOOSING THE REPORT LAYOUT AND PAGE ORIENTATION

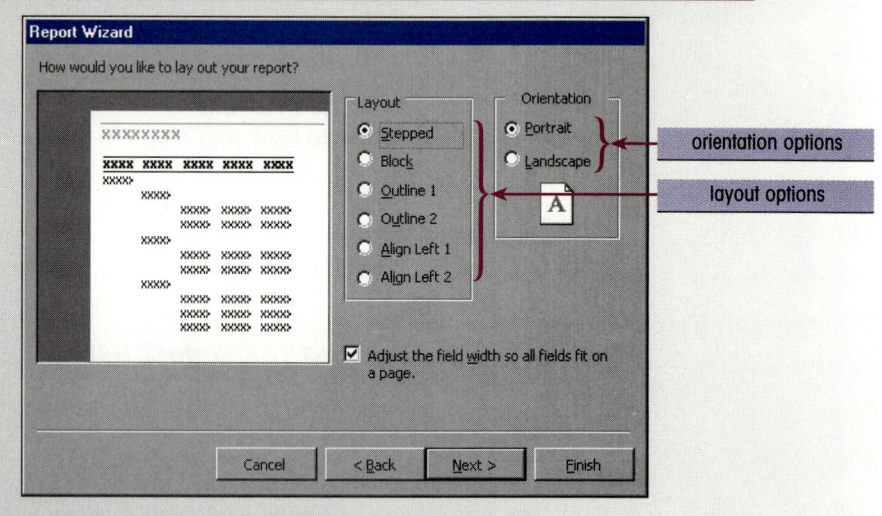

orientation options

layout options

A sample of each layout appears in the box on the left.

4. Click each layout option and examine each sample that appears.

You'll use the Outline 2 layout option because it resembles the layout shown in Zack's sketch of the report. Also, because of the number of fields in the Position table, the information would fit better in a wide format; therefore, you'll choose the landscape orientation.

5. Click the **Outline 2** option button, click the **Landscape** option button, and then click the **Next** button. The next Report Wizard dialog box opens, in which you choose a style for the report.

    A sample of the selected style, or AutoFormat, appears in the box on the left. You can always choose a different AutoFormat after you create the report, just as you can when creating a form. Zack likes the appearance of the Corporate AutoFormat, so you'll choose this one for your report.

6. Click **Corporate** (if necessary), and then click the **Next** button. The last Report Wizard dialog box opens, in which you choose a report name, which also serves as the printed title on the report.

    According to Zack's sketch, the report title you need to specify is "Employers and Positions."

7. Type **Employers and Positions** and then click the **Finish** button. The Report Wizard creates the report based on your answers and saves it as an object in the Northeast database. Then Access opens the Employers and Positions report in Print Preview.

    To view the report better, you need to maximize the Report window.

8. Click the **Maximize** button on the Employers and Positions title bar.

    To view the entire page, you need to change the Zoom setting.

9. Click the **Zoom** list arrow on the Print Preview toolbar, and then click **Fit**. The first page of the report is displayed in Print Preview. See Figure 4-27.

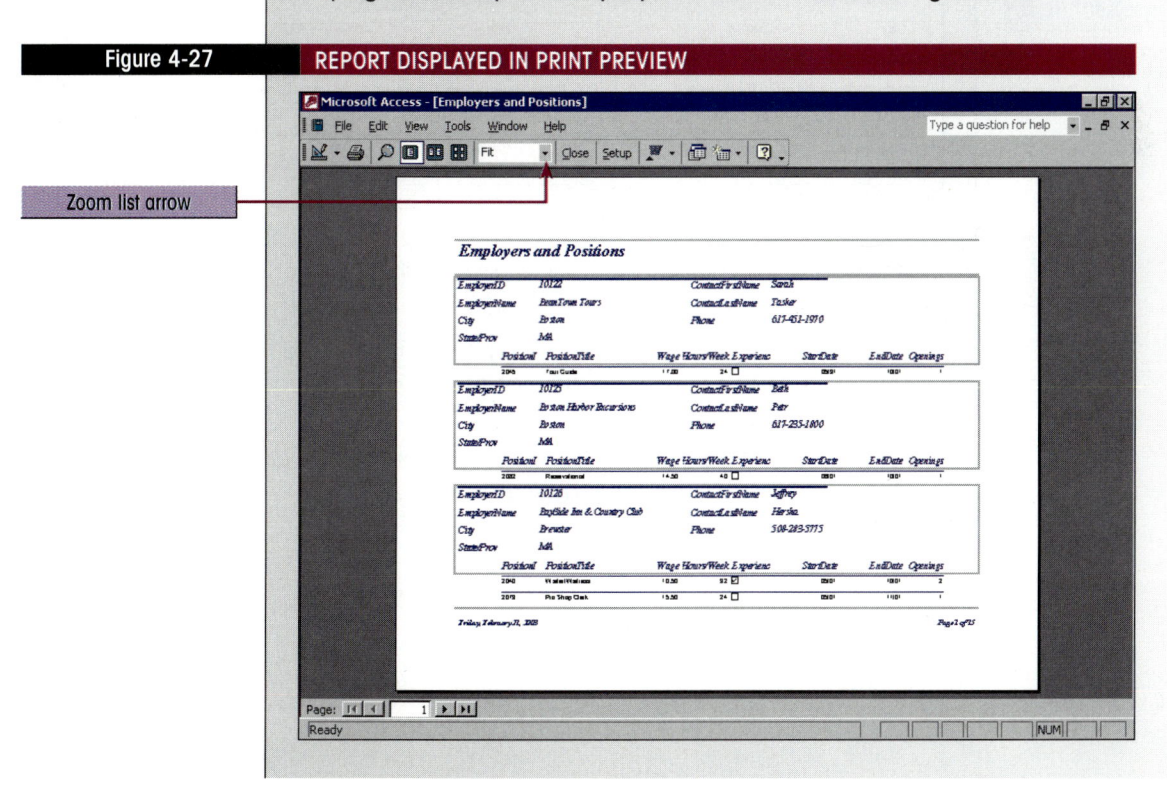

Figure 4-27   REPORT DISPLAYED IN PRINT PREVIEW

When a report is displayed in Print Preview, you can use the pointer to toggle between a full-page display and a close-up display of the report. Zack asks you to check the report to see if any adjustments need to be made. For example, some of the field titles or values might not be displayed completely, or you might need to move fields to enhance the report's appearance. To do so, you need to view a close-up display of the report.

To view a close-up display of the report and make any necessary corrections:

1. Click the pointer 🔍 at the top center of the report. The display changes to show a close-up view of the report. See Figure 4-28.

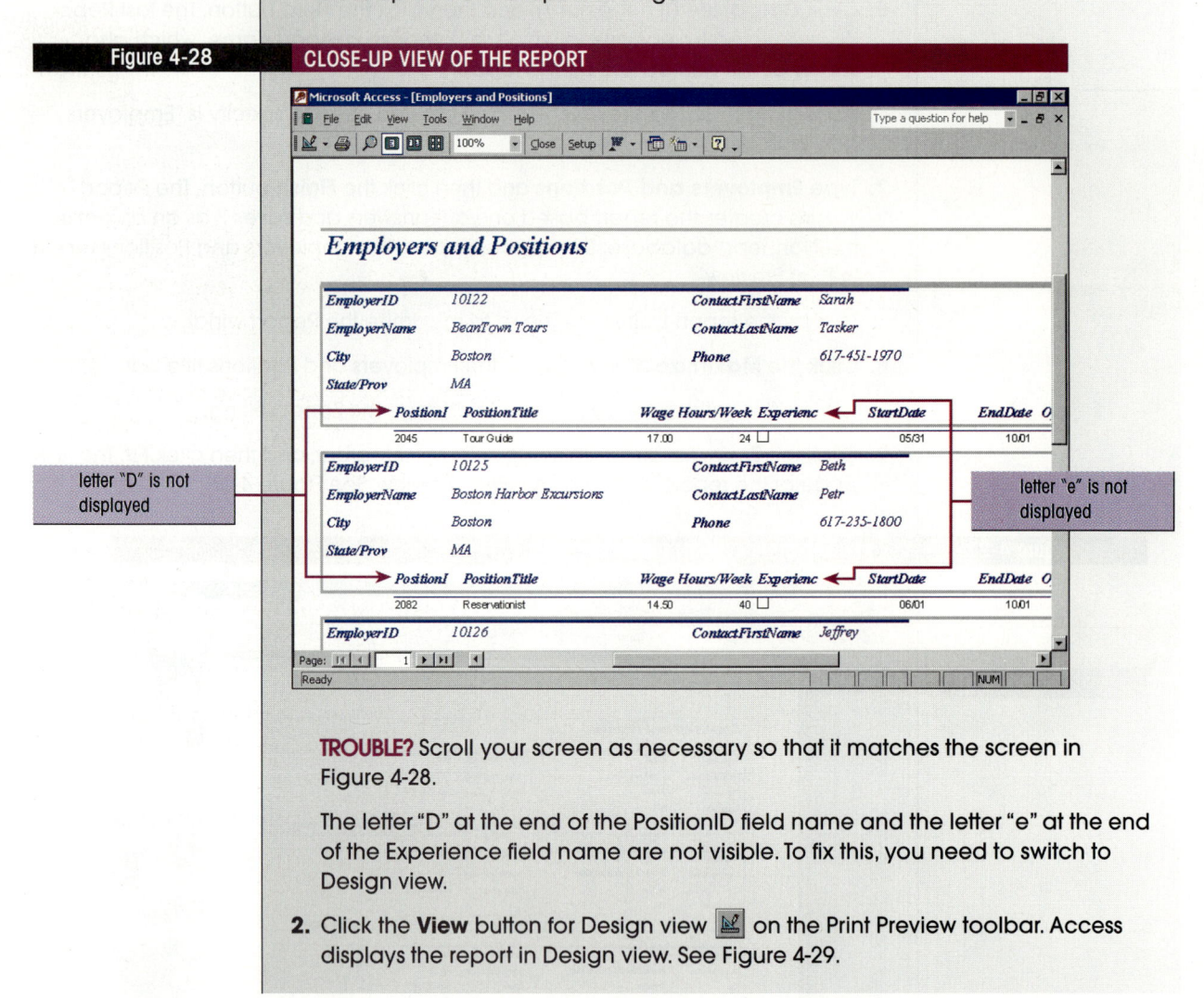

Figure 4-28   CLOSE-UP VIEW OF THE REPORT

letter "D" is not displayed

letter "e" is not displayed

TROUBLE? Scroll your screen as necessary so that it matches the screen in Figure 4-28.

The letter "D" at the end of the PositionID field name and the letter "e" at the end of the Experience field name are not visible. To fix this, you need to switch to Design view.

2. Click the **View** button for Design view on the Print Preview toolbar. Access displays the report in Design view. See Figure 4-29.

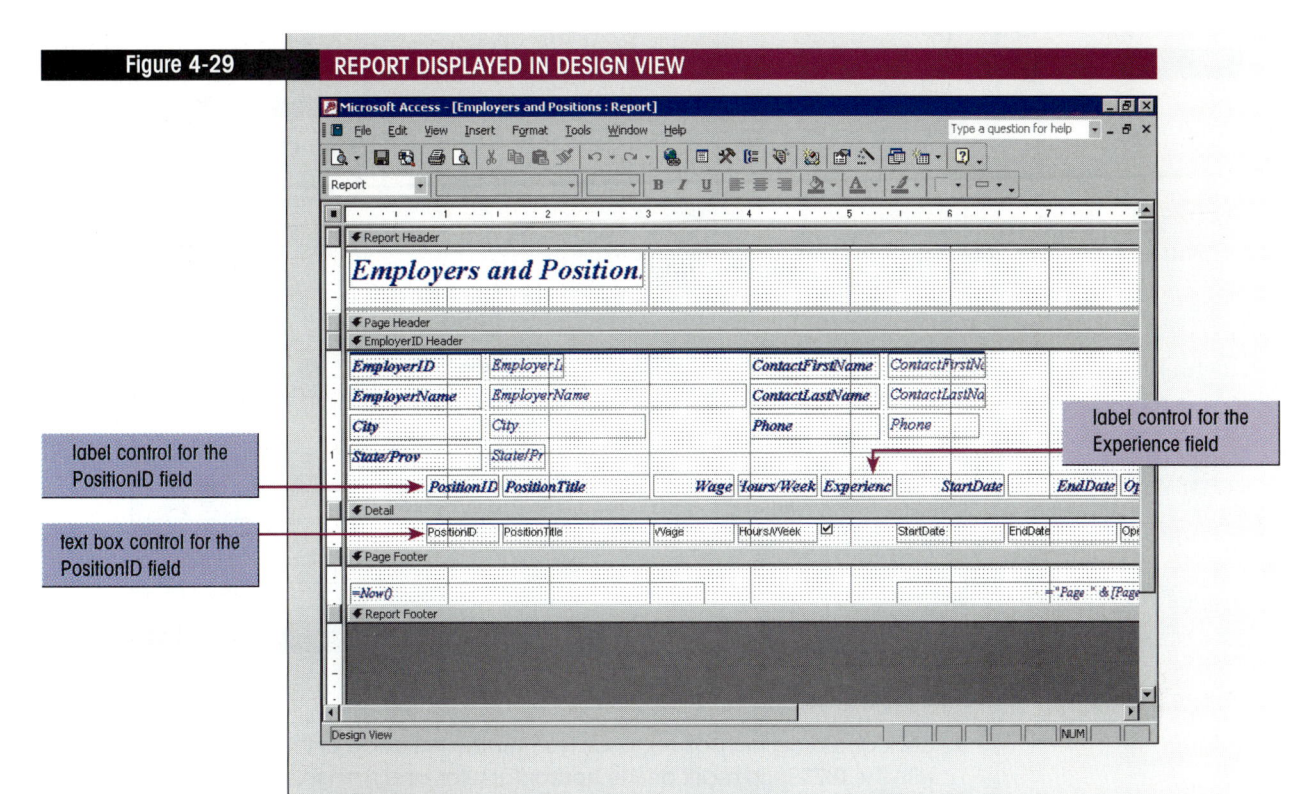

Figure 4-29   REPORT DISPLAYED IN DESIGN VIEW

(Screenshot of Microsoft Access Report in Design View titled "Employers and Positions: Report", showing Report Header with "Employers and Positions", EmployerID Header with fields EmployerID, EmployerName, City, State/Prov, ContactFirstName, ContactLastName, Phone, PositionID, PositionTitle, Wage, Hours/Week, Experience, StartDate, EndDate; Detail section; Page Footer with =Now() and "Page " & [Page]; Report Footer.)

Callouts:
- label control for the PositionID field
- text box control for the PositionID field
- label control for the Experience field

TROUBLE? If your screen displays any window other than those shown in Figure 4-29, click the Close button ⊠ on the window's title bar to close it.

You use the Report window in Design view to modify existing reports and to create custom reports.

Each item on a report in Design view is called a **control**. For example, the PositionID field consists of two controls: the label "PositionID," which appears on the report to identify the field value, and the PositionID text box, in which the actual field value appears. You need to widen the label control for the PositionID field so that the entire field name is visible in the report.

3. Click the label control for the PositionID field to select it. Handles appear on the border around the control, indicating that the control is selected and can be manipulated.

4. Position the pointer on the center-left handle of the PositionID label control until the pointer changes to a ↔ shape. See Figure 4-30.

Figure 4-30   **RESIZING THE PositionID LABEL CONTROL**

drag this pointer to the left to widen the label control

handles indicate the label control is selected

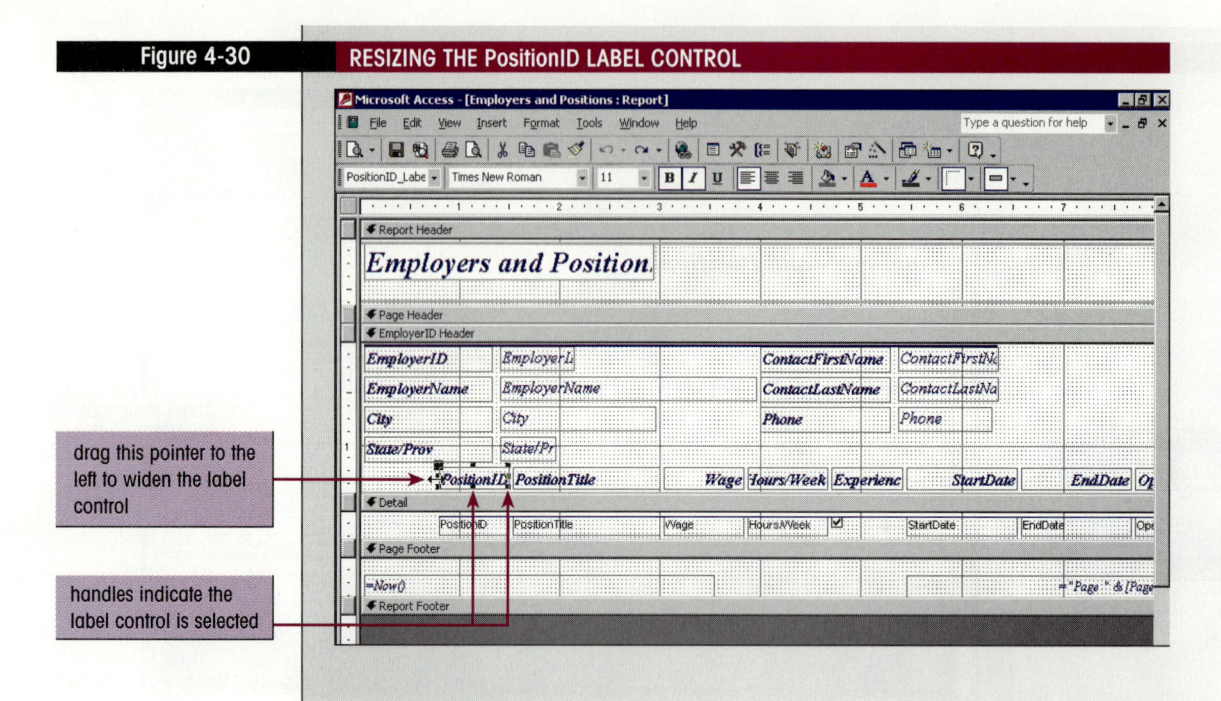

5. Click and drag the pointer to the left until the left edge of the control is aligned with the **0.75**-inch mark on the horizontal ruler, and then release the mouse button.

   To correct the problem with the Experience field name, you'll use the center-right handle.

6. Position the pointer on the center-right handle of the Experience label control until the pointer changes to a ↔ shape, click and drag the pointer to the right until the right edge is aligned with the 5.5-inch mark on the horizontal ruler, and then release the mouse button.

   Now you need to switch back to Print Preview and make sure that the complete names for the PositionID and Experience fields are visible.

7. Click the **View** button for Print Preview on the Report Design toolbar. The report appears in Print Preview. Notice that the PositionID and Experience field names in the label controls are now completely displayed.

8. Click **File** on the menu bar, and then click **Save** to save the modified report.

Zack decides that he wants the report to include a graphic image to the right of the report title, for visual interest. You can add the graphic to the report by inserting a picture.

Inserting a Picture in a Report

In Access, you can insert a picture or other graphic image in a report or form to enhance the appearance of the report or form. Sources of graphic images include files created in Microsoft Paint and other drawing programs, and scanned files. The file containing the picture you need to insert is named Globe, and it is located in the Tutorial folder on your Data Disk.

TUTORIAL 4 CREATING FORMS AND REPORTS   AC 4.31   ACCESS

To insert the picture in the report:

1. Click the **Close** button on the Print Preview toolbar to display the report in Design view. See Figure 4-31.

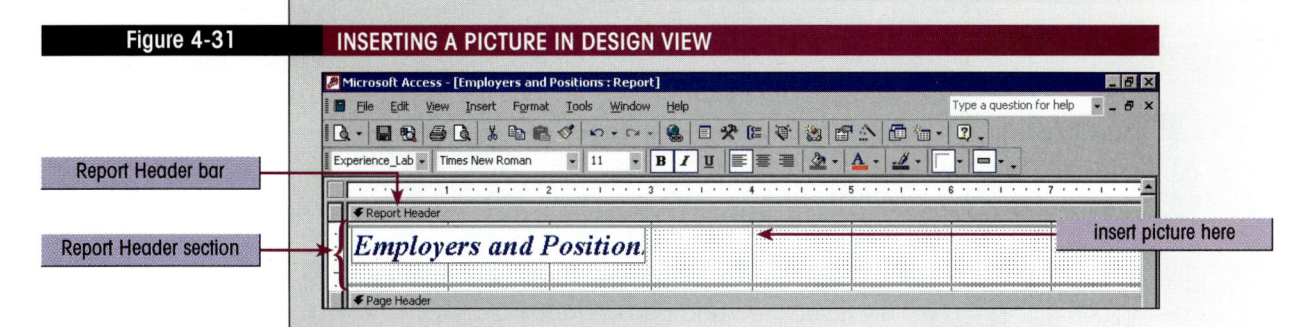

| Figure 4-31 | INSERTING A PICTURE IN DESIGN VIEW |

Report Header bar

Report Header section

insert picture here

Zack wants the picture to appear on the first page of the report only; therefore, you need to insert the picture in the Report Header section (see Figure 4-31). Any text or picture placed in this section appears once at the beginning of the report.

2. Click the **Report Header** bar to select this section of the report. The bar is highlighted to indicate that the section is selected.

3. Click **Insert** on the menu bar, and then click **Picture**. The Insert Picture dialog box opens. If necessary, open the **Tutorial** folder on your Data Disk. See Figure 4-32.

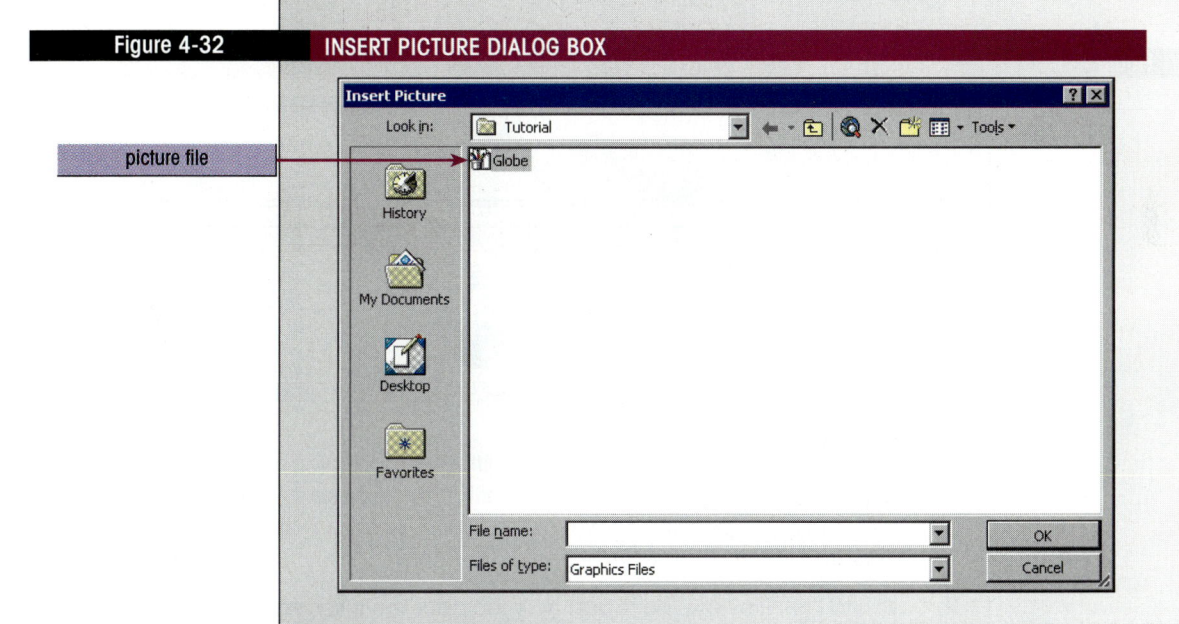

| Figure 4-32 | INSERT PICTURE DIALOG BOX |

picture file

4. Click **Globe** to select the picture for the report, and then click the **OK** button. The picture is inserted in the left side of the Report Header section, covering some of the report title text. See Figure 4-33.

Figure 4-33 PICTURE INSERTED IN THE REPORT

inserted picture

top border line of report

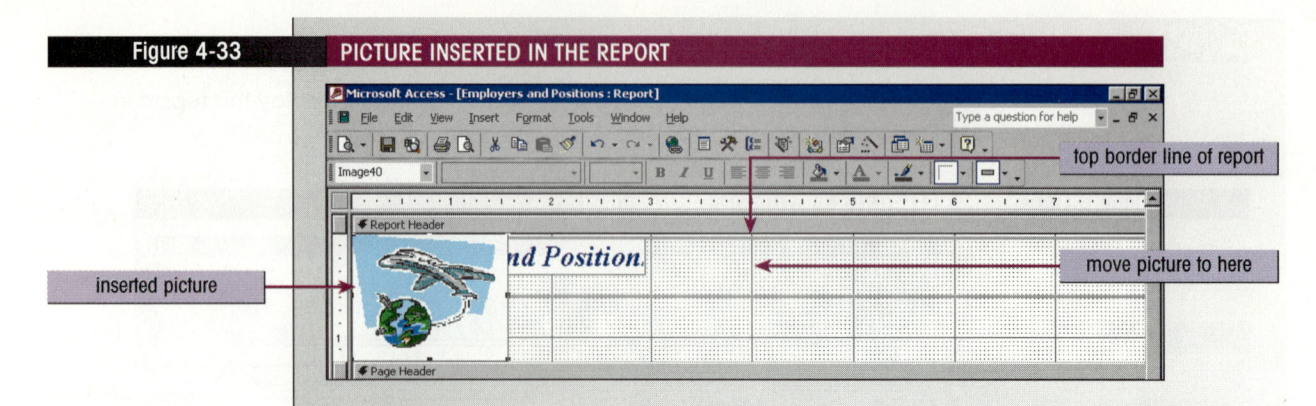

move picture to here

Notice that handles appear around the picture's border, indicating that the picture is selected and can be manipulated.

Zack wants the picture to appear to the right of the report title, so you need to move the picture using the mouse.

5. Position the pointer on the picture until the pointer changes to a 🖐 shape, and then click and drag the mouse to move the picture to the right so that its left edge aligns with the 4-inch mark on the horizontal ruler and its top edge is just below the top border line above the report title (see Figure 4-33).

6. Release the mouse button. The picture appears in the new position. Notice that the height of the Report Header section increased slightly to accommodate the picture. See Figure 4-34.

Figure 4-34 REPOSITIONED PICTURE IN THE REPORT

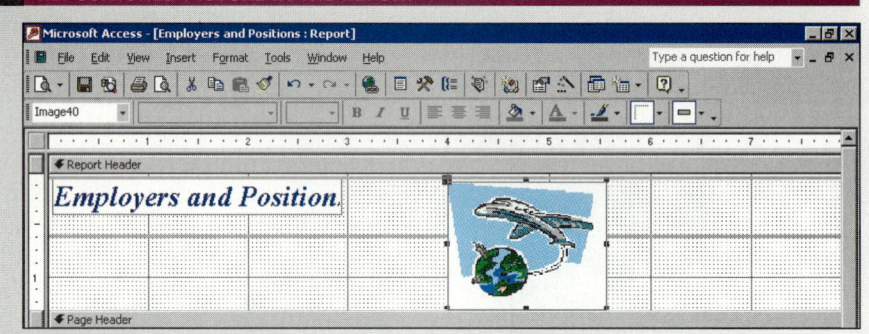

TROUBLE? If your picture appears in a different location from the one shown in Figure 4-34, use the pointer 🖐 to reposition the picture until it is in approximately the same position shown in the figure. Be sure that the top edge of the picture is below the top border line of the report.

7. Switch to Print Preview. The report now includes the inserted picture. If necessary, click the **Zoom** button 🔍 on the Print Preview toolbar to display the entire report page. See Figure 4-35.

Figure 4-35 PRINT PREVIEW OF REPORT WITH PICTURE

picture included in report

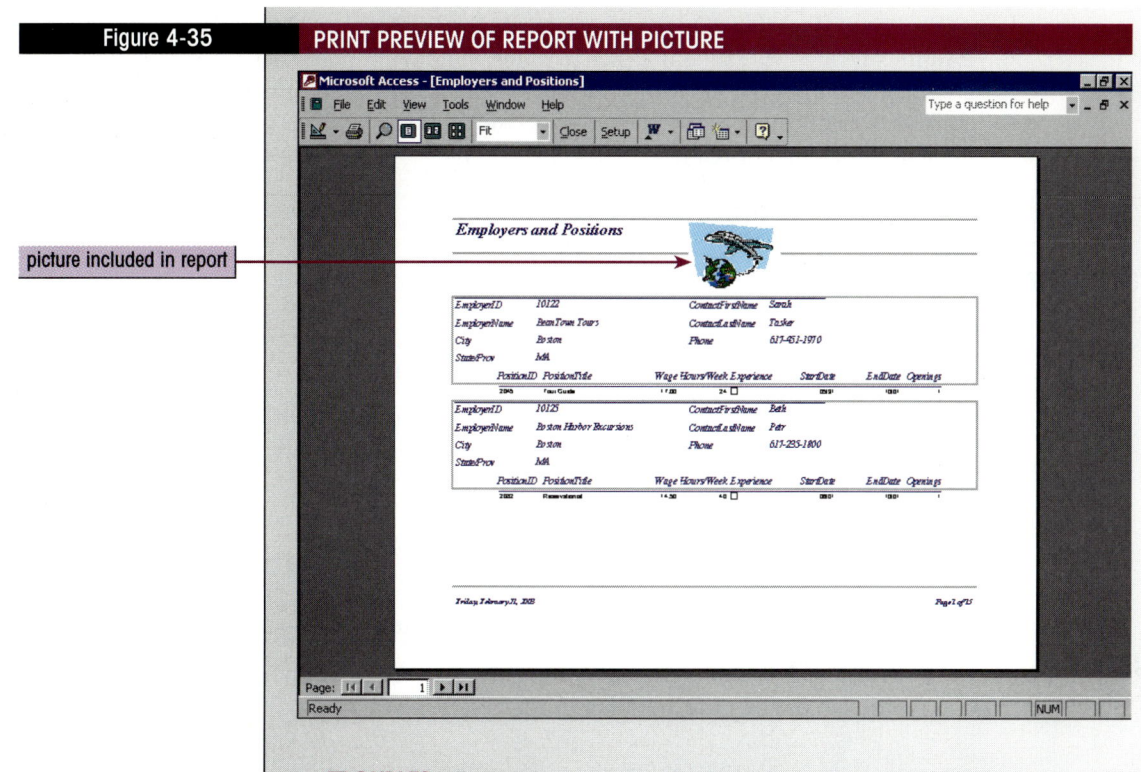

> **TROUBLE?** If the picture covers the gray line at the top of the report, switch to Design view and use the pointer to position the picture in the correct location. Then repeat Step 7.

8. Save the modified report.

The report is now completed. You'll print just the first page of the report so that Zack can review the report layout and the inserted picture.

To print page 1 of the report:

1. Click **File** on the menu bar, and then click **Print**. The Print dialog box opens.

2. In the Print Range section, click the **Pages** option button. The insertion point now appears in the From text box so that you can specify the range of pages to print.

3. Type **1** in the From text box, press the **Tab** key to move to the To text box, and then type **1**. These settings specify that only page 1 of the report will be printed.

4. Click the **OK** button. The Print dialog box closes, and the first page of the report is printed.

   Zack approves of the report layout and contents, so you can close the report.

5. Click the **Close Window** button ⊠ on the menu bar.

   TROUBLE? If you click the Close button on the Print Preview toolbar by mistake, you switch to Design view. Click the Close Window button ⊠ on the menu bar.

6. Exit Access.

Elsa is satisfied that the forms you created—the Position Data form and the Employer Positions form—will make it easier to enter, view, and update data in the Northeast database. The Employers and Positions report presents important information about NSJI's employer clients in an attractive and professional format, which will help Zack and his staff in their marketing efforts.

Session 4.2 QUICK CHECK

1. In a form that contains a main form and a subform, what data is displayed in the main form and what data is displayed in the subform?
2. Describe how you use the navigation buttons to move through a form containing a main form and a subform.
3. When you use the Report Wizard, the report name is also used as the _____.
4. Each item on a report in Design view is called a(n) _____.
5. To insert a picture in a report, the report must be displayed in _____.
6. Any text or pictures placed in the _____ section of a report will appear only on the first page of the report.

REVIEW ASSIGNMENTS

Elsa wants to enhance the **Recruits** database with forms and reports, and she asks you to complete the following:

1. Make sure your Data Disk is in the appropriate disk drive, start Access, and then open the **Recruits** database located in the Review folder on your Data Disk.

2. If your **Recruits** database is stored on drive A, you will need to delete the files **Seasons97.mdb** and **Seasons2002.mdb** from your disk so you will have enough room to complete the steps. If your database is stored on a hard or network drive, no action is necessary.

3. Use the Form Wizard to create a form based on the **Student** table. Select all fields for the form, the Columnar layout, the SandStone style, and the title **Student Data** for the form.

4. Use the form you created in the previous step to print the fifth form record. Change the AutoFormat to Sumi Painting, save the changed form, and then print the fifth form record again.

5. Use the **Student Data** form to update the **Student** table as follows:
    a. Use the Find command to move to the record with StudentID STO1323. Change the field values for FirstName to Nathaniel, City to Perth, and BirthDate to 4/2/85 for this record.
    b. Use the Find command to move to the record with StudentID KIE2760, and then delete the record.
    c. Add a new record with the following field values:
       StudentID: SAN2540
       FirstName: Pedro
       LastName: Sandes

City:	Barcelona
Nation:	Spain
BirthDate:	5/1/85
Gender:	M
SSN:	977-07-1798

    d. Print only this form record, and then close the form.

Explore   6. Use the AutoForm: Columnar Wizard to create a form based on the **Salaries with Raises** query. Save the form as **Salaries with Raises**, and then close the form.

Explore   7. Use the Form Wizard to create a form containing a main form and a subform. Select the FirstName, LastName, and SSN fields from the **Recruiter** table for the main form, and select all fields except SSN from the **Student** table for the subform. Use the Datasheet layout and the Sumi Painting style. Specify the title **Recruiter Students** for the main form and the title **Student Subform** for the subform. Resize all columns in the subform to their best fit. Use Design view to resize the main form and the subform so that all fields are visible in the subform at the same time. Resize the Form window in Form view, as necessary, so that all fields are visible at the same time. Print the fourth main form record and its subform records. Save and close the form.

Explore   8. Use the Report Wizard to create a report based on the primary **Recruiter** table and the related **Student** table. Select all fields from the **Recruiter** table, and select all fields from the **Student** table except SSN, in the following order: FirstName, LastName, City, Nation, BirthDate, Gender, StudentID. In the third Report Wizard dialog box, specify the Nation field as an additional grouping level. Sort the detail records in ascending order by City. Choose the Align Left 2 layout and the Formal style for the report. Specify the title **Recruiters and Students** for the report.

Explore   9. Display the **Recruiters and Students** report in Design view and maximize the Report window. In the Nation Header section, change the Student_FirstName label control to "FirstName" and change the Student_LastName label control to "LastName." Widen both the Gender and StudentID label controls so that the labels are fully visible in the report. (*Hint*: You can resize the Gender control to both the left and the right, and the borders of adjacent controls can touch each other.)

10. Insert the **Travel** picture, which is located in the Review folder on your Data Disk, in the Report Header section of the **Recruiters and Students** report. Position the picture so that its left edge aligns with the 4-inch mark on the horizontal ruler and its top edge is just below the top border line of the report.

11. Print only the first page of the report, and then close and save the modified report.

12. If your database is stored on drive A, you will need to turn off the Compact on Close feature before closing the **Recruits** database because there isn't enough room on the disk to compact the database. If your database is stored on a hard or network drive, no action is necessary.

13. Close the **Recruits** database, and then exit Access.

CASE PROBLEMS

Case 1. Lim's Video Photography Youngho Lim wants the **Videos** database to include forms and reports that will help him track and view information about his clients and their video shoot events. You'll create the necessary forms and reports by completing the following:

1. Make sure your Data Disk is in the appropriate disk drive, start Access, and then open the **Videos** database located in the Cases folder on your Data Disk.

2. Use the Form Wizard to create a form based on the **Client** table. Select all fields for the form, the Columnar layout, and the Blends style. Specify the title **Client Data** for the form.

3. Change the AutoFormat for the **Client Data** form to Standard.

4. Use the Find command to move to the record with Client# 338, and then change the Address field value for this record to 2150 Brucewood Avenue.

5. Use the **Client Data** form to add a new record with the following field values:

   Client#:   351
   ClientName: Peters, Amanda
   Address: 175 Washington Street
   City: Berkeley
   State: CA
   Zip: 94704
   Phone: 510-256-1007

   Print only this form record, and then save and close the form.

6. Use the Form Wizard to create a form containing a main form and a subform. Select all the fields from the **Client** table for the main form, and select all fields except Client# from the **Contract** table for the subform. Use the Tabular layout and the Standard style. Specify the title **Contracts by Client** for the main form and the title **Contract Subform** for the subform.

7. Print the seventh main form record and its subform records, and then close the **Contracts by Client** form.

8. Use the Report Wizard to create a report based on the primary **Client** table and the related **Contract** table. Select all the fields from the **Client** table, and select all the fields from the **Contract** table except Client#. Sort the detail records in ascending order by Contract#. Choose the Align Left 2 layout and the Casual style. Specify the title **Client Contracts** for the report.

9. Insert the **Camcord** picture, which is located in the Cases folder on your Data Disk, in the Report Header section of the **Client Contracts** report. Position the picture so that its left edge aligns with the 4-inch mark on the horizontal ruler and its top edge is just below the top border line of the report.

10. Print only the first page of the report, and then close and save the modified report.

11. Close the **Videos** database, and then exit Access.

Case 2. DineAtHome.course.com Claire Picard continues her work with the **Meals** database to track and analyze the business activity of the restaurants she works with and their customers. To help her, you'll enhance the **Meals** database by completing the following:

1. Make sure your Data Disk is in the appropriate disk drive, start Access, and then open the **Meals** database located in the Cases folder on your Data Disk.

2. Use the Form Wizard to create a form containing a main form and a subform. Select the Restaurant#, RestaurantName, City, Phone, and Website fields from the **Restaurant** table for the main form, and select all fields except Restaurant# from the **Order** table for the subform. Use the Datasheet layout and the Industrial style. Specify the title **Restaurant Orders** for the main form and the title **Order Subform** for the subform. Resize all columns in the subform to their best fit. Print the first main form record and its displayed subform records.

3. For the form you just created, change the AutoFormat to SandStone, save the changed form, and then print the first main form record and its subform records.

4. Navigate to the third record in the subform for the first main record, and then change the OrderAmt field value to 107.80.

5. Use the Find command to move to the record with the Restaurant# 118, and then delete the record. Answer Yes to any warning messages about deleting the record.

Explore 6. Use the appropriate wildcard character to find all records with the word "House" anywhere in the restaurant name. (*Hint*: You must enter the wildcard character before and after the text you are searching for.) How many records did you find? Close the **Restaurant Orders** form.

Explore 7. Use the Report Wizard to create a report based on the primary **Restaurant** table and the related **Order** table. Select the Restaurant#, RestaurantName, Street, City, OwnerFirstName, and OwnerLastName fields from the **Restaurant** table, and select all fields from the **Order** table except Restaurant#. In the third Report Wizard dialog box, specify the OrderDate field as an additional grouping level. Sort the detail records by OrderAmt in *descending* order. Choose the Align Left 1 layout and the Bold style for the report. Specify the title **Orders by Restaurants** for the report.

8. Insert the **Server** picture, which is located in the Cases folder on your Data Disk, in the Report Header section of the **Orders by Restaurants** report. Leave the picture in its original position at the left edge of the Report Header section.

Explore 9. Use the Ask a Question box to ask the following question: "How do I move a control in front of or behind other controls?" Click the topic "Move one or more controls to a new position," and then click the subtopic "Move a control in front of or behind other controls." Read the information and then close the Help window. Make sure the **Server** picture is still selected, and then move it behind the Orders by Restaurants title.

Explore 10. Use the Ask a Question box to ask the following question: "How do I change the background color of a control?" Click the topic "Change the background color of a control or section." Read the information and then close the Help window. Select the Orders by Restaurant title object, and then change its background color to Transparent.

11. Display the report in Print Preview. Print just the first page of the report, and then close and save the report.

12. Close the **Meals** database, and then exit Access.

Case 3. Redwood Zoo Michael Rosenfeld wants to create forms and reports for the **Redwood** database. You'll help him create these database objects by completing the following:

1. Make sure your Data Disk is in the appropriate disk drive, start Access, and then open the **Redwood** database located in the Cases folder on your Data Disk.

2. If your **Redwood** database is stored on drive A, you will need to delete the files **Redwood97.mdb** and **Redwood2002.mdb** from your disk so you will have enough room to complete the steps. If your database is stored on a hard or network drive, no action is necessary.

3. Use the Form Wizard to create a form based on the **Pledge** table. Select all fields for the form, the Columnar layout, and the Blueprint style. Specify the title **Pledge Info** for the form.

4. Use the **Pledge Info** form to update the **Pledge** table as follows:
   a. Use the Find command to move to the record with Pledge# 2490, and then change the FundCode to B11 and the TotalPledged amount to 75.
   b. Add a new record with the following values:
      Pledge#:   2977
      DonorID: 59021
      FundCode: M23
      PledgeDate: 12/15/2003
      TotalPledged: 150
      PaymentMethod: C
      PaymentSchedule: S
   c. Print just this form record.
   d. Delete the record with Pledge# 2900.

5. Change the AutoFormat of the **Pledge Info** form to Expedition, save the changed form, and then use the form to print the last record in the **Pledge** table. Close the form.

6. Use the Form Wizard to create a form containing a main form and a subform. Select all the fields from the **Donor** table for the main form, and select the Pledge#, FundCode, PledgeDate, and TotalPledged fields from the **Pledge** table for the subform. Use the Tabular layout and the Expedition style. Specify the title **Donors and Pledges** for the main form and the title **Pledge Subform** for the subform.

7. Display record 11 in the main form. Print the current main form record and its subform records, and then close the **Donors and Pledges** form.

Explore

8. Use the Report Wizard to create a report based on the primary **Donor** table and the related **Pledge** table. Select the DonorID, FirstName, LastName, and Class fields from the **Donor** table, and select all fields from the **Pledge** table except DonorID. In the third Report Wizard dialog box, specify the FundCode field as an additional grouping level. Sort the detail records in *descending* order by TotalPledged. Choose the Align Left 2 layout, Landscape orientation, and the Soft Gray style. Specify the title **Donors and Pledges** for the report.

9. Insert the **Animals** picture, which is located in the Cases folder on your Data Disk, in the Report Header section of the **Donors and Pledges** report. Position the picture so that its left edge aligns with the 4-inch mark on the horizontal ruler and its top edge is just below the top border line of the report.

Explore

10. Use the Ask a Question box to ask the following question: "How do I add a special effect to an object?" Click the topic "Make a control appear raised, sunken, shadowed, chiseled, or etched." Read the information, and then close the Help window. Add the Shadowed special effect to the **Animals** picture, and then save the report.

Explore

11. Print only pages 1 and 7 of the report, and then close it.

12. If your database is stored on drive A, you will need to turn off the Compact on Close feature before closing the **Redwood** database because there isn't enough room on the disk to compact the database. If your database is stored on a hard or network drive, no action is necessary.

13. Close the **Redwood** database, and then exit Access.

Case 4. Mountain River Adventures Connor and Siobhan Dempsey want to create forms and reports that will help them track and analyze data about their customers and the rafting trips they take. Help them enhance the **Trips** database by completing the following:

1. Make sure your Data Disk is in the appropriate disk drive, start Access, and then open the **Trips** database located in the Cases folder on your Data Disk.

2. Use the Form Wizard to create a form containing a main form and a subform. Select the Client#, ClientName, City, State/Prov, and Phone fields from the **Client** table for the main form, and select all fields except Client# from the **Booking** table for the subform. Use the Datasheet layout and the Standard style. Specify the title **Clients and Bookings** for the main form and the title **Booking Subform** for the subform. Resize all columns in the subform to their best fit. Print the ninth main form record and its subform records.

3. For the form you just created, change the AutoFormat to Stone, save the changed form, and then print the ninth main form record and its subform records.

4. Navigate to the second record in the subform for the ninth main record, and then change the People field value to 7.

5. Use the Find command to move to the record with Client# 330, and then delete the record. Answer Yes to any warning messages about deleting the record.

6. Use the appropriate wildcard character to find all records with a City value that begins with the letter "D." How many records did you find? Close the form.

7. Use the Report Wizard to create a report based on the primary **Client** table and the related **Booking** table. Select all fields from the **Client** table, and select all fields except Client# from the **Booking** table. Sort the detail records by the TripDate field in ascending order. Choose the Outline 1 layout and the Compact style. Specify the title **Client Bookings** for the report.

Explore 8. Display the **Client Bookings** report in Design view, and then widen the Phone text box control so that the Phone field values are completely displayed in the report.

9. Insert the **Raft** picture, which is located in the Cases folder on your Data Disk, in the Report Header section of the **Client Bookings** report. Position the picture so that its left edge aligns with the 2-inch mark on the horizontal ruler and its top edge is just below the top border line of the report. (If the picture blocks part of the bottom border line of the header, that is fine.)

Explore 10. Insert the same **Raft** picture in the Report Footer section of the **Client Bookings** report. (Items placed in the Report Footer section appear only once, at the end of the report.) Position the picture so that its right edge aligns with the right edge of the report, at approximately the 6.5-inch mark on the horizontal ruler. Save the report.

Explore 11. View the first two pages of the report in Print Preview at the same time. (*Hint*: Use a toolbar button.) Use the Page navigation buttons to move through the report, displaying two pages at a time. Print only the first and last pages of the report, and then close the report.

12. Close the **Trips** database, and then exit Access.

INTERNET ASSIGNMENTS

Student Union

The purpose of the Internet Assignments is to challenge you to find information on the Internet that you can use to create effective documents. The actual assignments are updated and maintained on the Course Technology Web site. Log on to the Internet and use your Web browser to go to the Student Union on the New Perspectives Series site at **www.course.com/NewPerspectives/studentunion**. Click the Online Companions link, and then click the link for this tutorial.

QUICK CHECK ANSWERS

Session 4.1

1. The AutoForm Wizard creates a form automatically using all the fields in the selected table or query; the Form Wizard allows you to choose some or all of the fields in the selected table or query, choose fields from other tables and queries, and display fields in any order on the form.
2. An AutoFormat is a predefined style for a form (or report). To change a form's AutoFormat, display the form in Design view, click the AutoFormat button on the Form Design toolbar, click the new AutoFormat in the Form AutoFormats list box, and then click the OK button.
3. the last record in the table
4. datasheet
5. the question mark (?)
6. as many form records as can fit on a printed page

Session 4.2

1. The main form displays the data from the primary table, and the subform displays the data from the related table.
2. You use the top set of navigation buttons to select and move through records from the related table in the subform, and the bottom set to select and move through records from the primary table in the main form.
3. report title
4. control
5. Design view
6. Report Header

OBJECTIVES

In this tutorial you will:

- Learn about the World Wide Web
- Create and view a static Web page
- Create and view a dynamic Web page

CREATING WEB PAGES WITH ACCESS

Creating Web Pages to Display Employer and Position Data

CASE

Northeast Seasonal Jobs International (NSJI)

Elsa Jensen recognizes the value of the data stored in the Northeast database, both for promoting NSJI's business activities and for maintaining important information about NSJI's employer clients and student recruits. To increase efficiency and facilitate the sharing of information, Elsa wants to display certain information in the form of Web pages. **Web pages** are special documents you can view using a program called a **browser**. The two most popular browsers are **Microsoft Internet Explorer** and **Netscape Navigator**. The browser retrieves files from a type of computer called a **Web server** and displays those files on a computer in the form of a Web page.

Web pages are connected to each other through **hyperlinks**, which are words, phrases, or graphic images that you click to move to another location in the same Web page or a different page. Text hyperlinks are usually underlined and appear in a different color than the rest of the text in the page. The collection of linked Web pages that reside on computers throughout the world is called the **World Wide Web**, or simply, the **Web**. These computers form the largest and most widely used computer network in the world—the **Internet**. Most companies maintain a **Web site**, which is a group of related Web pages that provides information about the company and allows interaction with it. Each Web site has its own Internet address, which is called a **Uniform Resource Locator (URL)**. For example, the URL www.microsoft.com is the address for Microsoft Corporation. Most companies, including NSJI, also maintain internal private networks, called **intranets**, for sharing information only with other members of the organization.

Most Web pages are created using a programming language called **HTML (Hypertext Markup Language)**. You can create a Web page by typing all of the necessary HTML code into a text document and saving the document with the .htm or .html file extension. Because a Web page contains HTML code, it is also called an **HTML document**. Some programs, including Access, have built-in tools that convert objects to HTML documents for viewing on the Web. In this tutorial, you will use these built-in tools to convert objects in the Northeast database to HTML documents.

Working with the Web

When you create Web pages based on Access database objects, the pages can be either static or dynamic. A **static Web page** shows the state of the database object at the time the page was created; any subsequent changes made to the object, such as updates to field values in a record, are not reflected in the Web page. A **dynamic Web page** is updated automatically each time the page is viewed and reflects the current state of the database object at that time. The type of Web page you create depends on how you want the information to be shared and manipulated by other users.

Creating and Viewing a Static Web Page

Elsa wants you to create a Web page based on the Employer Positions query, which shows selected fields from both the Employer and Position tables. She wants this information to be available to NSJI employees when they work out of the office and make a dial-up connection to NSJI's intranet from their laptop computers. Because Elsa does not want the employees to be able to make changes to this information, you'll create a static Web page.

In Access, you create a static Web page by exporting a database object to an HTML document.

> *To export the Employer Positions query as an HTML document:*
>
> 1. Place your Data Disk in the appropriate disk drive, start Access, and then open the **Northeast** database located in the Tutorial folder on your Data Disk.
>
> 2. Click **Queries** in the Objects bar of the Database window, right-click **Employer Positions** to display the shortcut menu, and then click **Export**. The Export dialog box opens, displaying the type and name of the object you are exporting in its title bar (in this case, the Employer Positions query). In this dialog box you specify the filename, file type, and location for the exported object. You need to save the Employer Positions query as an HTML document in the Tutorial folder.
>
> 3. Make sure that the Save in list box displays the Tutorial folder on your Data Disk.
>
> 4. Click the **Save as type** list arrow, and then scroll down the list and click **HTML Documents**. The query name is added to the File name text box automatically. See Figure 1.

CREATING WEB PAGES WITH ACCESS   WEB 3   ACCESS

Figure 1: EXPORT DIALOG BOX

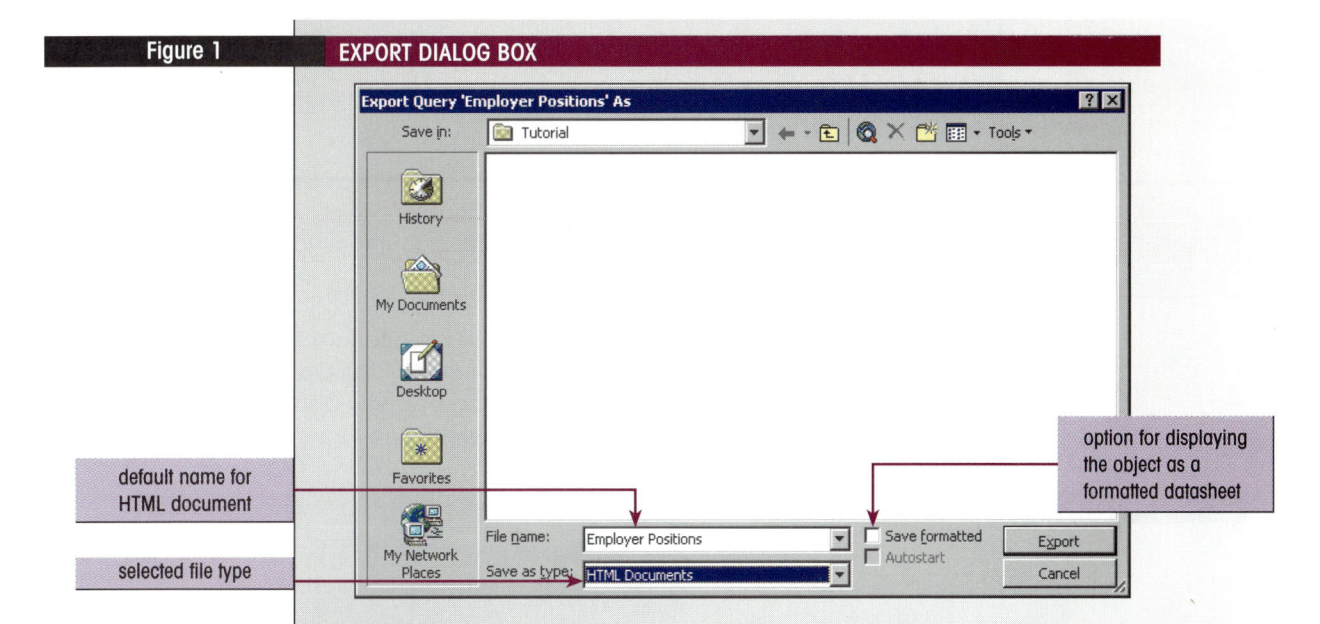

- default name for HTML document
- selected file type
- option for displaying the object as a formatted datasheet

Notice the Save formatted option. This option allows you to display the object in a format similar to its appearance in Datasheet view, with all the column headings, shading, and so on. If you do not choose this option, the object will appear without the field names as column headings and the appropriate spacing between columns. Elsa wants the Employer Positions query to appear in datasheet format.

5. Click the **Save formatted** check box, and then click the **Export** button. The HTML Output Options dialog box opens. See Figure 2.

Figure 2: HTML OUTPUT OPTIONS DIALOG BOX

- option for choosing a template
- option for using the default format

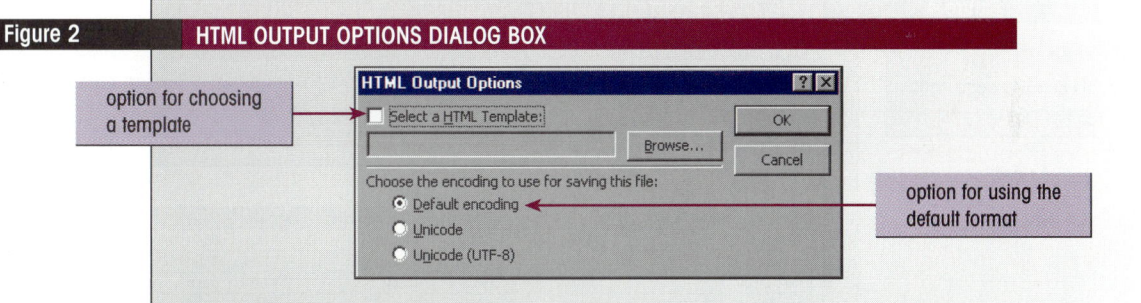

This dialog box provides options for choosing an HTML template in which to display the Web page, or for using the default format. A **template** is a file that contains special instructions for creating and displaying a Web page with both text and graphics. Elsa does not want to use a template for the Employer Positions query, so you can accept the default settings.

6. Make sure that the **Default encoding** option button is selected, and then click the **OK** button. Access exports the Employer Positions query to an HTML document named Employer Positions in the Tutorial folder. The HTML document does not exist in the Northeast database as a database object; it is a separate file stored on your Data Disk.

NSJI uses Microsoft Internet Explorer as its Web browser. You will now use Internet Explorer to view the Web page you just created.

To view the Employer Positions query Web page:

1. Click **View** on the menu bar, point to **Toolbars**, and then click **Web**. Access displays the Web toolbar.

2. Click the **Go** button on the Web toolbar, and then click **Open Hyperlink**. Access displays the Open Internet Address dialog box, in which you can specify the URL of the Web site or the name of the HTML document you want to view.

3. Click the **Browse** button. The Browse dialog box opens.

4. Make sure that the Look in list box displays the Tutorial folder on your Data Disk, click **Employer Positions** in the list, and then click the **Open** button. The Address list box in the Open Internet Address dialog box now displays the address for the Employer Positions HTML document. See Figure 3.

Figure 3 — OPEN INTERNET ADDRESS DIALOG BOX

- path to the Employer Positions Web page (yours might be different)

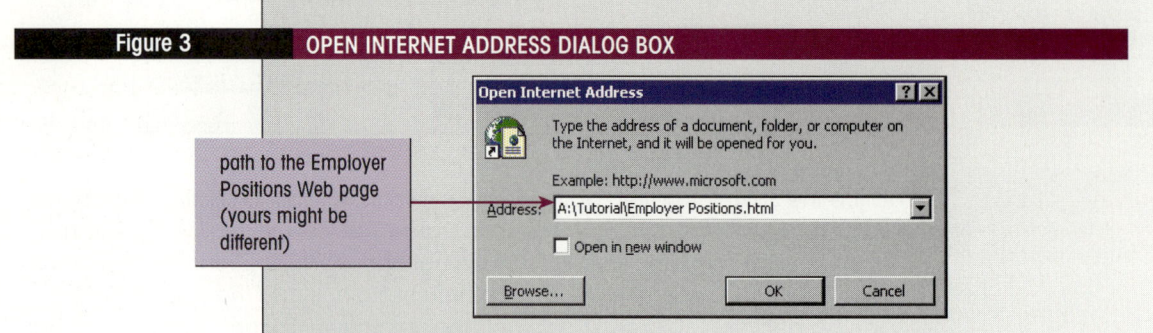

5. Click the **OK** button. Internet Explorer starts and opens the Employer Positions Web page. See Figure 4.

Figure 4 — EMPLOYER POSITIONS QUERY DATASHEET IN THE INTERNET EXPLORER WINDOW

- HTML document filename appears as the Web page title
- address for the Employer Positions Web page (yours might be different)
- records from the Employer Positions query datasheet

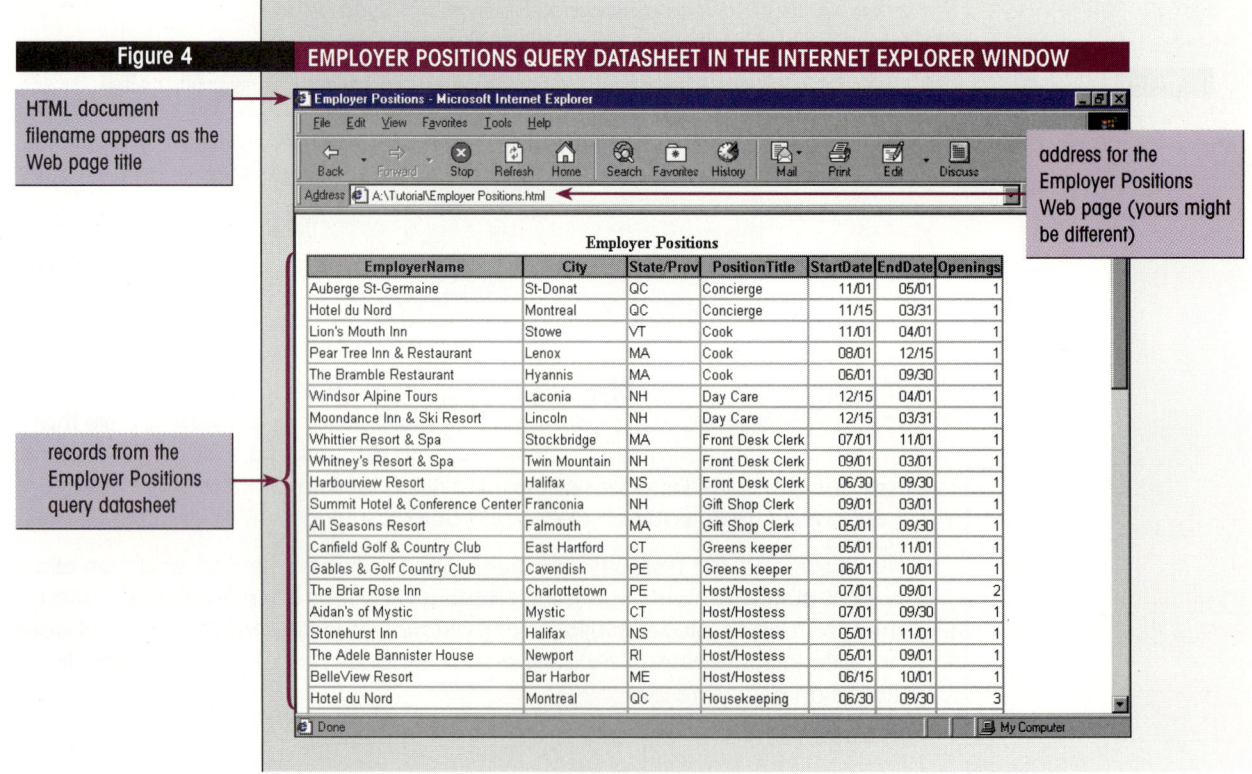

Employer Positions

EmployerName	City	State/Prov	PositionTitle	StartDate	EndDate	Openings
Auberge St-Germaine	St-Donat	QC	Concierge	11/01	05/01	1
Hotel du Nord	Montreal	QC	Concierge	11/15	03/31	1
Lion's Mouth Inn	Stowe	VT	Cook	11/01	04/01	1
Pear Tree Inn & Restaurant	Lenox	MA	Cook	08/01	12/15	1
The Bramble Restaurant	Hyannis	MA	Cook	06/01	09/30	1
Windsor Alpine Tours	Laconia	NH	Day Care	12/15	04/01	1
Moondance Inn & Ski Resort	Lincoln	NH	Day Care	12/15	03/31	1
Whittier Resort & Spa	Stockbridge	MA	Front Desk Clerk	07/01	11/01	1
Whitney's Resort & Spa	Twin Mountain	NH	Front Desk Clerk	09/01	03/01	1
Harbourview Resort	Halifax	NS	Front Desk Clerk	06/30	09/30	1
Summit Hotel & Conference Center	Franconia	NH	Gift Shop Clerk	09/01	03/01	1
All Seasons Resort	Falmouth	MA	Gift Shop Clerk	05/01	09/30	1
Canfield Golf & Country Club	East Hartford	CT	Greens keeper	05/01	11/01	1
Gables & Golf Country Club	Cavendish	PE	Greens keeper	06/01	10/01	1
The Briar Rose Inn	Charlottetown	PE	Host/Hostess	07/01	09/01	2
Aidan's of Mystic	Mystic	CT	Host/Hostess	07/01	09/30	1
Stonehurst Inn	Halifax	NS	Host/Hostess	05/01	11/01	1
The Adele Bannister House	Newport	RI	Host/Hostess	05/01	09/01	1
BelleView Resort	Bar Harbor	ME	Host/Hostess	06/15	10/01	1
Hotel du Nord	Montreal	QC	Housekeeping	06/30	09/30	3

> **TROUBLE?** If your computer has Netscape Navigator installed as its default browser, Netscape Navigator will start automatically and open the Employer Positions Web page. If this is the case, your screens will look slightly different from those shown in the figures.
>
> **TROUBLE?** If your computer does not have a browser installed on it, ask your instructor or technical support person for assistance.
>
> 6. Scroll through the Employer Positions Web page to view its contents. Notice the Print button on the Standard Buttons toolbar, which you could use to print the Web page, if necessary.
>
> 7. Click the **Close** button ⊠ on the title bar to close Internet Explorer. You return to the Northeast database in the Microsoft Access window.

Because you exported the query object to an HTML document, you created a static Web page. Therefore, any future changes made to the underlying data in the Employer and Positions tables will not appear in the Employer Positions Web page. Elsa will need to export this information periodically, perhaps once a week, so that the NSJI employees who view this page will have updated information.

Next, Elsa wants you to create a Web page showing the information in the Employer table. She wants this page to be dynamic, so that any changes made to the data in the Employer table will be reflected in the Web page. Furthermore, Elsa wants NSJI employees to be able to use the Web page to make changes to the Employer table. To meet Elsa's needs, you'll create a data access page.

Creating and Viewing a Data Access Page

A **data access page** is a dynamic HTML document that you can open with a browser to view or update current data in the Access database object on which the data access page is based. Unlike an exported HTML document, such as the one you just created, a data access page exists as a database object with a link to the HTML document on which it is based. This HTML document, however, is stored outside the database.

You can create a data access page either in Design view or by using a Wizard. To create the data access page for the Employer table, you'll use the AutoPage: Columnar Wizard.

> ### To create the data access page for the Employer table:
>
> 1. Click **Pages** in the Objects bar of the Database window to display the Pages list. The list box does not contain any pages.
>
> 2. Click the **New** button in the Database window. The New Data Access Page dialog box opens. This dialog box is similar to ones you have used to create new forms and reports.
>
> 3. Click **AutoPage: Columnar** to select this Wizard, click the list arrow for choosing the table or query as the basis for the page, click **Employer**, and then click the **OK** button. After a few moments, the AutoPage: Columnar Wizard creates the data access page and displays it in Page view. See Figure 5.

Figure 5   DATA ACCESS PAGE CREATED BY THE AUTOPAGE: COLUMNAR WIZARD

first record from the Employer table →

Employer	
EmployerID:	10122
EmployerName:	BeanTown Tours
Address:	105 State Street
City:	Boston
State/Prov:	MA
PostalCode:	02109
Country:	USA
ContactFirstName:	Sarah
ContactLastName:	Tasker
Position:	Office Manager
Phone:	617-451-
WebSite:	☑
NAICSCode:	56152

Employer 1 of 45

Record Navigation toolbar

TROUBLE? Your data access page might appear with an AutoFormat applied to it. This will not affect your work with the page; simply continue with the steps.

Notice that the Phone field value is not completely visible. You can fix this quickly in Design view.

4. Click the **View** button for Design view on the Page View toolbar. The data access page opens in Design view.

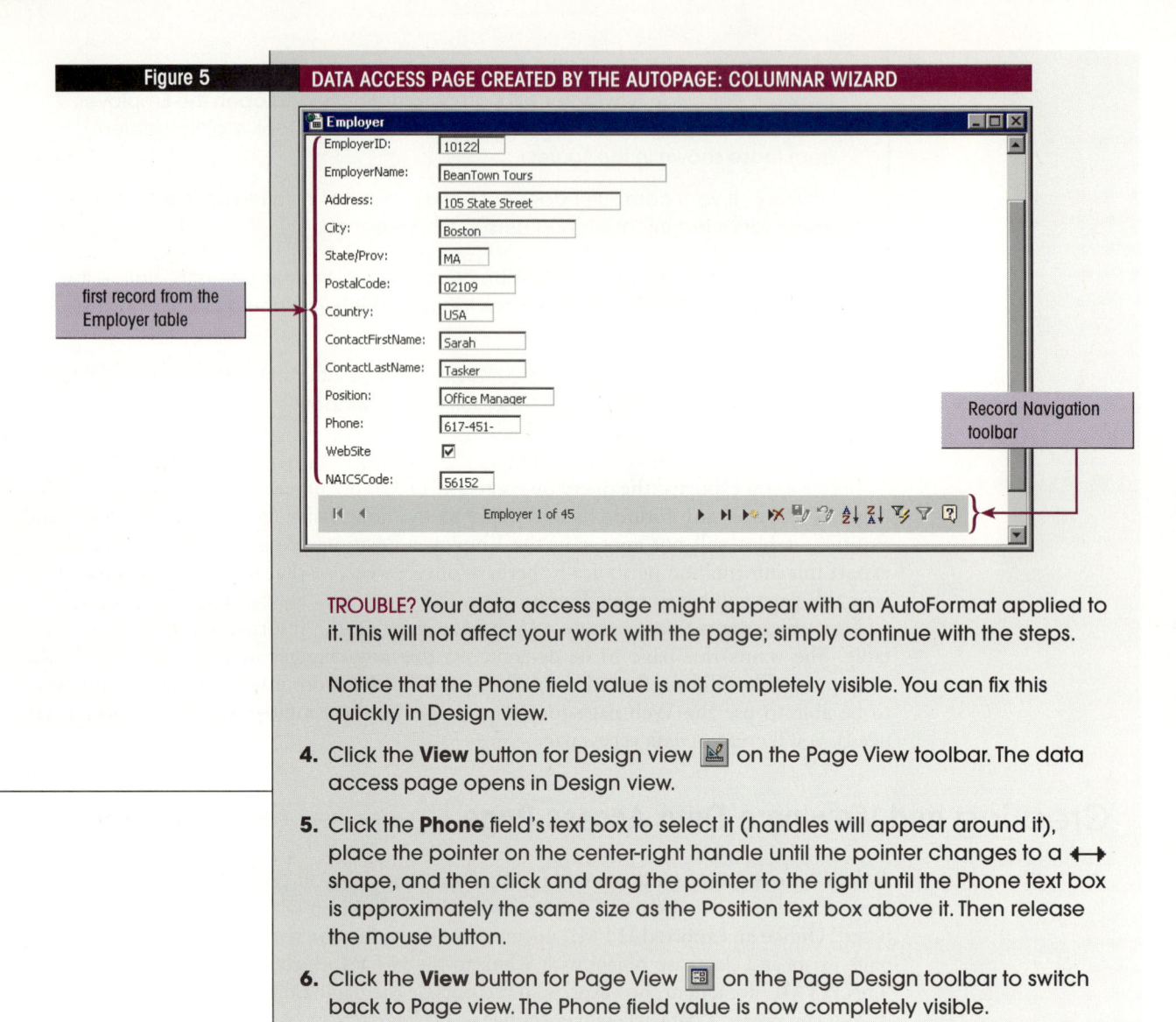

5. Click the **Phone** field's text box to select it (handles will appear around it), place the pointer on the center-right handle until the pointer changes to a ↔ shape, and then click and drag the pointer to the right until the Phone text box is approximately the same size as the Position text box above it. Then release the mouse button.

6. Click the **View** button for Page View on the Page Design toolbar to switch back to Page view. The Phone field value is now completely visible.

The data access page displays the fields for the first record in the Employer table in a format that is similar to a form. Notice the Record Navigation toolbar, which appears below the record. This toolbar provides buttons for moving between table records, similar to the buttons you use to move between records in a form, and buttons for adding and deleting records, sorting and filtering data, and so on.

Elsa has a change to make to one of the records in the Employer table. The Bayside Inn & Country Club has a new General Manager, so the contact first and last names for this employer need to be changed. You can make the necessary changes directly in the data access page, which at the same time will update the Employer table in the Northeast database. Before making the changes, you will save the data access page.

To save the data access page and update the contact information in Page view:

1. Click the **Save** button on the Page View toolbar. The Save As Data Access Page dialog box opens.

2. Make sure that the Save in list box displays the Tutorial folder on your Data Disk, and then click the **Save** button to save the data access page with the default name "Employer."

   TROUBLE? If a message box opens with a warning about the connection string, click the OK button and continue with the steps.

   Now you will change the necessary field values in the Employer table.

3. Use the Record Navigation toolbar to move to record 3 (for the Bayside Inn & Country Club), double-click the entry **Jeffrey** in the ContactFirstName field, type **Mary**, double-click the entry **Hersha** in the ContactLastName field, and then type **Russell**.

   You can save changes you make to a record in a data access page either by moving to another record or by clicking the Save button on the Record Navigation toolbar. You'll save your changes.

4. Click the **Save** button on the Record Navigation toolbar.

5. Click the **Close** button on the Employer window title bar. The data access page closes, and you return to the Database window. Notice that the Employer data access page is listed in the Pages list box.

You have created the data access page and viewed it in Page view. Now, you'll see how the page looks in Internet Explorer.

To view the Employer data access page in Internet Explorer:

1. Right-click **Employer** in the Pages list box, and then click **Web Page Preview**. Internet Explorer starts and opens the Employer data access page. See Figure 6.

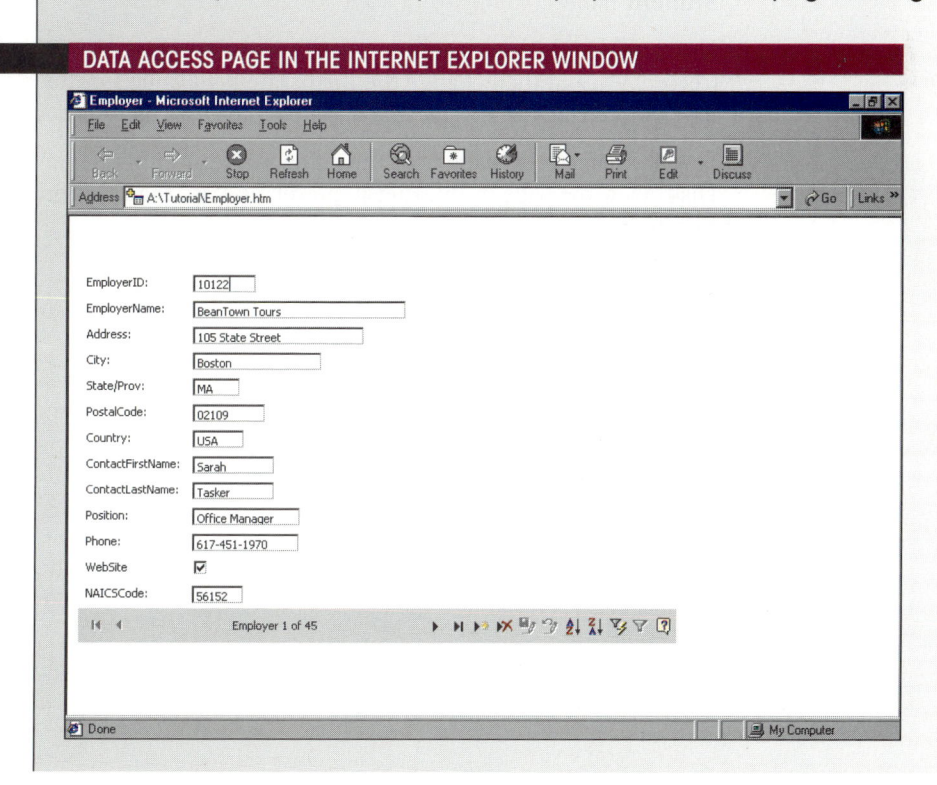

Figure 6   DATA ACCESS PAGE IN THE INTERNET EXPLORER WINDOW

> Now NSJI employees can use the company's intranet to view and update Employer data in Internet Explorer. Any changes that employees make using the Employer data access page will also be made to the Employer table.
>
> 2. Close Internet Explorer. You return to the Database window.
>
>   To confirm that the changes you made earlier to the contact information are reflected in the Employer table, you'll open the table now and view the record.
>
> 3. Click **Tables** in the Objects bar of the Database window, and then open the **Employer** table in Datasheet view. Scroll to the right and notice that the contact information for the Bayside Inn & Country Club is now Mary Russell.
>
> 4. Exit Access.

REVIEW ASSIGNMENTS

Elsa is pleased with the Web pages you created for the **Northeast** database. Now she would like to you create Web pages based on objects in the **Recruits** database. Complete the following:

1. Make sure your Data Disk is in the appropriate disk drive, start Access, and then open the **Recruits** database located in the Review folder on your Data Disk.

2. Create a static Web page named **Recruiter** based on the **Recruiter** table. Specify the option for displaying the data in a datasheet format and do not use a template. View the resulting Web page in Internet Explorer, use the Print button on the Standard Buttons toolbar to print the page, and then close Internet Explorer.

3. Use the AutoPage: Columnar Wizard to create a data access page based on the **Student** table.

4. Use the Record Navigation toolbar to move to the last record in the **Student** table (record 34), and then change the BirthDate field value for the last record to 11/16/84. Save your change using the appropriate Record Navigation toolbar button.

5. Save the data access page with the name **Student** in the Review folder on your Data Disk. View the page in Internet Explorer, and use the Print button on the Standard Buttons toolbar to print the page.

6. Close Internet Explorer, and then exit Access.

INDEX

A

Access. *See also* **Access database; Access table; database**
  exiting, AC 1.13
  in general, OFF 6
  starting, AC 1.07–1.10, AC 3.03
Access database. *See also* **database**
  copying records from, AC 2.29–2.31
  editing mode, AC 2.34
  importing table from, AC 2.32–2.33
  navigation mode, AC 2.34
  record modification, AC 2.35
Access table. *See also* **table**
  in general, AC 1.10–1.11
    column selector, AC 1.11
    datasheet view, AC 1.11
    field selector, AC 1.11
    record selector, AC 1.11
    row selector, AC 1.11
  modifying
    adding field, AC 2.24–2.26
    changing field properties, AC 2.26–2.29
    deleting field, AC 2.23–2.24
    in general, AC 2.22-2.23
    moving field, AC 2.24
Access window, AC 1.10
aggregate functions, in query, AC 3.38–3.40
AND logical operator, AC 3.28, AC 3.29–3.30
Ask a Question box, OFF 21
AutoForm Wizard, AC 1.18

B

backup, database, AC 1.23
browser, WEB 1
button, Office, OFF 13

C

calculations, with query, AC 3.33
closing, Office, OFF 16–18
column selector, AC 1.11
compacting, database AC 1.24–1.25
comparison operator, AC 3.22
  using to match values, AC 3.26–3.28
composite key, AC 2.03
  See also **key**

D

data
  filtering, AC 3.19–3.21
  finding with form, AC 4.08–4.10
  maintaining in form, AC 4.12–4.14
  sorting, in general, AC 3.14–3.15
  updating, AC 3.07
data organization, AC 1.04
data redundancy, avoiding, AC 2.03
data type, field data types, AC 2.05–2.06
database, OFF 6. *See also* **Access; Access database**
  backup and restoration, AC 1.23
  compacting and repairing, AC 1.24
    automatically, AC 1.24–1.25
  converting, AC 1.25–1.26
  creating, AC 2.07–2.08
  data organization, AC 1.04
    common field, AC 1.05
    field, AC 1.04
    field value, AC 1.04
    record, AC 1.04
    table, AC 1.04
  design guidelines, AC 2.02–2.04
  in general, AC 1.04
    primary key, AC 1.05
  management, AC 1.23
  opening, AC 1.07–1.10
  relational database, AC 1.04–1.08
  relational database management system, AC 1.06
  saving, AC 1.12–1.13
  updating
    changing records, AC 2.34–2.35
    deleting records, AC 2.33–2.34
    in general, AC 2.33
database management system (DBMS), discussed, AC 1.06–1.07
database program, OFF 6
database window, in general, AC 1.10
datasheet, AC 1.11
  changing appearance, AC 3.25–3.26
  navigating, AC 1.11–1.12
    current record symbol, AC 1.11
    navigation buttons, AC 1.11
    Specific Record box, AC 1.12
datasheet view, table, AC 1.11
DBMS. *See* **database management system**
deleting
  field, AC 2.23–2.24
  record, AC 2.33–2.34
design grid, AC 3.04
Design View, form modification, AC 4.19–4.22
detail record, AC 4.22. *See also* **record**
document. *See also* **report**
  entering text into, OFF 16–17
  Word, OFF 4

E

editing, Access database, AC 2.34
entity integrity, AC 2.16
Excel
  in general, OFF 4
  starting, OFF 10–11
exiting
  Access, AC 1.13
  Office, OFF 23
expression, AC 3.33
Expression Builder, AC 3.34

F

field. *See also* **field properties; field selector**
  adding, AC 2.24–2.26
  calculated, AC 3.33
    creating, AC 3.34–3.38
  common field, AC 1.05
  defining, AC 2.09–2.16
  deleting, AC 2.23–2.24
  in general, AC 1.04, AC 2.02, AC 2.03
  moving, AC 2.24
  null value, AC 2.16
  properties, AC 2.04
  sorting, AC 3.16–3.19
field list, query, AC 3.04
field properties
  changing, AC 2.26–2.27
  field data types, AC 2.05–2.06
  Field Size property, AC 2.06–2.07
  guidelines, in general, AC 2.04
  naming fields and objects, AC 2.04–2.05
  setting, AC 2.04
field selector, table, AC 1.11

Field Size property, AC 2.06–2.07
field value, database, AC 1.04
file
  closing, OFF 18
  modifying, OFF 18
  opening, OFF 18–20
  printing, OFF 20–21
  saving, OFF 18
  switching between, OFF 12–13
file extension, OFF 16
filename, OFF 16
Filter By Form, AC 3.20
Filter By Selection, AC 3.20
filtering, data, AC 3.19–3.21
Find command, AC 4.08
  wildcard character, AC 4.09
form. *See also* **form record**
  AutoForm Wizard, AC 1.18
  AutoFormat changes, AC 4.05–4.08
  creating
    with Form Wizard, AC 4.02–4.05, AC 4.16–4.19
    main form and subform, AC 4.16–4.22
    navigating and, AC 1.18–1.20
  detail record, AC 4.22
  finding data using, AC 4.08–4.10
  modifying, in Design View, AC 4.19–4.22
  Position Data form, changing the record, AC 4.12.–4.13
  table data
    maintenance, AC 4.12–4.14
    spell checking, AC 4.14–4.15
form record. *See also* **form; record**
  previewing and printing, AC 4.11–4.12
Form Wizard, AC 1.18
  form creation with, AC 4.02–4.05, AC 4.16–4.19

G

Group By operator, AC 3.40
Groups bar, AC 1.10

H

Help, Office, OFF 21–23
HTML. *See* **Hypertext Markup Language**
HTML document, WEB 1
hyperlinks, WEB 1
Hypertext Markup Language (HTML), WEB 1

I

integration, Office, OFF 7–9

J

join, tables, AC 3.08

K

key
  composite key, AC 2.03
  foreign key, AC 1.05
  primary key, AC 1.05, AC 2.03
    specifying, AC 2.16–2.17
  sort key, AC 3.14
keyboard shortcut, Office, OFF 13

L

logical operator, AC 3.28
   AND logical operator,
      AC 3.28, AC 3.29–3.30
   OR logical operator,
      AC 3.28, AC 3.31–3.33

M

menu
   Office, OFF 13-16
   personalized, OFF 13–14
menu command, OFF 13
Microsoft Access 2002.
   See **Access**
Microsoft Excel 2002.
   See **Excel**
**Microsoft Internet Explorer,
   WEB 1**
Microsoft Office XP.
   See **Office**
Microsoft Outlook 2002.
   See **Outlook**
Microsoft PowerPoint 2002.
   See **PowerPoint**
Microsoft Word 2002.
   See **Word**

N

navigation
   Access database, AC 2.34
   datasheet, AC 1.11–1.12
   form, AC 1.18–1.20
   query, AC 1.15–1.18
navigation buttons, AC 1.11
Netscape Navigator, WEB 1
null value, AC 2.16
number field. *See also* **field**
   property settings, AC 2.06

O

objects, naming, AC 2.04–2.05
Objects bar, AC 1.10
Office
   closing, OFF 16–18
   exiting programs, OFF 23
   in general, OFF 4–7
   Help, OFF 21–23
   menus and toolbars, OFF 13–16
   opening file, OFF 18–20
   program integration, OFF 7–9
   saving, OFF 16–18
   speech recognition, OFF 15
   starting, OFF 9–12
   switching between programs
      and files, OFF 12–13
Office Assistant, OFF 21
opening
   database, AC 1.07–1.10
   query, AC 1.13–1.15
**OR logical operator,
   AC 3.28, AC 3.31–3.33**
Outlook, in general, OFF 6

P

**picture, inserting in report,
   AC 4.30–4.34**
PowerPoint, in general, OFF 5
presentation, in general, OFF 5
**presentation graphics program,
   OFF 5**
primary key, AC 1.05, AC 2.03
   specifying, AC 2.16–2.17
printing
   file, OFF 20–21
   form record, AC 4.11–4.12
programs. *See also* ***specific
   programs***
   switching between, OFF 12–13
properties. *See* **field properties**

Q

QBE. *See* **query by example**
query. *See also* **query window;
   table**
   creating, AC 3.05–3.07
      multi-table, AC 3.13–3.14
   creating, sorting, navigating,
      AC 1.15–1.18
   for calculations
      aggregate functions,
         AC 3.38–3.40
      calculated field creation,
         AC 3.34–3.38
      in general, AC 3.33
      record group calculations,
         AC 3.40–3.41
   for data updating, AC 3.07
   in general, AC 1.13, AC 3.02
   multiple selection criteria
      AND logical operator,
         AC 3.29–3.30
      in general, AC 3.28
      multiple Undo and Redo,
         AC 3.30–3.31
      OR logical operator,
         AC 3.31-3.33
   opening, AC 1.13–1.15
   record selection criteria
      changing datasheet appear-
         ance, AC 3.25–3.26
      comparison operator use,
         AC 3.26–3.28
      in general, AC 3.22
      specifying exact match,
         AC 3.22–3.25
   recordset, AC 3.02
   running, AC 3.04,
      AC 3.05–3.07
   select query, AC 3.02
   sorting data
      in general, AC 3.14–3.15
      multiple fields in design
         view, AC 3.16–3.19
      toolbar button for,
         AC 3.15–3.16

query by example (QBE), AC 3.02
query window
  discussed, AC 3.02–3.05
    design grid, AC 3.04
    field list, AC 3.04
Query Wizard, AC 1.15

R

record. *See also* **form; form record; table**
  adding to table, AC 2.19–2.22
  changing, AC 2.34–2.35
    in form, AC 4.12.–4.13
  copying, AC 2.29-2.31
  current record symbol, AC 1.11
  database, AC 1.04
  deleting, AC 2.33–2.34
  detail record, AC 4.22
  modifying, AC 2.35
  orphaned, AC 3.09
  record group calculations, AC 3.40–3.41
  sorting, AC 3.14
  Specific Record box, AC 1.12
record selector, AC 1.11
recordset, AC 3.02
Redo command, multiple, AC 3.30–3.31
referential integrity, AC 3.09
relational database. *See also* **database**
  discussed, AC 1.04–1.08
report. *See also* **document; Report Wizard**
  closing and saving, AC 1.23–1.24
  creating, with Report Wizard, AC 4.22–4.30
  creating, previewing, navigating, in general, AC 1.20–1.21
  inserting picture in, AC 4.30–4.34

Report Wizard
  report creation, AC 4.22–4.30
  detail record, AC 4.22
row selector, AC 1.11

S

saving
  database, AC 1.12-1.13
  Office, OFF 16–18
  report, AC 1.23–1.24
  table, AC 2.17–2.18
ScreenTip, Office, OFF 21
search. *See* **Find command**
sort key, AC 3.14
  nonunique, AC 3.16
  primary, AC 3.16
  secondary, AC 3.16
  unique, AC 3.16
sorting
  data, AC 3.14–3.15
  fields, AC 3.16–3.19
  query, AC 1.15–1.18
  Sort Ascending, AC 3.15
  Sort Descending, AC 3.15
speech recognition, Office, OFF 15
spell checking, table data, AC 4.14–4.15
spreadsheet program, OFF 4
starting
  Excel, OFF 10–11
  Office, OFF 9–12
  Word, OFF 11–12

T

table. *See also* **Access table; query; record; table relationships**
  adding records to, AC 2.19–2.22

creating
  field definition, AC 2.09–2.16
  in general, AC 2.08–2.09
  primary key specification, AC 2.16–2.17
  saving, AC 2.17–2.18
  data maintenance with form, AC 4.12–4.14
  database, AC 1.04, AC 2.02, AC 2.03
  entity integrity, AC 2.16
  importing, AC 2.32–2.33
table relationships
  defining, AC 3.09–3.12
  in general, AC 3.08
  join, AC 3.08
  one-to-many, AC 3.08–3.09
    orphaned record, AC 3.09
    primary table, AC 3.09
    related table, AC 3.09
  referential integrity, AC 3.09
    cascade deletes, AC 3.09
    cascade updates, AC 3.09
text
  entering in document, OFF 16–17
  Zoom box, AC 3.34
toolbar
  Office, OFF 13–16
    personalized, OFF 14–15

U

Undo command, multiple, AC 3.30–3.31
Uniform Resource Locator (URL), WEB 1
URL. *See* **Uniform Resource Locator**

W

Web page, WEB 1
   data access, creating and viewing, WEB 5–8
   dynamic, WEB 2
   static, WEB 2
      creating and viewing, WEB 2-5
Web server, WEB 1
Web site, WEB 1
What's This? command, OFF 21
wildcard character, AC 4.09
Word
   in general, OFF 4
      documents, OFF 4
   starting, OFF 11–12
word processing program, OFF 4
workbook, Excel, OFF 4
World Wide Web (WWW), WEB 1
   working with, WEB 2
WWW. *See* **World Wide Web**

Z

Zoom box, AC 3.34

TASK REFERENCE

TASK	PAGE #	RECOMMENDED METHOD
Access, exit	AC 1.13	Click ✕ on the program window
Access, start	AC 1.07	Click Start, point to Programs, click Microsoft Access
Aggregate functions, use in a query	AC 3.38	Display the query in Design view, click Σ
AutoFormat, change	AC 4.05	See Reference Window: Changing a Form's AutoFormat
Calculated field, add to a query	AC 3.34	See Reference Window: Using Expression Builder
Column, resize width in a datasheet	AC 2.29	Double-click ↔ on the right border of the column heading
Data, check spelling of	AC 4.15	Click [ABC✓]
Data, find	AC 4.08	See Reference Window: Finding Data in a Form or Datasheet
Database, compact and repair	AC 1.24	Click Tools, point to Database Utilities, click Compact and Repair Database
Database, compact on close	AC 1.25	See Reference Window: Compacting a Database Automatically
Database, convert to another Access version	AC 1.26	Close the database to convert, click Tools, point to Database Utilities, point to Convert Database, click the format to convert to
Database, create a blank	AC 2.07	Click [icon] on the Database toolbar, click Blank Database in the Task Pane, type the database name, select the drive and folder, click Create
Database, create using a Wizard	AC 2.07	Click [icon] on the Database toolbar, click General Templates in the Task Pane, click the Databases tab, select a template, click OK, type the database name, select the drive and folder, click Create, follow the instructions in the Wizard
Database, open	AC 1.07	Click [icon]
Datasheet view, switch to	AC 2.19	Click [icon]
Design view, switch to	AC 2.23	Click [icon]
Field, add to a database table	AC 2.25	See Reference Window: Adding a Field Between Two Existing Fields
Field, define in a database table	AC 2.10	See Reference Window: Defining a Field in a Table
Field, delete from a database table	AC 2.23	See Reference Window: Deleting a Field from a Table Structure
Field, move to a new location in a database table	AC 2.24	Display the table in Design view, click the field's row selector, drag the field with the pointer
Filter By Selection, activate	AC 3.20	See Reference Window: Using Filter By Selection
Form Wizard, activate	AC 4.02	Click Forms in the Objects bar, click New, click Form Wizard, choose the table or query for the form, click OK
Object, open	AC 1.10	Click the object's type in the Objects bar, click the object's name, click Open

TASK REFERENCE

TASK	PAGE #	RECOMMENDED METHOD
Object, save	AC 1.20	Click 🖫, type the object name, click OK
Picture, insert on a report	AC 4.31	Select the report section in which to insert the picture, click Insert, click Picture, select the picture file, click OK
Primary key, specify	AC 2.16	See Reference Window: Specifying a Primary Key for a Table
Property sheet, open	AC 3.37	Right-click the object or control, click Properties
Query, define	AC 3.03	Click Queries in the Objects bar, click New, click Design View, click OK
Query, run	AC 3.06	Click ❗
Query results, sort	AC 3.17	See Reference Window: Sorting a Query Datasheet
Record, add a new one	AC 2.28	Click ▶*
Record, delete	AC 2.33	See Reference Window: Deleting a Record
Record, move to a specific one	AC 1.11	Type the record number in the Specific Record box, press Enter
Record, move to first	AC 1.12	Click ▏◀
Record, move to last	AC 1.12	Click ▶▏
Record, move to next	AC 1.12	Click ▶
Record, move to previous	AC 1.12	Click ◀
Records, redisplay all after filter	AC 3.21	Click ▽
Redo command, use to redo multiple operations in a database object	AC 3.31	Click the list arrow for ↻, click the action(s) to redo
Relationship, define between database tables	AC 3.10	Click 🞀
Report Wizard, activate	AC 4.23	Click Reports in the Objects bar, click New, click Report Wizard, choose the table or query for the report, click OK
Sort, specify ascending in datasheet	AC 3.15	Click A↓Z
Sort, specify descending in datasheet	AC 3.15	Click Z↓A
Table, create in a database	AC 2.08	Click Tables in the Objects bar, click New, click Design View, click OK
Table, import from another Access database	AC 2.32	Click File, point to Get External Data, click Import, select the folder, click Import, select the table, click OK
Table, open in a database	AC 1.10	Click Tables in the Objects bar, click the table name, click Open
Table structure, save in a database	AC 2.18	See Reference Window: Saving a Table Structure
Undo command, use to undo multiple operations in a database object	AC 3.30	Click the list arrow for ↶, click the action(s) to undo

Access Level I File Finder

Note: *The Data Files supplied with this book and listed in the chart below are starting files for Tutorial 1. You will begin your work on each subsequent tutorial with the files that you created in the previous tutorial. For example, after completing Tutorial 1, you begin Tutorial 2 with your ending files from Tutorial 1. The Review Assignments and Case Problems also build on the starting Data Files in this way. You must complete each tutorial, Review Assignment, and Case Problem in order and finish them completely before continuing to the next tutorial, or your Data Files will not be correct for the next tutorial.*

Location in Tutorial	Name and Location of Data File	Student Creates New File
Tutorial 1		
Session 1.1	Disk1\Tutorial\Seasonal.mdb	
Session 1.2	Disk1\Tutorial\Seasonal.mdb *(continued from Session 1.1)*	
Review Assignments	Disk2\Review\Seasons.mdb	Disk2\Review\Seasons2002.mdb Disk2\Review\Seasons97.mdb
Case Problem 1	Disk3\Cases\Videos.mdb	Disk3\Cases\Videos2002.mdb Disk3\Cases\Videos97.mdb
Case Problem 2	Disk4\Cases\Meals.mdb	Disk4\Cases\Meals2002.mdb Disk4\Cases\Meals97.mdb
Case Problem 3	Disk5\Cases\Redwood.mdb	Disk5\Cases\Redwood.mdb Disk5\Cases\Redwood.mdb
Case Problem 4	Disk6\Cases\Trips.mdb	Disk6\Cases\Trips2002.mdb Disk6\Cases\Trips97.mdb
Tutorial 2		
Session 2.1		Disk1\Tutorial\Northeast.mdb
Session 2.2	Disk1\Tutorial\Northeast.mdb *(continued from Session 2.1)* Disk1\Tutorial\NEJobs.mdb Disk1\Tutorial\Seasonal.mdb *(continued from Tutorial 1)*	
Review Assignments	Disk2\Review\Elsa.mdb	Disk2\Review\Recruits.mdb
Case Problem 1	Disk3\Cases\Videos.mdb *(continued from Tutorial 1)* Disk3\Cases\Events.mdb	
Case Problem 2	Disk4\Cases\Meals.mdb *(continued from Tutorial 1)* Disk4\Cases\Customer.mdb	
Case Problem 3	Disk5\Cases\Redwood.mdb *(continued from Tutorial 1)* Disk5\Cases\Pledge.mdb	
Case Problem 4	Disk6\Cases\Trips.mdb *(continued from Tutorial 1)* Disk6\Cases\Rafting.xls Disk6\Cases\Groups.mdb	
Tutorial 3		
Session 3.1	Disk1\Tutorial\Northeast.mdb *(continued from Session 2.2)*	
Session 3.2	Disk1\Tutorial\Northeast.mdb *(continued from Session 3.1)*	
Review Assignments	Disk2\Review\Recruits.mdb *(continued from Tutorial 2)*	
Case Problem 1	Disk3\Cases\Videos.mdb *(continued from Tutorial 2)*	
Case Problem 2	Disk4\Cases\Meals.mdb *(continued from Tutorial 2)*	
Case Problem 3	Disk5\Cases\Redwood.mdb *(continued from Tutorial 2)*	
Case Problem 4	Disk6\Cases\Trips.mdb *(continued from Tutorial 2)*	
Tutorial 4		
Session 4.1	Disk1\Tutorial\Northeast.mdb *(continued from Session 3.2)*	
Session 4.2	Disk1\Tutorial\Northeast.mdb *(continued from Session 4.1)* Disk1\Tutorial\Globe.bmp	
Review Assignments	Disk2\Review\Recruits.mdb *(continued from Tutorial 3)* Disk2\Review\Travel.bmp	
Case Problem 1	Disk3\Cases\Videos.mdb *(continued from Tutorial 3)* Disk3\Cases\Camcord.bmp	
Case Problem 2	Disk4\Cases\Meals.mdb *(continued from Tutorial 3)* Disk4\Cases\Server.bmp	
Case Problem 3	Disk5\Cases\Redwood.mdb *(continued from Tutorial 3)* Disk5\Cases\Animals.bmp	
Case Problem 4	Disk6\Cases\Trips.mdb *(continued from Tutorial 3)* Disk6\Cases\Raft.gif	
Creating Web Pages with Access		
Tutorial	Disk1\Tutorial\Northeast.mdb *(continued from Session 4.2)*	Disk1\Tutorial\Employer Positions.html Disk1\Tutorial\Employer.htm
Review Assignments	Disk2\Review\Recruits.mdb *(continued from Tutorial 4)*	Disk2\Review\Recruiter.html